Smith Wildman Brookhart

"I would rather be

right than be regular."

—SMITH WILDMAN BROOKHART

SMITH WILDMAN BROOKHART

*Portrait by Allen Philbrick, 1928.
"It is Brookhart in action," said his old
friend, Edgar Harlan. "If it has a
certain crudeness, it is the crudeness
of the physical fearlessness
of the champion and advocate."*

Smith Wildman BROOKHART

Iowa's Renegade Republican

George William McDaniel

*For Bill,
with gratitude for all your
support through the years.
George McDaniel
Aug 10, 1995*

IOWA STATE UNIVERSITY PRESS / AMES

THE REV. GEORGE W. MCDANIEL
is professor and chair of the Department of History
at St. Ambrose University, Davenport, Iowa.

© 1995 Iowa State University Press, Ames, Iowa 50014
All rights reserved

Authorization to photocopy items for internal or personal use, or the internal or personal use of specific clients, is granted by Iowa State University Press, provided that the base fee of $.10 per copy is paid directly to the Copyright Clearance Center, 27 Congress Street, Salem, MA 01970. For those organizations that have been granted a photocopy license by CCC, a separate system of payments has been arranged. The fee code for users of the Transactional Reporting Service is 0-8138-2107-X/95 $.10.

♾ Printed on acid-free paper in the United States of America

First edition, 1995

Parts of Chapters 2, 3, 4, and 10 were originally published as "Martial Sons of Martial Sires," by George McDaniel, *The Palimpsest* 70 (Spring 1989); "Smith Wildman Brookhart: 'The Man Who Taught the Army How to Shoot,'" by George McDaniel, *The Palimpsest* 75 (Spring 1994); "Prohibition Debate in Washington County, 1890–1894: Smith Wildman Brookhart's Introduction to Politics," by George McDaniel, *The Annals of Iowa* (Winter 1981); "The Republican Party and the Defeat of Smith Wildman Brookhart," by George McDaniel, *The Annals of Iowa* (Winter/Spring 1987). Copyright 1981, 1987, 1989, and 1994, State Historical Society of Iowa. Reprinted by permission of the publisher.

Library of Congress Cataloging-in-Publication Data

McDaniel, George William.
    Smith Wildman Brookhart: Iowa's renegade Republican / George William McDaniel.—1st ed.
       p.   cm.
    Includes bibliographical references (p.   ) and index.
    ISBN 0-8138-2107-X (alk. paper)
    1. Brookhart, Smith Wildman, 1869–1944. 2. Legislators—United States—Biography. 3. United States. Congress. Senate—Biography. 4. Iowa—Politics and government. I. Title.
E748.B8464M33 1995
328.73'092—dc20
[B]   95-12116

To my parents Merritt and Dolores McDaniel

And my brothers John and David

With love and appreciation

CONTENTS

ACKNOWLEDGMENTS, *xiii*

INTRODUCTION, *xv*

1. The Farmer's Son, *3*
2. The Establishment County Attorney, *10*
3. The Soldier and Citizen, *19*
4. The Sharpshooter, *32*
5. The Making of a Progressive, *50*
6. The Railroad Reformer and Senatorial Candidate, *68*
7. The Cooperationist and Republican Insurgent, *93*
8. A Victory with National Implications, *121*
9. In Washington and Europe, *135*
10. The Defeat of the Disrupter, *153*
11. The Disrupter Victorious, *184*

CONTENTS

12. The Regular Republican and the Fight
    for Farm Relief, *199*

13. The Populist Becomes a Democrat, *242*

14. The Republican New Dealer, *270*

NOTES, *299*

BIBLIOGRAPHY, *347*

INDEX, *367*

Illustrations follow pages 86, 174, and 234

ACKNOWLEDGMENTS

This work began as a seminar paper at the University of Iowa, grew into my doctoral dissertation, and finally evolved into this book. Through this long process I have incurred many debts to people who have supported me and my work.

I am grateful to the faculty members of the Department of History at the University of Iowa who were so supportive. I would especially mention Professor Malcolm Rohrbough and my thesis supervisor, Professor Ellis Hawley. Professor Hawley has maintained an interest in the project and has quietly urged me to get it finished and published.

I am grateful for all the help I have received from librarians. Everywhere I have worked, librarians have responded quickly and efficiently to make my research easier. I would particularly like to thank the librarians in the Manuscripts and Government Documents divisions of the University of Iowa Libraries; the Des Moines and Iowa City Libraries of the State Historical Society of Iowa; and the staff at the Herbert Hoover Presidential Library in West Branch. Of all the places I worked, in many ways the most pleasant was Brookhart's and my hometown Washington Public Library.

The Herbert Hoover Presidential Library Association generously provided two research grants that were of great assistance. Ray S. Johnston also gave special support. St. Ambrose University provided faculty development grants to assist in my research. I am especially grateful to St. Ambrose for a sabbatical leave and financial support from the Baecke Chair of Humanities which enabled me to finish the manuscript.

I cannot fail to mention support from my colleagues in the Department of History at St. Ambrose: Professor Richard Geiger, the late Professor Francis W. J. Duncan, the late Professor Wayne DeJohn, and Dr. Jon Stauff. Through the years they have been very patient as I have told them more about Smith Brookhart than they really wanted to know. My students, too, have shown great forbearance as I have talked about Smith Brookhart over

ACKNOWLEDGMENTS

the years. They have also shown genuine interest in how the book was progressing and for that I am grateful.

I began this project in my pre-computer days. All of the final copy for the dissertation was done by Janet Minor of the Word Processing Department at St. Ambrose. Michelle Threet in Word Processing helped me to blend the new material with the old. I am grateful for her patience when I have asked for revisions that created additional work for her. At Iowa State University Press Bill Silag encouraged me from the beginning and in the latter stages of the book my editor, Jane Zaring, proved herself indispensable.

When I began this project in 1976, I had the help of three of Brookhart's children, Smith W. Brookhart, Jr., Florence Brookhart Yount, and Edith Brookhart Millard. They answered questions about their father, shared the materials they had, and never failed to respond quickly to a request. I regret that all three have since died and thus are unable to see the final product. The family support has continued into the next generation, however, with Smith's son, Charles E. Brookhart, and Florence's son, John Yount.

My mother and father and my brothers John and David have contributed more to this book than they can ever know, and to them this book is dedicated.

INTRODUCTION

Of all the men who have represented Iowa in the United States Senate, few were as well known in their own time as Smith Wildman Brookhart. During his Senate years, 1922 to 1933, newspapers from the *New York Times* to the *San Francisco Examiner* covered his speeches and expressed editorial opinion about him. Articles by and about him appeared in the *Saturday Evening Post*. He was in the very first issue of *Time* magazine. A favorite target of editorial cartoonists, especially the *Des Moines Register*'s Ding Darling, Brookhart was called a radical, an insurgent, a progressive, a socialist, a communist, a Bolshevik, a buffoon, and was numbered among the Senate's "sons of the wild jackass."

Most studies of the New Era, if they mention Brookhart at all, list him as one of several progressive or radical senators following the leadership of Senator Robert M. La Follette or Senator George Norris. Separate treatments of Brookhart have, with one exception, been unpublished theses. The exception is Jerry Alvin Neprash's, *The Brookhart Campaigns in Iowa, 1920-1926*, a 1932 study of the seven elections during those years in which Brookhart was a candidate for the Senate.[1] It is interesting but incomplete. For one thing, it does not include the last Senate campaigns wherein Brookhart lost as spectacularly as he had won in the earlier ones.

During the 1920s the Republican Party often wished Brookhart would disappear from the scene, and many party members worked very hard to bring about that end. Two modern works carry this attitude forward. One, *The Republican Party, 1854-1966* (1967) by George H. Mayer, comments about Brookhart:

> For nearly a decade Brookhart, whose middle name, appropriately enough, was Wildman, had espoused a variety of extreme measures for agricultural relief, and he continued to harass the regulars throughout the 1920's. . . .

The volatile Iowan stirred farmers into millennial ecstacy by impassioned denunciations of Wall Street.[2]

Another study, Malcolm Moos' *The Republicans, A History of Their Party* (1956), commenting on the losses suffered by the party in 1922, said that it was in Iowa that the Republican fold became "effectively unhinged." Then, having named Brookhart as the cause of this unhinging, Moos called him a "lusty bedouin," and said of "'Wildman' Brookhart" that "newspapermen were fond of setting off his middle name in quotes."[3]

Because of his wide publicity, it was easy to get the wrong impression about Brookhart. He was not the political gadfly his opponents would have had the public believe. His program for the problems of his era had its roots in nineteenth-century populism and early twentieth-century progressivism. But his program was often hidden by the fervid political rhetoric he used and that his opponents used against him.

Brookhart served in the Senate during years of great economic growth and great economic collapse. His analysis of the economic situation, especially as it applied to agriculture during the 1920s, said that Wall Street, big business, and the Federal Reserve Board had conspired to depress prices and restrict credit. Not only farmers but all producers, including industrial laborers, were exploited by this system. Brookhart believed that farmers and laborers ought to join in a political and economic coalition to protect their own interests. And where they were powerless to protect themselves, the progressive Brookhart said that it was the function of the government to protect them.

At the institutional level, Brookhart believed that the current economic system, with its emphasis on competition, was a failure, leading only to wars and discord. In its place, Brookhart would substitute a cooperative system of banks and marketing organizations with profits limited and with producers sharing dividends above profits according to the degree of their participation in the cooperative. In this way farmers and laborers would achieve economic independence and equality.

But an even larger question to be examined is the puzzle of Smith Brookhart himself. Like most young attorneys in nineteenth-century Iowa, he began his political career as a Republican. Over a period of years, however, he would reevaluate the position of the party, especially as it related to the question of railroad rates. In the first decade of the twentieth century, his study of the subject would lead him to ally himself with the progressive wing of his party. Unlike other Iowa progressives, he would never waver from his commitment to progressivism with its faith in government regulation to insure economic equality and justice.

When he went to the Senate in the 1920s, Brookhart joined the group of insurgent progressive senators who formed a minority within the business-dominated Republican Party. Prominent members of this group included, among others, George Norris (Republican, Nebraska), Robert M. La Follette, Sr. (Republican, Wisconsin), William E. Borah (Republican, Idaho) and Henrik Shipstead (Farmer-Labor, Minnesota). The progressive minority, however, was often so fragmented that it was unable to mount a coordinated, effective program to challenge the prevailing political climate. Undaunted by this, Brookhart remained true to his populist-progressive roots and continued to serve as a voice for Iowa farmers and labor he felt were not well served by the Republican Party. By the eve of the New Deal, he had come to realize that his vision of America was best represented by the Democratic Party and its candidate, Franklin Delano Roosevelt.

Brookhart was one of many characters on the political stage, but nobody dominated Iowa politics in quite the way he did during the 1920s. He was the lightning rod that discharged the discontent of farmers during those years of depression. He was also so strong a catalyst in the political mix that it was impossible for all other politicians not to react to his presence. Iowa politics in the 1920s was largely characterized by the struggle between the regular Republican Party and Smith Brookhart for the support of Iowans.

Although politics formed the principal arena for his activities, rifle shooting was another major interest in his life. As a member of the Iowa National Guard, he found his niche in training marksmen. He came to have definite views on the subject and he fought for them as vigorously as he fought for his political ideals. During World War I his methods were adopted by the military and at the beginning of his senate career he was often identified in the newspapers as the "man who taught the army to shoot." In time his marksmanship activities also took him to the national stage and he served for a time as the president of the National Rifle Association.

Brookhart's life serves as a mirror reflecting the changes taking place in the United States from the end of the Civil War to the end of World War II. Even before he became a political progressive, he was progressive in the sense that he believed that forward movement was good and necessary. But he also believed that progress should not take place at the expense of individual rights and the loss of those values and opportunities he believed were rooted in the founding of the nation.

He was most prominent in a period which current scholarship portrays as characterized by the acceptance of corporate values and by private enterprise initiatives seeking to create the conditions for an ordered growth of the economy.[4] The order was to come particularly through associational activities undertaken by modernizing elites, with some governmental assistance and cooperation but without the kind of statist intervention that could lead to a welfare or regulatory state. The ordered growth, it was held, would benefit not only business but society as a whole, and by limiting the role of the state essential freedoms would be preserved.

This side of the 1920s, however, should not obscure other facets of the period. Despite the prominance of corporate values and their influence on public policy, other value systems and perspectives remained alive and would regain some of their previous influence in the 1930s. One of these was the populist critique of corporate structures, a critique that viewed them as "monopolies" and "tyrannies." It tended instead to idealize the "people," the people's associations, and a people's government that could smite their enemies, serve as their advocate, and preserve the "independence" of citizens and communities.

This outlook became a fixed part of Brookhart's thinking by the beginning of the 1920s, and during the decade he would remain firmly attached to it, deny that modernization and economic growth required its abandonment, and show that it still had appeal for distressed farmers who found in it an explanation of their economic plight. The mainstreams of state-building and agricultural policy were moving in other directions, toward a bureaucratic state and bureaucratic mechanisms rather than populist ones. But men like Brookhart showed that the resistance could be strong, that populist ideals could be kept alive, and that politicians might have to make accommodations to them, as the New Deal would to some extent do after 1933. In this sense, he was representative of a significant aspect of the New Era and particularly of Iowa politics in the New Era.

Smith Wildman Brookhart

1

The Farmer's Son

In 1910 Smith Wildman Brookhart wanted to run for Congress from Iowa's first district. But to get to Washington he had to defeat three opponents in the June primary. The first was the incumbent congressman, Charles A. Kennedy, whose name was on the primary ballot. The others were the regular party organization and the Chicago, Burlington & Quincy Railroad, whose names were not on the ballot. It was not the last time that Brookhart would see himself as taking on more than one opponent. Nor was it the last time that he would see the real issue in a campaign as being the nature of Republicanism.

As he would in most of his subsequent contests, Brookhart opened the 1910 campaign with a speech at the Graham Opera House in his hometown of Washington, Iowa. On a stage decorated with a big stick, he began by noting the "sharp differences" between himself and "the distinguished gentleman now representing this district in Congress" as to "the fundamental definition of Republicanism." The Republican Party, he said, had been born in opposition to slavery. It had been an "aggressive fighting party" that had used the Emancipation Proclamation and later constitutional amendments to defeat the slave-holding oligarchy, not one that had embraced the notion of "Let well enough alone." But in the years of prosperity following the Civil War huge fortunes had been built, and to perpetuate themselves the great capitalists had sought political power. They had "poured sand in the journals and slowed down the wheels of progress." Great wealth had stepped in "to rule where men had been supreme." And a "fighting party" had become a "standpat" one, a position to which Congressman Kennedy was still committed. He had not responded when a new leader, in the person of Theodore Roosevelt, had again unfurled the banner of "progress."[1]

Brookhart, however, was ready to answer this new call to arms. He would help to make Republicanism a people's movement fighting against "monopoly, greed and corruption" as it had once fought against a slaveholding oligarchy. More specifically, he would support regulatory controls imposed through a people's government, especially where corporations did business "under a public franchise or [exercised] the right of eminent domain [and were] in the public service and . . . engaged in interstate commerce."[2]

The *Washington County Press* thought the speech made "good reading" and that "its clear-cut sentences" left "no question as to where [Brookhart] stands on matters of import in national politics."[3] It was hardly a ringing endorsement from the hometown Republican newspaper. But Brookhart was hardly a regular Republican and newspapers in the district took note of his relationship to the party.

The tone had been set earlier when Howard A. Burrell, former owner of the *Press*, had referred to Brookhart as an "assistant Democrat," a label that his opponents now used repeatedly. The Burlington *Hawk-Eye* referred to a Brookhart speech at Winfield as one of the "best democratic speeches ever delivered." The *Mount Pleasant Journal* noted that Brookhart and the Democrats were opposed to President William Howard Taft, the tariff, and the rate bill, two important Republican issues. And the *Keokuk Daily Gate City* commented:

> First district Republicans are called upon to choose between a loyal Republican who will stand by the President and aid him in his efforts to redeem the pledges the party made to the country in its national platform, and a man who claims to be a Republican but who has publicly announced his opposition to the President and given notice that he intends if elected to vote with the Democrats to nullify Republican principles and policies. No one would hesitate a moment in making a choice between these two candidates.[4]

Brookhart lost the election, receiving only 37.7 percent of the vote. Of the seven counties in the district, he won only Washington. Still, it was remarkable that a progressive had done even that well and Brookhart refused to be discouraged. "I was buried deeper than anybody else under the avalanche," he wrote Senator Jonathan Prentiss Dolliver, "but have already crawled out and ground my battle ax for the next encounter. I would rather be right than be regular any day."[5]

By 1910 Smith Brookhart was a thoroughgoing member of the progressive wing of the Republican Party. "I'd rather be right than regular" was not an entirely new sentiment for him. But it had now become one to which he was firmly and permanently committed. It stood as a harbinger of what was to come during his public career.

Smith Wildman Brookhart was born in a log cabin in Scotland County, Missouri, on February 2, 1869.[6] His middle name, which was to follow him as an epithet all his life, was his mother's maiden name. His father, Abram Colar Brookhart, farmed the hilly soil of northern Missouri.

The same week Brookhart was born the newspaper noted that two local men were building the first velocipede in Memphis, the county seat. This early version of a bicycle meant it was "good-bye horse" which the paper judged was too "slow for *Young Americans.*" The same edition of the paper also noted the continuing efforts to get the railroad to come through Scotland County. Railroads would "create, develope (sic) and build up the country." Railroads meant progress and Scotland County had cast its lot with progress.

Meanwhile that spring, farmers plowed under winter-killed wheat they had planted the previous autumn so they could try their luck with corn. Farm work was halted by heavy June rains and in July more heavy rains washed out bridges and swept away fences. It was estimated that the rains and floods had caused up to $200,000 worth of damages. But the next spring Colar Brookhart and his neighbors made another act of faith and put in their crops.

In the years following the Civil War many Americans were on the move in search of greater opportunity, and Colar Brookhart was no exception. Land in southern Minnesota sold for up to thirty-five dollars an acre, a price the local paper said was "worth the money for wheat growing and dairying." Lured by newspaper accounts of ninety cent wheat and the promise of "unprecedented prosperity," thousands of immigrants moved to the Upper Midwest. A local Minnesota paper reported that prairie schooners passed through town by "threes and fours." Colar Brookhart's dream was to "plow a wheat field in virgin soil," so in 1875 he moved his family, now numbering four sons, to Taopa in southern Minnesota.[7]

The work was hard but there was still time for fun. Smith remembered the July 4 celebration where he first drank red lemonade and where there were clowns on horses called Raggy Muffins. The risks, however, were high. Bad weather or insects could ruin the prospects for a profitable crop and southern Minnesota had both in the harvest season of 1876. Heavy rains destroyed what plagues of grasshoppers had not eaten. The paper warned that with a poor wheat crop and the prospects of more grasshoppers the following year people were well advised to live within their means.[8]

Having planted his wheat field, Colar was unable to sell the crop at a profitable price and in 1877 decided to return to Missouri. After sending his wife and three younger sons ahead on the train, he and Smith made a seven-day trip across Iowa by covered wagon. He later said, "I came back from Minnesota with four sons and a dollar fifty."[9]

The family stayed in Missouri for about two years and then moved to

Iowa, first to Jefferson County and in 1885 to Van Buren County. While the father taught his sons the skills needed to farm, Cynthia Wildman Brookhart concerned herself with the education of her growing family. Years later Smith recalled that his mother "would sacrifice almost anything to get a book for her children." Her cousin, John Grinstead, the county superintendent of schools, gave her all the sample copies of books that were sent him. Smith could count to a hundred before he entered school. Subsequently, he learned to spell from an old green-backed spelling book, doing well enough to win a spelling prize.[10]

In Iowa Smith went to school in a redbrick schoolhouse. Speaking a "piece" (his first speech) at a "literary," he was puzzled when the audience responded by stamping their feet. In general, he received high marks, but one time he failed to study and was spelled out at a spelldown. He felt so ashamed he redoubled his efforts so that it would never happen again. He also excelled at arithmetic, and a later teacher advanced him to the highest group in the subject at school. He remembered being a "little bit of a fellow walking up front and sitting by big May Taylor and Minnie Copeland."

A good student, Smith also stood his ground outside of school. Once Bill Phillips, the largest boy in school, got into a fight with the teacher, and after school all the students took Bill's side except for the smaller Smith. When the others wanted to "trim him up" so as to bring him "into line," Bill, perhaps amazed at Smith's courage, would not let them. Bill, however, was usually on the other side in the childhood game of "Old England and Yankee Doodle." He led Old England and, given his size, threw the biggest clods. Still, the much smaller Brookhart's Yankee Doodles usually held their own.

Brookhart also worked. He did farm work and was reported to be the best hay-stacker in the area. He had his own patch of wheat and one season proudly reported thirty-nine bushels to the acre. Later he chopped wood for his mother's cousin, John Grinstead, and used the money to buy Barnes' *Brief History of the World*.[11]

It was Grinstead who suggested that Brookhart go to Bloomfield for high school. There he did well, graduating with a class of six boys and six girls on April 30, 1886. Each student participated in the graduation program. Brookhart's speech on the topic of "Personal Responsibility" was pronounced to be "strikingly original" and "gave evidence of a studious mind and high intellect."[12]

Brookhart next enrolled in the Southern Iowa Normal and Scientific Institute at Bloomfield. In addition to his studies Brookhart joined the Philomathean Literary Society. The Philomathean was a debating society and Brookhart held various offices, including president. He also took a role in the monthly debates and declamations on a wide variety of topics. One month he took the affirmative on the proposition: "That patriotism is a greater virtue than philanthropy." The next month he spoke on "The Power of Ideas" and to celebrate the centenary of the inauguration of President Washington, he took as his theme "The Surrender of Burgoyne."[13]

The local papers usually gave him good marks for attempting difficult subject matters and on one occasion noted that he was an "earnest, emphatic [speaker who] carried his audience with him." These debates helped him to hone the skills he would use throughout his public career. His last speech as a Normal student was at his graduation in June 1889. His later political opponents might have suggested that his topic, "Political Eccentricities," could have been self-descriptive.[14]

During these same years Brookhart taught in various country schools. His first teaching position was at Brock School in rural Scotland County, Missouri. His students were mainly farm children who attended between fall harvest and spring planting. One remembered that he would fascinate the children by writing on the blackboard with both hands at the same time. If this made him popular with the students, his insistence that they learn algebra made him unpopular with their parents who made up the local school board. The board did not think that algebra would be of any use to them and told Brookhart he could not add it to the curriculum. He taught it anyway, at recess.[15]

Another term Brookhart taught in Jefferson County, at a salary of $22.50 a month, and the year after that in Bloomfield. His teaching, combined with summer jobs, enabled him to save enough to buy a farm for his father, the first farm Colar Brookhart had ever owned. The farm was on the Fox River east of Cantril in Van Buren County where the land was fertile but swampy and the river "overflowed a good bit." At times fishing was the best crop.

Summers he returned to Bloomfield and continued his association with Southern Iowa Normal. In 1890 he taught school in Bloomfield and was back on the programs of the Philomathean and took a part in a play at Lloyd's Opera House. The newspaper said that as could be expected, the amateur cast "lacked the life and vim that ought to characterize a theatrical play." He also spoke at the Normal commencement where his stage presence was said to be "too much like that of a prize-fighter" but that the speech itself was a "splendid production" which was "roundly applauded." The next summer the alumnus served on a committee to petition the board of directors of Normal and the people of Bloomfield to allocate money to enlarge the buildings at the school.[16]

Brookhart was rated as a "successful teacher" and had been invited by the board to return to Bloomfield for another year of teaching to begin in the fall of 1891.[17] But school teaching proved to be only a short-term occupation for him. Years before when he left the farm, his father had suggested he study the law; and in the spring of 1891, Brookhart started to read the law, first with Dillon H. Payne and George T. Sowers in Bloomfield, and the next year with William Walker in Keosauqua.

One of his first cases occurred only two months after he began to read law. The case involved a lawsuit against a railroad which had killed a farmer's livestock. On its merits the case was a small one but the novice lawyer used his debating skills to make it a big case. Although the jury could not agree on a verdict, the judge seemed impressed by Brookhart's efforts and was surprised to find that the young man had only been studying law for two months.[18] In another case the opposing attorney objected that Brookhart was not a member of the bar. The judge overruled his objection: "If the Court doesn't care," he declared, "why should you? The Court doesn't care!"

In October 1892, Brookhart passed his bar examination and began the practice of law. This would be his living. But his real passion in life had already become the practice of politics. While reading law with Dillon Payne, he had met Payne's brother-in-law, General James B. Weaver, who by that time was already a legendary figure in Iowa. A Civil War general, Weaver had served one term as a Greenback congressman and two subsequent terms as a Democrat and Greenback-Laborite. In 1880 he had been the Greenback candidate for President and in 1892 would be the Populist candidate for the same office.[19] Brookhart often visited the Weaver home, both before and during the 1892 campaign. And in 1912, following Weaver's death, he would write:

> We knew him best when he was at the zenith of his career. . . . This acquaintance gave us a profound and keen respect for the pure, patriotic character and clear and fearless intellect of one of Iowa's greatest men. . . . When he first questioned the corporation leadership of the Republican party, the spirit of partisanship was so bitter that even his old comrades in arms turned upon him as a vicious and dangerous enemy. He was never daunted but continued straight ahead in the course that seemed to him right. . . . As a statesman he is a pioneer in many of the reforms that are now agitating the whole country and promising a revolution of political systems.[20]

Despite his relationship with Weaver, however, Brookhart gave his support to the Republican Party in 1892, acknowledging years later that he had not at that time properly appreciated the "prophets of progress of our country."[21] He took to the stump for the Republican candidates—Benjamin Harrison for President and John H. Gear, running to reclaim the First District House seat he had lost two years before. At one rally in Van Buren County, Brookhart attacked Dr. Wiley A. Jones, the local Democratic leader and postmaster. To the great delight of a crowd that had come as much for entertainment as politics, he listed, one by one, the Democratic "political crimes" that the long-standing Democrat had "pleaded guilty to." Jones, in a reply to the speech published in the *Van Buren Democrat*, questioned whether anyone from the swamps of the Fox River could know about politics. The speech was understandable, he said, when one considered that it was amid the frogs, mosquitos, crayfish, and calamus weeds that young Brookhart, the "Calamus Swamp Orator," had gained his political wisdom.

In the first twenty-three years of Brookhart's life can be found the statement of many themes that would be played out during the rest of his life. Cynthia Brookhart encouraged her son to study, to learn about the world beyond the narrow confines of the Fox River Valley; and Colar Brookhart supported his wife's plans. Regarding farming as a marginal enterprise, he apparently had no plans to pass the farm on to his eldest son. Smith had also learned early in life how the farmer was buffeted by forces beyond his control, how heavy rains could turn fertile bottomland into a swamp, and how changeable marketing conditions could frustrate a man's dream of raising his family amid bountiful wheat fields. In Bloomfield, he had been exposed to partisan politics and through Weaver and others he had come into contact with the Populist theories and remedies that he would later make his own.

In 1892, however, Brookhart's efforts to apply such theories were still three decades in the future. In the meantime, he set about finding a place to practice law.

2

The Establishment County Attorney

On December 9, 1892, the *Washington* (Iowa) *Gazette* carried a small notice that "S. W. Brookhart, a bright young lawyer from Keosauqua, has formed a partnership with Jackson Roberts under the firm of Roberts and Brookhart." It was the culmination of Brookhart's search for a place to practice law, a search that had led him first to Oskaloosa and then to Fairfield where Roland J. Wilson, son of Iowa Senator James F. Wilson, had suggested that he try Washington and had given him a letter of introduction to William R. Mount, a Washington storekeeper. Mount, in turn, introduced Brookhart to Roberts. Brookhart later remembered that he had arrived in Washington with ten dollars in his pocket and a pair of shoes with holes in them.[1]

In 1890 Washington County, Iowa, had a population of 18,468; the county seat of Washington had a population of 3,235 which would increase by over 400 people within five years. Washington was typical of countless county seat towns in the Upper Midwest.[2] It received a steady flow of citizens coming to transact business with the county officers and also served as a market and trading center. It was served by several passenger trains each day and the hotel register regularly included guests from across the Midwest.

At the time Brookhart arrived the city was in something of a building boom as new houses went up and expanded the boundaries of the city. Old businesses were growing, new businesses started, and the newspapers urged the formation of a businessmen's association to encourage more growth.

Still the newspaper betrayed some ambivalence about what all the progress might mean. Writing in 1895 the editor of the *Washington Evening Journal* wrote that "Washington is quite a place for meetings this week, revival, temperance meetings, populist meetings and court. All these ought to affect some change for the betterment of Washington, but we think the town is not very bad yet anyway."[3]

The city was served by a good school system that included a post-high school academy. Many religious denominations were represented with active congregations. Included in these were the Roman Catholics with their own school and an African Methodist Episcopal Church for the small African-American community.

Four newspapers, three weeklies and a daily, kept the citizens informed about local and world news. The world was brought even closer to home when the papers published letters from local boys in Cuba and the Philippines during the Spanish-American War and from China during the Boxer Rebellion. Those who chose to do so could learn more from lecturers who regularly appeared at the Graham Opera House, or in later years, at the annual Chautauqua. Over a period of years such speakers as Mary Ellen Lease, Russell Conwell, William Jennings Bryan, Robert M. La Follette, Booker T. Washington, James B. Weaver, and Carrie Nation appeared in Washington. Local groups also sponsored lecture series, including an extension course from the University of Chicago.

Entertainment ranged from the Buffalo Bill show to the Iowa-born Cherry Sisters, who made off-key singing an art form. On the eve of the Spanish-American War, John Philip Sousa brought his band to Washington and the town proudly boasted that Washington was the smallest town in the nation to get Sousa's band. A steady stream of theatrical troupes brought Shakespeare, comedies, melodramas, and such perennial favorites as "Ten Nights in a Bar Room." At least once a year a company brought "Uncle Tom's Cabin" to town.[4]

The citizens also created their own entertainment. Athletic activities included a bicycle club, a golf club, tennis courts, and by the end of the century an active baseball team. At various times there were at least two bands as well as amateur theatrical groups. Proud of its role in the Civil War, the town turned out for the annual GAR Camp Fire and to remember the dead on Decoration Day.

As a young attorney new to town Smith Brookhart would eventually take an active role in its life. But his introduction to a public role came through politics and the issue of liquor. In the 1890s both Washington County and city were solidly Republican. Both were also bone dry; and when Brookhart arrived, both were served by two weekly Republican newspapers, the *Washington Press* and the *Washington Gazette*. The former was edited and published by Howard A. Burrell, who used it to articulate the moderate Republican view on prohibition, which maintained that one could be a Republican and a wet. The latter was run by D. H. Logan and Samuel Wakefield Neal who equated Republicanism with strict prohibition.[5]

Having established himself as a lawyer, Brookhart wasted no time in getting involved in Washington County Republican politics. In August 1893, he was elected chairman of the county convention and, in the words of the *Gazette*, "made a good speech, bristling with points."[6] He and thirteen others were then selected as delegates to the state convention, which was scheduled to meet later the same month.

In planning the convention, the Republican State Central Committee hoped to devise a platform, and especially a prohibition plank, that would unify the dry and moderate factions of the party. Their solution was a plank which declared that "prohibition is no test of Republicanism," and which advocated local option. The prohibitionists tried to remove the local option portion from the plank, but this failed by a vote of 613 to 590.[7]

The fight over the prohibition plank brought into the open the rift between Republicans in Washington County, a rift already reflected in the positions of the *Gazette* and the *Press*. Logan and Neal were the first to comment. "It is hardly necessary," they declared, "to say the [prohibition plank] is not the plank which the *Gazette* favored." It meant that the issue would now have to be entrusted to "good Republicans" in the General Assembly. Burrell, on the other hand, thought the plank adopted was the "sensible, manly thing to do."[8]

During this same period, county chairman Brookhart was busy with a county-wide tour. Between October 18 and November 4 he spoke in seven of the fifteen townships in the county, often appearing with Colonel William B. Bell, D. H. Logan, Jackson Roberts, and W. R. McClean. One of these performances was at Highland, where, according to the *Press*, "Brookhart made a forcible discussion of the national issues" and McClean spoke strongly in favor of the dry position. Between them, the correspondent noted, they had left "Old Highland . . . so hot she sizzles."[9]

The Republicans recaptured the statehouse, and in 1894 a number of liquor bills were introduced into the Iowa legislature. But the one generating the most comment was the proposal for a "mulct law." Based on a similar law in Ohio, this would levy a tax of six hundred dollars against anyone, other than a registered pharmacist, who sold liquor and would then allow those who paid the tax to operate without fear of prosecution. The mulct was not to be construed as a legalization of liquor, thus satisfying the drys. Yet at the same time, it would allow local option sales of liquor, the goal of the moderates. In cities of five thousand or more inhabitants, the law could become operative only upon signed agreement of a majority of the voters in the previous election. In smaller communities (such as Washington) 65 percent of the voters in the county had to agree to it. In essence, local governments, in return for tax payments, would allow the law to be broken.

After a month of debate the mulct bill passed both houses of the General Assembly, fifty-three to forty-five in the House of Representatives and twenty-six to twenty-four in the Senate. The governor signed the bill on March 29 and it become effective upon publication in the newspapers. Predictably, Logan and Neal of the *Washington Gazette* were opposed to it. They preferred "straight prohibition."[10]

The drys clearly saw the mulct as another form of local option that could mean the sacrifice of gains made under the prohibition laws of the 1880s. Washington County had once had its saloons and breweries. "For years," according to an account subsequently published by the Anti-Saloon League, the city had experienced "saloon fights, drunken father, brother, and sons [which] made nights hideous; heavy taxes, full jail and poorhouse were the order of the day." But prohibition had changed this, so that by 1889 the saloons were gone and "there were no saloon fights, seldom a drunken man on the streets, happy homes, well-fed and clothed women, with peace and quiet day and night." To insure that these changes were not undone, the drys were determined to control the county's law enforcement machinery, especially the office of county attorney through which the new state law was to be administered.[11]

In 1894 the incumbent Washington County attorney, Charles James Wilson, announced that he would not be a candidate for reelection. Two men announced their candidacies: A. S. Folger, a local attorney and insurance man, and Smith W. Brookhart. In the *Gazette* Folger was described as "an old soldier, a good honest man" while Brookhart was seen as "a very bright young attorney," who would be "a good stumper and would add strength to the ticket." In the *Press*, Burrell noted that both were reputable men. Folger was "familiar with the work" since he had been a county attorney in Indiana, and Brookhart was "a young man of reading, industry and considerable experience."[12]

Actually, Burrell and the moderates seem to have had another candidate in mind. As a *Press* editorial would put it some eighteen years later, "Burrell had cooked up the cutest little deal to beat Brookhart and nominate another man for a fifth term."[13] Apparently, the "cute little deal" was to have Wilson declare his non-candidacy and then have the county convention draft him.

As it turned out, Burrell and Wilson were unable to control the convention in the way envisioned. The drys had been busy organizing to secure the nomination for Brookhart, and this meant solid support for his candidacy. Among those who "made" him county attorney in 1894, Brookhart would later note, were D. H. Logan and Wake Neal, editors and publishers of the *Gazette*; Colonel William B. Bell, a long-time Republican and temperance man and currently state representative; John Alex Young, a banker who had been county auditor and mayor; Jackson Roberts, Brookhart's law partner; Vint Nash, Sam Thompson, Joseph H. Huston, Eusebius W. H. Ashby, farmers; Dr. Joseph Sheafe; and Benjamin F. Brown, farmer,

Anti-Monopoly state representative, and member of the Farmers and Laborers, Greenback, and Populist parties. "Others," he said, "were also involved, but these were the leaders."[14]

In general, the group of men who supported Brookhart represented an older generation of professional men and successful farmers. In 1894 their average age was fifty-four (Brookhart was only twenty-five), and six of the group had been Civil War veterans. All were long-time Republicans. Young had won his first election when Brookhart was two years old; Roberts, Young, Huston, and Neal had been delegates to the county convention in 1879; and Bell had gone to the congressional convention in 1879. In addition, they had long been associated with the temperance movement. Logan and Neal had made the *Gazette* into a spokesman for the dry cause, a stance clearly congruent with Neal's position as superintendent of the Methodist Sabbath School. Bell had been one of the founders of the Washington County Temperance Society and as state representative had voted against the mulct law. And Brown's Anti-Monopoly platform of 1874 had included a strong pro-temperance plank.[15]

At the county convention meeting on August 25, the work of the group paid off. Brookhart was named the party's candidate for county attorney on the second ballot, receiving sixty-one votes to thirty for Wilson and thirteen for Folger. The *Gazette*'s editors noted, perhaps with tongue in cheek, that "C. J. Wilson . . . made a good run although not a candidate." The party then closed ranks, at least publicly. On October 31 the *Press* endorsed Brookhart as having "the stuff and work in him," and in November Brookhart won easily, polling 57.6 percent of the vote.[16]

The drys of Washington County were in a position to protect their former gains. And while many counties adopted the mulct law, Washington and some fifty other counties did not. They continued, between 1895 and 1900, to operate under the prohibition laws. The result for the state as a whole was a kind of local option that did seem to satisfy both drys and moderates. As one writer later noted, the mulct law was "as illogical a law . . . as can be found anywhere," but it had apparently been accepted as "the final solution of the liquor problem."[17]

Brookhart's first political candidacy had been in advocacy of a cause. As the new young man in town, who wholeheartedly believed in the cause of prohibition, he had found an office waiting for him. Later in his political career Brookhart himself would become the issue. But in 1894 he was the political figurehead for a debate that had been raging in the county and state for several years. From the experience he had learned first hand that politics was something more than the entertainment he had enjoyed while debating with Democrats in the Fox River Valley. It could, as James B. Weaver no doubt told him, be a means to greater ends, in this case, a way to maintain the status quo. Having learned this, however, he was content to settle into a lifestyle indistinguishable from that of others who were similarly situated in the small towns of Iowa and the Midwest. It was only later that he would seek to use politics to attack the status quo and bring about a new order.

Meanwhile, Smith Brookhart settled into his life as county attorney. Following his election, he dissolved his partnership with Roberts, moved into a room behind a doctor's office, and quickly got down to work.[18] For the next six years he looked after the county's business and built his own practice.

The county work consisted of the full range of lawbreaking, from larceny to fraud to a recurring concern for vagrants who came to town by rail and tried to remain for a while. The people's business often meant that he travelled to other towns in the county and sometimes to Des Moines to appear before the Supreme Court for appeal proceedings. Not surprisingly, however, enforcement of the liquor laws took the largest share of the county attorney's time.

He had been elected as a dry and he was determined that his county would be as dry as he was. Brookhart attacked the problem on all fronts. Individual bootleggers, businesses that tried to sell liquor, and railroads that carried liquor through town were all called into court. The railroads also became targets when they would try to off-load liquor to an individual for resale. But liquor cases were difficult to prosecute and Brookhart's conviction record was mixed. Although the public appeared to support their county attorney one paper suggested that too many "nuisance" cases were brought on flimsy evidence.[19]

In May of 1896, Brookhart took time out from his practice to make the first of many trips from Washington, Iowa, to Washington, D.C. He attended the Supreme Court to hear a case argued and the dry county attorney was shocked to find "drunken Congressmen . . . in the House restaurant." Upon his return the *Press* reported:

> S. W. Brookhart's eastern trip was full of instruction and recreation: he saw how the great men in Congress don't do it, went to soldier's home, Mt. Vernon, Alexandria, Norfolk; saw how cannons and ships are made; went round by sea to New York and never heaved once. Travel, to a prepared mind, is the best educator in the world.[20]

Later that summer he was renominated by acclamation for a second term. "He has prosecuted with energy and good judgment," Burrell wrote in the *Press*, "and his record as fine collector and replenisher of the treasury is unexcelled." Logan and Neal concurred. Brookhart, they said, "has been County Attorney for one term and has made a record that has done him credit. He has done his duty without fear or favor and the people know a good officer when they have tried him." He was reelected in the fall.[21]

In the meantime Brookhart's private law practice grew. In 1895 he took on a young man from the community who read law in his offices. That same year he was admitted to practice in federal courts. His practice soon outgrew the single room behind the doctor's office and in 1897 he moved into the offices of his old partner, Jackson Roberts, who had recently retired from practice.[22]

One consequence of Smith's growing practice was that it enabled him to give support to his family. In 1894, for example, he brought his brother James to Washington. Two years younger than his brother, Jim Brookhart followed a course very similar to that of his older brother. A high school graduate at seventeen, Jim taught school for several years before coming to Washington to enroll in the Washington Academy. He graduated in 1896, taught school in Washington, and became a school principal. But like Smith, he also read law and was admitted to the bar in 1898.[23]

Smith and Jim Brookhart formed a law partnership which grew quickly and in 1902 they added an abstract business. That same year the *Journal* commented that they "numbered among our substantial citizens." Their partnership extended beyond their legal practice. Together they invested in a number of businesses and they shared a common interest in politics. In 1911 a third brother, Thompson (Thomps), would enter the firm. A Washington Academy and Iowa Law School graduate, Thomps would tend to the everyday business of the firm while Smith and Jim tended to outside interests.[24]

Because of their law partnership and other common interests, Smith and Jim were usually referred to by the collective, "the Brookhart brothers." Alike in many ways, in temperament, however, they were different and seemed to complement one another. Jim was an outgoing, social man who appeared in local plays, sang in a popular male quartet, played golf and other sports, and whose name often appeared in the social columns of the newspapers. Smith, on the other hand, cared little for such activities. A much more distant and remote man, his life was focused on the law. Beyond that his only public interests were a passion for politics and the National Guard.

Organized in 1877 by Civil War veterans, Company D, Iowa National Guard was one of the oldest continuous companies in Iowa. Over the years generations of young Washingtonians had enlisted, as much for the socialization as the military training. In June 1894 Smith enlisted as a private and within a year he was promoted to corporal. National Guardsmen elected their officers and in 1897 Brookhart defeated two other candidates to become a second lieutenant. His election by the men confirmed the opinion of the *Journal* that he was "one of the best posted men in military tactics in the business."[25] Over the next few years weekly drills and the annual summer camp would be added to the rhythm of his life.

His family was important to Brookhart and he made periodic trips to his parents' home in Van Buren County. In January 1897 however, the *Journal* noticed the visits were "becoming more frequent of late." The reason was Jennie Hearne. Seven months younger than Brookhart, Jennie had graduated from Iowa Wesleyan College where a classmate said that she was "respected by all as one of the brightest as well as model" women at the school.[26]

Smith and Jennie had first met in Bloomfield at an 1891 Epworth League dinner. As a schoolteacher from Keosauqua, she had been in town for a school meeting and was serving giblet gravy at the dinner. Smith managed an introduction and decided then and there that he was going to marry her. The courtship continued by mail until Brookhart decided he could just as well read law in Keosauqua as in Bloomfield.

"We had no money to spend on pleasure," Jennie recalled, "but there were hayrides, barn dances and rolling green hills for Sunday hikes, and an inexhaustible fund of common interests." This continued for five years while Smith tried to save enough money so they could be married. He gave her a ring, although "it wasn't much of a ring," and finally, on June 22, 1897, they were married. "We got so tired of waiting," Jennie said, "that we got married anyhow."[27]

Following a honeymoon among the northern lakes, the couple arrived in Washington and moved into a house on Green Street. The next evening they were given a shivaree by members of Smith's National Guard company.[28]

The house on Green Street was only temporary quarters for the newlyweds. By autumn work had begun on a new house at 302 East Jefferson Street. The Brookharts moved into their "elegant home" in early December. They were barely settled when family members began to arrive for Christmas. Smith's parents came from their home in Cantril. Jennie's father came from Keosauqua and her sister and brother from their studies at Iowa Wesleyan in Mt. Pleasant. Another of her brothers joined them from Oskaloosa. The following September the household grew by one with the birth of Charles Edward Brookhart, the first of their seven children.[29]

The new family quickly settled into the routine of small town life. Smith had his work, his continuing involvement with politics, and was becoming more involved with the National Guard. Occasionally they had friends in for dinner and parlor games; the newspapers commonly reported that such evenings were great successes and that Jennie was a "charming hostess."[30] But probably more typical was the evening Jennie described in 1899:

Evenings we usually read. We are still on *Les Miserables*. He reads the French, translating into English as he goes, and I keep with him in my English edition and if a difficult rendering comes up I read mine. It improves his French and we enjoy the book itself. He also reads some Spanish quite often. He is reading one of Wilkie Collins' novels, translated into Spanish . . . and he puts much emphasis upon enunciation and proper setting of lips, tongue and teeth.[31]

Evenings at home would become rare for the Brookharts. As they both became more involved in community activities, evenings would often find them out of the house to attend meetings. Moreover, as Smith's interests broadened beyond the borders of Washington County he would be away from home more frequently. In their later years politics, railroad issues, and rifle interests would separate them, but in 1898 it was war that took Smith away.

3

The Soldier and Citizen

On February 14, 1898, Washingtonians gathered in the Graham Opera House to hear John Philip Sousa's band play a concert that included the recently composed "Stars and Stripes Forever." Whether the Brookharts attended the concert is unknown, but events nearly 1,400 miles away would soon put an end to their peaceful evenings at home. The next day the American battleship *Maine* blew up in the harbor in Havana, Cuba, with the loss of 260 American lives. For months the papers had carried reports of the fight by the Cuban people to overthrow their cruel Spanish masters. Now the papers blamed the loss of the *Maine* on a Spanish mine, urged Americans to avenge the deaths of American sailors, and gave the nation a new battle cry: "Remember the *Maine!*"[1]

In the weeks following the *Maine* disaster public outcry for war increased steadily. Finally President William McKinley called for war and on April 25 Congress declared war with Spain. In the subsequent mobilization Iowa was called upon to supply 125,000 men, and Governor Leslie Shaw began preparations to call the four Iowa National Guard regiments to duty. The men of Company D in Washington would soon join their comrades from across Iowa to carry the stars and stripes into battle.

A few days after the *Maine* had blown up the *Journal* polled its readers and found that, like most Americans, they believed the explosion to be the work of "those treacherous Spaniards." Most seemed to be in favor of turning loose the "gods of war." Local ministers discussed the possibility of war from their pulpits. Downtown at the New York Store the merchant used dry goods to create a replica of the *Maine* with a flag, a picture of President McKinley, and the premature statement that "War had been declared." And in mid-March the *Journal* ran an ad: "Twenty able-bodies, intelligent young men to join Company D. Call and leave name at east side restaurant with Captain D. W. Harvey."[2]

Meanwhile, as Brookhart and Company D prepared to go off to war, the citizens of Washington reflected on the last time local boys went off to war. Company D boys had grown up hearing stories of the Civil War. Many were sons of veterans of that war and the Grand Army of the Republic (GAR) was an active part of the life of Washington. Many Company D boys hoped that war would come so they could go off to free the oppressed Cubans as their fathers had gone off to free the slaves.

As the day of departure of Company D neared, the old veterans, including some who had given Brookhart his start in politics a few years before, organized a banquet to give him and his men a proper send-off. On the following Monday night, April 25, the National Guard Armory was filled as seemingly the whole town gathered to bid the boys farewell. Following a sumptuous banquet prepared and served by the ladies, the old veterans told again the stories that the young soldiers had grown up hearing. There were toasts, songs, and the presentation of a flag that the citizens had raised money to purchase. Accepting the flag for the company, Lt. Smith W. Brookhart assured the townspeople that if necessary they would defend it with their lives.

The next morning school was dismissed and an estimated 5,000 people assembled to escort Company D to the train. At the head of the parade was the Palma Band, at least one member of which was experienced in sending men off to war. E. T. Hebner, a local monument carver, had been a fifer in the Mexican and Civil wars; now the old man saw another generation go to war.[3] The parade also included the hose and fire company as well as a second band. Marching alongside Company D, the men of the GAR carried the old torn flag that had been presented to them when they left in 1861. Arriving at the station, the Company broke ranks for a final farewell to family and friends.

In the late afternoon the train arrived at the state fairgrounds, renamed Camp McKinley. Company D quickly settled into the confusions and discipline of an army taking shape. The commander of the Iowa troops was James Rush Lincoln, long-time professor of military science at Iowa State College in Ames. Born in Maryland, and not related to the Civil War president, Lincoln had been a Confederate cavalryman at Gettysburg and had been with Robert E. Lee at Appomattox. Now he would lead the sons of those who had been his enemy. The first full day in camp Lincoln had all the Iowa troops assemble in formation and the sight of 2,500 men in blue thrilled the men of Company D.[4]

Throughout their weeks at Camp McKinley they continued the preparations for war. As officer in charge for most of the period, Brookhart filled their days with drills, exercises, mock combat, target practice, reviews, and the other activities necessary to build an army. Still they had a great deal of time on their hands, and so they quickly learned the universal lesson of armies to "wait patiently and ask few questions." Although they claimed to find it easy to get in the habit of "lazying" around and doing nothing, in fact they filled their time with great creativity.[5]

A number of the men, including Brookhart, used some of their time to write regular reports for the newspapers back home. They engaged in impromptu wrestling matches and songfests and occasionally one of the regimental bands would play a concert. Many of the companies adopted mascots and D was no exception. For a time they had two mascots, a mongrel called "Pokerine" and a water spaniel named "Craps" who would accompany them for their entire tour of duty. Brookhart said it would take "a grand jury to find out the meaning" of the names, but the suspicion was that at least one was named for a favorite game played in a "dark corner" of their quarters.[6]

After three weeks of drills and examinations Company D and the other companies were sworn into federal service on May 18. Now part of the Fiftieth Regiment Iowa Volunteer Infantry, most knew they would be going south soon, they hoped to Cuba.

Before Brookhart could go south, however, he had to make arrangements for the county attorney's office. One proposal was to continue to pay him a salary even though he would be unable to fulfill his duties of the office. Brookhart considered that to be charity, however, and refused to accept the offer. Instead, he resigned and in July the board of supervisors appointed Jim Brookhart to fill out Smith's term. Although some had misgivings because Jim had just been admitted to the bar, most realized that Jim would only serve until the election in November. The *Press* remarked that Jim's appointment was "a graceful compliment to both of the brothers."[7]

The orders finally came that the Fiftieth was to leave Des Moines for Florida on May 21. Roused awake that morning at 4:00 A.M., they marched to the railway station in a downpour, a presage of much of their stay in Florida. Despite the cheers of passersby, including some of their own townspeople who now lived in Des Moines, the men of Company D seemed quiet. A few shed tears.[8]

After a celebration in Davenport and a layover in Chicago, they boarded their railroad car, ironically named the "Maine." A soldier remarked that he hoped that they would not be as "unfortunate as the occupants of that notable vessel."[9] The train rolled south through Indiana, and on through Kentucky, Tennessee, and Georgia.

In the evening of the second day out they pulled into Jacksonville, Florida, where they immediately began to set up camp. Company D set up its "street" within the Fiftieth Iowa campsite at Camp Cuba Libre, as it was now named, and quickly got down to work. They began the daily routine of drills, inspections, exercises, mock battles, and the various activities that make an army. In charge of instructional activities Brookhart regularly took the men to the rifle range and he established a company school for noncommissioned officers. The work began to pay off. Following a drill at the end of June their brigade commander, General William A. Bancroft, said that Company D was the best drilled in the regiment. Former Confederate officers who frequented the camp agreed, adding that Company D was better drilled and made a better appearance than any other northern group.[10]

Most days were deadeningly the same. Most of the men had no money, which Brookhart thought was probably a good thing. As early as June 6 Smith Brookhart would write his wife that his was a lazy life and that "unless we go to Cuba soon and get some fighting to do, I am afraid my hitherto industrious habits will be seriously impaired."[11]

Brookhart was not entirely idle, however. He served in a number of positions during his time in Florida. In addition to his duties with the company, he served with the Judge Advocate, as officer of the guard, as head of the commissary, and for a time was a candidate for aide to the commanding general. In whatever capacity he served he was well regarded by the men. Brookhart "is one of the most reliable and best posted men in our regiment," one wrote, "and when they have an important position they want filled and filled right away they know he is the man to do it."[12]

In his spare time he and a few others from Company D hired a Cuban refugee to teach them Spanish. "It cost us twenty-five cents each per lesson at three lessons per week," he wrote his wife, "and I know of no other way so good to kill time." "If we stay here a few months," he thought, he would know Spanish "quite as well as French and German and better in conversation." Brookhart hoped that the men would take advantage of the opportunity to learn Spanish but he also saw the lessons as a way to occupy their time. Moreover, the prohibitionist knew very well how they might occupy their time and he told Jennie that he thought it a good idea "to keep a barrel of lemonade all the time" so that they "would not go to the saloons so much."[13]

As the Fourth of July approached, and they were still in Florida, Company D began to think it would never get to Cuba. But the men intended to celebrate the holiday like they would have had they been at home. They awoke to firecrackers which continued throughout the day, but rain postponed the afternoon parade in Jacksonville. Pooling their money they bought provisions for a banquet, complete with cigars. As they ate, news reached them that the Spanish fleet had been defeated at Santiago harbor in Cuba. With that the real celebration began and continued long into the night. One remarked that "if Washington people had laid low and listened I believe they could have heard the yelling done by Company D."[14]

But as summer wore on the soldiers in Florida grew increasingly restless. The victory over the Spanish fleet at Santiago and the surrender of the Spanish garrison there on July 17 spelled the virtual end of the war. The war finally ended on August 12 when the Spanish and American governments signed a protocol that provided for a peace treaty to be written.

For the men of Company D in Florida, however, peace did not mean the end of the threat of death. Disease had been a constant concern ever since Company D had first arrived in Florida. Throughout June and early July, the health of Company D was good. In mid-July, however, the rainy season began, resulting in the frequent flooding of their camp.

During the first weeks of August the sick call list began to grow, and along with it more reports of deaths in the Fiftieth Iowa. On August 23 Company D lost its first man: Albert Huff of Kalona died of typhoid. One week later "taps sounded" for Ralph Conger, another "of the good soldiers of Company D." Conger's death was felt even more because he was from Washington itself. When the body arrived home it seemed that all of Washington turned out for Conger's funeral and it served to remind the citizens of the danger that all of Company D faced in Florida.[15]

The war was barely over when Brookhart arrived home on a thirty-day leave. The reason for his leave is unclear but it could have been the fact that Jennie was in the last month of her pregnancy. Or it could have been the fact that the Republican county convention was scheduled for mid-September. His weekly columns in the *Press* had kept him in the public eye:

> Lieutenant Brookhart's letters in the *Press* are widely copied. They are terse, meaty, and hit the salient points. Brookhart has been growing fast in the esteem of our people, both as a man and a lawyer, and we have heard many Republicans express the hope that the war may soon be over, that they may honor themselves as well as him by renominating this able attorney for county attorney.[16]

Nevertheless, he was warmly greeted. He was the "color of a Cuban" and had lost twenty pounds, but otherwise he looked well.[17]

A few days after he arrived home, Brookhart went to an Old Settlers' meeting in Wellman. Although not on the program he was the center of attention. Prevailed upon to speak he told about the Washington County boys still in Florida. It turned out that his talk was "probably . . . the best received address of the day."[18]

Throughout Iowa pressure mounted on Shaw to bring the Fiftieth and other Iowa regiments home. Brookhart reported to his townspeople that although the camp was on high ground, the city sewage dump and swamps were but seventy-five yards away. In Brookhart's opinion six more weeks would be very bad for Company D. The group voted unanimously to appeal to all appropriate officials in Des Moines and Washington, D.C., to bring the boys home.[19]

Brookhart went to Des Moines to present the case directly to the governor. He was unsuccessful and returned from Des Moines disgusted with Shaw's seeming unwillingness to act. Years later Brookhart spoke about the meeting in a speech and without giving any details the newspaper report said he "did not throw large bouquets to Mr. Shaw." But Brookhart's effort did not go unnoticed in Florida. One of the columnists wrote that the "boys are pleased to learn of the good work being done by Lieutenant Brookhart at home, in regard to having our regiment mustered out."[20]

Shaw was in a spot. He knew that although the war was over, there was still a need for an army and he was reluctant to have the War Department think that Iowa was unwilling to do its part. Yet privately, he was angry with the War Department's claims that the men in Florida were receiving adequate health care. Shaw had visited the camp in August and had seen the sick lying untended in their beds with dead soldiers in the cots next to them. For a day or so he wavered, then he took action. He asked the Secretary of War to bring the Fiftieth Iowa home.[21]

Company D started home on September 13. The trip home retraced their route of nearly four months before. The company let out a great shout as they crossed the Mississippi River into Iowa. At DeWitt the train stopped long enough for the sickest to be taken off and sent directly to Washington, including Fred Crawford who would die of typhoid after he arrived home. The rest would go on to Des Moines and report to Camp McKinley. Three days later Company D was given a thirty-day leave but had to return in November when the company assembled at Camp McKinley to be mustered out.[22]

With the military formalities completed, the former Company D, now civilians, arrived home on December 1. That evening the Ladies' Aid Society gave a banquet. Everyone sensed that this would be their last time together. They came back from the war not heroes but survivors. Their experience in

Florida had been one of frustration and boredom. When it had become apparent that they would not see active service, their enthusiasm waned, and under threat of death by disease they asked to be brought home.[23]

Nevertheless the war touched them. As a county official and veteran of the recent war, Brookhart was often in demand for speeches on Memorial Day, July Fourth, or GAR campfire observances. Such holidays were the occasion for picnics and family gatherings. But the celebrants were not allowed to forget the serious nature of the day. One early Brookhart Memorial Day speech was filled with flowery patriotism. Extolling the virtues of freedom and democracy, Brookhart reminded his listeners that those virtues were won at a great price:

> The graves of some we decorated today, but many are far away and if perchance a flower were dropped upon them it was by the hand of a stranger or former foeman. . . . Their sacrifice was complete and without reward. They were denied the plaudits of a grateful nation and the unspeakable joy of a welcome home; cut off from a life of honor and pride; perished amid the gloom of defeat or the uncertainty of victory and while the bloom of youth was yet upon their brow.[24]

To emphasize the contribution Washington had made Brookhart read the names of 314 men who had served in wars, including the three Company D men who died in Florida. He said the best way to teach children patriotism was to read this list to them. The *Journal* said the list was "interesting and represents a great deal of work on the part of Mr. Brookhart." Such dogged attention to details and research was typical of Brookhart. In politics, the law, and other interests in his life, facts were important and he would often amass facts to build a case. The fact of war was that men died, and how better to make the case than to present their names?[25]

Twenty years later, in 1919, at the end of yet another war, some of the Company D men would gather to form the Albert M. Huff Post of the Veterans of the Spanish-American War. As veterans, they acknowledged that the war of twenty years before had brought more to the government in spoils than it had cost. Nevertheless, for the men of old Company D the proudest boast seemed to be that they had come home from the war and made good.[26]

Once home, they quickly returned to the lives they had interrupted six months before. Most returned to the jobs they left in May; others returned to school. Like his comrades in arms, Brookhart endeavored to make up for lost time. He had a new son and his new status in the community as a veteran brought new clients to his law firm. Jennie reported that he was well, had gained back the lost weight, and now was up to 166 pounds. "He is reading Spanish for amusement," she also reported, "he learned it pretty well—had a fine teacher and learned to converse."[27]

His immediate concern, however, was the fall election. Meeting on September 17, the county convention nominated him, reportedly "with enthusiastic vim," for the remainder of his own term and the full term beginning in 1899. "Lieut. Brookhart needs no introduction," the *Press* editorialized just before the election. "He has served as County Attorney, and the people were eager to renominate him. He is a rising young man, full of pluck, talent, industry and hard work. Smith is all right." Although elected for both terms, he was not mustered out in time to qualify for the short term, but took office for his third term in 1899.[28]

In addition to his work as county attorney his private law practice was growing. Most of his work was routine but occasionally a case would catch the public interest. One case that drew huge crowds to the courthouse involved whether a liquor permit should be issued to Ed C. Carris, a local druggist. Under Iowa law druggists could sell liquor for medicinal purposes. Brookhart, his brother Jim, and a third attorney from Fairfield appeared for the Young People's Good Citizenship Union who opposed the permit. Arguing that the county was totally dry, Brookhart presented a petition from 1,000 citizens who wanted to keep it that way. Following three days of testimony the permit was denied.[29]

Brookhart's various interests meant he traveled a great deal. The local papers frequently reported that he left on the morning train or had returned the previous night after some trip. Such travel was not without its hazards. Once when he and D. H. Logan drove a team and wagon to Dublin where each was scheduled to speak, the neck pin of the wagon broke and the team bolted. Brookhart jumped out of the wagon but Logan was thrown out and broke his collar bone. Although badly shaken Brookhart was able to give his speech. In reporting the incident the newspaper suggested in good-natured jest that Brookhart had "succeeded in having Logan hurt that he might occupy the full time of the evening."[30]

On another trip to Missouri, rains made the roads impassable and Brookhart had to make the long return trip on horseback. Automobile travel was not always an improvement. Following a trip to Iowa City one November, he reported that although it took only one hour, fifteen minutes to return the thirty miles, it was "rather cold for such rapid automobile riding."[31]

Washington was a growing community in the years following the turn of the century. Brookhart joined in a variety of efforts to build the community and improve the life of its citizens. In 1900, for example, citizens hoped to convince the state to build a normal school in Washington. Brookhart joined other businessmen to form an association to work for the school.[32]

A few years later Brookhart joined with others in a series of meetings that resulted in the Commercial Club, formed for the "material, the social and the moral good of the community." A building was secured that included meeting rooms, a gymnasium, and a bowling alley. Over the next decade the Commercial Club became the center of social activities for the businessmen of Washington. Whenever anyone had an idea for progress in the community it would be brought before the club for discussion. Brookhart took an active role in the club and in 1910 he was elected president.[33]

Still another group was formed to encourage industry to settle in Washington. Speaking before the founding meeting of the Industrial Association in 1906, Brookhart urged the members to work together in securing industry. The only way to succeed, he said, was to create an open system where the rights of all would be respected. Brookhart bought shares of stock in the association and was elected to the board of directors.[34]

Whenever there was a new project for Washington, Brookhart could be counted on to support it. When the Carris Novelty Company wanted to expand its operations he was among those who bought stock in the new Carris Manufacturing. Another time he used his good offices to help the Mills Seed Company obtain a loan to build a new building.[35]

Brookhart was a strong advocate of education. He had brought several of his brothers and sisters to Washington to attend the local academy. He had joined the group to get the state to build a normal school in Washington. When another group wanted to bring a series of teachers from the University of Chicago, Brookhart was among the subscribers who underwrote the lectures.

Beginning in 1905 Washington businesses organized a Farmers' Institute, a one-day exhibition for farmers. In 1911 Brookhart urged that the Farmers' Institute be expanded to include courses taught through the extension service of Iowa State College. He raised money to finance the project, and served as general manager for the so-called "short course" held early in December 1911 and again in 1912.[36]

In 1900 he was elected a vice-president of the Loan and Building Association and served in that capacity until 1913 when he was elected president. Founded in 1886, the association provided over half a million dollars in loans that helped build hundreds of homes in Washington. He also was a founding director of the Farmers' and Merchants' Bank. As a state bank the Farmers' and Merchants' Bank could provide a more liberal loan policy than the local National Bank. Brookhart remained a director until the bank failed in 1924.[37]

Not all of Brookhart's projects were strictly community service. His growing law practice gave him the means to enter speculative ventures as well. One was an interurban railroad to be built from Iowa City south through Washington and on to Mt. Pleasant, Fort Madison, and Keokuk. Washington was well-served by several east-west rail lines but north-south travel by rail was difficult. This venture would help to correct this difficulty.

In 1903 Brookhart was among the investors who formed a corporation to build the road and served on the board of directors. Development was slow, however, and it took nearly three years for the surveys to be completed. The engineers reported that a route was feasible and in 1906 the board of directors began to discuss ways to finance the three million dollars it was projected would be necessary to build the road.[38]

Brookhart worked hard to gather support for the project. Appearing in Mt. Pleasant in March 1907, he debated the issue with a representative of the Chicago, Burlington and Quincy Railroad, which had a branch line that ran from Burlington to Washington. The railroad argued that the proposed interurban was not necessary and would not create the kind of business growth its advocates claimed. Brookhart disagreed and said that the interurban would give the area another route to the south. This would benefit the area by making it possible for additional goods to be delivered to citizens. Moreover, he argued, the competition of the interurban with the C. B. & Q. would result in lower freight rates for shippers.[39]

Brookhart kept up the campaign for better rail service. Speaking before the Commercial Club the next year he urged the members to petition the Iowa Board of Railroad Commissioners to improve the service to Washington and the surrounding area.[40] Meanwhile, the interurban proposal gathered scattered support in the communities it would have served, but it would never be built. Brookhart had approached the project in the hopes it would benefit the community; those hopes were unrealized. Moreover, he hoped to make money on the project. In this too, he failed.

Another speculative venture was more successful. George H. Paul, a local land speculator, and Jim Brookhart had been selling land for some time in the area around Corpus Christi, Texas. In November 1907 Brookhart joined them to form the George H. Paul Company with a capitalization of $50,000.[41] Smith Brookhart did legal work for the corporation but he did not actively sell land.

The business grew rapidly and Paul regularly bought more Texas land. In 1908 Smith Brookhart went with Paul to Cincinnati, Ohio, to see Charles Taft, the brother of the president, to negotiate a deal to buy land from Taft to add to the Paul holdings. Later that year Brookhart went to Des Moines to get the necessary state permission to increase the capital holdings of the company.[42]

The papers were full of optimistic reports from Washingtonians and others who had made the journey to Texas. Jim Brookhart made regular trips with prospective buyers. Smith went twice in 1908 and like most of those who went he not only inspected the lands, he took time to hunt deer. Following the second trip his stories about the number of game he and his party killed made the *Journal* wonder just how many deer were left in Texas. But such stories helped the business to prosper. Soon one Texas newspaper called the Paul Company the "largest retail operators of Texas lands in America."[43]

At the annual meeting in January 1909, the company reported that it had sold 80,000 acres of land in 1908, up from 27,000 the year before. Plans were announced to bring excursion cars from Nebraska and from as far east as Pittsburgh. At the same meeting Smith was elected to the board of directors. At the next annual meeting in January 1910, the company reported that sales in 1909 had been about 65,000 acres, down somewhat from the previous year. But in the nearly three years the company had been in existence, it had sold 200,000 acres of land for about seven million dollars. At this meeting the Brookhart brothers sold their interest to George Paul for $115,000. Smith's share was $59,000.[44]

The company had grown to the point that Brookhart could no longer do its work and maintain his law practice. Moreover, his growing family, as well as his political and other interests, demanded more of his time. The parting was amicable and the brothers maintained their law office in rooms at the Paul Building, headquarters of the land company.

Smith Brookhart's involvement with George H. Paul would come back to haunt him in later years. Although the company was legitimate, there was a public perception that Texas land companies were unsavory and so he was tainted by his involvement. Moreover, his profits from the sale of his stock put him in an economic bracket much higher than the small farmer he claimed to be. This perception was enhanced when a few years after Brookhart left the company, George Paul formed a new company and moved to Texas. At about this time the city of Washington took as its motto, "The Cleanest City in Iowa," to which a local wag added, "Yes, and George H. Paul cleaned it!"[45]

With the law practice, his political activities, and his business interests Brookhart had become a community leader. He did not, however, join the organized social and fraternal organizations that existed in towns like Washington. While he still lived in Bloomfield he had joined the Knights of Pythias. But after his first few years in Washington he rarely took part in the activities of the organization. The only other local organization to which he belonged was the Bar Association which he helped to found in 1905.[46]

Still he would occasionally join in the informal events typical of midwestern small towns. For a time the local professional groups challenged one another to baseball games, and when the lawyers played the doctors Brookhart joined the team. On another occasion his boast that he was the "best straw stacker in fourteen counties" resulted in a challenge. A local farmer offered his straw field and a crowd gathered to watch the event. The contest took place with a great deal of bantering and disputes about proper method, as well as frequent stops for rest. The *Journal* reported that the contestants did better at the dinner table than at the straw stack.[47]

The focus of the Brookhart social life was not in community organizations but in their home. Smith and Jennie were both close to their families and the Hearnes and Brookharts often came to visit from Keosauqua. On one occasion the Brookharts welcomed Jennie's brothers home from military service in the Philippines with a party that included decorations and artifacts from the Spanish-American War. Another evening they entertained Jennie's friends from Iowa Wesleyan College. On Valentine's Day they had local friends in to exchange greetings of the day. Jennie was known as a "charming hostess" who knew "well the art of entertaining." The Brookharts had the ability of "killing all formality at the very start and putting their guests at perfect ease."[48]

Unlike Smith, Jennie did join some local groups. She joined the PEO sisterhood, was active in the Methodist church, and served in the hospital auxiliary. But Smith's frequent absences put more of the household burdens on her. Their family was growing. Following the birth of their first son in 1898, three more sons were added to the family, John in 1901; Samuel Colar in 1903; and Smith Wildman, Jr., in 1905. The first daughter, Florence, was born in 1908 and in 1911 the *Journal* commented that the birth of Edith made "two daughters in a family which ran pretty strongly to boys for several years." The seventh child, Joseph, was born in 1915.[49]

The house on Jefferson Street soon became too small for the growing family. In April 1909 they broke ground for a new house on the east edge of town. Caring little for style and design, Brookhart insisted on two qualities for the house: it must be "fire proof and child proof." The result was a large structure with a concrete floor and supports, brick walls, and, at Brookhart's suggestion, a roof of concrete with asbestos shingles, the first roof that the architect had ever heard of being so constructed. The six bedrooms upstairs each had hot and cold running water so, as the *Press* reported, "It will never be necessary for members of this household to retire with their faces clouded with leftover complexions or to appear at breakfast with traces of dreams in the corner of their eyes." "It's only a plain farmhouse," Brookhart said, "and built to raise my [family]." Brookhart's "plain farmhouse" and the barn cost him $13,000 which he paid for with money from the sale of his George Paul stock.[50]

The following April the family celebrated the opening of their new home with a dinner for all the nearly fifty workmen who built it. The house and large acreage soon became a magnet for the children and all their friends. The large size gave them plenty of room to play and the unique construction made the house nearly impervious to damage. A favorite play activity was roller skating on the concrete floor of the attic.[51]

A concrete and brick barn was soon added to accommodate the horses and the other livestock they raised. Brookhart sent to Iowa State College for information on apple raising and within a few years had a large orchard. The children were expected to help with the chores, especially in the orchard. During his early years in the Senate the family supplemented their income with the sale of apples.

Thereafter he insisted on calling himself a "common, ordinary farmer." Speaking before the opening of the annual Farmers' Institute in 1910 he talked about his move to the country. He noticed that since the move he had fallen into the habit of "curling up his nose at city people" but also noticed that they were "always glad to have us farmers come to town." He also spoke about the recent census figures which indicated a loss of population for Iowa. He said it was not his fault because his household had doubled during the same period.[52]

The brick house would be home for the Brookharts for the next sixteen years. But by the time it was built Smith's activities would take him more frequently away from home. A small town entrepreneur, attorney, and politician, he now had his sights set on a larger world. Politics and an activity stemming from his National Guard service, rifle shooting, would take him from Washington and Iowa to a national stage.

4

The Sharpshooter

When Company D was mustered out of federal service in November 1898, the company itself ceased to exist. Before Brookhart left Des Moines, however, he spoke to Brig. Gen. Melvin H. Byers about organizing a new Company D. Writing Byers a few days later Brookhart said he would supply a list of names of those who wanted to join and formally apply to establish the new company. The list he sent Byers early the next year included some members of the old company as well as a number of new recruits. By the end of January forty-four men had enlisted and had been given physicals.[1]

Two weeks later the men unanimously elected Brookhart as captain and General Byers came to Washington to swear in the new company. Over the next few weeks Brookhart worked to equip and train the company. In May new Springfield rifles arrived from the Rock Island Arsenal and Brookhart immediately ordered extra drills with the new weapons to get ready for the Memorial Day parade. The new rifles also gave Brookhart the chance to pursue what would become one of his passions over the next thirty years: rifle marksmanship.[2]

Marksmanship had not been particularly important in the Civil War, given the weaponry and the battle tactics. Although the standard muzzle-loaders lacked precision, the rows of soldiers advancing side by side did not. If the musket ball missed one soldier, it would probably hit someone else down the row. But after the Civil War, new breech-loading guns could be much more accurate in the hands of a trained shooter. This launched a movement for rifle training, headed by militant journalist William Conant Church, founder of the National Rifle Association (NRA) in 1871. According to Church the purpose of the NRA was to make National Guardsmen into "sharpshooters."[3]

Although several former Union officers helped found the NRA, the U.S. Army ignored their call for rifle training; sharpshooting would encourage individualism, an undesirable trait in enlisted men. Instead, the NRA focused on training interested citizens and National Guardsmen. With the help of the New York legislature, the NRA built a one hundred acre rifle range called Creedmoor on Long Island and began to sponsor competitions. By 1874, in its first international match, the American team hit the bull's-eyes a half mile away with amazing accuracy and beat the reigning champion from Ireland.

Building on this success, the NRA sponsored numerous competitions and trained Guard units. "Rifle clubs and ranges popped up at an astonishing rate across the country," according to Osha Gray Davidson's history of the NRA. But the popularity of rifle competitions began to fade, and the NRA lost state funding of the Creedmoor matches.[4]

From its founding in 1877 Company D had a tradition of prize-winning rifle marksmanship teams. In the 1890s the current team and former teams would challenge each other to competitions. The competitions were neither formal nor regular, rather, a notice would appear in the paper that one group challenged the other to a shoot. Such events were always the occasion of bonhomie and good-natured wagers. One time, for example, the notice read: "From Co. D, to the fossilized shooters of the city." The next day the "fossilized shooters" chided the young team that it was "trying to get out of [its] class" by challenging them. On another occasion when an oyster supper was on the line, the young team lost and thus had to treat. The paper reported that "some of the boys, when the feast was ended, looked like the Irishman's stone wall—he built it four feet high and six feet wide, so if it tumbled over it would be higher than it was in the first place."[5]

Brookhart participated in most of the challenge shoots in the years before the Spanish-American War. His first recorded score came in a National Guard shoot in Muscatine when he got 124 out of a possible 225. Another time the paper reported that he hit a telegraph pole and a nearby window but rarely the target. Eventually his scores improved; in 1897 he qualified for the sharpshooter's medal. But he would never become a great shooter; his real skill was in training others to shoot.[6]

In time he developed a philosophy and method for the shooter. Brookhart believed it was not enough to simply fire at random and hope to hit something. Rather each man should practice until he could hit the target exactly. Factors such as wind, temperature, humidity, distance, and body position had to be taken into account. Shooting, however, was much more than a mechanical process. The shooter had to believe in himself and to believe that he could hit the target. Writing in 1918 Brookhart said that the necessary mental attitude was: "A belief in straight shooting. An enthusiasm for straight shooting. A pride in straight shooting."[7]

Equally important was one's physical condition, what Brookhart termed the "normal condition." In fact, he said, "I am a crank for the normal condition." This meant first a proper diet of water, milk, plain foods in moderate quantities and without strong seasoning. Moreover, tobacco and other such stimulants should be avoided. "The proper attitude of mind will give every man more pleasure in conquering a habit than in submitting to it. To win over the smoking habit is an achievement of which to be proud and it improves the scores."[8]

Finally, the rifleman had to avoid alcohol. Throughout his years in the National Guard, Brookhart considered that the use of alcohol in camp was a "capital offense." Usually, however, he fought a losing battle as more men went to town for liquor than stayed in camp to drink Brookhart's Florida lemonade. But as a shooting instructor he exercised more control and occasionally dropped a shooter from the team for alcohol use. He even forbade the temperate use of alcohol, arguing that any man who needed a drink to steady his nerves was unfit to be on the team. "Total abstinence, bone dry," he wrote, "is the only safe rule."[9]

In rifle shooting Brookhart found an activity that was a perfect complement to his own personality and predilections. It required study and discipline, and once mastered, the elements of it were uncomplicated: aim, pull the trigger, hit the target. He neither smoked nor drank and his habits were simple. In other words, he was what he advocated, "a man in normal condition." He believed that the normal condition made for "efficiency" in shooting, in the military "or in any other line of human service if you want all the facts." "Straight shooter" described Brookhart the rifleman, Brookhart the politician, and Brookhart the man.[10]

During the war Brookhart often took his men to the rifle range. Frustrated because he had been issued only thirty rounds of ammunition per man for practice, he said he knew he "couldn't train anybody to be expert at anything doing it 30 times." The ammunition problem was solved shortly after he took command of the new Company D when he found 18,000 rounds of ammunition that a previous captain had requisitioned but had never expended.[11]

He immediately set about building a rifle range on a site two miles west of town along a creek which had a thirty-foot bluff behind it. On June 7 he wrote Byers to say that he had finished the range and to ask him to reimburse the fifteen dollars he had spent. He also asked Byers for targets so that the men could begin rifle practice. The range served the company for two years; then Brookhart built a longer range so the men could use larger weapons and practice charging.[12]

While rifle shooting became a special interest, Brookhart enjoyed all aspects of the National Guard. The order and discipline of the military agreed with his own sense of discipline. Military rules and protocol became new subject matter for him to study and master. He worked hard to improve Company D to make sure that it got the best equipment available. At one point he used his own money to purchase a building in the hopes of remodeling it into an armory. When that did not come about, he worked to get the legislature to appropriate money to build an armory.[13]

Since most of the men of Company D did not intend to make the Guard a career, they did not always share their captain's enthusiasm for military drill and discipline. Although some of them were Spanish-American War veterans, most were new recruits. For many of them the Guard's obligatory two-hour drill each week was really a night out with "the boys," and the August encampment was a chance for adventure. Moreover, the ten cents an hour they received was a welcome addition to their income.[14]

Brookhart grew up in an era when Civil War veterans had kept their titles and used them as a means of entry into politics or status within the community. Ambitious for other political office once his term as county attorney ended, Brookhart's position in the National Guard would keep him in the public eye. When the position of major in the 50th Regiment opened up, Brookhart presented himself as a candidate for election. The 50th included the counties of southeast Iowa, and although he was not a leading candidate for the office, the *Journal* reported that "everyone in Washington will be glad to see him elected." He received all the votes of Company D, as well as two other companies, but did not receive the promotion.[15]

Throughout the summer Brookhart drilled the men to get them ready for their first summer encampment in August. As the company left for camp in Burlington the *Journal* commented that Brookhart was a "strict disciplinarian," who believed that he was responsible for the behavior of his men. But, the paper continued, "He has good men in the company and will hardly need to enforce any rigid rules."[16]

Nevertheless, he soon found himself defending his reputation as a commander. During a raid on a sutler's stores some private property was stolen. The allegation was made that the raiders were members of Company D and that Brookhart had known of the raid in advance and had done nothing to stop it.

Brookhart said that he had been awakened by a commotion near the sutler's tent and that he had ordered the tent guarded. The sutler, however, had dismissed the guard and given away what remained of his goods to the men, four of whom were from Company D. Furthermore, Brookhart said that General Byers had done him a "personal wrong" by charging him with "neglect of duty." Finally, he said that Byers had exceeded the law when he withheld part of the wages of the entire regiment to reimburse the sutler. "I am as strong for discipline and as diligent at enforcing it as any officer in the Guard," he told Byers, "but I am also for justice." He also said, discipline "will never be attained by punishing men for offenses they did not commit." Apparently the matter was dropped with no further consequences.[17]

A local community was largely responsible for the support of its guard company. Brookhart sometimes invested his own money in the company. The state picked up other expenses but still there was never enough. For additional support Brookhart apparently followed an established custom and deducted an annual four dollar "dues" from the camp pay of each man to pay for lights and fuel. Some of the men resented the loss of pay and sent a petition with twenty-one names to Byers calling for Brookhart's removal.

A few weeks later Brookhart dismissed the two ringleaders, Jasper Neiswanger and George Williams, for "inability to attend drills." Neiswanger, however, claimed that the real reason he was dismissed was because of the petition. In his defense Brookhart said that the petition was public knowledge, was "demoralizing" to the company, and had "impaired discipline." But the last straw came when Neiswanger came to drill and attacked Brookhart with "violent language." Brookhart then had no choice but to dismiss him. He chose the grounds of non-attendance because it was "most favorable" to them and would not unduly affect their future. Upon review the General sustained Brookhart's action as being in the "best interests of the Guard."[18]

Over the next few weeks several of the men expressed their regrets about the petition and Brookhart worked to put the matter behind him. Nevertheless, the issue smoldered throughout the winter. In March three men, including two who had signed the petition, refused to answer the roll at muster and Brookhart dismissed them for "insubordination." Writing Byers he said that he hoped that "this is about the last of the Neiswanger rebellion in my company."[19]

His hopes were unrealized, however, as morale and efficiency continued to decline. In April 1902 inspectors visited the company and reported that at least eight men had applied for discharge because they were unable to attend drills. Moreover, many of those attending drills were unable to satisfactorily perform the basic drill exercises. The inspectors learned that apparently a number of men were willing to enlist in the Guard but would not do so as long as Brookhart was in command. The inspector recommended that Brookhart and all other officers resign at once, that the company be mustered out, and a new company formed.

Brookhart admitted that he had not given the Guard his full attention. He was a candidate for district judge which took him away from town a great deal; if he won the judgeship he would resign his commission. Even if he lost, however, his growing law practice and other business interests would necessitate his resignation in the fall. But by early May the pressure to resign was too great and on May 14 he submitted his resignation.[20]

For the next five years Brookhart concentrated on politics, his law practice, and other business interests, but he also maintained his interest in rifle shooting. His hard work began to show results. In 1907 LeRoy Schilling of Washington won the Allison trophy given for outstanding scores at the state shoot. For years Schilling represented Iowa at the national matches.[21]

That same year Governor Albert B. Cummins appointed Brookhart the Inspector of Small Arms Practice for the state of Iowa with the rank of Colonel. The appointment recognized Brookhart's work and expertise in rifle shooting. The *Journal* noted that he "is a man who goes into his work thoroughly and conscientiously always, and friends and political antagonists alike will be pleased to hear of the honor that has so worthily come to him."[22]

The new inspector set out at once to build a state rifle range which would cover 287 acres of land and cost over $40,000. In the meantime he began to select the team that would represent Iowa at the national matches at Camp Perry, Ohio. First held in 1903, the matches brought together state National Guard teams, military teams, and private shooting clubs for competition and instruction.[23]

The national matches were an indication of a renewed interest in marksmanship on the part of the War Department. This new popularity can be attributed to the guerrilla Afrikaners in the Boer War: they had not defeated the British, but their sharpshooting had impressed them enough that the British military began to emphasize target shooting. Canada, and then the United States, picked up on the trend, and the NRA pressed again for training programs and governmental support. In 1903 the U.S. War Department founded the National Board for the Promotion of Rifle Practice to encourage rifle practice and to produce qualified marksmen in the event of war. Quasi-governmental, the National Board was instructed to stage shooting competitions, build and maintain rifle ranges, and "create a public sentiment in respect to the necessity of rifle practice as a means of national defense."[24]

The national matches at Camp Perry were cosponsored by the National Board, the War Department, and the NRA. Iowa had participated since 1904, when it placed fifteenth out of nineteen teams. More teams entered, and Iowa improved, staying consistently in the top half. By 1907, Brookhart's first year, Iowa placed twenty-first out of forty-eight. In 1910 his team finished fourth, bringing home a Congressional medal and prize money.[25]

Brookhart's emphasis on practice meant that he saw any shooting competition as an opportunity for instruction. Here he could instill his ideas in the officers who attended, who would then take them home to their men. In these "schools of instruction," the step-by-step basics of rifle shooting were taught by Morton C. Mumma, who would head the military program at the State University of Iowa from 1909 to 1912, and again later in the decade. He and Brookhart soon became close friends. "These schools were not only pleasant and enjoyable," Brookhart recalled later, "but they also brought out the most practicable and scientific instructions the Iowa National Guard has ever received."[26]

Brookhart's greatest honor as a coach came in 1912 when he was selected to lead the American team to the Palma Trophy competition. The Palma had once been a truly international competition, dating back to 1876, when the United States won against teams from Ireland, Scotland, Australia, and Canada. Participation dropped off throughout that decade, and the contest was not revived until 1901 and then only sporadically, the last time being in 1907.[27]

Now, in 1912, the United States would take on the Canadian team in Ottawa. Brookhart chose Mumma as his adjutant, and together they arranged a competition to select the twelve-member team. The only disappointment for Brookhart came when John Jackson, his Company D student, had to withdraw because of illness in the family.[28]

On September 10 the omens in Ottawa were not good. First the luggage did not arrive. The next day while returning from practice one of their trolley cars was struck by lightning. The weather on the two practice days was windy and chilly. Saturday, the day of the competition, was warm but cloudy. The shooting began and at the half-way point the Canadians were ahead by five points. While Mumma reportedly "chewed up a perfectly good two-bit Perfecto," Brookhart "just wore that same old satisfied grin of his and made figures on a pad. His self-control was something to wonder at."[29]

In the second half of the contest the Americans pulled ahead and finally defeated the Canadian team by eight points. World records were broken that year by both teams, and Brookhart telegraphed the victory news to President

William Howard Taft who sent back his "hearty congratulations."[30]

But perhaps the most touching tribute for Brookhart was a local one a week later. Working in his office late one night he was surprised when a group that included his brother Jim, the mayor, and about fifty men arrived. Aware of Brookhart's pride in having enforced prohibition laws while he was county attorney, they joked with him that they were thirsty; he joked back that he could not comply "on account of certain arid conditions that have existed in this community." The men offered their congratulations on his success in Ottawa. Brookhart told them about the competition and said that in addition to shooting they had been "dined and feted until they were nigh unto undone." After he had finished speaking the Washington band came in and played a few tunes. The last speaker was one of Brookhart's old political mentors, John Alex Young. Stating that he always rejoiced in the accomplishments of a Washington boy, Young wished Brookhart continued success.[31]

Brookhart's reputation as a rifle expert now extended beyond Iowa. Already a life member of the National Rifle Association, in 1911 he published the first of many articles in its magazine, *Arms and the Man*. The article was reprinted in the *London Territorial Service Gazette*, which commented that Brookhart "speaks with some practical, as well as theoretical knowledge."[32]

Moreover, his annual trip to Camp Perry for the national matches brought him in contact with shooters from across the nation. And although the national match at Camp Perry had been canceled in 1912 because of the Olympics and other international matches, a Company D shooter, John Jackson, was on the Olympic rifle team and won a bronze medal. And now Brookhart's American team had won the Palma.[33]

September 1912 brought yet another honor: he was elected to the board of directors of the NRA and the next year he was named second vice-president. Over the next thirteen years he would serve on the executive committee and as second vice-president and finally, from 1921 to 1925, as president. Calling the presidency of the NRA the "greatest honor accorded in the shooting game," he stated: "I am going to try to represent the riflemen of America, and to aid them in developing the shooting game, wherein knowledge is power, just as it is in any other field of effort."[34]

A year after his election to the NRA board, Brookhart joined the National Board for the Promotion of Rifle Practice. Now he was a member of the boards of the two groups most responsible for rifle shooting competitions in the United States. No doubt Brookhart was pleased to see the participation of National Guard teams increase and their records improve. He realized that the Camp Perry matches could effectively develop qualified shooters who could become instructors in their own communities. To him, the annual match was "the greatest school of rifle practice in the world." The U.S. Army saw it differently.[35]

Except for 1912, the matches had been annual events since 1903. At its January 1916 meeting the National Board for the Promotion of Rifle Practice adopted Brookhart's motion that the national matches "be held this year and every year." But the War Department refused, citing the expense involved and time lost by regular army personnel in administering the matches.[36]

Worried that this would "discourage rifle practice in the National Guard," Brookhart protested to Secretary of War Newton Baker and asked for a hearing on the matter. Baker explained that the army could not participate but that he had been "assured" that the matches could be held without army teams. In the short term Brookhart's side prevailed and the War Department hastily scheduled the matches for December 1916. But areas of disagreement between Brookhart and the army remained.[37]

Funding for the matches was part of a long-standing tension between the regular army and the National Guard. According to the army, the state forces did not maintain proper standards of training or operation and were of little use anyway. The army did not believe that the matches were helping the Guard improve their shooting and was reluctant to "waste" its money on the national matches when the army had plenty of uses for the funds.[38]

Brookhart interpreted the army's reluctance to fund the matches as part of its larger goal, namely, to weaken, if not destroy the Guard. Brookhart strongly supported the idea of a citizens' army of volunteers who devoted part of their life in service to the country. Militias had served the nation well since the American Revolution, Brookhart reasoned. Although he recognized the necessity for regular army officers at the highest level, he believed officers should come up through the ranks; in guard units, the men were equals who elected their officers in democratic fashion. The current system, Brookhart alleged, had created an elite caste of career officers, trained at the military academy to feel inherently superior to the men they led. Such a system, Brookhart contended, "makes a snob and autocrat of every officer." He also disdained the practical training West Pointers received, claiming that they had "150 official hours of dancing and 30 hours on the rifle."[39]

Brookhart believed that the training the Guard received was as good, if not much better, than the regular army. As an example he cited the Iowa Guard during its Mexican border service. Mexico had experienced a series of revolutionary changes of government that gave rise to raids on American border towns by Mexican bandits, including Pancho Villa. The Iowa National Guard went to Brownsville, Texas, as part of the force sent to protect American citizens on the border.

To get ready for border service the Iowa Guard drilled in Des Moines under their own commanders. But once in Texas regular officers took over the troops and the level of proficiency they had achieved in Des Moines declined. For example, the regular artillery instructor had reportedly not seen a battery in years and the Iowans were compelled to wait until "their instructor could brush up" on his skills.

Rifle practice was the worst of all. When the Iowans' commander asked for time to practice he found that the range was wholly inadequate. The Iowa Guard returned from Texas with no rifle practice at all, and Brookhart said that in Texas the regular army taught

> the caste distinction between officers and men and we are proud to state that most of our Iowa officers have refused to learn it. They have found it so important that an officer should keep his coat buttoned to the neck in 100 degree temperatures as to issue an order to that effect, but in six months they have not permitted our men to fire a shot with the rifles they must use if the clash of battle ever comes.[40]

In time his ideas led him to develop a proposal for universal military training. Under this plan all male citizens at age eighteen would register for military training; the only exemptions would be for physical or mental illness. After registration each man would then be obligated to one year of training and then he would return to his home. Once a year he would return for a brief drill period. Brookhart claimed that this system would protect the nation better against aggression than under the system of regular army and National Guards. Moreover, each man would serve his country and still "look forward to a civilian life, and [be] better equipped physically, mentally and morally for it."[41]

Brookhart also had a standing quarrel with the Ordnance Department about the necessity of rifle marksmanship. The old school of professional soldiers had long believed that marksmanship in the heat of battle was not possible. In their view, the soldier had only to scatter as many shots in the direction of the enemy as possible, on the assumption that some would find their target. This view had been developed in Germany, adopted by West Point instructors, and disseminated through the ranks of professional soldiers. According to the army, therefore, rifle marksmanship as advocated by Brookhart, the NRA, and the National Board, and developed through competitive matches, was a waste of time and money.[42]

Brookhart said flatly that the "German theory is all wrong," claiming that it used resources inefficiently and endangered soldiers' lives. Furthermore, rifle training and matches were not recreational but were an integral part of the training of all soldiers and Guardsmen. Soldiers were not trained merely to win sharpshooter prizes but to protect their own lives and they deserved the "best possible training in the use of their weapons."[43]

He was also outspoken in criticizing the army in other matters. The army insisted that the weapons be spotless and pass a white-glove inspection. Soldiers spend considerable time in cleaning their guns, sometimes using an abrasive that Brookhart believed damaged the weapon. "They would shine all right; they were beautiful inside," Brookhart said, but they would not shoot accurately. On another occasion he rejected some reconditioned rifles that the army had sent to the Iowa Guard. He said the guns were "worn out and worthless," and should never have been repaired in the first place. His men would "not be able to hit anything with them."[44]

In the spring of 1916, the army made a critical move by changing the composition of the National Board for the Promotion of Rifle Practice. Acting on a request by the General Staff and War College faculty, Secretary of War Baker expanded the Board from nine to eleven members and filled the new positions with army representatives. Brookhart's term had expired at the end of 1915 and in the reorganization he was not reappointed.[45]

Rifle shooting, the National Guard, and politics took Brookhart away from home more and more often. And when he was home he usually seemed preoccupied with his current interest. A lively conversation could take place at dinner, and he would suddenly interrupt with a question that had nothing to do with the subject at hand. Edith remembered that when he was working on a problem he would pace around the living room. "Joe would get on one foot and I'd get on the other and we'd ride around and after several minutes he would say, 'Well, where'd you chaps come from?'" They understood that their father was like that. Once when a neighbor asked the youngest son, Joe, about his father, the boy replied that he was sick. When the neighbor asked the nature of the illness Joe replied, "He's got the politics."[46]

Another favorite memory was Sunday morning after church. Brookhart himself rarely attended church. But Jennie made sure all the children went to church after which they would go to their father's law office to pick him up and spend Sunday together. When they would ask their mother about his non-attendance she replied simply that "he lives nearer the Golden Rule than any man I know." Years later his son, Smith, recalled:

> I think he had all the instincts and the moral feelings that you attribute to a Christian. And certainly he was decent and clean and never profane, at least in female company, or ever obscene or in any way disreputable in dealing with people.[47]

The Brookharts taught their children to be self-reliant; if they wanted anything they worked for it or built it. Once John wanted a boat, so his parents supplied the materials and he built it. It was the same story when Florence wanted a tennis court. The children also were expected to help with the work on the farm. They attempted different crops using the latest information from Iowa State College. Generally, they approached the problem like their father approached rifle shooting—methodically. For a time they tested seed corn to find which variety gave the best yield. It was reported that once they had 10,000 ears of corn in the basement as part of their experiment.[48]

In spite of his involvement with rifle shooting, Brookhart rarely hunted. He had guns in the house and all the boys took up hunting. This led to a tragedy in early 1916. John celebrated his fifteenth birthday with a party of his friends. Following the party John and thirteen-year-old Sam took a Remington rifle that the company had given their father and went shooting. When they returned home John left the rifle downstairs and told his mother it was not loaded. Later that evening as he carried it upstairs to put it away, it went off and hit Sam in the head. Their father ran upstairs but it was too late. Sam died within minutes.[49]

Sam was "undoubtedly the brightest one of the bunch," his brother Smith later remembered, and was very popular in Washington. The community rallied around the grieving family and the funeral two days later was very large. Ironically Sam's death did not deter Smith Brookhart from his interest in rifle shooting. If anything it probably made him more resolute about proper rifle procedures.[50]

Even after Congress declared war in April 1917, the United States was slow to enter the war in Europe. But as General John J. Pershing toured battlefields and conferred with allied commanders, he became convinced that rifle marksmanship was necessary. In September, and again the next month, he cabled his superiors in Washington that "infantry soldiers should be excellent shots." Pershing recommended that instruction in small arms begin immediately.[51]

The NRA greeted Pershing's message with relief. An editorial in its magazine said that the American commander intended to fight the war based on "American ideas" to "insure an American victory in an American way." When the War Department proposed bringing European instructors to train Army riflemen, however, the NRA pointed out that the War Department had invested a great deal of money over the years for the national matches. These matches had produced more than enough expert American riflemen, like Brookhart, capable of training the soldiers. "The fact now stands out clear and plain that *our men must be taught to shoot,"* and that Americans should do the training.[52]

Like thousands of other guardsmen Brookhart asked to be called into service. But as an outspoken critic of the army, he had been blacklisted (a story he would often tell years later), and only the collusion of two old friends had gotten him on active duty. An old ally, Colonel Ira L. Reeves, had become Assistant Chief of the Militia Bureau and found a list with Brookhart's name at the top. When his superior was out of the office, Reeves submitted a list of names, including Brookhart's, to the Assistant Chief of Ordnance. This man, also a friend of Brookhart's, waited until his chief was out of the office and then issued the orders to put Brookhart on active duty. Both officers neglected to inform the personnel section until Brookhart had reported for duty. Protests were made about this procedure but ultimately the Judge Advocate General ruled in Brookhart's favor. At long last he was in the army. "After I was in," he would recount years later, "it was harder to put me out than it was to keep me from coming in."[53]

In mid-November, in Des Moines, Brookhart was mustered into service with the rank of major. Soon in Washington, D.C., he reported to the Chief of Ordnance who assigned him to the Small Arms Division. Brookhart remained in Washington long enough to write a report, with his old friend Col. Morton Mumma, recommending that the army establish rifle-training camps.[54] Next he was sent to New Haven, Connecticut, for ten days. There he toured the Winchester rifle plant and worked on its assembly line to get a better sense of the rifle.

His stay in New Haven reveals much about his no-nonsense approach to life. First quartered in the Taft Hotel, he switched to thriftier accommodations in a Yale University dormitory that had been made available to the army. He purchased a meal ticket for the campus dining room and found his forty-five cent meal there much better than the dollar and one-half meal at the Taft. On Thanksgiving he strolled through the Yale University Museum. Its famous collection of Greek vases he dismissed as the "oldest collection of kitchenware" he had ever seen. Two pianos reportedly played by Haydn and Beethoven did not impress him; when he plunked out "Yankee Doodle" on one he found that the piano was so out of tune it "sounded like a Russian constitutional convention."[55]

He spent an interesting but lonely Thanksgiving afternoon in the museum. Brookhart was a utilitarian, with little sense of the aesthetic. Years before when he had read *Les Miserables* it was as much for the language practice as for literary content. Now Greek vases were "kitchenware" and pianos were useful only if in tune, no matter who had played them or owned them. To underscore his impressions he wrote home that his solitary afternoon in the museum was spent "without interference, obstruction or enlightenment."[56]

Brookhart was soon ordered to report to Camp Dodge in Des Moines to train rifle shooters in the 88th Division. He stopped in Washington, Iowa, on December 21. Despite the approaching holidays he stayed only three days with his wife and six children. He reported for duty at Camp Dodge on the day before Christmas, only to find that most of the officers were away from camp for the holiday. Brookhart would have to wait until December 26 for his students.

Over the next three weeks he instructed over two thousand officers in rifle marksmanship. The original schedule had called for officers to attend only one hour a day at their own discretion. Most of the officers stationed at Camp Dodge were regular army, so Brookhart expected a cool reception. But he was pleased and surprised when he was cordially received. Many officers went beyond their scheduled one hour and spent the entire day honing their rifle skills only to return for further work at night. He concluded that perhaps opposition in the regular army to marksmanship had come from officers in the bureaucracy and not those in the field. Brookhart considered this the busiest month of his life, but he regretted leaving because of the friends he had made.[57]

Back in Washington, D.C., at the end of January, Brookhart prepared a report of his activities at Camp Dodge. The report found its way to the desk of Secretary of War Baker who ordered Brookhart to come see him. Since Baker's reorganization of the National Board, General Pershing had kept up the pressure for rifle instruction and now Baker wanted Brookhart to explain his theories.

Brookhart repeated again why the German theory of marksmanship was wrong and why its supporters (the War College and Ordnance generals) were wrong. He explained why he was no longer on the National Board and how the War College memorandum to Baker had precipitated the board reorganization and shift of power. Reportedly this angered Baker, who had not realized he had been a pawn, but Brookhart reassured Baker that recent appointments, which included Mumma, had helped restore balance. Finally, when Baker asked him about rifle training for the army, Brookhart outlined a plan for a rifle school that could serve the whole army and be taught by a ready-made corps of marksmen trained at the national matches.[58]

Baker had heard enough. He ordered that planning begin. On April 15 orders were signed to establish the small arms school at Camp Perry. Classes would begin in late May.⁵⁹ Mumma was put in charge of the project, assisted by Brookhart and other national match shooters. Meanwhile, Brookhart tested rifles at nearby Camp Meade and wrote a series of articles for *Arms and the Man* entitled "Rifle Training in War," which appeared in six parts in April and May of 1918.

The articles gathered in one place the ideas Brookhart had used so successfully since the late 1890s. Here he articulated his emphasis on the shooter; not just on his weapon. He restated his now familiar ideas on alcohol and tobacco. He detailed the problems of flinching and being gun-shy (called "buck fever"). His constant theme was that the shooter must be in complete control of himself and his weapon.

There was nothing new in the articles; Brookhart had been teaching these same ideas for years. But now the timing was right; the war gave his ideas added weight. "We are now going out to shoot at targets that will shoot at us first if they can," he wrote. "The importance of fire discipline, fire direction, fire control and fire distribution is brought home to us with a personal meaning." The NRA and the National Board published the articles in a pocket-size book entitled *Rifle Training in War*. This became the army's standard rifle manual during 1918.⁶⁰

As chief instructor at Camp Perry, Brookhart reminded his students that they were not training for rifle matches but for war, a "great test of liberty of the world." "Preliminary training, if done right, means finished training," he cautioned. "You make haste by starting slowly." The students settled quickly into a routine of daily instruction and practice on the ranges. To remind them of the fundamentals Brookhart wrote the "Ten Commandments of the Firing Point," a checklist that included gripping the weapon, breathing, and squeezing the trigger. He had these printed on a small card and required all instructors and students to wear them pinned to their sleeves.⁶¹

The students moved through the course rapidly and soon second, third and fourth classes were formed with as many as 1,100 in each class. Although Brookhart kept the men busy there was still time for recreation. Many took advantage of the officers' club for evening games and singing. Occasionally baseball games were organized. On weekends they went fishing or into nearby Toledo for shopping or to attend a dance put on by some local group. Wives of permanent staff members joined their husbands and were pressed into service knitting sweaters and making arm badges for the men. Distinguished visitors also came to see the camp and impress upon the men the serious nature of their work. Another reminder of their patriotic work occurred on June 29 when 530 immigrants became citizens of the United

States at Camp Perry.[62]

Jennie did not join Smith at Camp Perry. She was much too busy caring for their large family and the farm. Probably, however, Smith was too busy to be of much company even if she had come. He did, however, celebrate one milestone when he took his first ride in an airplane. A pilot from an airfield in Michigan landed at Camp Perry and took Brookhart up. Once in the air the plane headed for Lake Erie but ran into rain and they were forced to land in Toledo. The next morning they took off again but were forced down by engine trouble. Brookhart said he knew something was wrong when he noticed that the pilot periodically shut off the engine. After a forced landing in an oats field the oil was changed and they continued their flight to Detroit. He reported that from the air the huge Ford automobile plant "didn't look as big as a beehive." Brookhart became an enthusiastic advocate of the new means of transportation. "The trip did not make me sick in the slightest degree," he bragged, adding that he would go again if offered the chance.[63]

The Small Arms Firing School was a success. In July the army instructed Mumma to begin plans to extend the work of the school to other army bases. Mumma immediately appointed Brookhart to a committee to prepare the plans. Camp Perry instructors would select likely students as instructors at the new sites.[64]

Meeting at Camp Perry in June, the National Board decided to hold the annual matches in September. Certainly this was a victory for Brookhart; the army could have protested that the matches would divert time and money from the war effort. But Brookhart was not satisfied. He pushed for the creation of a Department of Small Arms Practice within the army. Under the current system all small arms training was a specialization that required the soldier to be sent away from his unit. The strength of Brookhart's proposal was that small arms training would now become an integral part of all army duty and would allow the men to remain with their units. Brookhart's proposal was adopted.[65]

Another item of business at the summer meeting concerned the eventual closing of Camp Perry. Situated on the banks of Lake Erie the camp was of no use once winter weather set in. Mumma proposed that the work of Camp Perry be moved to Jacksonville, Florida, at the end of November. Instead Congress appropriated money to build a new facility near Columbus, Georgia. First called the Infantry School of Arms, it was later renamed Fort Benning. In the interim, Camp Perry instructors were reassigned. Brookhart, newly promoted to lieutenant colonel, was sent to Camp Dodge near Des Moines.[66]

Camp Perry had served well. Nearly 6,000 officers graduated from the facility in just over five months. Years later Col. Harry L. Cooper, commander of the 88th Division during the war, acknowledged "the benefit of training under such men as Colonel Brookhart."[67]

The Infantry School of Arms did not open its doors until February of 1919, three months after the war ended. As the army began to scale back, some of the small arms instructors left to return to their pre-war jobs. In February, Mumma resumed his position in the military program at the University of Iowa, where he would stay until 1928. Brookhart remained in Georgia for a few months where he headed the marksmanship department. That summer, however, he was stricken with influenza and in the fall he left the army to return to Iowa.[68]

In the years following the war Brookhart continued to urge the necessity of proper rifle training. At the first post-war meetings of the National Board for the Promotion of Rifle Practice and the National Rifle Association in January 1919, Brookhart again offered resolutions that a Department of Small Arms be established within the army. His long experience had been that the army could not be trusted to undertake this important work in the system that prevailed before the war. "Training in marksmanship cannot be left to the systems which work in ordinary drill training," he said. He urged that in every division there be "an officer especially charged with such matters." He also supported the continuation of the national matches.[69]

The matches were held annually through 1925 and Brookhart continued to play an important role. As the president of the National Rifle Association during those years, he spoke even more forcefully in support of the matches. Moreover, following his election to the U.S. Senate in 1922, he exerted influence to insure that Congress continued to appropriate money to fund the matches.

Never content to sit on the sidelines, Brookhart joined Mumma and others to teach shooting techniques at matches at Camp Perry. The purpose of the schools, as Mumma described it, was to "provide instruction for the uninstructed in the use of arms" thereby "increasing their effectiveness as potential soldiers." In 1920, 842 shooters entered the school and within three years the number of entrants was over 1,000.[70]

Yet the costs were mounting. By 1926 an economy-minded Secretary of War eyed the $500,000 price tag and refused to provide the funds. The match was held, but on a much smaller scale. The matches were held the next year, but only after a period of uncertainty about funding from the War Department.[71]

The NRA and National Board lobbied for legislation that would mandate the War Department to fund the matches. The first attempt was a bill introduced by Congressman John C. Speaks (Republican, Ohio) to appropriate the money. The Speaks bill passed in the House of Representatives but when it reached the Senate Brookhart added an amendment to enlarge the membership of the National Board. These added members would be appointed by governors of the states, an obvious attempt to tip the balance away from the army. The president vetoed the bill because governors would have been appointing members to a federal board, thus violating the division of powers between the states and the federal government.

A new bill was immediately introduced, Brookhart agreed not to offer his amendment, the bill passed quickly, and was signed by President Coolidge. The continuation of annual matches now seemed assured. But in 1931 the Great Depression did what match opponents had been unable to do and the matches were dropped.[72]

In the last fifteen years of his life Brookhart maintained his interest in rifle shooting but did not participate. When he attended matches it was in the role of an "old shooter," to whom respect was paid but whose time was past. Years before, the army had supplanted *Rifle Training in War* with a new manual. He still was called on to test new military rifles and on occasion he testified before a congressional committee about new weapons. But in his testimony he tended to refight the old battles with the opponents of marksmanship and the committee seemed more courteous than interested.[73]

Rifle shooting was never a recreational activity for Smith Brookhart. Nothing really was. He approached rifle shooting as he did the other interests of his life, with a single-mindedness that bordered on obsession. He studied it, tried to master it, and did become a world-class expert on the teaching of marksmanship. The interest in rifle marksmanship that began in late nineteenth-century Iowa took him from Washington to a national stage. So did the other interest of that same period—politics.

5

The Making of a Progressive

The first fifty years of Brookhart's life were filled with a variety of activities: a county attorney and private lawyer, a county seat politician, an entrepreneur and community leader, a rifle expert, and a family man. His profile during these years is not much different from that of men in countless other small towns during the same years. What set him apart, and brought him renown beyond the boundaries of Washington County, was his growing passion for politics as an agent of change.

Brookhart entered elective politics when Iowa was still a solidly Republican state. Iowa would remain a Republican state for most of his career. But at about the same time he ran for his second term as county attorney, the nature of Republicanism began to change. Writing on January 16, 1897, Council Bluffs attorney John Y. Stone told James S. Clarkson that

> things have changed in the state though some of the landmarks can still be recognized. New hopes and ambitions are overlapping the past and spreading for the future. New interests are arising—new friends are following the old and never-changing selfishness exhibits its never-releasing grasp.[1]

Stone, who had served as Speaker of the Iowa House, Attorney General, and Republican National Committeeman, and Clarkson, one of the owners of the *Des Moines Register* and former chairman of the Republican National Committee, were among the leaders of the party that had controlled Iowa politics since the Civil War. They were part of a political establishment that had elected all of Iowa's postwar senators and fifty-eight of its seventy-three postwar congressmen.[2] They had also, with the exception of the two recent terms of Democrat Horace Boies, controlled the governor's office. And under the leadership of United States Senator William Boyd Allison, who was just finishing his fourth term, they expected to continue their political dominance.

Also functioning as part of this establishment was an "invisible government" of men who exercised power without holding public office. Joseph W. Blythe, for example, a New Jerseyite who had come to Burlington as assistant attorney for the Chicago, Burlington and Quincy Railroad and later became the railroad's General Counsel, was by 1897 the chief member of the so-called "Regency," a small group said to control the Republican Party in Iowa. Through this group Blythe wielded great power, especially on the "Reservation," the name given to the southern three tiers of counties through which the C. B. & Q. passed. The Reservation included Iowa's First Congressional District, of which Washington County was a part.

One source of Blythe's power was his ties to politicians he had helped to elect. Among these, for example, was John H. Gear, Governor of Iowa, twice a congressman, from 1895 until his death in July of 1900 a United States Senator, and also Blythe's father-in-law. Another was four-term First District Congressman Thomas Hedge, Blythe's law partner. In addition, Blythe's power extended into each county on the Reservation through railroad attorneys, local attorneys kept on retainer to look after railroad interests, physicians used for the same purpose, and newspaper editors.

Blythe also provided these men, as well as countless state legislators, political party workers, and convention delegates, with railroad passes. With these he insured a large and faithful attendance at party functions across the state, reaping the rewards at election time. And when new men appeared and were nominated for office, they were provided, as future Governor Dan Turner was in 1904, with "a 2,000 mile book from Blythe." Viewed by *Harper's Weekly* as a "master mind in politics," Blythe was clearly a major power in shaping public policy.[3]

Into this situation came Albert Baird Cummins. Born in Pennsylvania in 1850, the same year as Blythe, Cummins attended Waynesburg College and after a period of wandering through various jobs, had read law, passed the bar examination, and in 1878 moved to Des Moines. Subsequently, he served one term in the Iowa House and then set his eye upon the only political office he ever really wanted—the United States Senate. In 1894, when Senator James F. Wilson retired, Cummins was the most prominently mentioned of several Republican candidates for the position. But Blythe and his machine thought otherwise, and their support went to the sixty-nine-year-old John Gear, who after several ballots in the legislature was elected. The *Dubuque Weekly Times* commented of the C. B. & Q effort that there "never was ... a more relentless machine at work than now."[4]

The next major clash between the Cummins supporters and the established party leadership came at the Republican convention of 1897, particularly in regard to the Republican nomination for governor. There, after a long and confusing battle, Leslie M. Shaw, Joseph Blythe's candidate, was nominated over Abraham B. Funk, who later became an important Cummins supporter. According to Thomas R. Ross, Jonathan Dolliver's biographer, the strains this contest placed on Iowa politics had "lasting significance:"

> It marked the definable beginning of the division of the party in [Iowa] into what by 1901 came to be called the "Progressive" and the "Standpat" factions; for certainly at first that schism was one of personalities not issues, a matter of Cummins-Funk and Company *vs.* Blythe-Hubbard Incorporated.[5]

Gear's reelection campaign in 1900 was very similar to the 1894 contest, except that now there was only one other candidate—Albert B. Cummins. To elect Gear, so the Cummins forces charged, was to elect a "dead man." For Gear, now seventy-five, was in failing health. But again the Blythe machine prevailed and in the end Gear was elected by acclamation.[6]

In six months Gear was dead; and while Blythe wanted Governor Shaw to resign and have himself appointed to the Senate, Shaw was reluctant to advance himself in this fashion. Blythe then had his brother, James E. Blythe, a Mason City lawyer, suggest to Shaw that he appoint Congressman Jonathan Prentiss Dolliver. Although Dolliver was not Blythe's first choice, he was the strongest candidate after Shaw; and since he and Cummins shared many of the same supporters, he was presumably someone Cummins would not oppose. In 1902, even though both Senate seats would be up for election, Cummins would not be a candidate. He felt that he could not run against Dolliver, and he realized that he had no chance against the other Senator, William Boyd Allison, who was arguably the most powerful man in the Senate and was unassailable by anyone.

Cummins then turned his attention to winning the gubernatorial nomination, and here he was finally successful. When, on August 7, 1901, the Republican State Convention selected Albert B. Cummins as its nominee for governor, it was, as Fleming Fraker has written, "the first significant defeat suffered by the 'standpatter crowd' in over thirty years." In an editorial entitled "An Iowa Dynasty Fallen," the *Washington County Press* noted the growth of Iowa along the river and the "quiet, but potent political dynasty [that had] held the state in its grip for over thirty-five years." In the northern half of the region it had been Senator Allison of Dubuque, in the southern half a succession of former Governor and Senator James W. Grimes of Burlington, former Senator and Secretary of the Interior James Harlan of

Mount Pleasant, former Senator James F. Wilson of Fairfield, and the late Senator Gear of Burlington. But when Gear died, the Blythe machine had been unable to find someone to replace him. "The old dynasty died hard," the *Press* concluded, "but it is dead."[7]

If not dead, the machine did seem to be on its last legs. In seven years Allison would be dead. In eight Blythe would follow. But before their passing, they would deal one more blow to Cummins' hopes for the Senate, and as governor he would have to face a standpat legislature hostile to the political reforms that he proposed. Nevertheless, Cummins' victory was real and is best understood in terms of the geographic shift that the *Press* pointed out. Beginning with Cummins, power in the Republican Party shifted from the old Mississippi River towns to central and western Iowa. Republicans would now look to Des Moines, Fort Dodge, Mason City, Sioux City, Cedar Rapids, as they had once looked to Burlington and Dubuque.

It remained for another James S. Clarkson correspondent, this time his brother Richard, editor of the *Des Moines Register*, to summarize the change. Writing his brother after Cummins' gubernatorial victory in the general election of 1901, Richard Clarkson observed:

> The Cummins juggernaut political machine is as relentless as the juggernaut of ancient times. . . . It will roll over every anti-Cummins man who is a candidate for an office or position the Cummins men can control. He is still a candidate for U. S. Senator, and, as he told me a year ago, he is to have a Cummins man placed in every position possible. That is the reason he was a candidate for governor, and that will be the cause of his defeat, if his opponents are worthy of being termed opponents.[8]

In Washington, Smith Brookhart was not initially involved in the Cummins-Blythe battles. In 1896 Brookhart helped organize a "Sound Money Club" to support the Republican candidate for President William McKinley in his battle against William Jennings Bryan and silver. Three years later he was among the Company D veterans who played a prominent part when Speaker of the United States House of Representatives, David Henderson, spoke in Washington.[9]

Although he was chairman of the Republican county convention in 1900, he did not go to the state convention.[10] And since he decided not to seek a fourth term as county attorney, he was not a contestant in the election of 1900. The Republican nominee for the position was Marsh W. Bailey.

Brookhart's involvement in the election of 1900, aside from his convention chairmanship, was to make speeches for other Republican candidates. There was nothing remarkable in his speeches that year, nothing that hinted of the progressive Brookhart to come. Following one speech before an overflowing crowd in rural Washington County, the *Journal* noted only that "Republicans speak highly of [the speech]."[11]

The only controversy involving Brookhart that year was a post-election lawsuit maintaining that Bailey's election as county attorney was legally void and that Brookhart should remain county attorney until January of 1902. In the election the voters had approved the so-called Titus amendment to the state constitution, providing for biennial rather than annual elections, stipulating that these should take place in odd numbered years beginning in 1901, and stating that those terms of office normally ending on the first Monday of January 1901 (Brookhart's term was one) would be extended for one year. The approval of this amendment, so Brookhart alleged, meant that he was county attorney until 1902.[12]

Shortly after the election the out-going Attorney General, Milton Remley and the in-coming Attorney General, Charles W. Mullan, met with George Titus, the author of the amendment and they agreed that the situation in Washington County would make a good test case in the courts. Titus came to Washington to meet with Brookhart and Bailey about the matter. Both men agreed to waive all procedures that would have delayed the case so that a quick ruling could be handed down.[13]

Bailey sued in District Court, arguing that the Titus Amendment had a technical flaw and ought to be set aside. It was an argument with which Washington District Court Judge Almon D. Dewey agreed, and Brookhart then appealed to the Iowa Supreme Court, where oral arguments were heard on January 23, 1901. In presenting his case, Brookhart argued for a liberal interpretation of the amending process under which the Titus Amendment would stand. Bailey, of course, argued the opposite, and on February 1 the Supreme Court agreed with his line of reasoning and held the Titus Amendment to be null and void. The constitution had not been amended, and hence Bailey rather than Brookhart was county attorney.[14] The Court heard Brookhart's arguments on the point, said the *Press*, "and turned 'em both down, upset 'em. The decisive 'nub' in the case was this: The legislature did not adopt the amendment in the way the constitution says it shall." With not a little glee, Editor Burrell also noted that Bailey, in his oral and printed argument, had "laid special emphasis on the very point the court made the basis of its decision, viz., the precedent in the prohibitory amendment opinion."[15]

Smith Brookhart lost the case, the appeal, and his office. But he gained a friend when he met Albert Baird Cummins who presented arguments in support of Brookhart's position. For the first time Brookhart and Cummins were allied on an issue, and from this would grow a political alliance stretching over twenty years.

The relationship grew slowly. Brookhart was not a delegate to the state convention where Cummins challenged the "standpatters" and won. The *Journal* said the local standpats took the defeat in good grace, adding that the "victory of Cummins . . . means a stir in Iowa politics." Brookhart said later that "I looked on in wonder and drifted with the corporation crowd." The next month at the county convention Brookhart was a member of the resolutions committee which mourned the dead President McKinley, praised the new President Theodore Roosevelt, and commended Cummins' "broadminded policy in becoming the candidate of the whole party, and whole people, and [we] believe in his triumphant election."[16]

Early the next year Brookhart, as President of the Young Men's Republican Club, invited Cummins to speak at its Lincoln Day Banquet. And while Cummins had to decline because of a previous engagement, he seemed receptive to visiting Washington and finally did so in April. Arriving for a G.A.R. Campfire, he was greeted by Brookhart.[17]

April 1902 was also when Brookhart began a campaign for the seat on the three-man Sixth Judicial District that had been held for the past twelve years by local attorney Almon R. Dewey. In the precinct caucuses, meeting in April, Brookhart was quite successful, receiving seventy-eight votes to only thirty-four for Dewey; and at the county convention meeting the next week, a roll call on whom to recommend to the coming judicial convention registered seventy-two votes for Brookhart to forty for Dewey.[18]

At the subsequent judicial convention meeting in Grinnell on June 4, each county had its man; and, the *Press* asked, "Will 'Brook' come home with his shield, or on it?" It turned out to be the latter. Brookhart lost badly. But the *Press* reported he was "chipper and gay," not disappointed because he had not expected to win, and ready to "buckle down to the hard work he loves for ten years or more to come."[19]

Howard Burrell's comment that Brookhart was ready to settle down for ten years was more wish than reality. He was a delegate to the county convention meeting in May 1903, and while there was chosen by Colonel David J. Palmer, Civil War hero, former State Senator, and since 1898 a member of the state railroad commission, to be one of the delegates to the state convention. That Palmer, a standpatter, selected Brookhart indicates that the latter was still in the fold, albeit on the edge of it. He went to the state convention, his first, "on a [railroad] pass." But once there he found himself intrigued by the Iowa Idea for tariff reform and by Cummins' arguments on the convention floor. Clearly impressed by Cummins, Brookhart "wondered why nearly all the congressmen and both senators were leagued together against a man so brilliant and so valiant."[20]

Brookhart, as noted previously, had begun his political career on the conservative side of the liquor issue, taking in effect what would later be called the "standpat" position. His opponent had been C. J. Wilson, whose position had been championed by Howard Burrell in the *Press* and opposed by Logan and Neal in the *Gazette*. In the years following that first battle, Brookhart had won two elections, lost one election case in the Supreme Court, and been rebuffed at the judicial convention. He had also been listening to Albert Cummins talk of railroad control of the political process, with the result that it was a different Smith Brookhart, now not quite a progressive but certainly no longer a standpatter, who accepted an invitation from a boyhood friend, Hugh B. Sloan, to meet him in Burlington.

Brookhart's activities in Washington County had come to the attention of Joseph W. Blythe.[21] Brookhart met Sloan sometime in late December of 1903 or early January 1904 at the Delano Hotel and Sloan suggested that they go see Blythe. Brookhart knew that Sloan had been a Cummins supporter and was somewhat surprised at the suggestion. But he was open to it. Although he was listening to the Cummins' message, he was still "inclined to be against Cummins" because Cummins was a wet.[22] An alliance with Blythe was still not out of the question.

Blythe's greeting was cordial and open, and Brookhart felt honored to be consulted by the great man. Blythe then told Brookhart that he had watched his career with interest, and that since "our Republican leaders are dying or retiring from politics" there was a need for "young and competent men to assume their honors and take up their burdens." The key to political success, he said, was organization. It was organization that had elected governors, senators, representatives, and various other officials down through the court house level. Cummins, he continued, was a good man. But he was working outside the organization, and after finishing his current term would "disappear." In closing, Blythe showed Brookhart a stack of letters from grateful public officials thanking him for his help and seeking his advice on various matters. The message was clear: "Young man if you want anything in politics, the only place to get it is through the organization, and the organization in Iowa is Joseph W. Blythe."[23]

Brookhart later told everyone he "went out of Joseph W. Blythe's office determined to fight the railroads and drive them out of our politics."[24] That, however, was the way he remembered it in 1923. In reality he seems to have thanked Blythe and said he would think it over. He had, after all, attended enough caucuses and conventions and listened to enough of Cummins' speeches to know how the system worked and how railroad control of the political process was exercised.

Still, he apparently had been surprised by some of the correspondence that Blythe had shown him, especially that with Senator Allison. In one letter Allison had asked Blythe who should be named a federal judge, and in another he had enclosed a note from President Roosevelt written on a White House menu, a note that Blythe later used against Roosevelt's programs.

Upon his return to Washington, Brookhart went to see *Gazette* editor Wake Neal, who had been one of his first supporters in 1894 and, like Brookhart, was a fervent dry. They discussed the issue many times over the coming months, with both having the same reservations about Cummins—he was wet. In all probability, Brookhart also told others about his experience in Burlington, perhaps prompting the *Press* editorial of February 17, 1904, defending Blythe, whose picture was printed in the editorial page, against his critics. The *Press* said:

> His enemies have at different times tried to make him out a political boss . . . he is a man of power . . . His effort is always to keep down "bad blood." He cultivates the amenities rather than the asperities of life. He is a man of whom Iowa, and especially the First District, should be proud.[25]

Meanwhile, Brookhart kept busy with his law practice and allowed others to speculate about his political alignment. In August the Washington *Democrat* expressed the view that the "Blythe crowd" would probably run Colonel David Palmer for governor while "the Brookhart-Cummins crowd" would "bring out Mr. [John Alex] Young." "Gosh," it said, "we don't care. Both are good men and if we have to have a Republican for governor, take one from this county." Later that fall, the *Democrat* noted that there were a number of prominent local Republicans at a campaign meeting but that they did not include "the half breeds, the La Follette people. Bill McClean, S. W. Brookhart, Wake Neal, D. H. Logan, Marion Crawford and all the rest of the La Follette people were conspicuous by their absence."[26]

Brookhart and Neal continued to talk and watch Cummins; and while they still had some reservation about his wetness, they noted that he was enforcing the prohibition law. They were faced now with a choice between a man whose control of the political process was odious to them and a man with whom they disagreed on a very fundamental issue but who had enough integrity to enforce laws with which he had personally disagreed. They wrote for an appointment with Cummins, and in mid-February, 1905, they went to Des Moines to confer with him. Cummins already knew Brookhart, and State Senator John Alex Young, a Cummins ally in the legislature, sent a letter of introduction for Neal.

At the meeting Cummins told them of his belief in the people and in the role that government should play in insuring popular rights. He deplored the role big corporations played in the political process and reiterated themes that he had set forth in his inaugural, namely that while "incorporate wealth" had many rights and privileges, it had no right to vote, to sit in political conventions and legislative chambers, or to determine what "our laws shall be and who shall execute them."[27] He noted, however, that it would not be easy to defeat the Blythe machine and that there would be little reward for trying. He had, he told Brookhart, no jobs to offer, nothing in fact but trouble and fight and, maybe in the end, defeat. "If you want to go with me," he declared, "you will have to be a crusader and be prepared to be licked again and again."[28]

That did it. The two Washingtonians told Cummins that they would join him in his fight. And a few days later, in acknowledging Young's letter of introduction, Cummins noted, "I had a very good talk with Mr. Neal and Mr. Brookhart, and I hope that before long there will grow up a union among the better elements of your part of the country that will help on the cause of good government everywhere."[29]

In March, Senator Young recommended to Cummins that he appoint Brookhart to the governor's military staff. Cummins could not do so, since Colonel David Palmer was already on the staff and it seemed unwise to appoint another Washington County man. But, Cummins wrote, "I would otherwise be glad to have Brookhart,"[30] and subsequently he did find another job for him. In the fall, Cummins named Brookhart as a delegate to the Interstate Commerce Law Convention, meeting in Chicago.

The Interstate Commerce Law Convention had been formed in 1900, when a group of midwestern grain dealers, millers, and others interested in the railroad rate problem met in St. Louis.[31] The group was initially led by Edward Bacon of the Milwaukee Chamber of Commerce, and at its initial meeting had endorsed legislation designed to lower and equalize railroad rates. Bacon had then worked to get a rate bill (the Corliss-Nelson bill) through Congress, but had little support from the membership of the convention. As a result, railroad leaders had been able to combine portions of the Corliss-Nelson bill with their own Elkins bill, producing a measure that was wholly unsatisfactory to Bacon.

In 1904, an election year, there had been a renewed interest in the question of railroad rates; and at the Interstate Commerce Law Convention that year, meeting as the first one had in St. Louis, newly interested commercial associations had helped to transform the formerly midwestern group "into a major business organization."[32] Among those who had attended and spoken at this meeting had been William Larrabee, who as a former state legislator and governor had mounted an earlier challenge to the rate structure of the C. B. & Q. It was Larrabee who had secured legislation establishing Iowa's first Board of Railroad Commissioners, and it was as the "grand old man" of the railroad question—the veteran of reform efforts, author of *The Railroad Question* (1893), and a founder of the Interstate Commerce Law Convention—that he had spoken in 1904.[33] The burden of his message had been that rate increases amounted to a "transportation tax," that they must therefore be discussed with those to be "taxed," and that the best way to insure this was for shippers and farmers to organize politically and change the structure within which rates were being made.[34]

It was against this background that the 1905 convention, the one to which Brookhart was a delegate, opened in Chicago. As the delegates arrived, they read a *Chicago Tribune* story from Washington, D.C., stating that whether there was to be railroad reform in the current session of Congress depended "entirely upon the extent and magnitude of public opinion that is developed on the subject." It was clearly an observation with which most of the delegates agreed; and so did another group arriving in Chicago, namely the representatives of railroads and large eastern manufacturers under the leadership of National Association of Manufacturers President David M. Parry. This anti-reform group sought to gain entrance to the convention. But Bacon demanded that each delegate, as a condition of entry onto the floor, sign a pledge to support President Roosevelt's call for legislation that "would confer on the Interstate Commerce Commission the power to revise rates."[35] Refusing to sign such a pledge, Parry's group moved across the street to another hall, and for the next two days the two groups exchanged rhetorical barbs.

"I expected this convention to be a tame and formal affair," Brookhart reported in the *Gazette*, "but the actions of the railroads injected enough spice, fire, and lightning to create the greatest interest." He was especially indignant over the use of railroad passes to bring in men seeking to sabotage and undermine the work of the legitimate delegates. "Upon these points I was a tender-foot," he admitted, but "my fund of knowledge has been considerably enlarged."[36]

One of the principal speakers at the convention was Frank T. Campbell, a former Iowa Lieutenant Governor and Railroad Commissioner who had later moved to Ohio, and a man that Brookhart called a "grand old war horse against railroad domination in Iowa politics." In his speech Campbell warned that if there was not government control of the corporations, "the people" would "take this question in their hands and go further than we want them to." The people, he said, had given land to the railroad corporations so they could build their lines. In return, the railroads conceded the right of control to the people. Yet when this control was demanded, those doing so were labeled "socialists." If that was the case, he continued, "count me a socialist." For on one side was the railroads and all their money, "on the other side the sovereignty of the people, which is greater than all wealth and all corporations."[37]

The Convention Chairman, William E. Hughes of Denver, also made a similar speech. The convention, he declared, did not want to take rate making away from the railroads. But when a rate was challenged, there must be an impartial body to decide upon its fairness, and if necessary, substitute a temporary rate. The railroads, he conceded, had done a great deal for the West. But the real heroes were those who had heard the "mystic voices from the west" and had moved there and developed the country. Hence, it was time to establish popular control by prodding Congress into action and following the leadership of a president who was not only a real "representative of individualism" but stood for all that was "best and cleanest in American life and government."[38]

In response to such rhetoric, the convention passed resolutions in support of Roosevelt's program for amending the Interstate Commerce Act. It "specifically" agreed with Roosevelt that the Interstate Commerce Commission should be empowered to arbitrate disputed rates and "fix" them where necessary. And it accepted the view that while the Constitution had vested control of interstate transportation in the Congress, this had been usurped by individuals and corporations bent upon "devising new ways . . . for increasing the cost of necessities of life in the United States."[39]

As deliberations drew to a close, Governor Larrabee spoke, praising Bacon for his fine work and noting the failure of the "rump" group to undermine the convention. He then said:

> The remedy that we have sought to encourage, the object of this convention, has been to encourage the people to arouse themselves and to make a demand upon their Congressmen and upon their Senators to favor the measure we advocate. And so long as we keep up that pressure I have no fear whatever of the result. A public officer, when he feels the people are back of him, is given courage. He is willing to go forward. . . . The greatest enemies to the railways, to the stockholders, are the kind of men who have got control of them at the present time.[40]

Brookhart was swept away. In an article for the *Gazette*, he stressed "the injustice and oppression of present freight rates," a matter that was "too plain for controversy" and amounted to an "infernal system" of rate discrimination. The railroads, he argued, had watered their capital, to the extent of about $31,000 per mile over the railroad's real value; and it was this "dirty water" that had entered into their rate making processes and required high rates in order for them to pay dividends. In addition, he noted that railroads typically bought their supplies from subsidiaries and by placing an inflated book value on such supplies could claim high expenses and low profits despite their excessive rates. "This convention," he said, "made it plain that the people do no longer intend to submit to the lawlessness and anarchy of the big corporations."[41]

Brookhart expected that Republicans would endorse Roosevelt and his program but the Democrats who did so surprised him. John W. Kern, later a Democratic senator from Indiana, challenged any Republican to surpass his endorsement of Roosevelt. And in Virginia, a Democratic leader had warned the railroad companies that "when a Democrat like me stands for Theodore Roosevelt . . . there is thunder in the air." "As for me," Brookhart wrote, "I must quit being a Cummins man. His pace is too slow. I am a Roosevelt man."[42]

Albert Cummins, so it seems, had taken Smith Brookhart to the top of the mountain. But once he was there it was Theodore Roosevelt's voice speaking from the cloud. And for Brookhart, Roosevelt's personality and his claim to speak for a popular and just cause apparently made a difference. He would rally to other such men in the years ahead—to Iowa Senator William S. Kenyon, Nebraska Senator George Norris, Wisconsin's Robert M. La Follette—but Roosevelt was the first and seemingly with Brookhart the most influential. Later, to be sure, historians would note that Roosevelt did more talking than "trustbusting." But this was not apparent to Brookhart in 1905. He swore allegiance to a personality and a cause, and for him these kinds of loyalty would soon become more important than any loyalty to party.

This tendency, to be sure, had been apparent as early as the temperance fight of 1894. But when that was over, Brookhart retreated back to party regularity. Now he was ready to get off a sinking party ship, even if his critics told him it was "rats" who went first. In his view from the mountaintop, he had been able to see how extensive the railroad's control over the "people" had become and how, in the face of protest, their "system" was organizing "every precinct in Iowa with its passes and its patronage, its rebates and its discriminations" so as to "defeat the rights of the people defended by the greatest president they have ever had."[43] In later years, Brookhart would go on to fight other enemies of the "people," among them Wall Street, the Federal Reserve Board, and big business.

Brookhart came down the mountain a zealot. He sent Cummins a copy of his *Gazette* article and suggested that passenger fares in Iowa be reduced to two cents. Other delegates at the convention, he assured Cummins, were favorable. In addition, he asked Cummins for facts and tables about railroad rates.[44] And with the enthusiasm of the reborn, he made a convert, Clifford Thorne, another Washington, Iowa, attorney. Thorne would go on to a distinguished career as a rate attorney.

In 1906 Cummins ran for a third term,[45] and this time Brookhart did not "watch and wonder." He was all over the First District looking for Cummins supporters. Brookhart's campaign speeches included ringing criticism of Blythe and the railroad machine. He said he would be willing to work with the standpat Republicans but not if harmony meant railroad control. He knew that his position would only add fuel to the fire of those who opposed him but that did not slow him down. The night before the election he admitted that he was "in a sense, temporarily at least, a political corpse," but he would retain the right of a corpse to raise a "stink." "You must be omnipresent," Cummins had written in March, "for I hear of your work everywhere. I did not believe it was possible for you or anyone to infuse such energy into the campaign as is now manifest in your part of the state."[46]

Still Cummins lost the First District by 6,000 votes, coming close in Washington County, but winning only in Lee County.[47] The Reservation continued to hold firm for its chief.

Smith Brookhart, meanwhile, had been rewarded for his work in the 1906 campaign. Cummins had appointed him to his military staff as General Inspector Small Arms Practice with the rank of Colonel. Consequently when Theodore Roosevelt came to Keokuk in October 1907, Brookhart had ridden horseback in the parade honoring the President's arrival.[48]

About this same time Brookhart apparently began to give some thought to running for Congress in the First District. But in December 1907, when the *Press* had listed nine men as possible candidates, Brookhart had not been among them. The next month, however, he said in an interview that the time was "ripe for an open, aggressive fight in the First District for progressive principles." He thought that such a fight could be won but was undecided whether he should be the one to carry the banner. He certainly did not act like a candidate. He was not a delegate to the county, district, or state conventions in 1908. And while he did attend the national convention in Chicago, he did not do so as a delegate.[49]

Meanwhile, in 1908 Cummins challenged incumbent Senator William Boyd Allison who was running for a seventh term in the Senate. Brookhart made a series of speeches for Cummins that carried him to the northern part of the state and as far west as Shenandoah. The most notable of these came on April 28, when he went to Burlington to "beard the lion in his den." Speaking there before the Taft-Cummins Club, he told how he had come to be a Cummins supporter, recounted his famous 1904 meeting with Blythe, and outlined how Blythe was trying to influence the current election. The speech gained notoriety when it was published as a campaign broadside and circulated throughout the state.[50]

Allison's health was so bad he was unable to campaign. Still the party regulars were able to muster enough votes to defeat Cummins. But then on August fourth Allison died. After Allison's death, Brookhart was sure that Cummins would be his successor. "Cummins is the logical candidate," he remarked, "and he will represent Iowa in the Senate as sure as two and two are four." To help insure that his arithmetic would be correct, Brookhart again made speeches for Cummins, this time, however, only in Washington County. There Cummins lost. But statewide, he garnered 59 percent of the vote, an outcome, the *Press* noted, that had made Colonel Brookhart "the happiest fellow in town."[51]

Clearly, the fortunes of Iowa's progressives seemed to be turning. Cummins was now in the Senate, and the other Senator, Jonathan Dolliver, was sounding more like a progressive every day. In Iowa the progressive forces received an unexpected boost with the sudden death in March 1909 of Joseph Blythe. Under the circumstances, Brookhart began to shed his earlier reluctance and to think seriously of running for Congress in 1910.

The *Evening Journal* ran a long article in October about Brookhart. The paper said his candidacy was promising but that it would be difficult as Brookhart had "tramped on some tender toes." Noting that Brookhart would be a Roosevelt progressive the paper alluded to the former President's large family and said that Brookhart's four sons and one daughter were "undisputed evidence of the Colonel's faithfulness to the Roosevelt policies." But when the *Press* asked Brookhart about the speculation in the *Journal*, Brookhart said that he had made no decision. He was grateful, however, for "so big a gratis write-up."[52]

As noted previously, Brookhart finally did enter the 1910 congressional primary and waged a strenuous campaign against Congressman Charles Kennedy. His campaign was part of a larger battle between progressives and standpats that included the formation of Taft Republican Clubs. Financed from outside the state the purpose was to elect standpat candidates to Congress and begin to build an organization for Taft's reelection in 1912. One of the other battlegrounds was the fight for governor between the incumbent B. F. Carroll, a standpat and the progressive candidate Warren Garst. Although he supported Garst, Brookhart hoped to avoid taking sides in that race so he would not alienate the standpats in the First District. In January he said it would be a mistake to oust Carroll. Later in the campaign he tried to keep pro-Garst speakers out of the district, prompting the *Brighton Enterprise* to comment that "we did not know that Brookhart owned this district." And in May, when Cummins and Dolliver returned to Iowa from Washington to speak at a Cummins-Dolliver-Garst rally in Des Moines, Brookhart viewed the speech with "alarm." Garst was defeated in the June primary.[53]

Blythe may have been dead but the standpat machine he created in the district was not. District newspapers attacked Brookhart regularly in their editorial columns. One said the choice in the First District was between a loyal Republican [Kennedy] and one opposed to Taft, a pseudo-Democrat [Brookhart]. Another said that Brookhart was not taken "very seriously" in the district. The *Burlington Hawk-eye* questioned how Brookhart would vote on the issues before the current Congress. The candidate replied that if the paper would read the platform it would know how he would have voted. Brookhart added that before the campaign ended it could also prove that he "would have voted against the Declaration of Independence and the Emancipation Proclamation," but he assured his listeners that he was "still sound on the rule of three and planting potatoes on Good Friday."[54]

Kennedy, meanwhile, used his office to the best advantage. In January he had introduced a bill in Congress to build a federal building and post office in Washington, Iowa. Now in April and May the administration announced a number of postmaster appointments in the district. The appointment causing the most comment was of William W. Copeland to be postmaster in Burlington. Brookhart was reported to be "very much disconcerted" over the appointment. A progressive, Copeland had been Brookhart's strongest supporter in the district and the appointment made it seem that Copeland had deserted Brookhart.[55]

Kennedy also used the Department of Agriculture to good advantage. It was the custom for Congressmen to have the department send free packets of garden seeds to constituents. Kennedy flooded the district with seeds prompting one paper to comment that the campaign was a battle between Kennedy's "garden seeds" and Brookhart's "sophomoric oratory."[56]

Brookhart continued to press the same progressive issues throughout the race: congressional and tariff reform, and Lincoln-Roosevelt Republicanism. He portrayed his candidacy as a fight for principle rather than personal honor. In late May the *Journal* said that he would "make a credible showing at the polls."[57] As has been noted, however, he lost the election but not his spirit and his commitment to the progressive cause.

In the general election in the fall, Brookhart supported Kennedy, a move that impressed the *Keokuk Gate City* as attesting to his "Republicanism," and being "highly credible in every way." Brookhart's support of Kennedy, however, did not mean that the Republicans were united, either in the First District or across the state. Evidence of the continuing rift came in late October, when Senator Dolliver died after a sudden illness. Once again, as after the deaths of Gear and Allison, there was a scramble for the vacancy, and during it the cleavage between standpatters and progressives was much in evidence. Since Dolliver's death came too late in the year for a special primary, the governor proceeded to appoint Lafayette Young, editor of the *Des Moines Capital*, to serve until the General Assembly could elect a successor. The voting on this began on January 18, with the standpats casting their votes for Senator Young while the progressives split theirs among several candidates. Receiving votes on the progressive side were former railroad attorney and Assistant United States Attorney William S. Kenyon, former Iowa Attorney General Howard W. Byers, and Spirit Lake newspaperman Abraham B. Funk.[58]

In Des Moines for the first days of the balloting, Brookhart worked from "early morning until early morning" lobbying for the progressives, his first choice being Byers, and if not him, then Funk. After a few days, however, the progressives settled on Kenyon. The standpats, in the meantime, had swung their support to Supreme Court Justice Horace Deemer, Young having decided to withdraw; and the Democrats were now backing former state legislator Claude Porter. The contest remained deadlocked until April 12, the last day of the session, when on the sixty-seventh ballot Kenyon was elected.[59]

During the balloting Brookhart had opposed Kenyon because of the latter's former ties to the railroads. Later in the same year, however, when Kenyon came to Washington and met with Brookhart in his office, Brookhart began to see him as more of a progressive than he had thought earlier.[60] In time he would put Kenyon alongside Lincoln and Theodore Roosevelt in his pantheon of Republican heroes.

In 1911 Brookhart's candidate for the Republican presidential nomination was Robert M. La Follette of Wisconsin. Despite the First District's reputation as a "citadel" of standpattism, he assured La Follette, there was strong sentiment for him. And in correspondence with Walter Houser, La Follette's campaign manager, he observed that "we have never advanced any by waiting for a more favorable time, but have gained ground every time we made a determined fight."[61]

In November of that year Brookhart gained a new weapon when he bought the *Washington County Press*. To no one's surprise the new owner said the paper would espouse progressive principles. Writing his first editorial he said that progressives were at war to restore the functions of government to the people. The *Press,* would be "a soldier clear through this war. Its weapons will be facts and arguments and good will."[62]

Editors across the state took note of the change of ownership. The *Journal* welcomed Brookhart to the journalism fraternity and said that he had "convictions" and wanted others "convicted." In neighboring Ainsworth the editor of the *Clipper* said that with Brookhart "at the head of the editorial department, it will have to be progressive from the devil at the ink rollers up to the front door." The *Sioux City Journal* said that with a "hustler for reform" at the helm of the *Press*, "the newspaper situation in Washington is likely to be more exciting" than it had been.[63]

Brookhart's first hope was to use the *Press* to boost the candidacy of La Follette and he promptly informed the La Follette committee to put the newspaper on its mailing list.[64] In January of 1912, however, when Cummins let it be known that he was available for the nomination, Brookhart withdrew his support from the La Follette campaign and gave his backing to Cummins.

The year 1912 was a banner year for Brookhart. At the county convention, in March, the "progressives" finally ousted the "standpats" in what the *Press* called a "clean-cut" victory, one that clearly put Washington County "on the side of progressive principles" and ousted "standpattism" from "one of its original strongholds."[65]

In June he attended the tumultuous Republican National Convention. The party was split between the candidacies of President Taft and former President Theodore Roosevelt. When the party chose Taft, Brookhart said the people wanted Roosevelt but the nomination was stolen by Taft. The convention, he said, had "stirred up a political cyclone" and he predicted trouble for the Taft wing of the party. He was correct in his analysis of the damage done to the party but incorrect when he predicted that from the maelstrom would come reform:

> The whole convention came under the microscope of public opinion and it stands condemned. It is an organized system of greed and graft. It will be displaced by universal primaries. Never again will a candidate for president be nominated in such a seething caldron of fraud and corruption.[66]

The next month Brookhart was chosen as chairman of the Republican State Convention. The *Muscatine Journal* reported that:

> Brookhart for years had been one of the chief leaders of that gallant band of progressives, who in season and out of season have assailed the citadels of the old guard in the reservation territory of the First District. Never compromising, never giving back, accepting defeat, abuse and ridicule with the same indifference, fighting always they slowly marched on to eventual victory.[67]

Throughout the fall Brookhart worked for Roosevelt in his unsuccessful Bull Moose campaign. Brookhart was willing to work for Roosevelt because he understood the Progressive Party platform as true Republicanism. The next year he was invited to preside at a banquet for former Indiana Senator Albert Beveridge, one of the founders of the Progressive Party in 1912. Beveridge opposed the fusion of the Progressives and the Republicans. Brookhart would always resist separation of the two and so he declined the invitation to preside at the banquet. He did attend, however, and praised Beveridge's stand on human rights and progressive reforms.[68]

The meeting in Joseph Blythe's office had been a watershed event for Brookhart and, although in his frequent retelling of it throughout his life he no doubt over-dramatized it, the constant reference to it is testimony to his realization of its importance for him. What he learned there did not come as a sudden revelation—he was not thrown to the ground like Saul on the road to Damascus. It was, rather, a confirmation of the darker side of politics; the letters were hard evidence that what many had been saying about the political system was true. Smith Brookhart had been leaning toward a rejection of politics as usual and this meeting was the catalyst that completed the change. If the move from Blythe to Cummins was slow in coming, the reason had little to do with Blythe and a great deal to do with Cummins' position on liquor. Brookhart rarely compromised, and that he was willing to compromise enough to ally himself with a wet is another indication of the importance of the meeting with Blythe.

When Brookhart enrolled as a progressive he signed on in what he believed was a righteous cause. As he saw it there was a natural order for America: "government for the people and business for the corporations." But the natural order had been disturbed by the intrusion of business into government, and Brookhart's response, as shown in the 1908 speech in Burlington, was one of anger and indignation. "I know full well the hardship" you have undergone, he told the audience, "and the cunning, treachery, and duress that has threatened you at every step." In Burlington one man, W. W. Copeland, had stood in opposition to railroad control and in describing Copeland, Brookhart could well have been speaking of himself. In Copeland, he said,

> You soon found a leader worthy of any cause, a man who asked nothing for himself; with everything to lose, nothing to gain; who brought down upon himself the wrath of every financial institution under the influence of the great Burlington railroad and never flinched; who reaped no reward but the consciousness of having stood for the right.[69]

This is the Smith Brookhart of the 1920s, righteous, angry, concerned that the people be able to control their own political and economic lives. In the first decade of the century Joseph Blythe personified all that was wrong with the American system, and the spectre of Joseph Blythe, embodied in other oppressors, would remain with Brookhart throughout his public career. Forty years after the event, in his last illness, Smith Brookhart retold the story of the event that gave birth to Senator Brookhart.

6

The Railroad Reformer and Senatorial Candidate

In 1912 Brookhart had been a thoroughgoing Bull Mooser; and when Roosevelt lost, he had pronounced the "bi-partisan alliance of business and politics" to be the "most immoral thing in our country today." Even though he more often spoke in terms of justice, equality, and common sense than in terms of morality, he had written a highly emotional editorial denouncing the system he had been fighting and indicating where, in his view, the fight would eventually lead:

> When the truth is known every county in the district will be like Washington County. Proud old Washington County! The first to kick out this gang and assert the independence that belongs to it. In this county a barber is as big a man as a railroad attorney, a section hand has as many rights as the vice president of the road. And these things are true not only in the Republican Party but also in the Democratic Party. That secret bi-partisan combination of railroad attorneys and editors that slated up both sides and built its organization upon free passes is "busted" higher than Gilroy's kite. Washington County has the proudest name in the state of Iowa today. It has won the most against the greatest odds. . . . You can not stop the great army of progress and Washington County leads the van.[1]

Smith Brookhart became a progressive because of his opposition to railroad control of the political process in Iowa. Regulation of the railroads was just one of many progressive reforms he advocated but it remained central to his thinking. In the years following the rate convention of 1905, he and Clifford Thorne made themselves rate experts. As usual they were not shy about telling others of their ideas. The *Journal* commented that they had been "preaching railway reform to their friends and their followers in their offices and in incidental conversation." Speaking at a Republican rally in

1906 they attacked Blythe's "Reservation" and the corruption of the system by the railroads. Opinion of their neighbors was divided about the merits of their case but everyone enjoyed the show. The *Journal* said, "It was a trifle Sam Jonesy in spots, Billy Sunday like in others, and Thorne and Brookhart like principally."[2]

Their reputation began to spread and soon they were representing clients in rate cases. In one they represented independent oil producers who alleged that Standard Oil conspired with the railroads to keep the rates charged to the independents high. In another their client was the Corn Belt Meat Producers Association in a complaint to the Interstate Commerce Commission against Iowa railroad companies. A few years later they were back before the ICC representing Iowa Mississippi River cities who charged that the railroads gave favorable rates to river cities in Missouri. Brookhart was quick to point out that these cases would have an impact on the entire state and not just in the river cities.[3]

Meanwhile, Brookhart had become increasingly frustrated and disappointed by the problems inherent in making a regulatory system work. Earlier, when William Jennings Bryan had urged government ownership and operation of the railroads, Brookhart had called the idea "socialist vagary." But by 1913 his studies of rate making, railroad finance, and the way competition had worked in the railroad industry were leading him to the conclusion that government ownership might be the only real solution. When Taft recommended that the government build the railroads in Alaska, Brookhart urged that it also operate them. "The government," he declared, "ought to have built every railroad in our country." Private ownership had been a "fatal mistake," resulting not only in exorbitant costs but in "the invisible government" of the big trusts. The idea that government could not economically operate the railroads, he added, was nothing more than railroad propaganda spread by a compliant press. It could certainly have done a better job than the "small group of stock watering grafters" who had got control of lines originally built with the "people's" money.[4]

Brookhart did not hesitate to proselytize opponents of the concept. For example, in 1914 his progressive hero, Theodore Roosevelt, wrote that in Chile government ownership was a "burden on the government and unprofitable to the citizens generally." Brookhart wrote Roosevelt to claim great savings by government ownership which would allow lower rates and increased wages for railroad workers. Moreover, Brookhart told Roosevelt, "The question is fast becoming a live political issue in this section of the country, and . . . I have no doubt it will become a national question soon." Finally, Brookhart and some other Iowans had just organized the National School of Public Ownership, for the "investigation of the feasibility of government ownership of railroads, and other public utilities." As chairman of the executive committee, Brookhart extended an invitation to Roosevelt to join.[5]

Still, if Brookhart had lost his faith in the ability of regulation to control the railroads, he had not lost his conviction that the "people" were and should be the government. In his vision of a publicly operated system, as other *Press* articles in 1913 had made clear, it was the "people" paying the transportation bill, not the railroad workers or the "overhead class" from railroad presidents down to railroad attorneys, that would set policy and make the system serve the "public interest." If his "people" tended to be shippers, as opposed to investors or occupational interests, this was disguised by his identification of them as popular and progressive forces and his condemnation of their opponents as "machine politicians," greedy profiteers charging "what the traffic would bear," and users of regulation to thwart the popular will. Popular government, he had noted, had done well in running the post office and building the Panama Canal, and it might have done equally well in bringing efficiency and good service to the railroad field. Nor did an expanded area of government enterprise necessarily mean an end for legitimate and useful forms of private enterprise. It had not done so abroad, and there was no reason why functions "fully and rightfully" belonging to the private sphere should not remain there. He was warning only that transportation was not one of them and should therefore be in the public domain.[6]

In his discussions of government ownership and operation, Brookhart had also exhibited a growing tendency toward apocalyptic statements designed to dramatize the issue. In November 1914 for example, in an editorial on "The Railroad Question," he had again reviewed the history of regulation and had then stated: "The great economic issue for the present generation is now clearly appearing upon the horizon. Who shall own and operate our railroads?" Serving similar purposes, too, was his "Invisible Government" feature, a page one boxed column in which he refuted statements made in railroad advertising and insisted that it was the merchants, farmers, manufacturers, and laborers, not the railroads, that constituted the "very life blood of the nation." "The railroad," he said, "is the servient agency and the producer is the dominant agency in our civilization. The railroads never did and never will make prosperity when the producer is not prosperous."[7]

For a time, moreover, the "Invisible Government" series had been given national exposure. In April 1915 the National Council of Farmers' Cooperative Associations had ordered fourteen of the articles printed in pamphlet form and had subsequently distributed some 25,000 of these pamphlets to commercial clubs and federal and state legislators. Through these pamphlets it had allegedly brought to light facts "purposely concealed" by the railroads.[8]

In December 1916 Brookhart had also journeyed to Washington, D.C., to testify before a joint Congressional committee studying, as President Wilson had put it, "whether there is anything else we can do . . . for bettering the conditions under which the railroads are operated and for making them more useful servants of the country as a whole." He had come at the invitation of Senator Cummins, a member of the committee, and having told the committee about his study of the rate question since 1905, he argued that for reasons of economy and efficiency, government ownership was not only "the ultimate solution" but the presently desirable one.[9]

In 1916 the committee had been hostile to the suggestion of government ownership. But in December 1917, when Brookhart returned to give further testimony, a committee concerned with the war-induced railroad crisis had been more receptive to his arguments. After repeating much of his earlier testimony, Brookhart predicted that government would "take over and operate all of the railroads before the grass grows again, if not before the new year dawns."[10] A few days later, President Wilson issued an executive order and took possession of the railroads.

In conjunction with his Washington visits, Brookhart had also continued to discuss the railroad question with Senator Cummins. On one occasion, he, Cummins, and Iowa's junior Senator William S. Kenyon had spent most of the night debating the pros and cons of government ownership. On other occasions, the subject had frequently come up. And once the debate over what should be done with the railroads after the war had begun to develop and become an important item of business for Cummins' Committee on Interstate Commerce, Brookhart had been consulted on the matter.[11]

This consultation had also continued in early 1919, when Cummins began preparing a bill defining the peacetime status of the railroads and Brookhart agreed to discuss "railroad reconstruction" before the Iowa Grain Dealers Association in Cedar Rapids. In part, Brookhart reiterated his pre-war case for government ownership. But drawing on his discussions with Cummins, he also pointed out the special feature of the war system and predicted that the new legislation would divide the railroads into several regional systems operated by private leases but with the government retaining the right to take over operation on a six-months' notice. He would have preferred to go farther, he said. But this was a progressive step along the lines recently taken by Canada and Great Britain, and he had no hesitation in urging its support.[12]

Following his Cedar Rapids address, Brookhart had continued to watch Cummins' progress toward railroad legislation. In March of 1919 Cummins himself had returned to Iowa and addressed a joint session of the General Assembly, speaking particularly about the importance of the railroad problem and denying that solutions envisioning government ownership were tantamount to "socialism." Even before the war, he said, all "thoughtful men" had concluded that there "must be a radical change in the system." This had been borne out by the war experience, even though government operation had not been able to show a profit. And whatever Congress did now, it must seek to implement three principles. It must insure, first of all, that there would be a fair and reasonable return on the capital invested, something, he thought, in the neighborhood of 4½ percent. Second, it must consolidate the railroads into not more than eighteen systems, merging the weaker roads with the stronger while retaining safeguards against monopolistic abuse. Finally, it must recognize that the government could not operate such a large, far-flung system, and provide for private operation.[13]

The eventual result would be the Cummins bill of October 1919 and beyond that the Esch-Cummins Act of 1920. But these would take forms disappointing to Brookhart. While there was to be voluntary consolidation, there was also to be a return to private ownership and operation, an even greater reliance on regulation, and new controls designed to prevent strikes and work stoppages. The most objectionable part of the bill was Section 15-A which directed the government to set rates that would guarantee an income to the railroads. Forced to compromise, Cummins would eventually defend and lend his name to a measure containing many items that Brookhart saw as being anything but progressive. If the year 1919 saw his maturation as a student of the railroad question, it also witnessed the coming of a new disappointment and the beginnings of a new attack on those making railroad policy.

During his years in the army, Brookhart continued his interest in politics. In 1916 he attended the Republican National Convention. He was not impressed by any of the speakers but expressed amazement at how easily a convention filled with standpatters could adopt a progressive platform on such issues as the tariff. When the progressives' hopes of a Roosevelt candidacy were dashed, the convention settled on Charles Evans Hughes of New York. Brookhart believed he would be elected in November.

Brookhart's only function during the convention was to serve as assistant sergeant-at-arms in the far reaches of the convention hall. His job was to keep out those without tickets. He admitted, however, that Iowans without tickets were "promptly and efficiently supplied with transportation over the underground railroad." Although they frequently had to move when the rightful ticket holder appeared, no Iowan failed to get into the hall. "We beat the Q railroad in its palmiest free pass days," he later bragged.[14]

The trips he made to Washington, D.C., to testify before Congress were also occasions to keep his hand in the political mix. The evenings he spent with Cummins included more than discussion about railroad questions.

Moreover, now that he was in the army he had even more opportunities to go to the Capitol.

In March 1918 he attended a reception at the Willard Hotel to celebrate the election of Will H. Hays as Chairman of the Republican National Committee. Brookhart was impressed by the unity in evidence after several years of discord and division. Only Senator Warren G. Harding seemed to stumble over the idea of party unity. The new chairman urged the Republicans to look to the future. "The spirit of Lincoln and Grant seemed to lead the Republican Party again," Brookhart wrote, "which means victory, equality, peace and prosperity for all our people."[15]

Brookhart delighted in rubbing elbows with the party elite. He met Congressman Joseph Cannon. Ten years before when Cannon had been Speaker of the House he was the target of progressive reformers. Now Cannon told Brookhart that "every once in a while he votes progressive himself." He also met Congresswoman Jeanette Rankin of Montana. The first woman ever elected to Congress, Rankin was already famous because she was among those who voted against the declaration of war the previous year. Brookhart was impressed with her courage, ability, and patriotism and said that "a few more like Jeanette Rankin in Congress would improve the whole outfit."[16]

Through October 31, 1919, Brookhart was still in the army but was contemplating his discharge and whether to run for Congress in the 1920 election. Aware of his political ambitions, Jennie had other hopes for their post-army life. "My dear Smith," she wrote,

> Jim [Brookhart] is going around giving his lecture against the league of nations . . . lots of people [are] urging him to run for Congress but he [will] not block your way. I think the political bee has stung him, and he likes public life. I surely hope you can see your way to throw the mantle on him. Since Mr. Eicher is gone the law is just as much as you want to make it and we surely have been a divided home long enough.[17]

The next day Jim wrote telling him of the speeches he had been making and of several candidates who were already at work campaigning for the First District Congressional seat still held by Charles A. Kennedy, Brookhart's 1910 opponent. Among these was William F. Kopp, a Mount Pleasant lawyer and friend of the Brookharts, who, according to Jim, was getting "a good many inquiries" but would not commit himself until he knew "what you wanted to do."[18] Politics was not the only thing on his mind. During his last weeks in service, he was ill with the flu; and when he finally arrived home, he was very thin and still quite weak.

He was also incredulous at what was now happening in Congress. The Cummins bill, as he saw it, would use the government to guarantee returns on watered capital; and in an article prepared for the *Des Moines Register* and published there on January 5, 1920, he predicted that such legislation would "prove to be the finest hatching of Wall Street chicks that ever came out of a railroad incubator." He had supported, he said, the plan that Cummins had presented to the Iowa General Assembly and had calculated that it would reduce transportation costs for Iowa counties by nearly 30 percent. But under what was being proposed now, the costs were likely to go even higher. Congress, in effect, was about to impose the counterpart of a new road tax, and farmers ought to be complaining about the prospect.[19]

In addition, Brookhart was troubled by the labor provisions of the bill. It seemed, in his view, to reflect the anti-labor impulses that had been apparent in the breaking of the coal, steel, and Boston Police strikes. And these, he thought, were impulses to which farm communities ought not lend their support. Farmers and laborers each bought the products of the other. Together they made up 95 percent of the population; and if they were to fight one another, the other 5 percent, big capital, would exploit them both. "Besides," he continued, "it is wrong in principle to prohibit strikes while organized capital owns and operates the railroads." Labor, in this situation, had to fight for its jobs, wages, and benefits, and it must have the strike and other tools with which to fight. A comparable tool for farmers was cooperative associations, and farmers would and should be angry if the American Federation of Labor asked for legislation to prohibit cooperatives.[20]

Brookhart was also strongly critical of the Cummins bill in a floor fight at the January 1920 convention of the Iowa Farm Bureau Federation. Under the leadership of James R. Howard, who in late 1919 had been elected national president of the Farm Bureau and was using that position to insist that laborers "owed an honest day's labor for an honest day's pay," the Iowa organization had become increasingly concerned about the "drift to bolshevism" and the "covetous tentacles" reaching forth from the radical foes of free enterprise.[21]

The Farm Bureau, it was said, was a movement of "hope and deliverance" from these pernicious influences;[22] and at the state convention, the resolutions committee had finally dropped a resolution endorsing the guaranteed returns provision of the Cummins bill but had retained one endorsing the labor provisions. This it took to the convention floor, apparently thinking it would pass easily. But two men on the floor thought differently. Former State Senator Asa L. Ames of Tama and Smith Brookhart both took the floor to speak against the resolution, with Brookhart reiterating many of the points made in his *Register* article. If the farmers joined the trusts and Wall Street against labor, he said, then who was to say that labor would not do the same against farmers. The result might well be that farmers would be included in future anti-trust acts and lose their right to form cooperative societies or join together in other ways.

Brookhart and Ames presented a substitute resolution favoring national and state legislation that would bring economic equality and thereby make strikes unnecessary. As Brookhart put it:

> Until the nation provides a sickness, old age and unemployment fund, and we insure men against loss of labor and wages by these measures, we are in no position to enforce a no-strike dictum. . . . Let us first make wage earning secure in time of sickness or in time of enforced idleness by reason of old age. Then we can say to labor that strikes are unnecessary.[23]

Somewhat surprisingly, Brookhart's substitute was passed.

Brookhart's actions at the convention led the *Des Moines Register* to speculate about his becoming "a candidate for Congress." And he could also take heart when the farmer-labor alliance he was advocating seemed to be forming. At a mid-January meeting of representatives of various farm and labor groups, among which were the State Federation of Labor, the United Taxpayers League, the Iowa Threshers Union, the Brotherhood of Railway Engineers, and the Iowa branch of the American Society of Equity, the notion of such an alliance dominated proceedings. Speaking there, Benjamin Marsh, secretary of the Farmers' National Council, declared that, "Any farm leader who, knowing Wall Street's game during the war, favors the return of the railroads before investigating the maladministration of the Wall Street manipulators, is betraying the farmers he represents."[24]

Brookhart's friends were also busy now, among them James M. Pierce, who since 1895 had been owner and editor of the *Iowa Homestead* and an important shaper of political opinion. In addition to his regular editorial column, "The Publisher's Views on the Topics of the Times," Pierce often wrote multipaged articles on topics of particular interest; and in early 1920 the topic that most interested him was the railroad bill and its provision for returning the railroads to private ownership. Senator Cummins, he thought, had given distinguished service to the state, but he had now wandered from his former path and was ready to give a failed system of private operation another trial. This betrayal of the progressive cause, he added, was clearly apparent in the opposition to Cummins' bill by such former allies as Senator La Follette, Clifford Thorne, and Smith W. Brookhart, the latter "one of the deepest students of railroad problems in the state of Iowa."[25]

Pierce considered Des Moines lawyer Howard J. Clark as a possible candidate for Cummins' senatorial seat. But he soon decided against him, primarily because Clark was little known outside Des Moines. Subsequently he had Brookhart tell Clark that the *Homestead* would not support him. For his part, Brookhart was still considering a run for the House. On February 22, when a *Register* article listed eight possible contenders for Cummins' seat, Brookhart was not among them.[26]

There was, however, some speculation to the contrary. The *Des Moines Capital* of January 21 did report that Brookhart was a likely opponent of Cummins and that since he was working with Fred Canfield, President of the State Federation of Labor, the labor provisions of the Esch-Cummins bill were likely to be the primary issue. After reading the *Capital* article, Mt. Ayr attorney R. H. Spence wrote to Cummins, informing him that "the warrior from Washington, Iowa, had his vision focused on your toga" and that Brookhart would be a formidable candidate. In his reply, Cummins spoke of the candidacy of "my former friend . . . [who] is an honest man and sincerely believes what he is saying to the people of Iowa." He had already told him, Cummins said, that he was "unintentionally misrepresenting" the provisions and consequences of the railroad bill.[27]

Brookhart held off from any announcement of his intentions, waiting in particular to see what would happen to the railroad bill in Congress and what Cummins might do there. The senator, after all, was an old friend and a national figure of major stature whose apparent loss of support among Iowa political groups might prove illusory. But in late February, when it became apparent that the Esch-Cummins bill would pass and that the President would sign it, Brookhart, supported by Pierce, made his move. Earlier, when Pierce decided against Howard Clark, he told Brookhart: "We have but one man in Iowa to make the race and [you are the one]. The farmers can depend upon [you] to fight to the finish."[28]

On March 19, at a meeting of the Washington County Republicans, Brookhart announced his candidacy. In a statement issued in the name of "farmers, laborers and businessmen" and signed by members of the Farm Bureau, Farmers' Union, American Legion, and Spanish-American War Veterans, he noted the "rising tide of farmer opposition" to a railroad act that legalized watered capital and guaranteed a return on it. The farmer, he said:

> is not and never will be a radical, but he is rapidly reaching the conclusion that the men who produce by the toil of hand and brain must unite and have a greater voice in the control of their government. This movement is taking concrete form throughout the country and it calls for a reconsideration of men and issues.[29]

In addition, he called for "a proper insurance plan" for the veterans of the World War; for cooperation among the "great producing and distributing classes . . . in their battle against the big combinations of capital"; and for providing greater economic protection for the aged, mothers, and the "several million children in the United States who are undernourished."[30]

Commenting on the statement, the *Washington Evening Journal* noted that it was written in the "blunt and plain language" that had been typical of Brookhart. It also recalled that Brookhart had been in many local battles and had suffered wounds, some of which were not yet healed. And while it could not always agree with Brookhart, it admitted that local pride would play a part in the primary and predicted that Washington County would stand behind him.[31]

Ten days later, on March 29, Brookhart delivered the opening speech of his campaign. Before an audience that filled the main floor of the Washington High School auditorium and included many laborers and farmers, the latter despite bad roads because of the spring thaw, he reiterated his by now familiar position on the railroads.[32] Cummins' retreat from the plan presented before the Iowa General Assembly, he declared, amounted to "a surrender of most of the reforms we have fought for during the past twenty years."[33]

In addition, Brookhart took positions on three other issues. He called, first of all, for adjusted compensation and a lifetime insurance plan for veterans. Four million men, he said, had been drafted to fight the war. Now capital should be drafted, through a tax on war profits, to provide needed veterans' benefits. Second, he was opposed to the recent discounting of the Liberty Bonds that citizens had purchased to help with the war effort. The policy on these should be reversed. And third, he called again for old age insurance, unemployment insurance, and aid to mothers and children. In this regard, he said, he welcomed the ballot for women. "When the women vote, these social questions that go to the life and security of the homes will receive due consideration and we will have insurance to protect the worker's life from infancy to old age against calamities he cannot avoid."[34]

Finally, Brookhart introduced a theme that would become familiar in the years ahead. The spirit of the time, he said, was democracy; and true democracy was incompatible with the rule of competition, whether for political supremacy or economic gain. Competition had led, in business and politics, to the creation of a small class of managers, czars, kaisers, corporate presidents. It had created "castes and monopolies at the top; ignorance, poverty, despair and anarchy at the bottom," overriding constitutional guarantees of equality and leaving power in the hands of fewer than 5 percent of the people. A substitute had to be found; and the one road, he thought, that held out "the promise of safety for all the good things of civilization" was a system of "cooperatives" founded on the Rochdale principle of one man, one vote, a limitation on capital, and dividends returned according to amount of participation. Power in a democratic order should come through men, not wealth, and this could be achieved only by "cooperation." "If I go to the Senate," he concluded, "it will be chiefly to lead in this great movement for a practical golden rule of the economic field."[35]

Although there were many Washingtonians present to watch the local man enter the national spotlight, a number were noticeable by their absence. Colonel David Palmer, Brookhart's old opponent Charles J. Wilson, Attorney Schuyler Livingston, and other local Republican Party leaders made no secret of their opposition to Brookhart. Nor did Brookhart expect help from local or First District Party organization leaders. He would, he said, "carry the county despite their opposition."[36]

Pierce was pleased. In the *Homestead* he called Brookhart's candidacy the "outstanding development" of recent months, "an answer to widespread demand that the farmers of Iowa have a representative in Congress who is one of them." In forwarding copies of Brookhart's statement and speech to Senator La Follette, he expressed optimism about the candidate's chances and noted that the railroad brotherhood, especially the Brother of Locomotive Engineers, had promised funds although these had not yet come in. Subsequently, La Follette met with B. of L. E. President Warren Stone, who assured him that the brotherhoods were ready to put forth "every effort to secure Colonel Brookhart's nomination."[37]

Pierce's associate editor, Austin P. Haines, agreed to manage Brookhart's campaign and in the *Homestead* Pierce ran editorials supporting the various positions Brookhart took and supplemented these with longer feature articles about Brookhart and against Cummins. He was supportive, in particular, of Brookhart's stand on the railroad labor issue. In supporting anti-labor legislation, he thought, the National Farm Bureau was "sowing the wind" that would turn into a "whirlwind against itself." Fortunately, the Iowa Farm Bureau Federation, in the January resolution that Brookhart had helped bring about, was showing greater wisdom.[38]

Iowa's other major farm journal, *Wallaces' Farmer,* disagreed. The farmer, it said, was "thoroghly (sic) fed up" with crippling strikes and was ready for a labor system that would, as the Esch-Cummins bill did, recognize the "rights of all three parties to the controversy, the public, labor, and capital." As for the rest of the bill, it added, no one was entirely satisfied with it. But it was the best that could be done at the present time. Its author, Senator Cummins, had stood with the farmer for twenty years and had given more thought to the railroad situation than anyone in the country.[39]

Brookhart, *Wallaces' Farmer* also insisted, was a dangerous radical who wanted the "continuation of industrial war" to the end of "industrial socialism [as] they have in Russia today." The real issue in the campaign was the "contest between . . . radical labor leaders and the rest of the people, particularly the farmers." And Brookhart was the candidate of the "radical labor leaders," a man who would not intentionally plunge the nation into the "pit of social anarchy" but one who "in his innocence and his ignorance" was being used by those who wanted to continue turmoil and unrest. He was "a good-hearted fellow, but to send him to the Senate in the place of Senator Cummins would be like sending a city kid out to run the corn planter when the season is three weeks late."[40]

The largest labor group in Iowa, the railroad brotherhoods, was strongly for Brookhart, and this was especially true of the Brotherhood of Locomotive Engineers and its Grand Chief Engineer (President) Warren Sanford Stone. Born on February 1, 1860, in Ainsworth, Washington County, Iowa, Stone had graduated from the Washington Academy, gone on to become an engineer on the Rock Island Railroad, and after joining the union advanced rapidly as a union leader, being elected Grand Chief Engineer in 1904. He had been instrumental in establishing the first pension system for union members and their widows, had been a founder of *Labor,* a weekly newspaper, and as a believer in cooperation had got the B. of L. E. to found a cooperative bank. In 1924 he would strongly support Robert La Follette's presidential bid.

Stone favored government ownership of the railroads and was therefore opposed to the Esch-Cummins bill. He supported instead the Sims bill, more commonly referred to by the name of its author Glenn Plumb, who was another Washington County native. Born in Clay in 1866, Plumb had later moved with his family to Illinois, attended Oberlin College and Harvard, and subsequently taken a law degree at Northwestern and begun practice in Chicago. In 1917 he had been retained by several railroad brotherhoods, including the B. of L. E., to represent them at hearings before the Interstate Commerce Commission.

Under the Plumb Plan the government would own the railroads with rates to be set by the Interstate Commerce Commission, but operation would be in the hands of a board of fifteen members representing the public, the operating officers of each line, and the classified employees. Surplus income after expenses was to be divided between the government and the employees, thus providing workers with a dividend for efficiency. In discussing the plan in a February speech, Stone declared that government ownership was "nothing new." It existed elsewhere in the world, and "it is coming in the United States."[41]

Stone supported Brookhart through the journal of the B. of L. E., the *Locomotive Engineers Journal.* He also gave financial support. In April he sent a check for $5,000 constituting over half the total that Brookhart would eventually raise. Two other major financial contributions also had railroad brotherhood connections. James Stedman of Vinton, Iowa, an engineer member of the Brotherhood of Locomotive Firemen and Engineer Men, sent $2,000; and Robert McBirnie, a brakeman and member of the board of the Brotherhood of Railroad Trainmen, sent $1,000.[42]

During the campaign, the railroad unions built upon a great resentment among their members against the Esch-Cummins bill. In the lower two tiers of counties in central and southwestern Iowa (part of Blythe's Reservation), noted *Des Moines Register* reporter L. J. Wilson, "antagonism among railroaders to Cummins seems general." Wilson also thought that Iowa labor in general was likely to endorse any candidate who supported labor principles. Although professing non-partisanship, labor leaders were urging their followers to enter the Republican primary and vote for Brookhart.[43]

Meanwhile, in Washington, D.C., Cummins had secured the support of the state's entire Congressional delegation. At a meeting called for this purpose, all were present except First District Congressman Charles A. Kennedy, who subsequently endorsed Cummins. There was feeling at the meeting, especially on the part of Sixth District Congressman C. William Ramseyer, that such action would give Brookhart a chance to talk against the "Federal bunch." But Cummins was willing to take this chance. He also rejected Ramseyer's suggestion that Brookhart simply be ignored. Brookhart and the Plumb Plan, he believed, had to be defeated. Labor was against him, he said, and he wanted to start people thinking and try to hold the farmers.[44]

Upon returning to Iowa, Cummins found many letters of support, most of them attacking Brookhart as a radical. "Colonel Brookhart has made a political blunder in his attack on your railway bill," wrote Burlington editor J. L. Waite. "The candidacy of Smith Brookhart against you has not taken away any of your strength here," wrote Fairfield editor Dean Taylor. "In fact it has brought scores to your support who never were for you before." And from Fort Dodge banker Frank Corey came the view that Brookhart was basing his campaign on the "most dangerous foundation . . . of class rule . . . a situation . . . approaching very closely that of Russia today." Brookhart's plan to unite farmers and union labor, as Corey saw it, was "absurd."[45]

Former Brookhart friends and supporters also wrote Cummins. W. W. Copeland of Burlington, a Cummins and Brookhart ally in the earlier battles between progressives and standpats, wrote to tell Cummins of the coalition of railroad union men and Farmers' Union members in southern Iowa. The Farm Bureau Federation, he noted, was strong in the northern half of the state and was made up of the "better class of farmers." But in the south the farmers were more radical and belonged to the Farmers' Union. In an earlier letter, Copeland had told Cummins that Brookhart was "dangerous . . . [without] a speck of honor, gratitude or good fellowship wrapped up in [his] hide"; and he now pledged to help in whatever way Cummins asked.[46]

No letter was more poignant, however, than one from Mt. Pleasant attorney Roger S. Galer, who had been principal of Southern Iowa Normal, had been one of Brookhart's teachers there, and had later introduced Brookhart at the opening speech of the 1910 Congressional primary campaign. Now, Galer wrote Cummins, "I cannot follow him in his present course and am very much grieved at the action he has taken. I regard him at present as advocating dangerous radical theories."[47]

For Republican progressives the choice was between two of their own; and for some, like Copeland and Galer, the choice was painful but obvious. They could not abide what they perceived as Brookhart's radicalism and therefore went with Cummins. Others, like Pierce, felt that Cummins had deserted the progressive cause and therefore supported Brookhart. As for the old standpats, who had lost control of the party in 1912, they were now hopeful that Cummins' need for their support would allow them to reestablish their dominance. "I wish to take the oath of allegiance," Charles J. Wilson wrote to Cummins. "I very earnestly hope that you will be elected. Heretofore in pre-convention and pre-primary contests I was not for you but always [supported] you when you became the choice of the party."[48] Indeed, no one in Washington County worked harder for Cummins than Charles Wilson.

Cummins' response to these various letters followed a general theme. Almost invariably he expressed shock or surprise or disappointment or regret that Brookhart had entered the race. He then denied any desire to attack Brookhart personally or to "disparage my old friend." And finally, he went on to say just how dangerous Brookhart really was.[49] Typical was his response to an editorial written by Cyrenus Cole, Cedar Rapids editor and later Congressman:

> Colonel Brookhart has succeeded in getting behind him more organizations with false and vicious principles than we often find in concert. The Committee of Forty-eight, a purely socialistic affair, headed by Pierce of the *Homestead*; the Plumb Plan League; and the alleged Triple Alliance, bring together, from my standpoint, about all that is objectionable in American political life. I am very glad to meet the issue and there is no better place to meet it than in Iowa, and if that kind of a combination can command anything like a majority of the Republicans in the state I would despair in my country.[50]

At the time, moreover, the association of Brookhart with radicalism was a potent weapon. Early 1920 was the time of the Palmer raids. Fear of "Bolshevism" was widespread, and in Iowa this fear was exacerbated by increased union activity and debates over the legitimacy of the strike as a labor weapon. In that context his government owner scheme seemed even more radical. Adding further fuel to the fire, too, was the Greater Iowa Association, an association of businessmen, local commercial clubs, and Chambers of Commerce originally founded for the purpose of boosting Iowa business and industry. Back in 1917 it had become the publisher of *The Iowa Magazine,* a small, slick-paper monthly full of pictures and articles about progressive towns and businesses. But as of February 1920, it had transformed this magazine into an anti-communist tabloid with a motto of "Thoroly (sic) American." The idea, it declared, was to meet "fire with fire" and undertake "an effective propaganda against those who would destroy our government."[51]

In the years ahead, Brookhart would frequently face the charge of being a radical, and not all would be as kind as Cummins was in 1920. Cummins seems honestly not to have imputed any destructive purpose to Brookhart, at least not in 1920. Rather, he thought Brookhart was being misled by the various organizations he named in the letter to Cole. In reality, Brookhart advocated government ownership only of the railroads, although later he would broaden this to include all public utilities. The threat posed by Brookhart, as Charles Metz pointed out in *The New Republic,* was not the threat of communism. For "only a brave and misguided man will stump Iowa's farms . . . in the interest of land nationalization." The threat came rather from his "attack upon the institution of privately and competitively managed distribution."[52]

Iowa newspapers were generally of two minds about Brookhart. One group, although not fully supportive, gave him credit for being forthright about the issues. The *Decorah Journal,* for example, felt that Iowans owed him thanks for not "trying to ride two horses, or play both ends against the middle." The *Mount Vernon Record* noted that he was not "the puppet of any man or any set of men." And the *Ames Tribune* credited him with standing firmly for the principle of equal opportunity for all. The other group followed *The Iowa Magazine* in depicting him as a dangerous radical and demagogue. The *Keokuk County News* had him "pawing the air with both hands and arms in his raving against Senator Cummins." The *Webster City Freeman-Journal* saw him appealing to class prejudice and drifting in a "socialist direction." The *Spencer News-Herald* found his platform to be "almost socialist in spots." And the *Eagle Grove Eagle,* in what was probably the most vicious of the ad hominem editorials, talked of three black crows sitting in a tree. The first was William Jennings Bryan, "imploring the pardon of heaven for electing Wilson." The second was James M. Pierce, "doing penance by sleeping on cockleburrs for electing W. L. Harding Governor of Iowa"; and the third was Brookhart, "wearing camels' hair and sitting in Iowa coal ashes in expiation for his twenty years of mistaken zeal in promotion of Senator Cummins' political ambition." Brookhart, it said, had stopped at nothing "crooked, demagogical or politically unmoral (sic)" to elect Cummins and was now reaping what he had sowed.[53]

Brookhart attacked the radicalism issue like he attacked everything else—head on. Cummins, he said, was setting up straw men that he could knock down, and if "that affords him amusement it does not bother me."

> I am not a socialist; not a member of the Committee of 48; and not a member of the Plumb Plan League. I am running on the same platform on which I have supported Senator Cummins in the years gone by, which he has deserted. . . . It is my contention that the question of what constitutes true Republican doctrine is something the voters have a right to determine at the polls, instead of having it dictated by a political machine.[54]

The Republican State Convention, meeting in April, walked a tightrope between Cummins and Brookhart. While each side wanted an endorsement for its man, neither was willing to push hard for it. The majority of the delegates, however, were for Cummins, their general attitude being, as the *Register* had said earlier, that if "the old man wants another term, he can have it." It was only the fear that Brookhart forces might walk out that kept Cummins' supporters from pushing an endorsement resolution. They settled instead for a resolution that did not mention either candidate by name but left little doubt as to where the party stood. It was, according to the resolution, opposed to socialism, communism, or government ownership, in favor of governmental intervention in business only when private enterprise had demonstrably failed, and committed to liberty, law, peace, good order, progress, and human and property rights.[55]

Cummins, as temporary chairman of the convention, gave the only real speech there, one in which he discussed general issues and defended the Esch-Cummins bill. Brookhart was neither mentioned nor invited to speak. Noticeably, too, especially to Pierce, was the way in which former opponents of Cummins gathered around him. The Senator, so Pierce thought, appeared "ill at ease" among these new "friends (?)." "Perhaps," he added, "the conservative atmosphere in Washington had had its effects on Cummins, as the latter once charged it had on Senator Allison. Perhaps he had simply come to the point where he is tired of the battle and wants peace."[56]

Cummins made only one other speech, at Winfield just past the Washington County line in Henry County. He then became ill and was confined to bed for the rest of the campaign. But he did continue to worry about who was going to vote in the open primary. Many of Brookhart's supporters, he noted, were socialists or Democrats; and hence, it was important to "keep the Republican primary pure; that is, to prevent men from voting a Republican primary ticket unless they are qualified under the law to do so."[57]

Meanwhile, Cummins' mail continued to reflect the realignment of Republicans. An editor from Preston, "who has never supported you," wrote to say he was now supporting Cummins because of the "fight that is being hatched against you by an element which should not be given an opportunity to gain a foothold in our government . . . the Bolsheviks and I. W. W. element." And George C. Call, a Sioux City bond and mortgage dealer, told of the need to get out the businessman's vote to counter labor. He assured Cummins that the "old standpatters are your loyal supporters in this town."[58]

Brookhart, in the meantime, was finishing the campaign with a flurry of speeches and articles. The *Locomotive Engineers Journal* published a point-by-point refutation of Cummins. The *Homestead* published an article entitled "Why I am a Candidate." And in the *Iowa Union Farmer,* the official organ of the Iowa Farmers' Union, a pose of non-partisanship was accompanied by articles extolling "cooperation" and urging members to look at the issues and decide who was for the farmer. Its May 19 issue also carried an article by Brookhart entitled "What Cooperation Means to the Iowa Producers."[59]

In addition, organized labor worked hard for Brookhart. On the Saturday before the election, railroad men distributed literature all over the state; and in an open bid for non-Republican votes, thousands of cards were distributed, instructing Democrats on how to get to polls and change their party affiliation and how to take out an absentee ballot. The cards concluded, "A vote for Colonel Brookhart on June 7 is a vote for the producers and consumers of Iowa."[60]

On election day *Register* political writer L. J. Wilson began his column with a "political forecast:"

> Clear and calm for the Democrats; no contest for nomination on either state or congressional ticket. Clouds of doubt hang low over Republican territory in Iowa. Sharp winds of opposition arising from Brookhart camp bid fair to rip up a few tent stakes in Cummins' encampment.

The weather, always a concern on election day, was even more so for the Cummins people. They hoped to try a new election tactic and use fleets of automobiles to bring farmers to the polls.[61]

Cummins won the election by a comfortable margin of 54.6 percent of the vote. Brookhart took only twenty-eight counties, sixteen of them in the lower three tiers once regarded as part of the Blythe Reservation. The remaining twelve were scattered across the state. He carried Monroe and Lucas counties, the center of the Iowa coal industry and mine union strength, by margins greater than 55 percent. He also carried Cummins' home county, Polk, by eighteen votes. But he lost such urban counties as Linn, Black Hawk, Pottawattomie, Scott and Woodbury; and the losses in the latter two, according to Pierce, were especially noteworthy. It was in their major cities, Davenport and Sioux City, that the Greater Iowa Association saw the "reddest red in Iowa and where the labor and socialist tickets have been recently victorious in city campaigns." In addition, the "get out the vote" efforts against Brookhart were a factor. He lost the 1920 primary with 5,000 more votes than Cummins had polled as a winner in 1914. Overall, 70,000 more votes were cast in the 1920 Republican senatorial primary than in the 1914 primary.[62]

Iowa Republicans were in Chicago for the Republican National Convention the day after the primary and were "frankly anxious" about the outcome. As the returns came in, however, the delegates, almost all pro-Cummins, greeted them with "real enthusiasm." Cummins' victory, it was believed, had been the result of work by the county Republican organizations, particularly since he had been unable to campaign himself. It was also the result, in the *Register's* view, of standpat support. "Had they not come to his rescue," it declared, "he could not have saved himself from defeat." And with this assessment a number of others agreed. "As a rule," wrote a Mount Ayr attorney, "the old standpatters supported you but every disgruntled and disappointed voter in the county was against you."[63]

Still, the strength of Brookhart's vote surprised Senator Kenyon. "I never dreamed," he wrote, that "the Brookhart forces could make the fight they did." What he had not taken into account, he thought, was the influence of the *Homestead* and its capacity for stirring up farmers who had formerly been Cummins' friends.[64]

In Washington, D.C., the election was a matter of "greatest interest." The *Homestead's* Washington correspondent reported:

> It threw the cold shivers into the little group of influential reactionaries, who fear the slightest approach to real representative government. They have more cold shivers coming to them—provided the farmers of American will stick together for a real economic program, and not be fooled by any substitute marked "Just as good."[65]

Cummins wrote to presidential nominee Warren G. Harding that the campaign was the "cruelest and bitterest fight ever known in this state." It was also one that had left him with concerns about the future of the Republican Party. If the forces he had faced in Iowa combined to form a third party, the Republicans would have continued success. But if they joined the Democrats, he told Indiana Senator James Watson, "we have before us the hardest fight in our history." And as he told Senator Kenyon, it would be particularly hard if waged on a platform that "politically speaking" was "a meaningless instrument," one that did not "catch the popular imagination" and had "nothing in it to impress the public mind."[66]

Brookhart had been a reluctant opponent of Albert Cummins. His earlier move to Cummins and the progressives had come only after months of thought and not by calculating its political advantages. And the move away from him had come after similar study and after waiting to be sure that the Esch-Cummins bill would amount to a sacrifice of the progressive principles to which this study had led him. In his biography of William Jennings Bryan, Louis W. Koenig notes that the Great Commoner was willing to sacrifice ideology and faith to personal ambition and calculated self-seeking, particularly on such issues as prohibition.[67] But the same could not be said about Brookhart. Once a prohibitionist, once a progressive, and once an advocate of government ownership, he would never waiver from these views. (Although in the case of Cummins, support for progressivism overrode distaste for wetness.) He ran in 1920, as he would run in future years, to advance a cause, in this case the fight against railroad control.

Cummins, like a number of other progressives after the war, was moving away from some of his earlier positions,[68] and eventually his political philosophy would diverge markedly from Brookhart's. But it was a political decision, in particular the decision by Cummins to "settle for what he could get" on the railroad bill, that led to the "fight" of 1920. Brookhart was not a politician in the same sense and could never "settle for what he could get," especially on matters of basic principle.

Cummins had been renominated. But over the next few years the discontented voices that he had heard in the summer of 1920 would be joined by others. And in Iowa they would look not to Albert B. Cummins for relief, but to his opponent that year, Smith Wildman Brookhart.

Smith Wildman Brookhart at Bloomfield High School. He graduated in 1886. *Courtesy, John Yount.*

Brookhart family group, 1901. Smith Brookhart (with bow tie) is in the center behind his wife Jennie (*seated*), who is holding son John. The Brookhart brothers are in the back row (*from left*), Thomps, Jim, Alan, Smith, George, Newt. The Brookhart sisters stand in front of them (*from left*) May, Myrtle, Della, with Lillian kneeling (*center front*). The Brookhart parents are seated, and Smith's mother is holding his son, Ned. *Courtesy, John Yount.*

Brookhart home on Jefferson Street in Washington, Iowa. Smith and Jennie are on the front porch. *Courtesy, John Yount.*

Lieutenant Smith W. Brookhart assured his townspeople that Company D would uphold their expectations in the Spanish-American War, 1898. *Courtesy, State Historical Society of Iowa.*

Camp Perry, 1911. *Courtesy, John Yount.*

United States sharpshooting team that won the Palma trophy in 1912. Col. Brookhart (*seated, center*) was team captain. Capt. Morton C. Mumma (*front left*) was adjutant.

Jennie Brookhart, 1900. *Courtesy, John Yount.*

The brick house, built in 1909 outside Washington. The basic construction is of poured concrete. Smith demanded a house that was "childproof and fireproof." *Courtesy, John Yount.*

Three generations of Smith Wildman Brookhart. Smith Jr. is standing behind his father. The Senator is holding his grandson, Smith III, the son of John and Marguerite Brookhart, 1935. *Courtesy, John Yount.*

The Brookhart family, June 1922 (*from left*) John, Smith Jr., Smith Wildman, Joe, Jennie, Edith, Florence, Ned. *Courtesy, John Yount.*

7

The Cooperationist and Republican Insurgent

After the primary of 1920 Iowans settled into a political calm. Albert Cummins went on to win the general election in November and to serve his third full term. The other Senate seat, Kenyon's, would not be contested until 1924; and hence many thought, and others hoped, that Smith W. Brookhart would not be heard from for at least another four years. The calm that followed the spring of 1920, however, proved to be short-lived. New clouds were already gathering on the horizon. The storm that struck took the form of an agricultural depression that would continue until the rest of the country joined the plight of farmers with the onset of the Great Depression in 1929.

The farm depression that began in late 1920 served as the catalyst for yet another transformation of Smith Brookhart. He had begun his political life as a regular Republican. Later he had moved into the progressive camp. Later still he had become disenchanted with progressivism and its regulatory solutions. And now his analysis of the farm depression and his search for a way to end it would take him back to his earliest political education—the populism of James B. Weaver.

During the war and immediate post-war years agricultural prices had risen dramatically, and, as a result of the higher prices and a favorable credit structure, farmers had expanded their operations, bought more land and equipment, improved their farms, and invested in new farm machines as well as automobiles. Then, beginning in the fall of 1920, prices began to fall. In the second half of that year average prices of ten leading crops fell 57 percent, and by the following spring, prices were one-third of what they had been the previous June. At the same time, the Interstate Commerce Commission granted higher freight rates to the railroads, an action that again brought the railroads under attack. In Congress, Senator Arthur Capper tried to repeal section 15-A (the guarantee clause) of the Esch-Cummins Act.[1]

Historians cite a combination of national and international economic conditions to explain the onset of the agricultural depression. But in the 1920s, as Brookhart saw it, the chief villain was the Federal Reserve Board. In May of 1920 it had met with the Federal Advisory Council and Class A Directors of the Federal Reserve Banks from across the country and had surveyed the credit situation. Alarmed at the continuing increase of speculative activity fueled by easy credit, it had then raised the rediscount rate and urged member banks to curtail credit and "discourage loans for capital and speculative purposes." The meeting had been held amid great secrecy and, although there were summary accounts in the press and the *Federal Reserve Bulletin*, it was not until 1923 that a full account would be published.[2]

By autumn banks across the country were tightening credit. In Iowa farm loans were called in, and to meet the call many farmers were forced to sell their crops early and take a loss. Large numbers of notes also proved uncollectible, which for some banks meant failure. In late October, as the situation worsened, the Iowa Bankers' Association and several farm groups sponsored a series of meetings. And at the one convening in Ottumwa, Smith Brookhart was an active participant.

Speaking first at the meeting, L. A. Andrews, president of the Iowa Bankers' Association, defended the action of the bankers. There were, he said, two reasons for the economic setback. One was "speculation and reckless . . . senseless buying of autos and luxuries of all kinds." The other was wartime inflation, which had put the credit system on a false basis. Farmers, he advised, must learn good saving practices and "realize that we are in a period of lower prices in all things." There would be a period of recession, but "sooner or later" the world would have to use Iowa crops "at fair prices." Other speakers included E. G. Nourse, head of the agriculture department at Ames, and E. H. Cunningham, State Secretary of the Iowa Farm Bureau Federation. The former urged careful farming marketing practices. The latter told the group that the Iowa banker was the best friend the farmer had.[3]

Smith Brookhart then took the floor, declaring that out of every dollar the working man paid for a farm product the farmer got only thirty-eight cents. And similarly, he went on, a dollar spent by farmers for the products of labor brought an even smaller yield for the worker. What, he asked Davenport banker Albert F. Dawson, were bankers going to do to remedy such an unjust situation? Dawson confessed that he knew less about the situation than did Brookhart, but asked whether Brookhart was a farmer or lawyer. Brookhart said he was a lawyer, but that a "manure box smelled as sweet . . . as a counting machine."[4]

One farmer asked the speakers if any banker had some "specific plan to cure these evils so they will not recur every year?" And when no one answered, there was a "painful silence," characterized by Brookhart as the "most important during the conference." The farmers, he urged, should support the work of the Committee of 17, appointed by the Farm Bureau the previous summer. The committee, he felt, would ultimately propose a "plan for cooperative credit associations among farmers, together with cooperative marketing organizations, which would bring the farmer more for his products, while the consumer paid less for them."[5]

As a progressive Brookhart had long espoused government intervention or regulation to secure rights and insure justice. But now it seemed that the government was part of the problem. The Federal Reserve Board's credit policies were ruining farmers. Hence, Brookhart said, farmers must take their fate into their own hands. The solution was populism; and for Smith Brookhart, populism meant James B. Weaver.

Brookhart had first met James Weaver in the early 1890s, just when Weaver was becoming involved in the People's Party. At the time he had seemed unimpressed with Weaver's ideas. But later, he said, he had come to see the wisdom of them.[6]

The general outline of Weaver's thinking in those days can be found in his book, *A Call to Action*. Written in 1891, it was sold the next year as a means of raising campaign funds for Weaver's bid for the presidency on the Populist ticket. As Weaver's biographer has noted, it was not a "patiently wrought out study of existing conditions," but consisted of the "substance of the matter" Weaver had been "presenting upon the platform and in Congress." Nevertheless, it provides a good indication of what Brookhart and Weaver discussed when Brookhart went to tea in the Weaver home.[7]

Weaver and the Populists looked back to a simpler time, a time of the Jeffersonian ideal of yeomen farmers working their land, a time of decentralized government, a time that probably existed only as a romanticized myth. Their heroes were Thomas Jefferson, with his belief that it was the "distribution" of powers, not their "consolidation," that brought about good government; and Andrew Jackson, fighting against the centralizing tendencies of a national bank.[8]

This ideal, according to the Populists, was enshrined in the Declaration of Independence and its proclamation that "all men are created equal," that governments derive "their powers from the consent of the governed," and that they are instituted to secure the rights of the people. Almost immediately, however, a compliant Congress had cooperated with an "aggressive plutocracy" of corporate barons to pass measures such as a national bank, to allow land speculation, and to give huge amounts of western lands, "the inheritance and hope of our children," to the railroads.[9]

The People's Party had been started as the instrument of transformation; and in its 1892 platform, upon which Weaver had run for president, it had promised to restore government to the "plain people" and to use a "people's government" to restore a land free of injustice, poverty, and oppression. The platform had also called for a "permanent and perpetual" union of all labor forces in the United States; a system under which the government would own and operate the railroads and the telephone and telegraph systems; a strengthening of the civil service; and a monetary system that assured the "distribution direct to the people" of the currency necessary to meet all their debts. And finally, declaring that the land was the "heritage of the people," it had demanded that all lands now held by the railroads "in excess of their actual needs . . . be reclaimed by the government and held for actual settlers only."[10]

As enunciated by Weaver, the Populist vision had been one in which the individual citizen would have the opportunity to make his own way. The goal was not equality of results but rather a society where each citizen had an equal opportunity to advance using his own abilities. What had once been a "fairly free field [for] individual enterprise" had allegedly been transformed into a "centralized government . . . administered by great capitalists," and for Weaver and other Populists the great cry had become one of "Equal Rights to All; Special Privileges to None."[11]

As a political force, the Populists of the 1890s had also drawn strength from a heritage of organizational activity among southern and northern farmers. In the years following the Civil War agrarian reformers had organized as Grangers, Anti-Monopolists, or Greenbackers; and beginning in 1877 the Farmers' Alliances had appeared and begun urging farmers to organize cooperatives through which they could take matters into their own hands. This had become the approach that was supposed to solve not only the marketing problem but that posed by an eastern-controlled credit system. Working together in cooperatives, the people had allegedly learned that:

> though the hour was late, the people could be rallied to defend the democratic idea. . . . Here, perhaps, was the heart of the Populist belief: though the democratic heritage was imperiled by the demands of the industrial culture, the people were not yet helpless victims.[12]

On these matters, Smith Brookhart came to believe the Populists had been right. They had identified the threat to a democratic order; and they had championed the idea that when a system of special privileges developed, the people had the right to band together to demand justice from their government and equal access to the benefits of commerce and society. As the farm crisis of the 1920s took shape and persisted, he urged Iowa farmers to "rally to defend the democratic ideal" and to take matters into their own hands by joining together in cooperatives based on the Rochdale principles.

These principles, of course, had been around for a long time. The Equitable Society of Rochdale Pioneers had been established in the early 1840s by a group of weavers in the northern English town of Rochdale. It was one manifestation of the utopian socialism characteristic of the period. But its goal had been the practical one of improving the lot of its members through retail cooperation, the result being a new kind of retail establishment based on three principles: (1) an open membership with each member having one vote; (2) a limit on profits; and (3) a trade dividend which returned profits to members based on the degree of their participation.[13]

In America, the Grange had tried to apply the principles. But earlier organizational failures and the meagerness of the cash that farmers could raise had meant that such efforts were largely unsuccessful. Nor had the Populists of the 1890s seen much potential in them, at least until the exploitive features of the existing monetary system could be changed. But in Brookhart's mind they could be successfully applied. The coming of a "new economic world" had made them particularly appropriate tools for restoring power and opportunity to the people.[14]

Brookhart had first learned about the Rochdale system from Daniel Wilde, a fellow townsman who had been born in Rochdale, had come to America in 1851, and after 1863 had operated a foundry in Washington and become one the town's most prominent citizens. It is difficult to say, however, just when Brookhart made this form of cooperation a part of his recipe for democratic progress. It may have been as early as 1914, when he told the Washington County Farmers' Protective Association that it should look to English cooperative societies as models of how to reduce the profits of middlemen and secure greater returns for farmers. Or it may have been 1917, when he proclaimed in a *Press* editorial that "Individualism has run its course" and that further progress would now require the building of "a great cooperative system" like the one for which the Nonpartisan League was working in North Dakota. That such a system could be seen as socialism did not seem to bother him. What the government was doing during the war could also be regarded as socialistic, and it was through the subordination of the individual to society on an equitable basis that progressive ideals were now to be realized.[15]

In any event, by the time of the 1920 senatorial campaign, Brookhart had become firmly convinced of the wisdom of cooperation. There was, he claimed in the May 19 issue of the *Iowa Union Farmer*, no "greater movement than the future development and growth of cooperation." And here, for the first time, he had urged the use of the Rochdale principles and said that the high cost of living would push all those who worked with "hand or brain" into the Rochdale class. Here too, more clearly than ever before, he had enunciated a theme that would become familiar throughout his public career, the common interests of farmers and industrial laborers. At the recent All-American Farmer-Labor Cooperative Congress, he thought, the "most important matter" had been the proper "attitude of the organized farmer toward organized labor."[16]

Characteristically, Brookhart tended to exaggerate what could be accomplished through the Rochdale form of cooperation. Yet he was also aware of the principal reason that it had failed in the past, namely its lack of access to credit. And for this, his remedy was changes in the law that would allow farmers to form cooperative banks. Only when farmers could control credit, he would tell the Senate, would there be a banking system "fit" for "the farming business."[17]

In the wake of the postwar Red Scare, Brookhart had also begun taking greater pains to distinguish the "cooperative system" he had in mind from socialism or from socialism's violent cousins, communism and bolshevism. Collectivisms of the latter sorts led "into jungles of ignorance, confusion, and blood." But cooperation, properly envisioned, held out "the promise of safety for all good things in civilization." And in dozens of subsequent talks, addresses, and hearings he would keep extolling what could be accomplished through it. It was, he insisted, not "a dream or theory" advanced by wild-eye radicals. Rather, it was the "oldest, best developed, and most successful business system in the world," the "Sermon on the Mount in business," and a practical way of applying the wisdom of the Populists and other upholders of the "democratic ideal."[18]

Cooperation, then, had now become Brookhart's remedy for crisis as well as injustice; and in the months following the Ottumwa meeting he advocated such a solution in a variety of arenas. In January 1921 he testified before a subcommittee of the Senate Committee on Interstate Commerce. Later in the year he was a witness before the Joint Commission of Agricultural Inquiry. And in April he attended the Farmers' Union meeting in Washington, D.C., where, as secretary of its Committee on Comparative Credit Extension he presented a report on the causes and cures of agricultural distress. The causes, the report declared, were profiteering by middlemen, credit restriction, and the rise in railroad rates; and the remedy was for farmers and laborers "to take over the distribution of their products from producer to consumer." Specifically, the report called for: (1) requiring the Federal Reserve Board to allot credit in proportion to resources and deny it to speculators; (2) enacting a cooperative banking code that would allow farmers to control their own deposits and surpluses; (3) authorizing the Federal Land Banks to provide long-term, cheap credit; (4) lowering and keeping down railroad rates; and (5) taxing war profits.[19]

Throughout 1921 the squeeze on farmers had become even more acute. Writing his son in April, former Senator Lafe Young said:

> As near as I can find out, the farmers are planting about as usual but are very blue. Of course, I have a chance everyday to know the troubles of the country banks. Many of them are right on the ragged edge, because the farmers refuse to sell their crops and thus have no money with which to pay their notes. . . . Property cannot come down fully until everybody surrenders and joins the farmers on the lower level.[20]

Brookhart, meanwhile, continued his push for "cooperation." Speaking at a Farmers' Union meeting at Fairfield in October, he asserted that the "control of credit is the source of economic power," and argued that farmers in the past had been "systematically robbed" because they were not organized with the same intelligence as big business. Similarly, at a meeting of the Conference of Farm and Labor Organizations in November, he urged a joint effort to legalize cooperative banks in Iowa. And when the same group met again in January 1922, he was the principal speaker and was appointed chairman of a committee to draft and organize support for a cooperative banking bill. Joining him on the committee were representatives of the Iowa Federation of Labor, the Farmers' Union, the railroad brotherhoods, and the Taxpayers League.[21]

Meanwhile, events in Washington, D.C., had been moving in ways that would soon affect Brookhart's future. There Senator William Kenyon had become the leader of the Senate Farm Bloc, a group of midwestern senators highly critical of the Harding administration's failure to bring relief to agriculture; and as early as October 1921 there had been rumors that the President planned to rid himself of a critic by appointing Kenyon to the federal bench. In reporting the rumor, the *Register* declared that some Senate reactionaries would "carry [Kenyon's] suitcase to the train." Subsequently, the Senator had met with Agriculture Secretary and fellow Iowan Henry C. Wallace, who urged him to remain in the Senate, and on October 7, four days after the rumor had first surfaced, he had announced that although he had wanted to be a judge since he first sat in a courtroom as a boy, he felt that for now he could be of greater service in the Senate.[22]

On January 31, 1922, however, when Harding again offered the judgeship to Kenyon, the Senator decided to take it. In the interval, the Farm Bloc had been successful in adding a farmer member to the Federal Reserve Board. Kenyon had also become irritated with party colleagues who had voted to sustain Michigan's Senator Truman H. Newberry against charges of campaign expenditure violations, and both of these matters apparently figured in his decision. Again there were charges that Harding was using the federal bench as a tool to rid himself of a political opponent. But as Harding's biographer notes, the President "did not create Kenyon's desire for a judgeship or his willingness to leave the Senate."[23]

To fill the vacancy, Governor Nathan Kendall announced that he would appoint a progressive committed to the policies of Senator Kenyon and that he would honor the "unwritten law" requiring senators to be from different halves of the state. This was challenged by one correspondent, who pointed out that the custom was only recent since it had not been followed when Dolliver was appointed to replace Gear. Furthermore, Kendall was told, since Cummins was from Des Moines he could be claimed by either half of the state. Kendall told his correspondent he had given him "information which I had not heretofore possessed." But in public he still maintained the fiction of the "unwritten law."[24]

The *New York Times* reported a dozen names as being mentioned for the appointment, among them Congressman Horace M. Towner of Corning, Farm Bureau President J. R. Howard, and Colonel Smith W. Brookhart. The *Register* listed four northerners: Congressman Charles E. Pickett, Vinton banker Michael J. Tobin, Cedar Rapids lawyer James W. Trewin, and American Legion National Commander Hanford MacNider of Mason City. In addition, it mentioned several current Congressmen as "possibilities." And if Kendall did go to the southern half of the state, it said, the prospects would include Brookhart, Secretary Wallace, Des Moines attorney Howard Clark, H. W. Byers, Justice Scott Ladd, and State Republican Chairman Charles A. Rawson. It seems the only Iowa politician who did not want the appointment was Kendall himself. He refused to resign and have his successor appoint him.[25]

The cause of each candidate was championed by supporters, and Brookhart was no exception. His partisans portrayed him as a man with "character . . . intelligence and . . . wisdom," a "man whom we can trust," and who would "support agriculture in every legitimate transaction." As Congressman William Kopp saw it, Kenyon's successor "should be brave and fearless and absolutely free from domination by the big interests," a description fitting "Colonel Smith W. Brookhart." Similar expressions of support came from Farmers' Union locals and labor organizations. And in the eyes of another supporter the fact that "justice, honesty, [and] the rights of the people [were] at stake" should override even "such a noble rule" as the "unwritten law."[26]

Nevertheless, Kendall continued to cling to the "unwritten law," partly perhaps because some of the letters he received about Brookhart were anything but favorable. Eleventh District Congressman William D. Boies, for example, thought it "well understood that the real Republicans in Iowa do not want Mr. Brookhart." Consequently, he hoped that Kendall would appoint someone, preferably Congressman Burton Sweet, who could defeat Brookhart in the June primary. Making an ad interim appointment of someone who would not run could mean a primary in which Brookhart might be a "dangerous man."[27]

Similarly, Washington County Republican Chairman J. D. Glasgow wanted a man "big enough to measure up to the standard of an Allison or a Dolliver." And apparently, he did not see Brookhart as such a figure. "We have," he told Kendall, "too many men like Alfred Hargrave in Lucile," who, according to the Owen Meredith poem, seemed able to "dazzle, but not to illumine mankind."[28]

In the nation's capital, Senator Cummins worried about the new opening for Brookhart, and in letters to friends in Des Moines he suggested that they urge Kendall to nominate a man who had strong ties to farmers and the American Legion and who was "sufficiently conservative to enlist the support of the business men" yet not so conservative as to be "obnoxious to labor." Admitting that such a man was "not easy to find," he suggested Iowa Farm Bureau Secretary Edward H. Cunningham, Congressman L. J. Dickinson, or Sweet. Pickett, he thought, could not defeat Brookhart; and Brookhart's nomination "would not only be destructive of the public interest," but "exceedingly humiliating to me personally."[29]

Kendall was in a difficult situation. Brookhart, as the strong loser in the primary of two years before, was a logical choice. Yet he was wholly unacceptable to the party. And while the Iowa congressional delegation seemed to favor J. R. Howard, the latter said that if named he would ask his board of directors whether he could accept, thus putting Kendall in the untenable position of having the board of the American Farm Bureau Federation turn down his appointment. As for an ad interim appointment of someone who would not run in the primary (Rawson was most often mentioned), he was being told that this would be dodging the issue; and on this he agreed. "I think you know me well enough to know that I never dodge," he told one correspondent.[30]

On February 17 Kendall dodged by naming Charles A. Rawson to replace William S. Kenyon in the United States Senate. Rawson, he said, "is recognized everywhere as the closest friend Kenyon ever had in the state" and hence was the logical man to serve until "a senator can be regularly chosen." Refusing to take the advice of Cummins and others, who had hoped for a strong primary candidate, Kendall had asked Rawson to promise not to enter the primary. In response to questions, he also promised that if the primary nominee wanted to take his seat immediately, Rawson would resign and he [Kendall] would appoint the nominee.[31]

In an accompanying statement, Rawson said that the governor was correct to rely on the primary for the selection of a senator. But as for now, he cautioned, he was "going to Washington with the intention of working with the farm bloc organization for the best legislation that can be secured for Iowa." Still, the farm organizations and their spokesmen were suspicious. C. W. Hunt, President of the Farm Bureau, charged that the governor had deserted farmers for political expediency. *Wallaces' Farmer* commented that it was hard for farmers not to be disappointed with Rawson, since he had no experience with farm associations. And in Washington the choice of Rawson took the Iowa delegation by surprise. The appointment, most felt, would lead to a "bitter struggle at the primaries" between Brookhart and Pickett.[32]

Brookhart, who was in Washington when the appointment of Rawson was announced, had earlier told Kendall that he would run unless the appointee was someone strongly supportive of the farm bloc's attempts to relieve agricultural distress. Rawson was clearly not that someone, and after discussing the situation with Kenyon he was ready to return to Iowa to gather support for his candidacy. Before leaving Washington, however, he met with William H. Johnston, International President of the Machinist Union, and H. E. Wills, Assistant Grand Chief and National Legislative Representative of the B. of L. E., who invited him to stop in Chicago on his way home and attend a conference of progressive groups to be held there on February 20 and 21. Brookhart made no commitment, but he had already planned a stop in Chicago to meet with Farm Bureau President J. R. Howard and would therefore be in the city at the time of the conference.

The group that came to be known as the Conference for Progressive Political Action was originally brought together by sixteen of the railroad brotherhoods. It was they who had issued the letter of invitation, declaring in it that a land of inexhaustible resources had now become a land of idle and unused factories, men without jobs, farmers unable to sell their products, and "agents of privilege" busily destroying the rights guaranteed by the Constitution. It was time for "progressive elements" to act, and accordingly, they were invited:

> to discuss and adopt a fundamental economic program designed to restore to the people the sovereignty that is rightly theirs, to make effective the

purpose for which our government is established, to secure to all men the employment of the gains which their industry produces.[33]

The delegates to the conference represented four general groups of organizations. The first consisted of progressive political associations, including various non-partisan leagues, farmer-labor parties, and socialist organizations. The second consisted of "public" organizations, among them the Plumb Plan League, the People's Legislative Service, the Public Ownership League of America, and the Methodist Federation for Social Service. A third group was made up of labor organizations, specifically the railroad brotherhoods, the Amalgamated Clothing Workers, and the United Mine Workers. And a fourth consisted of such farm organizations as the American Society for Equity, the United Society of Agriculture, the Grange, and the Farmers' National Council. Neither the Farm Bureau nor the Farmers' Union was represented.[34]

In Chicago the conference organized itself and recommended a union of farmer, labor, cooperative, and progressive political organizations to elect legislators sympathetic to the needs of the producing classes. Issuing a "Declaration of Principles" modeled on the Declaration of Independence, it reaffirmed the self-evident truths of the latter document and then listed a series of grievances, including the Newberry case, the Federal Reserve Board's credit policies, war profiteering, railroad abuses, and the use of the army to crush labor disputes. In conclusion, it declared, that the "invisible government of plutocracy and privilege must be broken . . . so that this may become once more in very truth a government of the people, for the people, and by the people."[35]

Brookhart arrived in Chicago the morning of the twentieth and had a few hours between trains. Hoping to get Howard and the Farm Bureau to endorse his candidacy, he went to Howard's office and spent several hours with him. He then went to see Dante Pierce at his hotel but found that Pierce was at the conference and had left word for Brookhart to join him there. He arrived just as the conference was adjourning, located Pierce, and was accompanied by him to his train for Washington, Iowa.[36]

Later in the campaign of 1922 Brookhart's opponents would make a great deal of his attendance at a convention of socialists and radicals. But in reality he had nothing to do with the conference, its reports, or its Declaration of Principles. His presence at the conference site was an accident, for if Pierce had been at his hotel, it is unlikely Brookhart would have gone there at all. Later in the year, however, Brookhart did defend the conference, calling it an attempt by moderate labor and agricultural leaders to head off more radical voices and pointing out that its national committee consisted chiefly of labor union officials. Only one Socialist Party member, Morris

Hillquit, was on the committee.[37]

It should also be noted that the conference's Declaration of Principles did contain the kind of patriotic, Populist rhetoric that Brookhart frequently used and in which he fervently believed. If he had not been involved in its formulation, he was clearly in sympathy with the views expressed. And being neither a hypocrite nor a cynic, he refused to do the expedient thing and disavow the conference's actions.

The day after Brookhart arrived home, he wired the Iowa Secretary of State for nomination papers and stated in the *Journal* that he was optimistic and believed now that he had an "exceptional opportunity" to win. The optimism, moreover, did seem justified since Rawson appeared to be the only Iowan with a chance to defeat him, and Rawson was precluded from running by his promise to Kendall.[38]

Under these circumstances, the party's regulars decided to take advantage of a provision in the law stipulating that if a primary candidate did not receive 35 percent of the vote, the state convention would choose the nominee. Their plan was to flood the field with several other candidates, each one appealing to a particular segment of Brookhart's support, and in this way insure that no one could get the necessary 35 percent. The decision would then go to the convention, which the regulars felt they could control.

In the meantime, candidates for the June primary had already begun to enter the field, and one of them, Charles Pickett of Waterloo, had already been campaigning for several weeks. A lawyer with a degree from the University of Iowa, Pickett had long been active in Republican politics; and had served two terms as Third District Congressman during the Taft administration. As he saw it, agriculture was the nation's basic industry and deserved political support. But the great issue of the campaign was between adherence to traditional Republican values and advocacy of dangerous, radical ones. Of Brookhart he said:

> You do not find Colonel Brookhart proclaiming his party sympathies. The reason is that he is not a Republican. I admire Colonel Brookhart, his admirable sincerity and his sturdy support of things in which he believes, but I must say that his program, if carried to its logical conclusion, will lead to socialism and his ideas have no place in the American plan of government.[39]

The second candidate to enter the field was Burton Sweet of Bremer County, also a lawyer with a law degree from the University of Iowa, and since 1915 the Congressman from the state's Third District. For Sweet the lowering of freight rates and the development of inland waterways were issues of great importance. But his major appeal was to veterans. In Congress, he had been the author of bills to provide war risk insurance, increase veterans' compensation, and improve hospitalization and vocational training for veterans; and this record of "experience and achievement," he thought, "should outweigh ninety days of campaign promises."[40]

The third candidate to announce was former State Senator Leslie Francis of Spirit Lake, still another lawyer with an Iowa degree. Like the other candidates, Francis thought that railroad rates were excessive. In addition, he blamed the current economic distress on postwar speculation, advocated a department of health, education, and home management to be run by the "broadest-minded, best-qualified woman to be found in America," and favored a veterans' bonus to be paid for through equal taxation rather than a war profits tax. "You may not by law name one a profiteer and another not a profiteer," he said in his platform. The general tone of his campaign was set in an opening speech in which he denounced "the radical" as the "enemy of the laboring man" and pronounced efforts to put one class against another to be "un-American and unpatriotic."[41]

As these candidates entered the contest, Brookhart was busy lining up support for his own campaign. He could again count on the *Homestead*, now run by James Pierce's son, Dante. The Farmers' Union could also be counted on for support. And in mid-March a number of labor leaders, representing such groups as the Iowa Federation of Labor, the railroad brotherhoods, the plumbers and steamfitters, and the miners, met to form a Brookhart for Senator Club. Noting that Iowa farmers wanted Brookhart, the labor group felt that his record showed him to be "exceptionally well qualified."[42]

In addition, Brookhart hoped to gain Farm Bureau support and in his quest for this had already become involved in a dispute between Farm Bureau President J. R. Howard and Wisconsin Senator Robert M. La Follette. Back in December, La Follette had accused the Farm Bureau and the Grange of meeting with railroad executives and agreeing to abandon their efforts to repeal section 15-A of the Esch-Cummins Act. This Howard had denied; and when La Follette had responded by citing minutes of the meeting as proof, Howard had claimed that the document was a bogus one put out by business interests. Brookhart, after talking with Howard in Chicago, was convinced that the Farm Bureau leader had indeed been "framed," and to La Follette he wrote that "the minutes themselves are a fraud." He also told La Follette how much Farm Bureau support meant to him and urged the Senator to write Howard and renew friendly relations.[43]

As Brookhart worked to patch up the feud between Howard and La Follette, he also turned his attention to a similar situation in Iowa. There Dante Pierce and Farm Bureau Secretary Edward W. Cunningham had been feuding over the railroad question, and Brookhart was anxious that the quarrel be ended. Accordingly, he arranged for them to meet on March 2 to "talk it over and bury the hatchet." Labor, he noted, was "solidly behind" him. So was "90 percent of the soldier vote." And with Farm Bureau support, he should be able to "get 50 percent against any kind of a field." As he saw it, moreover, there was more than his own election at stake. There was now an opportunity to forge the coalition of producers that he had first talked about in 1920. As he told La Follette:

> If I can come to the Senate with a commission like this it will be worthwhile and you are in a position not only to give me very great help but also the bigger purpose of getting the farm and labor organizations together in a common cause.[44]

Brookhart announced formally on March 15 and had his platform printed in the *Journal*. In it there was relatively little that was new. Again it called for repeal of the Esch-Cummins Act; for restrictions on Federal Reserve power; for cooperative programs to control credit, production, and marketing; for taxing war profits in order to provide veterans' benefits; for higher wages so that mothers could stay home with children; for reopening the Newberry case; and for retaining state autonomy in the building of roads. No honest man, he said could represent all interests, and he was therefore stating plainly:

> what blocs I will support and what oppose. I will not support the Railroad Bloc, the Oil Bloc, the Steel Bloc, the Tobacco Bloc, the Sugar Bloc, the Beef Bloc, the Money Bloc, the Wall Street Bloc, the U. S. Chamber of Commerce Bloc, or the Great Paternal Social Bloc. On the other hand, for 365 days in the year I promise to support and fight for the Farmer Bloc, the Labor Bloc, the Soldier Bloc, the Mother's Bloc, and that part of the business world which cooperates with these blocs for its prosperity.[45]

Before publishing the platform, Brookhart had sent a copy to Howard asking for suggestions; and Howard had suggested several changes. He had urged Brookhart to remain firm in his stand for repealing Esch-Cummins. "I think it better," he said, "to repeal it and rewrite it than to ever attempt to patch it up." He also suggested a non-banker for the Federal Reserve Board and told Brookhart to "hit" the section on cooperatives even harder than he had. Brookhart, moreover, had incorporated the suggestions, and having done so he felt confident of the support of the Farm Bureau organization. This was particularly true after the state president, C. W. Hunt, had stated flatly: "The Iowa Farm Bureau will not oppose Colonel Brookhart."[46]

Meanwhile, at the *Homestead* the son had taken up where the father had left off two years before. Writing an editorial entitled "Iowa Should Send Brookhart to Senate," Dante Pierce declared that he would do all in his power to see that Brookhart was elected. In 1920, he said, Brookhart had been right on a number of issues, among them Esch-Cummins, the potential losses to holders of deflated Liberty Bonds, and the need for adjusted compensation for veterans. Furthermore, he had "advocated the agricultural bloc before there was any agricultural bloc," and many of his ideas had become centerpieces of that group's program in Congress. In urging all readers of the *Homestead* to campaign for Brookhart, Pierce declared:

> Iowa needs a senator who will not be dominated by . . . Wall Street. It needs a senator who will not act as a wet nurse to the railroads of the United States. It needs a senator who has the courage to denounce the manipulations of our finances through the powers of the federal reserve bank, whereby the farmers and workers are compelled to bear so much more than their share of the burdens of taxation. Colonel Brookhart meets these tests.[47]

With Brookhart in the field, Iowa's Republican Party regulars found themselves in much the same position as the standpats had fifteen or twenty years before. They were facing a strong challenge by a popular candidate running on a platform of "people's issues," and in these circumstances they found it difficult to maintain party discipline. Their attitude was summed up well by a letter from Lafe Young to Colonel D. J. Palmer, who had sent Young a copy of Brookhart's platform. "I realize," Young said, "that Colonel Brookhart is not a Republican. If we sent him down there, he would join Borah, Johnson, and La Follette and would be a hindrance to the country. I hope this may not happen."[48]

Young and Palmer had always been standpats. But also in the regular camp now were many of their former opponents, most notably, of course, Cummins and a number of his supporters. William W. Copeland, for example, wrote Cummins to say that he feared the plan for flooding the field with candidates would not work and to suggest all of the others pull out in favor of one man. "I hope," he said, that "something can be done by which neither of you Senators will be obliged to sit in the halls of Congress with [Brookhart], who will resort to anything to accomplish a purpose." In response, Cummins noted that he was aware of the "danger" but confident that an "energetic campaign" could lay bare "the absolute falsehoods of Brookhart's platform." Brookhart, he thought, would get more votes than anyone else, but there would be enough "good Republicans in the fight . . . to make it reasonably sure that the nomination will go to the Convention," where it could be "settled by the men who have the good of the country and the party at heart."⁴⁹

Another old Cummins man, Marshalltown editor David W. Norris, wrote to say that the situation in Marshall County was "deplorable" and to ask about Brookhart's statements regarding 15-A. He was unable to see, he said, how Brookhart could make such allegations. In response, Cummins declared that:

> For a long time I tried to preserve my faith in Brookhart's sincerity, but I have given up the attempt. It is perfectly plain to me now that he intentionally misrepresents the whole railroad situation. . . . Brookhart's statements are not only malicious, but they are wicked, for when they are made to people who have no opportunity to investigate, they are accepted and general discontent is the result. . . . I would not vote for Brookhart if he were nominated. I would feel it my duty to openly bolt his nomination, for not only does he hold the most dangerous opinions representing public matters but his campaign of misrepresentation is eminently more immoral than a campaign of bribery and corruption.⁵⁰

As of late March, there were already three candidates opposing Brookhart, each appealing to a particular segment of voters: Sweet to the veterans, Pickett to the old Taft Republicans, and Francis to the newly enfranchised women. But the strategy was not working, since Iowa farmers were still heavily in favor of Brookhart. If he was to be stopped, someone would have to pull away a large segment of the farm vote, preferably someone with enough progressive credentials to appeal to the more radical Farmers' Union yet reasonable enough to bring in Farm Bureau votes. As early as March 2, moreover, in a letter from J. R. Howard, Brookhart had got his first inkling of who that someone might be. Clifford Thorne, he learned, had been thinking about the Senate and would probably have declared his candidacy if Brookhart had not been a contender. And since Thorne was now the Washington lawyer for the Farm Bureau, his entry, if it should come, seemed likely to take away a number of potential votes for Brookhart.⁵¹

The possibility of this was also heightened by the fact that the Farm Bureau leaders had not yet given Brookhart the endorsement he had hoped for. On the contrary, Howard had finally responded to inquiries by informing Iowa Farm Bureau President C. W. Hunt that neither he nor National Secretary J. W. Coverdale had any interest in the Iowa situation except as "individual citizens interested in the welfare of our public institutions." Any statements they made, he said, were purely personal and were not to be considered Farm Bureau policy.⁵²

Behind the scenes, moreover, Thorne had continued to seek support for his candidacy. He had called on La Follette to argue his case, telling him that no candidate would receive the necessary 35 percent and that the contest would then go to the convention where he [Thorne] could get the support of a number of organizations, including the Farm Bureau. La Follette, though, had been unreceptive. He told Thorne in no uncertain terms that his candidacy would split the progressive vote and elect a reactionary, and he urged him to get into the fight and support Brookhart.[53]

The next major development in the situation came on April 1, when Howard wrote Thorne expressing gratitude for his Farm Bureau work and telling him that "no other man" was "so well fitted" for the Senate vacancy as himself. He wanted, he said, "as an individual citizen," to sign a nomination petition and cast his ballot for Thorne.[54]

Writing to Brookhart on April 4, Howard disingenuously said that he had been ill for a couple of weeks and knew "little or nothing" about the situation in Iowa. Nevertheless, he was not now so sure that Thorne would stay out of the race. The latter had called him, requesting a letter of support in case he did enter, and adding that "quite a number of very leading men at Washington had promised him very vigorous support." Given his long association with Thorne, he continued, he felt obligated to write the letter; and since he did not "believe in any political maneuver that will cover up," he was informing Brookhart. "The statement that I made to you when here," he concluded, "namely, that *as the field then was* I was for you, is correct and still stands."[55]

Smith Brookhart was angry! He knew full well that the men in Washington to whom Howard referred were Cummins, Secretary Wallace, probably Rawson, and at least some of Iowa's congressmen. "I am considerably surprised at the stand you take," he wrote Howard, and "as a member of the Farm Bureau," he refused to "submit to any such situation." Continuing, he declared:

> Cummins cannot use Thorne as a cat's-paw in this state without a fight and the Farm Bureau leaders cannot endorse him without an equally furious fight. I regret this situation very much [having] reached the stage where everything was proceeding along the line of harmony when you permit all to be uprooted by this dictation from Washington. It will not work and Thorne will be the most discredited man in Iowa if he proceeds with this Benedict Arnold scheme.[56]

Brookhart's anger was well-placed. Howard had promised to endorse him and was now reneging on that promise. Furthermore, Thorne and Brookhart had similar constituencies, and Thorne had the potential to hurt Brookhart as no other candidate could, particularly through his connections with the Farm Bureau and its estimated 127,000 votes in Iowa. Along with the anger, there was also a note of bewilderment and disappointment in Brookhart's letter to Howard, bewilderment that Howard could go back on his pledge of support, and disappointment that his old friend and ally Thorne could acquiesce in the plan.[57]

In the April 6 *Homestead*, Dante Pierce made good on his promise to do whatever he could to elect Brookhart. In a byline article, "Brookhart Foes Seeking for a Judas," Pierce outlined for his readers the efforts of the railroad attorneys, public utility representatives, and machine politicians to defeat Brookhart by working on the personal ambitions of Clifford Thorne. His entrance now, Pierce said, would brand him as the "Judas Iscariot of Iowa politics" and in the end would only serve his long-time opponents. Brookhart, he continued, was simply too independent for the "hidebound party regulars." They wanted a senator with a "ring put in his nose" and the chain pulled by Senator Henry Cabot Lodge or some other easterner. Iowans, he declared, were in a fight to determine whether or not they would send to the Senate:

> a man who represents the tenant farmer as well as the mortgage holder; a man who represents the business man who pays freight bills as well as Wall Street holders of railroad securities; a man who believes that the modest borrower from a western bank is entitled to as liberal credit and as low a rate of interest as the speculator in stocks upon the stock exchanges; a man who will view affairs at Washington from the standpoint of men and women who have little understanding of the tricks and plots of politicians but who do want good government and justice to all.[58]

Thorne's activities had brought into the open not only the poorly disguised strategy of the party regulars but also the complicity of the Iowa Congressional delegation in that strategy. While Senator Rawson was still state party chairman and, publicly at least, had remained neutral, other Iowans in Washington were thought to be encouraging Thorne. Even Secretary Henry C. Wallace was said to be supporting Thorne and, therefore, by inference, so was the administration.

Still, everyone remained coy. Coverdale wrote Indianola editor Don Berry claiming that Howard had endorsed no candidate. He had only commented in advance on Brookhart's platform "as containing some very good material as, no doubt, the platforms of the other candidates also have some planks that are just as strong." Rawson sent a telegram to the *Register* denying again that he would be a candidate in the primary. And Thorne refused to admit that nomination blanks secretly taken out by former Lieutenant Governor Ernest R. Moore were actually for him. During a visit to Washington, Iowa, Thorne still said nothing for publication, but to friends he admitted that he could not win. His hope was that he could force the choice into the Convention, where he would have a chance.⁵⁹

Washington had had some experience with candidates running for state and national office. In recent years Colonel Palmer and Clifford Thorne had run in a number of elections for state railroad commissioner, and Brookhart, of course, had run for the Senate. But now with two candidates vying for the same Senate seat the local loyalties were severely tested. One local citizen, who voted for neither Republican candidate, watched in amusement.

Alex Miller, editor of the *Washington Democrat* since 1893, had been as partisan in the cause of Democrats as the *Gazette* and the *Press*, in their day, had been for their brand of Republicanism. Over the years Brookhart and he had regularly traded barbs about the politics of the other. Yet while they were political rivals, they were personal friends. The Millers and Brookharts often dined together, and inevitably, the talk would turn to politics. As Miller now saw it, half the Democrats were likely to vote for Brookhart, and the more candidates the Republican brought out the greater would be Brookhart's majority. The only result of Thorne's entry, he said, would be to hurt "his bosom friend, his advisor, his mentor, his political guide"; and while Democrats might like to see Thorne "muddy the waters," he did not think the much discussed entry was likely to materialize.⁶⁰

Miller, though, was wrong. On April 15 Thorne made his formal announcement, issuing no formal platform but saying that statements would be forthcoming. The *Journal* noted the "remarkable coincidence" of two candidates from the same town and observed that Brookhart had entered the race thinking that Thorne would support him. Hence Thorne's entry had brought "pains and surprises" and the result would not be any "pink tea affair."⁶¹

Two days later, on April 17, Thorne published a statement of his position on the issues of the campaign. The farmer, he said, wanted "real genuine work" rather than "lip service" from his representative in Congress; and in the former category, he listed restoration of the railroad laws to their pre-war status and fundamental revision of the Federal Reserve Act. In addition, he called for an end to the struggle between organized labor and organized business in such a way as to guarantee labor its rights without tearing down the great institutions of business. He gave, however, no specifics as to how this was to be done, only that the necessary legislation must be "practical, wise, sane, [and] constructive."⁶²

As Thorne prepared to return to Washington, D.C., he also released the text of the letter of endorsement from Howard and part of a similar letter from Kansas Senator Arthur Capper, the new leader of the Farm Bloc. After expressing his appreciation of Thorne's work for agriculture over the years, Capper added: "I do not believe there is a man in the West who has shown a finer grasp of the agricultural situation in all its phases than you have."[63]

J. R. Howard continued to act as though nothing had happened. On the seventeenth, two days after Thorne's announcement, he wrote Brookhart that he had not seen Thorne for two or three weeks and that he was not sure whether he was going to announce. It was past relationships, he said, that had compelled him to support Thorne, and at present he had "no thought of any active advocacy" of the candidacy. He then went on to relate what he had allegedly heard in Washington, D.C., namely that if Thorne entered it would be because of the *Homestead* attack on him. And as a further explanation of his backpeddling, he added:

> I had told you when you were here and stated that you were going to enter the race and were convinced from what Mr. Sweet told you that he would not enter it, and that the field would be Mr. Pickett and yourself, that in that field I would be absolutely for you. If Mr. Thorne does not announce and the field narrows to what you stated it would be while you were here, I could not consistently do otherwise than exactly what I said at that time.[64]

Brookhart responded with an amazingly calm letter for one who had been double-crossed. He was sure, he said, that Cummins and Wallace were behind Thorne's candidacy and that his [Brookhart's] defeat, and not the welfare of the Farm Bureau, was the primary motive. Clearly, he felt betrayed; and he ended by saying that "all these matters are water over the dam, and so far as Thorne and I are concerned it is a fight to the finish."

In the same letter, Brookhart also requested that he, as a Farm Bureau member, be given space in the organization's newsletter to offset the story it had carried about Thorne's resignation as Farm Bureau counsel. The request, however, was denied. Thorne's resignation, said the Bureau's Director of Information, was "real news" for the members and served to point out that the Farm Bureau was "not in politics." But to print Brookhart's platform would give the news service a "political complexion from which it would never be able to survive."[65]

Meanwhile, Brookhart's forces had been gearing up for the formal opening of his campaign, a speech to be given at the Graham Theater on April 18. Meeting on the fourteenth, a group of his friends began a "local movement for the spirited encouragement of the Colonel's candidacy," complete with a Brookhart for Senator Club. And on the appointed day a large crowd gathered at the theater and were entertained as they entered by Fred Mannhardt's Orchestra.[66]

After being introduced by former Mayor J. D. Glasgow, Brookhart made no attempt at oratory. Speaking "calmly and deliberately," he confined himself to restating themes expressed in the platform and earlier speeches and declaring that the campaign had been one of himself against the field. He alone, he said, stood for repeal of the railroad law; and in one of the highlights of the speech he offered his version of what his opponents would say when asked where they stood:

> The first one . . . answers in stentorian tones, "I am a Republican." . . . The second . . . tells you very humbly, "I voted for that bill under pressure . . . and if somebody will get the pressure off we will repeal a part of it anyhow." . . . The third . . . says, "As soon as I can get back from the golf links and the motor boat I will tell you all about it." . . . The last . . . tells you promptly, "I am a rate expert. Look at my record. I believe in free and unlimited coinage of rate law suits. They have many charming advantages. They enrich the rate lawyers, even if the farmers do go broke."[67]

After treating other issues in a similar fashion, Brookhart then turned to the matter of Clifford Thorne. From the beginning, he said, there had been a concerted effort to induce other candidates to enter the primary, an effort that Thorne had initially resisted. But in the end, Thorne had been "weak enough to fall for [the] unsavory scheme." "I defied him," Brookhart concluded, "and I now defy the whole combination."[68]

Thorne was still in the east when Brookhart spoke. But arriving home on the twentieth, he announced that "we will have a little party of our own at the Graham." He had "enjoyed the brainstorm," he said, with its "accompanying charming exhibition of political hysteria" and he had been amazed, he added, at how before entering he had been a wonderful person but had now become a "Wall Street tool, a weak unsophisticated fool." He would not, he said, refer to Brookhart's speech as "the vain mouthings and claptrap of an ambitious demagog, pandering to class hatreds." But he then went on to do just that and to say that the real issue was one of qualifications for office. The voters would decide who was best qualified "by character, ability, and training" to represent Iowa in the Senate.[69]

In late April and early May, Dante Pierce kept up the *Homestead's* attack on Thorne. Writing on April 20, he told how Thorne had stayed in Chicago to meet with a client rather than come home to vote for Brookhart. In effect, he had sold out Brookhart for a $10,000 fee. On May 4 he called Thorne a "Modern Carpetbagger," who for several years had lived and paid taxes in Illinois. And on May 11 he printed the correspondence between Brookhart and Howard, thus documenting Howard's initial support of Brookhart's platform and his subsequent switch to Thorne.[70]

Thorne, however, was not without his supporters. *Wallaces' Farmer* hailed his candidacy as "good news" for Iowa and urged its readers to elect him in the primary and not take a chance on his being chosen by the convention. "While others have talked," it said, "Thorne has acted—acted intelligently, forcefully, and fairly. He is not a dreamer, nor a visionary, nor the propounder of strange and untried theories of government." Similarly, Lafe Young thought that Thorne would be a reasonable progressive, much like Kenyon. Brookhart, so he told Mark Sullivan, was the "radical candidate,"—and not just on railroads. Brookhart was "radical on everything."[71]

Publicly, Cummins remained silent. But privately, he told old friend Web Byers what he thought of the candidates. Brookhart, he said, was "so objectionable" that he could not express his views on him in "parliamentary language." Thorne, on the other hand, while he disagreed with Cummins on the Transportation Act, was doing so "in an entirely different spirit," and "upon every other subject" the two seemed to be "in perfect accord." He was "a man of great power" who "would make an admirable senator."[72]

Still, the attacks on Thorne had been telling ones, forcing him on the defensive. This was apparent in his own Graham Theater speech, delivered on May 5 to an audience of some five to six hundred people. Between Dante Pierce's "Inferno" on the one hand, he said, and the "deep abyss" to which some railroad publications would consign him, he was "in very truth between the devil and the deep blue sea." His counsel, however, was to sit tight and "don't rock the boat" for "we shall soon be past the squalls." Iowa, he also avowed, needed a senator who would represent more than one class or one group, someone who while representing the farmer, would also represent the banker, manufacturer, and laborer. And he was equipped, he felt, to be of such service to the state and its people.[73]

Thorne's late entry seemed to many an obvious signal that his was a "get Brookhart" campaign, and some of his correspondents at the time were sorry to see him in this role. "Had you been one of the first to announce your candidacy," one Washington County resident wrote, "I don't think there is a man in the field that could beat you. But at this late hour, I think you will lose out in your fight." Another admitted that Thorne was a better candidate than Brookhart. "But," he continued, "under the conditions on which you entered the race your candidacy is viewed with suspicion . . . by me and with all those I have talked to."[74]

Thorne had been the fifth candidate to enter the race, but he was not the last. In late April, Claude M. Stanley, of Corning, a lawyer with a degree from Drake University and service both as city and county attorney, had announced his candidacy. As a member of the National Guard, a veteran of the Spanish-American and World Wars, and a colonel in the Reserves, Stanley was apparently expected to draw off more of the veteran vote, especially in western Iowa. It was now Brookhart against five others, and in the opinion of the *Register* he would either have to "reveal astonishing strength" or his opponents would have to prove "surprisingly weak" if the nomination was not to "go to the convention." From here on, it concluded, the race belonged not to "the strong but to the cunning."[75]

The organization, moreover, was clearly looking ahead to the convention. In the same issue, the *Register* also reported that several top Iowa Republicans, among them former Governor William Harding and Cummins advisors Louis Kurtz and Web Byers, had just "happened" to be in Chicago to meet with Senators Cummins and Rawson. There the subject of discussion had been how to prevent Brookhart's nomination at the convention; and from the meeting had come plans to assure that the "right kind" of delegates were chosen.[76]

Brookhart, meanwhile, was going ahead with his own campaign. On April 26, speaking in Oskaloosa, he had accused Thorne of being weak and allowing himself to be manipulated. The opposition, he said, amounted to a "non-partisan league of Wall Street," and he was going to defy the whole combination." Two days later he was in Des Moines for a debate with the other candidates, a debate that was billed as the "first such event ever held in the state of Iowa." All six candidates had been invited, but only Brookhart and Leslie Francis put in an appearance.[77]

In his Des Moines remarks, Brookhart defended himself against charges of anti-Americanism, noting that his father, grandfather, and great-grandfather had all served in past wars and that he himself had spent twenty-five years in the National Guard. "I am," he said, "a Brookhart American." And as for his Republicanism, he declared, "I am a Lincoln Republican . . . a Roosevelt Republican . . . a farm bloc Republican."[78]

Francis expressed regret that the other candidates were absent, especially the "other half of the Siamese twins of Washington, Iowa," repeated his position on the issues, and again proclaimed his regularity. Of the two debaters, noted the *Iowa Forum*, Brookhart was "the more aggressive," and the more able to find fault with "the body politic." But he had no sound answers, and a vote for him was clearly a vote to break up the Republican Party.[79]

In May, Brookhart criss-crossed the state, from Keokuk to Waterville to Estherville to Bedford, all the while finding fault with the "body politic." He also continued to receive strong support from the *Homestead*. And while the *Iowa Union Farmer* took no official stand, it did publish letters in support of Brookhart. One, for example, not only urged farmers to vote but to take their wives to the polls too. In addition, support came from outside the state. In his magazine Senator Robert La Follette discussed Brookhart's platform, saying that it reflected a life-long commitment to the common people and should command widespread support among Iowans. It was, he continued, "more than a mere campaign platform." It was "a searching flashlight of the man's mind and character."[80]

From labor groups, too, came expressions of support. On May 19 La Follette's Conference for Progressive Political Action sent a circular letter to Iowa laborers assuring them that votes for Brookhart would "hearten and encourage" those "throughout the whole Mississippi Valley" who were fighting against "special privilege." And on May 20, the railroad brotherhoods' newspaper, *Labor*, printed a special four-page Iowa edition devoted to Brookhart's candidacy and urging his election.[81]

In Washington, D.C., Senator Rawson's correspondents kept him apprised of the situation in Iowa. "Outside of a few men," one wrote, no one seemed "very much interested." And in the view of Iowa City attorney LeRoy Rader, the "senatorial campaign had not until just recently taken a very active place in the thoughts of the voter." The race in Johnson County, said Rader, was between Pickett and Brookhart, "with the chances at this time favoring Pickett."[82]

It remained, however, for two Spencer bankers to sum up the positions of the two sides. Writing on May 11 Citizens National Bank Vice President J. H. McCord told Rawson that the campaign lacked excitement but that of all the candidates Brookhart had the largest following. Regretting that "opposition" to Brookhart could not settle onto one man, McCord nevertheless assured Rawson that no one would receive 35 percent of the vote and that Brookhart could not win at the convention. Just two days earlier John Sieh, cashier at the Farmers Trust and Savings Bank, had written Brookhart to assure him of his continued support. No one had been fooled by the party tactics, Sieh told Brookhart, and everyone knew that Francis was "just brought in to split the vote in this territory." Assuring him that the tactic would not work, Sieh said that he had just talked to "two very influential farmers . . . and was surprised how well informed and how decided they were in this matter."[83]

Election day, June 5, dawned with bright skies and June temperatures, the good weather boding well for a high turnout at the polls. Also likely to contribute to such a turnout, said the *Register*, was the discontent of the farmers and the increased participation of women, the latter now "more wide awake to the responsibilities of citizenship" than in 1920.[84]

Whatever the reason, farmers, women, and Iowans in general did turn out in record numbers. In all there were 323,622 votes cast in the Republican senatorial primary, over 110,000 more than two years before. And to the surprise of the establishment, Brookhart was a clear winner. He carried seventy-seven counties while running second in the remaining twenty-two, showing strength particularly in the upper and lower tiers of counties. And more important, he received 41.1 percent of the total vote, enough to win outright and keep the choice away from the state convention. Thorne was next (80,000 votes behind) with 16.3 percent.[85]

It was a stunning victory that shook Iowa politics and sent shock waves across the nation. The *New York Times* reported it as a "blow to the 'Old Guard group,'" and the progressives in the Senate were quick to comment. La Follette saw it as a "most remarkable victory for the people in . . . 1922," one that would greatly strengthen "the cause of real representative government." Borah viewed it as a demonstration that "the people" were "doing their own thinking," and Norris pronounced it "an unmistakable indication of the rising tide against reactionism and misgovernment." Not surprisingly, neither Senator Cummins nor Senator Rawson was pleased with the result, although neither would say so for the record.[86]

The day following the election Senator Medill McCormick, Chairman of the Republican Senatorial Campaign Committee, issued a statement saying that the Committee would join the Republican National Committee and its Iowa counterpart to work for Brookhart's election in the fall. One senator, however, noting that Brookhart had won without regular support, suggested that he probably would not need such help in the general election. Needless to say, the Democrats in Washington were delighted. National Chairman Cordell Hull set the tone when he interpreted the primary as evidence of the dissatisfaction of farmers with the "reactionary leaders in control of the Republican party."[87]

In the weeks that followed, Dante Pierce urged his readers not to rest but to continue to work for Brookhart. Farmers, workers, and everyday citizens, he said, were still Brookhart's best friends, and their vote for him was "evidence that the old people are awake and thinking, and that the old political tricks are no longer effective." Similarly, Milo Reno of the Farmers' Union observed that Brookhart's support had come from "the common people of Iowa, that part of society who do the work of the world." And in the *Locomotive Engineers Journal*, the result was called "the greatest single victory of the farmers and workers" in any of that year's primary contests.[88]

As for *Wallaces' Farmer*, it admitted the obvious fact that Brookhart's victory was decisive. Thorne, it felt, would have been preferable. But the people had spoken; and "Colonel Brookhart," it said, was "capable of rendering excellent service." He should "grow with responsibility."[89]

National publications agreed with the Democrats that Brookhart's victory was a repudiation of the Harding administration. *The Literary Digest* called the result of the election a "New 'Iowa Idea'" and noted that the Iowa victory, when coupled with progressive victories in Pennsylvania and

Indiana, indicated widespread dissatisfaction. Another journal, *The Outlook*, said that there was more "enthusiasm than wisdom" in Brookhart's platform, "but, however that may be, it is certain that the success of such a programme in the tremendously Republican state of Iowa is a warning light to the Administration." It was something that it would "do well not to ignore."[90]

If Brookhart thought his victory was a warning to the administration, he was careful not to say so, at least directly. The closest he came was to interpret it as an "indication" that the people of Iowa wanted a senator "anxious to represent all the people" as Dolliver and Kenyon had done before. A few days later he also noted:

> The administration . . . was not mentioned in this fight except by Secretary Wallace putting Thorne in. The vote indicates that people resented dictation. My idea is that the vote is not a defeat for the administration but a registration of sentiment that will bring the administration over to our way of thinking. What is its bearing on President Harding, you ask? Mr. Harding is a likable man. For myself I think he is too much influenced by some fellows too close to Wall Street. He can now listen to real dirt farmer and labor sentiment and I think he will. I think he responds to public sentiment as fast as it is developed.[91]

Brookhart was now in the national spotlight, and letters of congratulations came in reflecting that fact. "The result," Senator La Follette wrote, "is still the talk of the Senate, and there are some gentlemen who are feeling mighty blue around here." He hoped, he said, that Brookhart could come to talk to Wisconsin farmers, as this "would have a tremendous and telling effect." Similarly, former Senator (now Judge) Kenyon praised Brookhart for his "bold position on public questions" and concurred with La Follette as to the effect on Capitol Hill:

> Your nomination certainly shook the old crowd to their foundations. I am more than ever pleased now that I resigned from the Senate as it gave a chance for the people to express themselves and they certainly have done so. . . . My judgment is you are going to have the largest majority any man ever received in the State.[92]

The citizens of Washington, Iowa, seemed to enjoy their new celebrity. The *Journal* commented on the pride felt by Washingtonians and in a notable understatement added that "the secret of Colonel Brookhart's remarkable victory . . . seems to lie in his independence." The *Democrat*, no longer owned by Brookhart's friendly political adversary, Alex Miller, but no less partisan under the new owners, also rejoiced at Brookhart's success in doing what no one else had ever been able to do—defeat the old standpat organization. To those who had charged Brookhart with radicalism, the *Democrat* responded:

> Colonel Brookhart isn't going to be the radical, fire-eating socialistic revolutionist in the United States Senate that some of his opponents would have some of the people of Iowa believe. The Colonel is a common ordinary citizen, a good deal like the rest of us. He thinks strongly, talks strongly, and acts strongly, but he can be counted on to do always what he believes to be for the best interests of the majority of the people of Iowa.[93]

The week after the election the citizens of Washington staged a public rally to honor the Republican candidate. In Central Park, several hundred people gathered to listen to a concert by the municipal band and a speech by Brookhart. Hugh McCleery, former newspaperman and now commercial calendar manufacturer, served as master of ceremonies and William Sutherland, President of the Washington County Farmers' Union, as the introducer of the honoree. Seemingly touched by the turnout, Brookhart told his audience that "it was your victory. I merely served as your mouthpiece and your leader—it was your votes and the votes of thousands of common people all over Iowa which did the business." He added that he would enter the Senate free from deals and understandings.[94]

At least one Washington resident, however, did not celebrate in Central Park. On election evening Clifford Thorne had sent his former friend and ally a terse, one-sentence letter: "I extend to you hearty congratulations on your great victory." Thorne, so it seems, had come into the race too late to get an effective campaign in operation, particularly since his late entry was seen as too obvious an attempt to "get Brookhart." Publicly, he attributed Brookhart's win not to his platform but "entirely [to] the bitter, vitriolic, sweeping misrepresentations and falsehoods of the Iowa *Homestead*." After returning to his practice in Chicago and giving some thought to a 1924 candidacy, he would decide to take his wife and daughter on a world cruise, which would end in London where he caught pneumonia and died.[95]

The week after the primary Brookhart went to Des Moines to attend a reception in his honor and file a campaign expense report showing a total of $187 in contributions and total expenses of $453. Not reported, however, were the many contributions in services, meals, and lodgings or those from supporters who drove him from one county to the next. Support from "farm organizations, labor organizations and newspapers," Brookhart said, was "at their own expense. Halls were furnished without cost."[96]

Staying in private homes along the way was typical of Brookhart, since he cared little for the pretensions that often accompany political life. A lawyer who often met him in the courtroom attributed his success before a jury to his ability to "use the farmer's language." "He got down to their level to talk to them . . . he was able to think the way the average juror thinks. And it's a marvelous ability." On the campaign trail, Brookhart used that same skill. In town after town, the local leaders would bring dignitaries to meet with him, only to find him off with a group of farmers discussing their situation. Clearly, when he spoke of the bad farm situation, farmers felt they were listening to a kindred spirit, someone who really understood their problems.[97]

It was this Brookhart that the people of Iowa voted for in 1922, and it was his independence that so rankled the party organization. It was not just that he won without the organization, but that he had won in spite of it. Smith Brookhart was a Populist, a man who had an abiding faith in the common sense of the people. In this he was now far closer to his first political mentor, the Populist James B. Weaver, than he was to his more recent progressive allies.

As noted, Weaver's *Call to Action*, had attributed falling farm prices to "speculators and monopolists," and urged the people to band together for joint protection. It had also warned its readers to expect that the "two well-organized and equipped political parties" would use money and a sense of a "community of danger" as weapons to defeat any new political force. And now, thirty years later, many farmers in Iowa were again blaming their depressed conditions on the actions of eastern financial forces; and Brookhart's message to them was the Populist call to join together for action.[98]

In 1922 and in the years that would follow, Brookhart demanded that farmers be allowed to share in the prosperity that was enjoyed by the rest of the country. To achieve this, he had tried to work through the system, especially in his wooing of the Farm Bureau and attempts at building a coalition of supportive groups. He would also have been glad to have the support of the party machinery. But when support was not forthcoming, he had gone his own way, attacking his opponents as a group and forcing them to respond to his charges.

Smith Brookhart was at his best when attacking, and in 1922 his opponents had responded to such attacks in the long established way. For two generations following the Civil War the Republicans had won elections by waving the "bloody shirt." And now, for veterans of another war, the party continued to wrap itself in the American flag. This time, however, Iowans did not respond to this tactic, apparently seeing it as an effort to obscure the real issues that Brookhart was trying to raise.

As June gave way to July, a thin disguise of unity had been drawn over the relationships between Brookhart and the Iowa Republican Party. Both were preparing now for the state convention and the general election in November.

8

A Victory with National Implications

With his impressive victory in the 1922 June primary, Smith Brookhart now had the upper hand, and the Iowa State Republican Party hardly knew how to respond. Senator Cummins, although expressing disappointment at the size of the Brookhart vote, let it be known that he would not oppose Brookhart in the fall campaign. Secretary Wallace told reporters that Brookhart would receive the support of the regular organization, a statement considered significant since Wallace was generally regarded as the force behind the Thorne candidacy. And Senator Rawson, while admitting that there had been factionalism in the party, said that Brookhart had been "selected at the Republican primary, will have the support of the State Republican organizations and will be elected."[1]

But these early expressions of support were short-lived. The party leaders were not reconciled to Brookhart's victory and could not bring themselves to close ranks and unite behind him. Brookhart had won the primary without them and, as we shall see, would win the general election in spite of their efforts to defeat him. Republican Party leaders might see him as an alien in their midst. But in the context of the farm crisis his Populist formulas could win votes, and he would now become the instrument through which a discontented Iowa electorate would seek to send a message to Washington.

The first crack in the mask of Republican unity occurred on June 25, when Rawson suggested that Iowa Republicans meet in Chicago. Many refused, saying that Iowa Republicans ought to meet in Iowa.

Brookhart agreed, probably because he was afraid he would be asked to make compromises that he was unwilling to make.[2]

The party's convention was scheduled to meet in early August and would, so most commentators thought, produce intraparty battles over the work of Senator Cummins and the workings of the primary system. Some people, so Senator Rawson told Iowa's Farm Bureau secretary E. H. Cunningham, wanted to write a platform that would embarrass Brookhart, leaving him no choice but to repudiate it, which would then free the Republican regulars to take their support elsewhere—maybe even to the Democratic candidate. Others, however, realized that if the election of Brookhart was viewed as a slap at the Harding administration, the election of a Democrat would be even worse. "My idea," he continued, "is that we want to write a platform which will endorse the State and National Administrations and that will not be so strong that Brookhart and the rest of the State candidates cannot stand on it."[3]

Brookhart was also trying to be conciliatory. He was willing, he said, to see the platform voted on as a whole, rather than plank-by-plank. And rather than blame Cummins for the railroad bill, he was ready to blame the Democrats for both it and the Federal Reserve system and to center his attack on the "nonpartisan league of Wall Street."[4]

Pleading the press of Senate business, Cummins had planned not to go to Des Moines. But after being selected to chair the Polk County delegation and considering the ramifications of not attending, he seemed unable to make up his mind. If Brookhart wanted to make an issue of the railroad law, he wanted to be present to defend it. He also hoped to see Brookhart moderate his position, although for "purely personal reasons" he thought it "impossible" that he could ever vote for him.[5]

Another area of conflict expected to develop at the convention was that over proposals to change the primary system. It was being criticized now as "unwieldy" and "unworkable." And while some wanted to make it more open and more nonpartisan, most of those urging change tended to agree with Charles Pickett, who thought that a system in which Democrats, Socialists, or anyone else could ask for a Republican ballot was already too open. The "main objective," he wrote in July, "should be the repeal or modification of the primary law."[6]

In the Harding administration, Secretary of War John W. Weeks also said publicly that the direct primary had now become a threat to the country. It had, he said, "so palpably lessened the quality of men willing to serve in public affairs that prompt action should be taken to greatly modify or entirely repeal it." When asked about the statement, Brookhart said that "it would be better to repeal Weeks."[7]

Consequently, as the party gathered in Des Moines on August 2, the talk of "harmony" sounded forced and hollow. Nor had Brookhart helped matters when, on the Friday before the convention, he had told the Young Republican Club and its assembled guests that he had no intention of backing down on his platform. Sounding anything but conciliatory, he had demanded the repeal of the Esch-Cummins Act, called the chairman of the Federal Reserve Board "an errand boy" for Wall Street, and advocated a constitutional amendment to draft capital as well as men in wartime. Then, in an archetypal statement, he had concluded by declaring: "I don't know whether I can accomplish what I propose to do, but I am not afraid to try. I don't care what they think of this platform out on millionaire row if the farmers, laborers, soldiers, and mothers are for it."[8]

Rawson, by contrast, did seem interested in keeping things smoothed over. In any event, he announced that he would not stand for re-election as state chairman, a move that would give the Brookhart forces a chance to name their own man. This was interpreted as a conciliatory action. But some were also saying privately that Rawson had plans to run against Brookhart in 1924 and could not honorably do so if he served as state chairman and worked for his election in 1922.[9]

Cummins did not put in an appearance, pleading the press of Senate business to explain his absence. He was, he said, in "continuous consultation with the President" about the current railroad strike and therefore felt he would be "deserting in the midst of battle" if he left Washington.[10]

Among the anti-Brookhart forces gathered at the convention, a group described by the *Des Moines Capital* as "'die in the ditch' standpats," the most conspicuous element was the so-called "Cedar Rapids Gang" led by William G. Dows. The latter had threatened to fight singlehandedly, if necessary, for an endorsement of the Esch-Cummins Act. But some of his friends were assuring party leaders that he could be "calmed down" and would go along with the tactic of ignoring the Esch-Cummins Act altogether. Taking it all in stride, Brookhart defiantly said: "What difference will it make if they do try a fight on me at the convention? It would not get them anywhere. They would be licked again. Enough people liked my platform to nominate me and enough liked it to elect me whether it is the platform of the Republican party or not." The next day he added: "If it comes to a showdown I will have the support of 75 percent of the delegates."[11]

One showdown, as expected, came on a proposal to endorse the Esch-Cummins Act offered by the conservatives on the resolutions committee. The Brookhart forces, led by Sibley editor Willis W. Overholser, responded with a substitute plank condemning section 15-A of the Act but not calling for repeal of the entire bill. Lengthy debate followed, with the substitute being tabled twice. Finally, the committee voted six to five to say nothing at all about Esch-Cummins in the platform.[12]

Brookhart did not do so well, however, on other planks in the platform. One mandated that the Republican State Central Committee have the 1924 state convention in February, thus allowing the party to select its candidates for the primary ballot in June. Another, although it did not mention Brookhart by name, condemned "demagogues" who "sought for their own selfish purposes to arouse passions and prejudice of the people and to array class against class." And still another endorsed and commended Secretary of Agriculture Wallace, Governor Kendall, the Iowa Republican Congressmen and Senators, and especially Senator Albert Baird Cummins for his "example of patriotic and self-sacrificing citizenship and fearless, sagacious and distinguished statesmanship." Nowhere did the platform mention the Republican candidate for the Senate, Smith Wildman Brookhart.[13]

On the convention floor, Dows and other irreconcilables threatened to fight for a railroad plank. But Rawson finally headed this off by telling Dows that the resulting split in the party would be the quickest way to elect a Democrat to the Senate and to defeat several Republican congressmen. The convention then proceeded with the reading of the platform by Resolutions Committee Chairman Jim Trewin. At the conclusion of the reading, the platform was approved by voice vote. And before the Brookhart forces could raise any objections, a move to adjourn had been made, seconded, and carried.

Although the platform did not contain the railroad plank that conservatives wanted, it was clearly a victory for the anti-Brookhart forces. Following its adoption, the standpats filed jubilantly out of the hall, congratulating themselves on their success in keeping Brookhart from speaking or even being mentioned by name. The Brookhart followers, on the other hand, filed out wearing what the *Register* described as "expressions that betokened anything but satisfaction." Brookhart himself, though, seemed unperturbed. The platform, he told the *Register*, had not repudiated any pledges he had made during the campaign, and its railroad plank did call for a reduction of rates, something he knew how to do. As for not being allowed to speak, he put his tongue in his cheek and said that the convention had "so much confidence in me and in my interpretation of the platform, that they did not even take the time to ask me to speak. They knew where I stood . . . so why take up valuable time in hearing things they already knew."[14]

To a Calhoun County Fair audience that evening, Brookhart also declared that "in a general way, the platform suits me fine." The federal reserve plank, he said, "is my plank," the agricultural plank was "excellent," the primary reform was needed, and the soldier bonus plank, especially where it endorsed the conscription of capital as well as men, was fine. On the railroad question, too, he was pleased to see the demand for relief and he was "especially pleased" that the platform had endorsed no part of the

Transportation Act and was therefore in line with relief through its repeal. Finally, in a slap at his opponents that he would repeat during the campaign, he declared that:

> I approve the declaration against demagogs and socialists. I believe every railroad attorney demagog ought to be kicked out of the party. I believe that every socialist grafter, who wants government guarantees on a cost plus basis, ought to be given a quit claim deed to the Democratic candidate. . . . I am strongly opposed to arraying class against class, and I am still more opposed to arraying class over class.[15]

During the week following the convention, Brookhart announced his intention to visit every county and disclosed that he had already turned down two hundred speaking invitations. Seemingly, Iowans liked what he was saying and resented the moves of the "old guard" at the convention. As one letter to the *Register* put it, the people had elected Brookhart, but "the reactionaries, . . . like the old Bourbons of France" had learned nothing, and "did not have political sense enough to keep their hand hidden after they lost."[16]

Still, if W. O. Payne of the *Iowa Forum* was in any way representative, the "bourbons" were in no mood to apologize for their actions. Writing to Cummins on August 6, Payne assured the Senator that the convention had contained no "bona fide adherents of Brookhart." Rather, he said, it was largely peopled by anti-Brookhart "hard-boilers" (Brookhart supporters were "pussy-footers") who had firm control of the party throughout Iowa. Declaring Brookhart to be worthless, with "not a particle of genuine Republican blood in him," Payne assured Cummins that "the Republican party in Iowa is not a Brookhart party by a great row of apple trees."[17]

Whether or not Payne had the apple trees on Brookhart's farm in mind when he wrote Cummins, he was apparently expressing an attitude characteristic of those who feared that men like Brookhart were rendering the party organization superfluous. If the Albert Cummins of twenty years before had not been a "regular," he had still worked within the organization, fighting his battles on the floor of the convention and emerging as the party's candidate through that process. Brookhart was something different. Through the primary and other direct linkages to the people, he could operate outside of and ignore the party organization, managing without it to win the nomination, brush aside its platform planks, and run his own campaign. As a result, men like Payne were furious and frustrated and had not yet given up their determination to defeat Brookhart.

The split, moreover, seemed heaven-sent to the Democrats. There had not been a Democrat from Iowa in the United States Senate since the 1850s, and the party's leaders believed that now was the time to elect one. Their candidate was Des Moines automobile dealer Clyde L. Herring, whose only previous candidacy for statewide office had been an unsuccessful run for governor in 1920.

Opening his campaign with a speech in Sibley, Herring responded to Brookhart's charges that the Esch-Cummins Act had been a Democratic measure. Congressional Democrats, he noted, had voted four to one against the bill, and he himself had been against it from the beginning. Most of his speech, however, he used to charge that Brookhart was a socialist, or, at least, had too many friends who were socialists. The Republicans, he said, had no genuinely Republican candidate in the field, and they should therefore join with the Democrats to prevent "the slander upon Iowa which exists in Smith Brookhart and his platform."[18]

Similarly, in a speech at an old settlers meeting in Marshalltown on August 24, Herring declared that the principles of American government were being threatened by the Brookhart candidacy. The two-party system, he maintained, had kept the nation free. But now Brookhart wanted to change the form of government to one that neither party had sanctioned. His true colors had been made evident by his attendance at the Socialistic Conference for Progressive Political Action in Chicago, and such a man was clearly one whose calls for Democratic support should be strongly rebuffed. The question of the election was "whether some scheming and plotting agitators and disloyalists can get together in Chicago and deliberately steal the name of a great party in Iowa as a means of setting up control of the government."[19]

In a Labor Day address in Des Moines, Brookhart mounted his counterattack. After praising labor for its part in building the republic, he discussed former Governor William Larrabee, who, he said, had taught him the greatest political doctrine in the world, the brotherhood of man, leading not to radicalism or socialism, but to "the highest type of citizenship." Opposed to this, he went on, was the "non-partisan league of Wall Street," a "financial soviet" of corporate wealth organized in both parties to "overthrow the government of the people . . . and substitute a dictatorship of corporate combinations." With his railroad bill, Cummins had become the Republican spokesman for the league in Iowa. And Herring, he charged, had now become the Democratic representative. In the new combination, "Cummins furnishes the brains, Herring the money and Wall Street the platform."

Brookhart then reminded farmers and laborers that he had stood with them in their fight against special privilege. Hence, the Cummins-Herring charges that he was a socialist were really directed at them. He had been at the Chicago conference, he said, but not as a delegate and purely by chance. And besides, he was "past twenty-one years of age" and his opinions had never been "corrupted by bad stories or bad company."[20]

The socialist issue, though, was not allowed to go away. The March 4, 1922, issue of *The New Majority*, a weekly publication of the Chicago Federation of Labor, had listed Brookhart as a delegate. And Herring, who had used this as the source of his information for the Marshalltown speech, now had the article reprinted at his own expense and sent copies to the state's newspapers. In Washington, the *Journal* received a copy, but defended native son Brookhart in the editorial pages. It pointed out that of the 124 delegates only five had been socialists, and it explained how Brookhart had only "incidentally" dropped in on the meeting. It also said that while Brookhart did not hesitate to listen to all points of view discussed, he was not a socialist. "He is a Republican in his party affiliations," the *Journal* concluded, "and such minor differences as may arise to party policies he feels can be settled within the party."[21]

Another piece of literature circulating during the campaign was an eight-page pamphlet published by the Iowa Anti-Socialist Society and entitled "Progress of Socialism in Iowa This Year." Quoting prominent socialists, including Kate Richards O'Hare, who, it said, was "jubilant" over Brookhart's nomination, the pamphlet asked whether Iowa was ready to adopt Socialism by voting for Brookhart. In this case, Dante Pierce came to Brookhart's defense, pointing out that the unsigned pamphlet was in violation of the law's requirement that such publications be signed by officers of the organization publishing them. Although refusing to say so directly, Pierce left no doubt that he believed the pamphlet to be the work of the Greater Iowa Association, a group that he labeled "An Unholy Alliance in Defiance of Law."[22]

The Anti-Socialist pamphlet also claimed that at a Burlington meeting in September the socialist candidate for governor, Dr. Perry Engle of Newton, had said that Brookhart advocated the principles of the party and had urged socialists to work for him. In early October the secretary of the Des Moines County Socialist Party denied this, saying that an endorsement of Brookhart had been considered but rejected. And later that month, the State Socialist Party Secretary issued a broader denial. Brookhart, he said, had never been a Socialist Party member; the party and its candidates had never endorsed him; a socialist candidate for the Senate had been nominated; and "any member voting for Brookhart or advocating his candidacy" would be liable to expulsion from the party."[23]

Mixed with such denials, however, were expressions of support from avowed socialists. On October 19, for example, the *Register* published a letter from a Davenport socialist who would have liked Brookhart to be more "radical" but nevertheless believed that his election would constitute an "entering wedge" toward achieving socialist goals. Brookhart, the writer thought, was "more of a socialist" than he would "publicly admit," and for this reason he was "together with every true socialist in Iowa, enthusiastically in favor of his election."[24]

As we have seen, Brookhart was not in fact a socialist. Although he advocated government ownership of the railroads and sometimes vaguely included government ownership of other utilities as well, he was not an advocate of basic change in the political and social structure of the country. His constituents were small farmers and laboring men, and the measures he advocated in their behalf were intended to insure that they could remain, in the words of Mark Sullivan, "home-owning, small capitalists."[25] In Brookhart's view, such people should be able to control their own lives; and merely to transfer outside control from Wall Street to Pennsylvania Avenue would be of little help to them. Government should be an aid to freedom, not an instrument of central management.

Brookhart's radicalism was not so much in his ideas as in his language. Saying what he thought, oftentimes saying it before he thought, he remained a fundamentally open man who could see nothing wrong with discussing issues with anyone, socialist or otherwise; or with attending a meeting where socialists were present; or, as he would later, making favorable comments about the conditions of the peasants in Soviet Russia. Such behavior was probably naive and was certainly impolitic, but Brookhart refused to take the expedient way out of anything.

It seems doubtful, moreover, that the majority of Iowans believed much of the propaganda about Brookhart. His ideas, they seemed to feel, could be accommodated with a progressive Republicanism, as other allegedly "radical" doctrines had been in the past. One pioneer Iowa Republican, whose first involvement in politics dated back to 1840 and who later worked for John C. Fremont in 1856, wrote a campaign jingle for Brookhart. And while the poetry suffered, the content of one stanza probably summed up the feeling of many:

> The Chicago meeting let's now discuss
> Why Brookhart's call should make any fuss,
> Was it waste, un-American, rotten to the core,
> Unfit for a Republican to enter the door?
> Brookhart was anxious to learn about
> What socialists, I.W.W.'s and other parties turn out,
> So he stopped and listened to all that was said
> And left, a better Republican, to push ahead.

If the old guard disagreed that listening to radicals would make Brookhart a better Republican, the last two lines of the poem must have made them absolutely shudder: "So in November next all Republicans bent/Brookhart for Senate, and then President."[26]

On September 22 Congress adjourned, ending the longest session in thirty-three years; and since he could no longer cite the press of business as a reason for staying out of Iowa, Cummins made plans to return home. He intended, he said, to stay out of the election controversies. But given his role in writing the Transportation Act, this seemed highly improbable.

Cummins was also thrust into the campaign when Clyde Herring, speaking in Marshalltown, read a letter from him to another Iowa Republican, doing so, as subsequent correspondence made clear, without the Senator's permission. It was a letter that left no doubt as to Cummins' feelings about Brookhart. In it he had strongly criticized Brookhart's platform, and had written: "If his power were commensurate with his apparent desires our government would not last a fortnight."[27]

The letter, so Brookhart now declared, proved that the Cummins supporters had joined forces with Herring to defeat him. They had failed at the convention and hence had now joined, under orders from Wall Street, to protect the Transportation Act by defeating him in November. Both Republicans and Democrats, he thought, would resent such interference, and he therefore expected to carry every county in the state.

The next day, in a telephone interview with *Register* reporter W. B. Kerr, Brookhart also went on to demand that Cummins resign if he [Brookhart] won the election. "If Cummins is butting into the campaign," he said, and "has complete confidence in his position on the railroad issue," then he should, if the election went against him, send a letter of resignation to the Governor.[28]

Thus when Cummins arrived home in early October there was no chance that he could stay out of the picture. He was again deploring a "most lamentable ignorance" about the railroad law, something he felt obligated to correct and admitting now that the letter Herring had read had been published without his permission, he went on to tell the *Register* that it was not unlike many others he had written at the same time. "I think my opinion of Mr. Brookhart was pretty well known before," he said, and he had not changed it in "the slightest."[29]

Meanwhile, Brookhart had decided to take a few days off from campaigning in order to attend the National Guard rifle matches being held at Camp Perry, Ohio. Passing through Washington on his way east, he told the *Journal* that he had been giving one to three speeches a day and that his schedule was so full that the previous week he had had to charter an airplane to fly him from Strawberry Point to Davenport.[30]

With Brookhart out of the state, everyone else seemed to pause for a time. But the respite was short-lived. It came to an end when Dr. George Harding, the President's father, came to Des Moines for a GAR convention and proceeded to urge Iowa Republicans to bolt the party and vote for Herring. Brookhart, Harding said, was a socialist, and there were already "enough of these socialists in Washington now causing trouble . . . If I were an Iowan," he concluded, "I would take to the stump to help elect Clyde Herring and to help read Brookhart out of the party."[31]

As if to agree, a group of fifty anti-Brookhart Republicans had already met in Des Moines and called for a statewide meeting to find the best means of defeating Brookhart. Calling their actions "a movement to save the Republican Party," they had proclaimed their patriotism and insisted that Brookhart's candidacy was "part of a nationwide conspiracy . . . to destroy constitutional government in this county."[32] The meeting, as they planned it, was to convene on October 3.

As September ended, Brookhart returned from Ohio and announced, upon his arrival in Washington, that President Harding, Republican National Chairman John T. Adams, and Senator Medill McCormick of the Republican Senatorial Campaign Committee had all promised to support him. He then went on to Des Moines where he told the *Register* that both the Republicans and Democrats were for him and that now the "old guard" was trying "to wish the socialists" on him too. He refused, however, to comment at all on Dr. Harding's remarks, saying instead that he had had a "fine shoot" while at camp, had come back "ready for anything," and would make a full statement in a speech in Clinton on October 2.[33]

Brookhart's trip to Des Moines had been for the purpose of conferring with State Party Chairman B. B. Burnquist, Governor Kendall, Lt. Governor Hamill, the other top elected officials of the state, and the executive committee of the party. This he had done; and after the meeting Burnquist had not only taken note of the national support of Brookhart but announced that Senators McCormick, Thomas Sterling of South Dakota, Arthur Capper of Kansas, and Frank Kellogg of Minnesota would all be in the state to speak for him.[34]

On October 2 Brookhart spoke for himself in Clinton. At camp, he said, he had tried to put politics aside for a time but found that he could not since the riflemen there were unanimous in their support for him. And while he was gone, he continued, a "sinister and treacherous hand" had been "grinding [its] stilettos to stab [him] in the back." A "band of fools and hirelings of the public utilities" were trying to do him in. But they had succeeded only in bringing him national support.

Brookhart was exactly where he liked to be—on the attack; and he was enjoying it immensely. After giving details of the Republican support he had received, he twitted the old guard further by declaring that he had not heard a word "from Kate O'Hare, Berger or Hillquit or even Dr. Engle." He wondered, he said, if the old guard had captured them, for it would "certainly be too bad if they fall into company like that." He then returned in kind the charges against him and urged Democratic farmers and laborers to vote for him because they had no real Democrat to vote for. Herring, he charged, was a "renegade Republican of the millionaire class" who had delivered the Democratic organization to the old guard Republicans trying to defeat him. Nor should "honest Republicans" believe the "false socialist propaganda" being spread against him.

> I want to say that I have been a Republican all my life, that I entirely repudiate all socialist support, and have never had any socialist associations. I never in my life attended a socialist conference, read a socialist book or heard a socialist lecture. If I am elected to the Senate you can count upon me to fight 365 days in the year for the party of Lincoln, of Roosevelt and of Kenyon.[35]

The speech was vintage Brookhart, and its excesses, no matter how entertaining to the audience, only served to strengthen further the resolve of the party regulars to defeat him. This was not the first and would not be the last of the unnecessarily inflammatory speeches that he would give. Yet it should be noted that no matter how tempered his speech or conciliatory his words, he probably could have done nothing to close the rift between him and the irreconcilable old guard Republicans, at least not in 1922. Perhaps a more temperate tone would have helped him in the long run. But he rarely thought "in the long run" and seemed only to meet events as they arose.

As of October 3 the event at hand was the meeting in Des Moines of the old guard, or as the conservatives styled themselves, the "Republican Party of Iowa." Convened under the chairmanship of former Governor B. F. Carroll, the gathering produced a round of speeches extolling private property and expressing alarm over the socialist incursion represented by Brookhart. One speaker, State Senator Milton Pitt, declared that it was such as Brookhart that had "inflamed the brain of 'the Russian revolutionist' who shot McKinley." Another, Coe College President H. M. Gage, stated that "two days after the news came over the wire that property had been nationalized in Russia, there came another dispatch that women had been nationalized." "Those things," he said, "go together." Taking formal action, the meeting resolved that the choice was between a socialist and a Democrat, who, although he was an "exponent of misguided political and economic judgment," was "nevertheless for constitutional government and American institutions." Good Americans, it believed, would choose the Democrat.[36]

Saying that he was glad to have the support of anyone, Herring reasserted both his Democratic credentials and his capacity for placing "true Americanism" above partisanship. Brookhart, on the other hand, called the Des Moines group "political cadavers" who represented almost no one but themselves. "They are not afraid of me as a socialist," he said. "They are afraid of me because they know I represent the common people."[37]

A few days later Brookhart called the Bolters Convention, as it came to be known, the "best asset I have." And he was probably correct. In the *Homestead*, Dante Pierce called the meeting a last desperate effort to defeat Brookhart. And privately, he wrote to Senator La Follette saying that "the bolt has blown up" and predicting that for every Republican vote Brookhart lost he would gain three Democratic votes.[38]

Such was also the perception of others. Senator Arthur Capper, speaking for Brookhart to audiences in Hampton and Waverly, reported "great" meetings with his praise of Brookhart being "heartily applauded." Roy Rankin, serving as Senator Rawson's secretary, noted that observers thought that the Bolters Convention would make "hundreds" of votes for Brookhart. And in late October a Baltimore *Sun* reporter said that the bolters knew they were beaten and were taking comfort in the fact that Brookhart's term was for only two years.[39]

The campaign finished with a flurry of speeches, debates, and political endorsements. Former Governor Leslie Shaw joined former Governor Carroll in opposition to Brookhart. But Governor Kendall endorsed him and urged other Republicans to do the same. And Farmers' Union President Milo Reno said that Brookhart would be the "first man in Iowa history who will honestly represent both the farmers and the laboring man." As election day neared, the state chairman of each party issued optimistic statements about the outcome. Democrat Ed Feuling said that Herring would win because "the people of Iowa are Americans, loyal and patriotic," while his Republican counterpart, B. B. Burnquist, predicted that Republicans would carry ninety counties, and elect the ticket "from top to bottom."[40]

Brookhart went home to vote, saying upon arrival that he was having a lot of fun, had gained twenty-five pounds on the banquet circuit, and would after the election make a "serious effort to reduce his girth." Reiterating earlier forecasts, he predicted that he would carry every county and win by a margin of 175,000 votes.[41]

Brookhart was not quite correct. He carried only ninety-four counties (thirty-four of them by a margin of 70 percent or more) and received only 63 percent of the total vote. He ran strongest in the north central, northwestern, and southwestern counties, losing Democratic Dubuque County by 1,500 votes, Jones and Johnson Counties by about 600 votes each, and Fremont County, in extreme southwestern Iowa, by 46 votes. In Linn County, home of the Cedar Rapids Gang and many of the bolters, he lost but only by 201 votes.[42]

Brookhart's figures compared favorably with the two most recent Senate elections. In 1918 Kenyon had won 65.3 percent of the vote and ninety-six counties, while in 1920 Cummins had got 61.4 percent overall and a total of ninety-three counties.[43] There was one difference, however, that made Brookhart's victory more remarkable—he had won without significant party support. Writing in *The Nation* shortly before the election, Austin Haines, a former *Homestead* editor, said of Brookhart:

> Meanwhile Brookhart goes his way, practically alone, saying nothing in commendation of the Republican Administration, asking no favors of the organization, and avoiding any strictly partisan appeal, confident of his strength with the mass of voters on Election Day.[44]

Claiming victory for farmers and laborers, Brookhart expressed the hope that Democrats who had voted for him would remain with him. The elections, he said, demonstrated that Republicanism was on the proper track and that Republicans could win on "a platform similar to mine." Telegrams were also promptly sent to the three people to whom he felt a particular debt. To Kenyon he wired: "My election is a vindication of your great record." To Mrs. William Larrabee he declared the election to be "a revival of the great principles of William Larrabee upon both transportation and agriculture." And to Mrs. James Pierce, he recalled her husband's support in 1920, acknowledged that it had given him "courage to make the first race," and pronounced "this winning race" to be "the logical sequence."[45]

State Democratic Party chairman Ed Feuling joined many national observers in seeing Brookhart's victory as part of a widespread protest against the Harding administration. Senator Rawson, on the other hand, called it a "protest against local conditions," and Republican Chairman B. B. Burnquist breathed a sigh of relief that so few Republicans had been defeated and that the entire congressional delegation had been reelected. An editorial in the *Register* said that Brookhart was going to Washington with a program wholly his own and with a constituency favoring that program. Brookhart did not win by accident, the *Register* said; his cause appealed to the people, and "it is not without reason that so aggressive a champion of the new west goes to Washington from Iowa."[46]

Local conditions were undoubtedly important. But in other midwestern states, men running on platforms similar to Brookhart's were also elected to the Senate in 1922. R. Burton Howell won in Nebraska, Nonpartisan Leaguer Lynn Frazier in South Dakota, and Farmer-Laborite Henrik Shipstead in Minnesota. All were products of the agricultural depression and farm crisis, and all were expected to strengthen the more radical wing of the congressional farm bloc. The program it would now embrace, said the *New York Times*, was likely to give "shivers" to the old guard.[47]

But if Brookhart's election had national ramifications, he was for the moment at least primarily a hometown boy made good. "Destiny moves in a mysterious way," wrote the *Journal*, "and one who has watched politics in Washington County for the past thirty years looks back over a kaleidoscopic shifting of scenes that bewilders, dazes and amazes." In 1894, when Brookhart had first run for office, the issue had been liquor, with Brookhart's personality being almost incidental. Subsequently, in his work for Logan and Cummins and his own congressional candidacy in 1910, the issue had been control of the party and of the political process, with Brookhart serving as a soldier in the trenches. But now in 1922, even though causes and party control were still part of the rhetoric, the real issue had become Smith Brookhart himself, and the arena in which he was beginning to operate was no longer local. "Colonel Brookhart's battlefield goes into the halls of Congress now," the *Journal* commented, and "there is plenty of room there; it's a big ring, the referee is the whole people of the United States."[48]

Before he went east, however, the hometown folks gathered for a reception to honor the new senator. There was a torchlight parade from the Brookhart home to the Commercial Club, and there something more than a thousand people came to shake hands, partake of refreshments, and hear the inevitable speeches. Among the speakers were childhood friends Edgar R. Harlan, curator of the Iowa State Museum and Archives, and U. S. Smith, President of Iowa Wesleyan College; Louis Cook, representing Dante Pierce; former Grand Army of the Republic Commander J. H. Mills, representing Governor Kendall; and former Senator Lafayette Young. The latter, apparently there to try to heal divisions within the party, predicted a long and useful career for the fifty-three-year-old Brookhart. Speaking last, the honoree expressed his appreciation and pledged his determination to represent the people.[49]

Once the program was over the people slowly dispersed, reluctant to leave as they savored the moment and realized that they too would share in Brookhart's prominence. In the years ahead they would not always like what Brookhart said and did, but for now old fights were set aside in a common pride for what their neighbor had become.

9

In Washington and Europe

In late November 1922 Smith Brookhart went to Washington, his term in the Senate beginning as soon as the Governor of Iowa had sent his credentials. Before leaving Iowa, however, he took time to recruit an office staff. As clerks he took two women from Washington, Iowa, Elizabeth Fisher from his law office and Anna Dawson, his former newspaper partner. And on the recommendations of Dante Pierce and Congressman W. F. Kopp, he decided to keep Senator Rawson's secretary, Roy Rankin. The latter had gone to Washington sixteen years before and had served successively in the offices of Congressman Kennedy, Senator Kenyon, and Senator Rawson. "He is really a remarkable fellow," Kopp told Brookhart, "he knows all the 'ins' and 'outs' of the Departments."[1]

When Brookhart arrived in Washington, Rawson took him around to meet other senators and did what he could to get him started. As a senator-elect, Brookhart had the privilege of the floor, and he wasted no time in taking advantage of it. There he was introduced by Senator George Norris, and for the first time since the election he saw Cummins. They shook hands, although no doubt more perfunctorily than cordially, and there was speculation about whether Cummins would honor custom and escort Brookhart down the aisle to be sworn in.[2]

In addition, he witnessed the swearing in of the first woman United States Senator, Mrs. Rebecca Latimer Felton. The ceremony, he said, "recognized the right of womanhood to the highest place in our legislative assemblies."[3]

Observing another ritual, Brookhart paid a courtesy call on President Harding. Upon arrival, he found three senators ahead of him. But the three were "lame ducks" and were therefore asked to come back another day while Brookhart was ushered right in. The President and Brookhart talked for forty

135

minutes, discussing among other topics an administration ship subsidy bill. Harding urged Brookhart to vote for it, and when Brookhart refused the interview was "abruptly ended."[4]

Subsequently, his credentials arrived, and on December 2, 1922, Smith Wildman Brookhart was sworn in as a United States Senator from Iowa. Wearing a red rose in his lapel, a gift from Henry C. Wallace, he was escorted down the aisle by Senator Cummins and sworn in by Vice President Coolidge. His first act as a senator was to write a letter to a Forest City woman, Mrs. Ingar Hylen, whose son had been a Brookhart supporter in Winnebago County and had been killed in an automobile accident while hurrying to finish chores in order to attend a Brookhart meeting. "I cannot help but feel that in some degree his life was a sacrifice for me and for our cause," Brookhart wrote the mother, and this first letter as a senator, he continued, was a way to do "some fitting honor to his name."[5]

As a new senator, Brookhart was appointed to five standing committees: Education and Labor, Expenditures in the Executive Department, Interoceanic Canals, Military Affairs, and Manufacturers. Later he would be appointed to a select committee to investigate the possibility of a navigable channel from the Great Lakes to the Gulf of Mexico. As the controversial new boy in town, he also received a lot of attention, "too much in fact," he wrote Jennie. And elsewhere in the country he had acquired a certain amount of fame. From Arkansas came word that poor farmers were naming their newborn children after him.[6]

Never a social animal, Brookhart went only to those affairs he could not avoid. In February, for example, he was the guest of honor at the Iowa Society. But more typical was the December evening he described to Jennie. "Farm bloc meets tonight," he told her, "and I will eat supper with the girls and go home afterward." To the voters he had promised to stay away from the "social bloc," and he was true to his word. After a year in Washington he sent E. R. Harlan some invitations to White House functions with a note: "I am enclosing [these] White House invitations for your collection. I never use them. I do not know how great their value may be in the history of the State, as I am going clear around the social bloc."[7]

Clearly enjoying himself, Brookhart was able to exhibit a sense of humor all too often missing in the acrimonious campaign just ended. Edgar Harlan sent him the proofs of a series of photographs, apparently for a bust since they were done from the front, back, and sides. Acknowledging their receipt Brookhart thought them "very fine, especially the one from behind." "As to measurements," Brookhart continued, "I wear a 16½ collar, 7⅛ hat, No. 8 shoe, but I cannot remember the size of the sock or undershirt. I am five feet, seven inches tall and weigh 200 pounds."[8]

Home briefly in January to speak before the Iowa Farm Bureau

Convention, Brookhart also spoke before a Joint Convention of the Iowa General Assembly. In a speech he characterized as "more gossip than statesmanship," he told the Iowa lawmakers about his first days in Washington and his swearing in ceremony:

> That all happened about six weeks ago and I want to call your attention to the fact that the government of the United States still stands, and up to the present time I have had no word from Kate O'Hare. Honestly, I believe the I.W.W.'s are clear blown up. Further, there is not an ex-governor in sight anywhere around here. Under these circumstances I want to say to you that service in the United States Senate is exceedingly pleasant.[9]

Brookhart's first speech as senator was not on Capitol Hill but across town at a National Conference of Progressives sponsored by the People's Legislative Service. Organized in December 1920 by a group of Congressmen and others (including Brookhart), the People's Legislative Service had the mission of keeping members of Congress and the public at large informed on legislation. Its director, Basil Manly, regularly published bulletins under the title "On Guard For the People." Senator La Follette, who was chairman of the agency's Executive Committee, used the pages of *La Follette's Magazine* for added promotion. And serving as another member of the Executive Committee was Smith Brookhart.[10]

Meeting on December 1, 1922, progressive senators and congressmen from both parties planned an agenda for the coming Congress under the fundamental purpose: "To drive special privilege out of control of government and restore it to the people." For each policy area—agriculture, labor, railroads, shipping, natural resources, credits, taxation, and Constitutional amendments—they established committees of legislators in "union" with "men of affairs and experts." And in line with their call for restoring government to the people, they proposed a nationwide campaign for open primaries (including a presidential primary) and corrupt practices legislation.[11]

The next day some 200 men and women met, endorsed the proposals of the progressive congressmen, and listened to a series of speeches. Senators-elect Lynn Frazier of North Dakota and Burton Wheeler of Montana and Governor John J. Blaine of Wisconsin spoke in the morning and were then followed, in the afternoon, by Nebraska Senator George Norris, labor leader Samuel Gompers, and the newly sworn in Smith Brookhart. The day concluded with a banquet given in honor of newly elected progressives; and there, as during the day, the speeches were highly critical of the Harding administration. The remarkable unity shown by the progressives, said the

New York Times, was likely to make them "a powerful factor in the next Congress."[12]

At the time of the Progressive Conference, Congress had been in special session. This had been called on November 20 to consider a shipping bill that would provide government subsidies to underwrite the private shipping industry. This was a bill Harding strongly supported, arguing that it would serve the "larger good of the nation" rather than a special constituency. But it was opposed by most midwestern progressives and had been denounced by Brookhart during the campaign. Indeed, he believed that his opposition to the measure had been one factor contributing to his success in the primary, and in the fall campaign Dante Pierce had told his readers that a vote against Brookhart was a vote for the subsidy.[13]

On December 4 the special session gave way to the regular (fourth) session of the Sixty-Seventh Congress, one that Brookhart and the progressives hoped would provide some real relief for the persisting agricultural depression,[14] but one that he feared would be dominated by the ship subsidy bill. With this on his mind, he entered the Senate Chamber on December 7, found that he would be sitting next to the new Senator from Michigan, James Couzens, and thereby gained an unlikely ally.

Born in Canada, Couzens had moved to Detroit as a young man and had eventually become an official in the Ford Motor Company, a bank president, and mayor of the city. Named to fill the vacancy created by the resignation of Senator Truman Newberry, he was sworn in on December 7 and assigned the desk next to Brookhart. As he sat down he said, "I am glad to be next to a progressive." A friendship was born, and four days later the two new senators sat at their desks discussing how to get the ship subsidy bill off the calendar so that the farm relief issue could be taken up. "Why don't you get busy and poll the Senate on this?" Couzens asked Brookhart. "Guess I will," Brookhart replied, and within one day had fifty senators, fifteen Republicans, and thirty-five Democrats pledged to bring up farm legislation immediately.[15]

The move, Brookhart insisted, was nonpartisan and was in no way "an anti-Administration movement." "We are simply agreed," he told the *New York Times*, "that the farmer is in more need of immediate aid than private shipping interests." In any event, the tactic worked. The ship subsidy bill was kept off the calendar, and Brookhart was pleased. Writing to his wife, he said, "Everything going good . . . will speak on ship subsidy in a few days."[16]

Probably no one really expected Smith Brookhart to honor the custom that freshmen senators were to be seen and not heard. Only nine days after taking office he had helped sidetrack an administration bill, and on December 18, just a week later, he made his maiden speech. Ostensibly, it was on ship subsidies, but what it really amounted to was a primer on Brookhart's political philosophy. For the occasion some sixty senators were on the floor. But those who expected the radical Brookhart to produce oratorical fireworks were disappointed. While his ideas were radical enough, the *New York Times* said, his delivery was "mild and unsensational." He spoke slowly, reading from a typed text, with his voice "clear but sonorous" and "his enunciation so pronounced that he appeared to accent nearly every syllable."[17]

Brookhart began by arguing that the common people, now united to gain their political and economic rights, had decided that "government aid to private enterprises for profit [was] fundamentally wrong." Yet they had seen such action taken with the passage of the Transportation Act, and now another private enterprise, the shipping industry, was to be subsidized. The great irony, he continued, was that when the government guaranteed money to big business it was called a "wise, business-like, conservative, and patriotic use of the Public Treasury," yet a similar guarantee to farmers was "unwise, socialistic, and treasonable." In presenting the shipping bill to Congress, President Harding had argued that its passage would be an asset for America in the event of war and would increase material self-reliance in time of peace. But Brookhart was unconvinced. Unfurling the "yellow flag of Wall Street above the Stars and Stripes" he argued, was not patriotism. Nor did ships built for private use contribute to the national defense. "On the contrary, national defense consists in making this Government a more efficient, a more American, a more patriotic Government in its business affairs and its economic affairs, as well as its military affairs."[18]

Turning next to the agricultural problem, Brookhart pointed out that most people thought in terms of individual farmers rather than agriculture as an industry. Yet the total capital investment in American agriculture was eighty billion dollars, making the American farmer "the big business man of the United States." Consequently, agriculture deserved to be represented on the Federal Reserve Board, as did labor and small business. Farmers should also take control of their own credit through establishment of cooperative organizations. And as a measure of immediate relief, Congress should pass the Norris Bill establishing a government corporation to build elevators and warehouses in which grain could be held off the market until prices recovered. This, Brookhart said, was a "drastic" step. But it would provide the immediate relief that farmers needed.[19]

Reaction to the speech was mild. Brookhart, said the *New York Times*, did not live up to his reputation. Although billed as a "fulminator," he actually seemed more like a professor "droning observations on the theory of relativity." And in the *Register*, it was noted that the eastern press was not as hard on Brookhart as had been expected.[20]

Brookhart, however, was pleased with the speech and with the role he was beginning to play in the Senate. When Columbus Junction editor

Brainard Shearer wrote to ask for a copy, he gladly sent one, along with a note that sounded uncharacteristically pompous:

> When a person fights the battle of the common people he is then practically listed by big business as dangerous to the welfare of the world. As long as I am in public life it is going to be my aim to see that the farmer, laborer, and soldier are given justice in the halls of Congress.[21]

In Congress the Republican progressives and their Democratic allies managed to keep the shipping bill off the calendar through January. But in early February, Harding again addressed a joint session, urging action on the bill, and on February 19 the administration forces succeeded in bringing it to the floor of the Senate. The progressives responded with a filibuster, one in which Brookhart was reportedly as active as "a flea on a hot griddle, restlessly trotting from one filibusterer to another with advice, encouragement, exhortation and good cheer—a combination guardian angel and Pollyanna." When it came his turn, Brookhart spoke for three and one-half hours. But by that time the Republican regulars knew that they could not break the filibuster. The day after Brookhart's speech, Senator Charles Curtis went to Harding to tell him so; and although Harding urged them to keep trying, it was to no avail. On February 28 the pro-administration senators gave up.[22]

In his speech during the filibuster, Brookhart justified its use. The bill, he said, was not in the best interests of farmers, as demonstrated by resolutions of opposition he had received from several farm organizations. And given the interests at stake, those who represented the farmers were justified in using every legal means to block it. "When I filibuster," he continued, "I want everybody to know it. I want my constituents to know that I have kept the promise I made to them to use every means in my power, within the rules and within the law, to defeat the bill."[23]

During the battles over the shipping bill, Dante Pierce had visited Washington and reported to the readers of the *Homestead* that Brookhart was "making good" in the nation's capital. At a committee hearing, he noted, where Brookhart was leading the questioning, a man soon to be a witness had whispered to Pierce, "He's a good one, all right. Whoever started this radical talk about him?" Similarly, the syndicated columnist Mark Sullivan wrote that the image of Brookhart as a "bellicose fire eater" was a misconception, created, he thought, by the tendency of newspapers to print only his more extreme statements. In fact, wrote Sullivan, "the tone of his voice and the substance of his speech, give the impression of a combination farmer and rural school teacher with a decided trait of idealism, a ready enthusiasm for new projects designed to better the common lot of man."[24]

This notion of Brookhart the "moderate," however, was something that his more persistent critics found difficult to credit; and this was particularly true after he proceeded, as he had promised during his campaign, to devise legislation that would repeal the Esch-Cummins Act and bring railroad rate reductions. In the eyes of the spokesman for the railroads, he was a "communist" whose talk about the capital valuation of the railroads being some five billion dollars too high amounted to "baseless and reckless misstatements" conducive to the introduction of a "socialist regime in the United States." His bill, said such publications as *Railway Age* and *Railway Review*, was part of a larger scheme to nationalize the industry and perhaps to overthrow the government. It was the work of the "most dangerous organization of radicals in the world, outside of Russia," and if the principles underlying it were applied generally, the United States would be swiftly converted "into a Russia."[25]

Introduced on February 24, the Brookhart Railroad Bill called for the repeal of most sections of the Transportation Act of 1920, leaving intact only those parts necessary to keep from shutting down the railroads altogether. Clause 15-A, guaranteeing income to the railroads, was among those to be repealed. In its place there would be a provision directing the Interstate Commerce Commission to revalue the railroads, the evaluation to be based only on the fair market value of stocks, bonds, and securities, with no consideration to be given to the unearned increment in real estate values.[26]

The same day that Brookhart introduced his bill, James C. Davis, Director General of the U.S. Railroad Administration, spoke in Des Moines and suggested that in view of the rise of "socialism" and "sovietism" elsewhere in the world, "private ownership" might be "making its last stand." The high railroad rates, he said, were not the result of the Transportation Act, but rather the result of the disruptions caused by the "abnormal conditions" of the war period. The railroads, he also pointed out, would now have to make large, nonproductive capital expenditures in order to meet the increased competition of waterways and hard roads. Hence, they needed credit and new investors, something that Brookhart's devaluation plan would deny them. And above all, they needed to be kept out of the "maelstrom of politics" until "natural laws" could "restore order out of . . . chaos."[27]

In such remarks and others one could detect the fear of the industry that the Brookhart Bill would, in the words of *Railway Age*, become the "rallying point" for the anti-business politicians as well as "various groups of socialists, single-taxers, plain radicals and—some say—Bolsheviks." There were, it felt, growing linkages between the so called "progressives" and "anti-constitutionalist radicals and labor union leaders." And indeed, among those sharing Brookhart's views on the railroad question were such organizations as the Conference for Progressive Political Action, La Follette's People's Legislative Service, and the People's Reconstruction League, a group of labor unions and railroad brotherhoods dedicated to "a reconstruction program for economic justice."[28]

A more specific fear on the part of the railroads was that such groups were uniting to help the senate progressives take over the Senate Interstate Commerce Committee and use it to promote their campaign for the nationalization of the railroads. And again, it was possible to point to a certain amount of interlinkage and collaboration. Brookhart's name was on the letterhead of the People's Legislative Service. He was among those attending a meeting called by New Jersey attorney George Record to consider "various suggestions" in regard to the railroad question. And although he was not at the founding meeting, he was on one of the committees of the National Conference on Valuation of American Railroads, a group set up by the organizations that the railroads saw as pushing nationalization.[29]

In 1923 the Brookhart Bill remained in committee, there being little time to consider it before the March 4 adjournment. But ultimately, it seemed likely to receive a hearing, and there was no letup in attacks on the bill and its author by railroad spokesmen. Putting aside whatever merits his bill may have had, the fact that it was Brookhart's bill seemed to guarantee that it would not be passed.

His colleagues seemed not to know how to deal with him, so they did not. Iowa congressmen, moreover, kept their distance, one of them commenting that "you must be wholly for him or submerge your own ideas or you get the impression that he thinks you are wholly against him." They could see little moderate about a man who told one interviewer that he had found the "financial classes . . . deeply entrenched in every department," and that the only way out was to organize a "militant and united political force." Such usefulness as he had, one of them thought, was in providing a peaceful vent for radical expression and making "standpats" see "another side of economics."[30]

Arriving home on March 12, Brookhart stayed there for only two days before leaving on a speaking trip to Des Moines, Monmouth, Illinois, and Detroit. He then returned on March 19 and went daily to his law office, which he was now using only as a mailing address. He had given up practicing law, telling his friends that one job at a time was enough.[31] In April he declined most of the speaking invitations sent him, but did speak in Red Oak before the Southwestern Teachers Association and in Davenport, where he went to inspect the lock and dam, and discuss the use of the rivers for navigation.

His constituents, of course, wanted to know about life in the nation's capital and especially about whether their junior senator would wear formal dress clothes to Washington parties. Keeping his campaign promise not to be part of the "social bloc," Brookhart had refused to be listed in the Washington social register and had worn his blue business suit to those few social functions he could not avoid. One eastern newspaper said that Washington residents had been placing bets on how long he would resist switching to formal attire, and the home folks were naturally curious. Responding to questions, Brookhart said that he had been elected to work for the interests of his constituents and not to "parade up and down Peacock Alley in dress suits."[32]

The home folks, moreover, were not the only ones interested. Throughout the country, newspaper articles on Brookhart's dress appeared, with the result that many Americans knew more about his wardrobe than they did about his legislative program. His declaration that he preferred overalls to evening clothes also prompted Iowa labor leader J. C. Lewis and the Farmer's Cooperative Association to send him a new pair of overalls. "We're proud of Brookhart," Lewis said, "we know where he stands . . . we're behind him [and] one way of telling him so is by mailing him a pair of overalls." In his home town, Brookhart took a good deal of good-natured kidding about the whole thing. But if those writing the stories enjoyed it, he said, "then let them rave."[33]

If Brookhart and the home folks did not care how he dressed, Jennie did. She considered it a great victory when she could persuade him to buy a new suit. When he finally agreed to buy a new overcoat, Jennie wrote their son in Washington, D.C., to go to the office and take the worn-out overcoat hanging in the closet and sell it at a second-hand store before the senator arrived back in town. Otherwise, she said, "he may want to wear it."[34]

In early 1923 a number of senators, including La Follette and Burton Wheeler of Montana, had made plans to visit Europe. And while Brookhart had initially ruled out the idea of such a trip, he had by April changed his mind. He wanted to study the cooperative movement, especially the workings of the Rochdale system; and on April 23 he accepted an offer from Secretary of Commerce Herbert Hoover to furnish him with a Commerce Department aide. He would, he said, meet with Hoover before sailing.[35]

Brookhart's intentions, as he planned the trip, were to visit most of the countries of Europe, study the cooperatives in them, and investigate the possibility of setting up an international cooperative to exchange American grain for European manufactured goods. His idea was to develop a kind of barter system and thus "tie the can on the international banker." When asked if he would go to Russia, he replied, "If they will let me in . . . Those

Russians," he explained, "will not let everyone into their country; they have turned down some American senators." "But," he said, "I'll try to get in anyhow." To prepare for the Russian leg of the trip he locked himself in his office for two weeks and studied Russian. He did not expect to be proficient in the language but hoped to learn enough to carry on simple conversations with the peasants.[36]

On April 26, after issuing Brookhart a special passport, the State Department sent a circular letter notifying all its European stations that "Senator Brookhart is making the trip for the purpose of investigation of political and economic conditions." On the same day the senator began his trip east, stopping in Chicago and Cleveland; and after spending the weekend in the capital, he went on to New York, where on May 2 he sailed on the U.S.S. *President Monroe*. His old friend Alex Miller had asked him what he thought about sailing on a ship named after a Democratic president, and Brookhart had replied that since he believed in the Monroe Doctrine it did not bother him.[37]

Arriving in Cherbourg, the senator was met by Hoover's representative, Alfred Pearce Dennis, a Princeton Ph.D. born in the same year as Brookhart and, since the war, commercial attache who had served first in London, later in Rome, and then as a special representative in central and eastern Europe. Given his eastern establishment background, Ivy League credentials, and firm commitments to business, Dennis seemed a most unlikely companion for Brookhart. But, unaccountably, they became good friends.

Although Dennis was prepared to show Brookhart all the usual sights of Europe, he quickly found that the senator wanted none of it. Having read the history of Europe and studied many travel books, Brookhart said that he would let the "dead past bury its dead" and get down to the business of taking "a look at the living present" and "raising as far as possible, the curtain of the dawning future." In Paris he did permit himself a pilgrimage to three shrines—a few minutes at Napoleon's tomb, a few more at Lafayette's, and a visit to nearby world war battlefields. But with those formalities over, he was ready for business.[38]

Paying a courtesy call on U.S. Ambassador Myron T. Herrick, Brookhart explained the purpose of his trip and was told by Herrick that he was on the "greatest mission in the world . . . The proudest heritage I have to claim," the Ambassador said, "is that my father successfully managed a cooperative store for twenty-four years." The two then discussed the cooperative movement in general and talked in particular about Warren Stone's efforts to establish a cooperative bank for the Brotherhood of Locomotive Engineers. Back in 1914, Brookhart learned, Herrick had published a book entitled *Rural Credits*. And he now received an autographed copy of the book along with further encouragement. The United States,

Herrick noted, was the only country that by law prohibited farmers and laborers from organizing their own cooperative banks; and in his view, "cooperation" could "never be a permanent success until it has such a system for its foundation."[39]

Crossing the Channel, Brookhart stopped briefly in London and then proceeded to Edinburgh, the site of the great Rochdale Conference he had come to attend. He was there as a fraternal delegate representing the Cooperative League of America, and Dennis saw to it that he was invited to address the convention and thus had an opportunity to declare his great faith in the Rochdale system and its prospects for the future. "Cooperation," he told his audience, "never made a millionaire and it never made a pauper." The speech, needless to say, was enthusiastically received.[40]

Buoyed by the experience, Brookhart sailed from Newcastle-on-Tyne to Bergen, Norway, and from there traveled on to Oslo, to Sweden, and then to Copenhagen, Denmark. In the latter country, 95 percent of the farmers were in a cooperative system, thus making it, in Brookhart's eyes, a model for American cooperators. While there he met with the Danish Minister of Agriculture, Madsen-Mygdal. But when he told the latter of his high regard for Lenin (calling him the "farmers' greatest friend in the world today"), the Minister said that he did not think that much could be learned in Russia. American Ambassador John Dynely Prince, on the other hand, thought that a visit to Russia might well have a sobering effect on Brookhart and make him less of a zealot for the cooperative idea. Writing to the Secretary of State, he said that he had not discouraged Brookhart for undertaking such a trip.[41]

The American attitude about Russia was generally hostile. Russia was the source of communism, and most Americans realized it was dedicated to overthrowing their capitalist system. The Red Scare of a few years before and the tactics that Brookhart's opponents used to try and defeat him gave evidence of the degree of hysteria many felt about the Soviet Union. At the same time, however, in the first years of the 1920s the American government, joined by many private agencies, had been engaged in a massive relief effort that fed millions of starving Russians.[42]

Torn by civil war, an unsuccessful economic policy, and a devastating drought, the Russian people were in the midst of a great famine. And while Secretary of Commerce Hoover had philosophical differences with the Russian government, he had responded to pleas for help from Russian officials and asked the head of the American Relief Administration, Colonel William M. Haskel, to establish a system to distribute food to the Russians. Initially suspicious of the several hundred ARA operatives in their country, the Russian officials had gradually become less so; and on the other side, a number of ARA men had become less opposed to the idea of trade and diplomatic relations with the Soviet Union. By the end of 1922, however, tension had again begun to mount, and early the next year Hoover had made the decision to withdraw the ARA from Russia. As of June 1923 the ARA had distributed 700,000 tons of food worth sixty million dollars to some 10.5 million people.[43]

In May, Brookhart had sent a telegram to Hoover asking that Dennis be allowed to accompany him to Russia. Hoover, though, feared that an official representative in Russia would "cause discussion." He turned down the request, offering instead to arrange for the services of John Ellingston, an agricultural expert serving with the American Relief Administration. He then told the State Department what he had done, making it clear that he had provided an aide for Brookhart in the hope that the senator would obtain "an accurate view of the situation and thus would be helpful when he returned to the United States." ARA help to Brookhart while he was in Russia, he thought, would be conducive to the same end. The State Department offered no objections.[44]

In Berlin Brookhart picked up a Russian visa. He then traveled on to Warsaw and took a train for Moscow, entering Russia on June 9. On the trip he was impressed with what he saw. The Russian train was clean, efficiently run, and on time, and outside his window he could see mile after mile of well cultivated fields with prospects of a good harvest.

Arriving in Moscow on June 10, Brookhart was met by John Ellingston, who had expected to "chaperone an 'implacable' friend" of Russia in favor of recognition for "sentimental reasons." Instead, he found Brookhart to be a "hard headed American farmer," friendly to Russia "not because it was writing a new declaration of the Rights of Man . . . but because it had given the peasant the land and . . . was supporting the cooperatives at the expense of the middleman." Accompanying Brookhart throughout his stay in Russia, Ellingston kept him supplied with interpreters—most of whom, Brookhart said, were former Czarists and therefore unlikely to give him information favorable to the present government.[45]

During his five days in Moscow, Brookhart saw as much as he could. He met with a number of government officials, including the man he came to regard as an "organizing genius," Leon Trotsky. The latter told him that the cooperative movement would soon be recognized as the foundation of national economic policy in Russia. He was also urged both by Trotsky and others to work for United States recognition of the Soviet Union.[46]

Another stop for Brookhart was the Peasants' House, a hotel for peasants who came to Moscow with complaints for the central government. Visiting with peasants there, and later in several villages, Brookhart found them generally happy with their situation since the war. They now had land to farm, they said, and were able to feed their families with a little left over to sell. The trips to various villages, outside Moscow and later outside Kiev and Odessa, also confirmed the impression that Brookhart had received from his train window, namely, that the land was being intensely cultivated and that there were good prospects for the coming harvest—so good, in fact, that the surplus from the previous year was being sold.

The crop outlook, in Brookhart's eyes, meant at least two things. It meant, first of all, that the ARA had been correct in its decision to suspend its operations in Russia. And second, it meant that hopes of selling surplus American grain to Russia were ill founded. What American farmers could gain from Russia, Brookhart thought, was not a market for their goods but knowledge about cooperative marketing procedures.[47]

Still another stop in Moscow was the Agriculture College where more Russian students than could be accommodated were being taught modern agricultural techniques. There Brookhart was impressed by the large library, which contained, he found, the latest crop reports from Iowa. His major criticism was of the policy that based admissions on class origins and thereby excluded children of the bourgeoisie.

Clearly, Brookhart was impressed with the new Russia. It now had, he said, the "most stable" government in Europe, and it had "already done more for the peasants of Russia than Czarism did in a whole thousand years." It was also "proof of the Soviets' good faith," he thought, "that even when foreign nations have to feed some of the famine stricken they do not seize what grain the peasants have managed to save." The United States, he believed, should recognize the Soviet Union, if for no other reason than that "such recognition would contribute directly to the peace of Europe."[48]

Brookhart would concede, to be sure, that the Soviet government was far from perfect. The election system was too much like the old "standpat Republican caucuses"; and stability, he would admit, had been obtained at the high price of revolutionary excesses and cruelty. He thought, however, that the Soviet leaders were aware of these things and were taking steps to correct them. And even with these imperfections in the system, recognition ought to come. It did not mean approval of the government, and besides, "we have recognized lots worse Russian governments than this one."[49]

One must ask, of course, whether the view that Brookhart got of Russia was an accurate one. Certainly he had not begun as a dispassionate observer. He wanted to believe that cooperation was working in Russia, and Trotsky told him what he wanted to hear. He also undoubtedly saw what the Russian government wanted him to see. Unhappy peasants in depressed villages were not put on his itinerary. Yet as historian Edward Carr has pointed out, in 1923 "a noteworthy revival was discernable in the Soviet economy," due in part to the "natural process of recovery" after years of foreign and civil war, in part to the good harvest of the year before, and in part to policies introduced in 1921. By 1923 the famine was over, and at the time Lenin was still alive, albeit mortally ill. The power struggle brought on by his death was still on the horizon. As for the peasants, Carr observed, the picture of a "prosperous and contented peasantry . . . represented a fair approximation to the truth." Brookhart had gone to Russia at an unusual time, a period Carr calls "the interregnum," when there was "an uneasy balance, marked by the pursuit of policies of compromise and marking time." And by doing so, he had seen Russia at the best it would be for a long time and had formed favorable opinions that would stick with him.[50]

Sailing from Odessa on an American destroyer, Brookhart crossed the Black Sea to Constantinople, traveled from there to Constanta, Romania, and then entrained for Bucharest where he rejoined Dennis. While there he dined with the American Ambassador Peter Jay, a grandson of John Jay. The Ambassador, a Harvard graduate and career diplomat was in full formal attire. But, as Dennis recalled with great relish, Brookhart came in a celluloid collar and unpressed pepper-and-salt suit.

Pressing his views about Russia on Jay, Brookhart said that he had not gone to Russia to learn anything "but to prove something." Undoubtedly, Jay pointed out in his report to the Secretary of State, the Soviets had put on their best appearance for Brookhart's benefit. And the latter, Jay concluded, was so "intensely sincere in his beliefs" that the Russian government had "little difficulty in convincing him of its moderation and stability by persuading him that it was endeavoring to gradually replace Communism by cooperation."[51]

Returning to his hotel that night, Brookhart told Dennis that Jay had qualities about him that he liked and that at bottom he was a "pretty good sort of fellow . . . The only trouble with him," Brookhart continued, was that he did not get "a right start in life. He would have turned out to be a good deal of a man if he had had the right kind of training." The next day Jay told Dennis: "Of course your friend Brookhart is absolutely ignorant about European conditions, but he's very decent fellow after all. The great trouble with the man is he got a wrong start in life, and never had any advantages."[52]

Continuing on across Europe, Brookhart passed through Hungary, stopped in Prague for a visit with Czechoslovakian Foreign Minister Eduard Beneš, and then went to Vienna to attend another cooperative congress.[53] There Dennis and Brookhart parted, the former concluding some six years later that Brookhart had been the "mouthpiece of inarticulate, unorganized people" who had a right to be heard if America's was to be a truly representative government. Brookhart's ambition, Dennis thought, was "to avoid turning conservative," as other radicals had done. And while they had begun their acquaintance with a certain natural wariness, they had parted with mutual respect. Earlier in the trip when Dennis was about to be given another assignment, Brookhart had cabled Hoover to ask that he continue on, which Dennis had agreed to do. "My orders came to stand by the senator as long as needed," he wrote:

> I had already come to admire and respect Mr. Brookhart and he interested me greatly as a human being filled with courage and devotion, and without a particle of pose or affectation. As Carylye said of Sterling, "Despite many unsuitable wrappages of Church-of-Englandism and other, my heart loved the man."[54]

Back in Paris, Brookhart told Herrick about his visit to Russia; and while a missed message kept him from meeting with French Premier Raymond Poincaré, he did meet with Poincaré's assistant, who welcomed his information about Russia. From Paris he then journeyed to Belgium, crossed the channel, and went to Ireland, where he met with George William Russell and with the great Irish cooperator, Sir Horace Plunkett.

In Ireland, Plunkett had been organizing agricultural cooperatives for the past thirty years and earlier in 1923 had visited the United States and talked with Brookhart there. Subsequently, he had asked for a copy of Brookhart's speech on cooperation and, having read it, had written to Brookhart saying that it was a "powerful plea for the principle which I hold to offer the best compromise between the capitalists and the socialists . . . Your remedy for the great inequalities in wealth," he continued, "is not confiscation, but the wider distribution of wealth through organized, voluntary effort." Clearly, as reflected in their correspondence and the meeting in Ireland, he and Brookhart were kindred spirits.[55]

The visit with Plunkett was a fitting capstone to Brookhart's study of cooperation in Europe. Following it, he sailed for New York, arriving there on July 17 and announcing upon his arrival that cooperation was the "only constructive idea that has survived the war." He also urged a special session of Congress to deal with the problem of agricultural surpluses at home and abroad. And speaking in glowing terms of his visit to Russia, he reiterated his earlier statements calling for the recognition of the Soviet Union.[56]

Returning to Washington, Brookhart proceeded, on July 19, to call on Secretary of State Charles Evans Hughes, intending to present him with a full report of his trip, and to recommend "unhesitatingly . . . that the United States arrange for a speedy recognition of the Russian republic." Hughes, however, was not very receptive. As Brookhart reported in a letter to Herrick, the Secretary had "exhibited a generally hostile attitude toward the Soviet regime."⁵⁷

Hughes' position became quite clear the next week when he published a letter he had written to Samuel Gompers on the question of Russia. Although addressed to Gompers, the letter was interpreted by many as an answer to Brookhart as well. Hughes objected to the autocratic form of government in Russia, which did not protect the liberties of its citizens or respect the property rights of foreigners within Russia. And an even greater obstacle to recognition, he thought, was the "conclusive evidence that those in control at Moscow have not given up their original purpose of destroying existing governments wherever they can do so throughout the world."⁵⁸

In Iowa, meanwhile, criticism of Brookhart's views of Russia had already begun. Writing to the *Register*, former Governor Beryl F. Carroll said that Brookhart was absurd to think he could learn all about Russia in such a short visit. And in the Chautauqua circuit, Alexander Schwartz, who claimed to be a former associate of Lenin and Trotsky, charged that Brookhart had been duped and was now "delivering the message the communists of Russia gave him to deliver." The senator, he said, had seen only what the Russians wanted him to see.⁵⁹

In late July, Brookhart returned to Iowa, stayed home a few days to take care of his mail, and then went to Des Moines, where in a long interview with the *Register* he took issue with those charging that he had seen only what the Russians wanted him to see. "I went about the country as freely as I do in Iowa," he said. And furthermore, he pointed out, his interpreters had all had reason not to like the Soviets: one's wife was in jail for anti-Soviet activities, another's husband was killed in the revolution fighting the Soviets, and a third had a large business taken away from him. While in Des Moines, he also met with Governor Kendall, visited with Dante Pierce, and had supper with his brother's family.⁶⁰

Subsequently, Brookhart made several speeches, mostly at county fairs and labor conventions, and mostly on the subjects of cooperatives in Europe and conditions in Russia. The most publicized incident in August, however, came at the State American Legion Convention held in Mason City, where Brookhart was in attendance but did not speak.

The main speaker at the convention was Judge Kenesaw Mountain Landis, a long-time United States District Court judge and since 1920 the Commissioner of Baseball. His speech was long and patriotic, expounding on the general theme that the United States was losing its moorings and beginning to drift toward some foreign form of government. It had got to the point, said Landis, where some were suggesting that the United States recognize the Russian regime and where this very subject had become "a matter of very concrete interest in the state of Iowa." Such a course, he continued, would not only encourage the Russians in their "war upon all existing governments" but would mean that the veterans of 1917–1918 had fought in vain. It would amount to madness; and Iowans, when confronted with "counterfeit concoctions" and the "dogma of error," had always "stood 100 percent sane."[61]

The only meeting between Landis and Brookhart was in the hotel lobby, where the two passed one another and exchanged polite greetings (Brookhart: "I'm glad to see you." Landis: "Same here, senator."). Later, however, Brookhart told a reporter that his critics had not been to Russia and did not know. "I've been there," he said, "and know."[62]

Many legionnaires expected a reply from Brookhart. But the next morning, when the state commander offered the platform to him, he was not present. The convention then took Landis' advice, "opted for sanity," and passed a resolution declaring that the "Lenin-Trotsky (sic) form of government is a dangerous experiment [that] tends to the destruction of civilization," and that consequently the Legion was opposed to the recognition of the Soviet Union.[63]

It was probably just as well that Brookhart did not address the convention. Given his penchant for intemperate oratory, it was unlikely that he could have made any converts and might well have alienated more of the legionnaires than he already had. As it was, most of the state leaders were strongly critical, and none more so than past National Commander Hanford MacNider of Mason City. Whereas Landis had been cool toward Brookhart when they met, MacNider had been openly hostile:

"How are you, Jack?" said Brookhart, extending his hand.
"I don't know whether I ought to shake hands with you or not after what you said about Russia," replied MacNider.
"I can explain that," from Brookhart.
"Well, you would have to do a lot of explaining," retorted MacNider.

They had not shaken hands; and after Brookhart had moved on, MacNider told a companion that "for any American to advocate recognition of a government whose avowed principal purpose is to destroy all other organized governments is little short of treasonable."[64] This brief exchange proved to be only the preliminary to a Brookhart-MacNider duel that would continue for the rest of the decade and would have a major effect on Iowa electoral politics over the next three years.

Probably few Iowans were surprised at Brookhart's actions during his first session as a senator. As expected, he quickly aligned himself with the progressive wing of the party, called for relief for farmers, attacked the subsidy for the ship-building industry, and worked to modify the Transportation Act. Likewise, probably few Iowans were surprised when he spoke in glowing terms about the European cooperatives he visited. The formation of cooperative enterprises to solve the farm problem was by now a familiar Brookhart theme. Even his pro-Russian statements might have gone unnoticed except for the publicity given them by his political opponents.

For many Republicans the 1924 Senate race had already begun in the summer of 1923. They were looking, in particular, for a candidate who could defeat Brookhart yet seemed to have no one in sight who could campaign aggressively or who enjoyed the same widespread popularity. As it turned out, most of the principal players in the tragicomedy of politics for the next two years were present in Mason City, and it was among legionnaires that Brookhart's most solid opposition began to form.[65]

10

The Defeat of the Disrupter

Brookhart had no sooner been elected in 1922 when discussion began about defeating him in 1924. Writing Robert M. La Follette in March 1923, Dante Pierce told the Wisconsin senator that the groundwork was being laid for a "very bitter fight" against Brookhart, but that in his view the support of farmers and small businessmen would give him the "largest majority any man ever had for public office" in Iowa. The following September, the *New York Times* reported that of thirty-one north and northwest Iowa editors, only three supported Brookhart. Eighteen were against him but were undecided as to who should be the nominee, and the remainder were for other candidates, the most frequently mentioned being Burton Sweet.[1]

Although he had run fifth in the six-man 1922 primary, Sweet wanted another chance in 1924. He had refused, at the urging of the party leaders, to withdraw in favor of Tenth District Congressman Lester J. Dickinson, and by the first of the year Senator Cummins was reluctantly admitting that "the only practical thing to do [was] to get behind Burton Sweet and make the best organization possible founded upon the fundamental principles of our institutions." In late January, Dickinson decided to run for reelection in the Tenth District and to withdraw from the Senate race.[2]

Iowa Republicans, however, were not sanguine about Sweet's chances to defeat Brookhart. One friend who had broken with Brookhart wrote to Cummins urging that "very judicious and strenuous methods" be taken to prevent Brookhart's nomination. Yet outside Sweet's own congressional district, Cummins could find only "lethargy" about organizing to support him. His candidacy did not take off; and in March, when a Cummins supporter suggested that Brookhart's election seemed a "practical certainty," the senator did not disagree.[3]

Brookhart, meanwhile, was building his organization. One of his strongest sources of support in 1922 had been organized labor, and in early January 1924, J. C. Lewis assured Brookhart of labor's continued support. He also seemed strong with Iowans in general. Writing Rawson in early February, Brookhart's secretary and political operative, Roy Rankin, told the former senator that nomination papers with "thousands of names" were arriving in the mail, along with other reports indicating that Brookhart was in "mighty good shape."[4]

Rawson wanted to be the new national committeeman to be chosen by the state convention in early March. But the anti-Brookhart forces, who were determined that Cummins should lead the Iowa delegation to the national convention, suspected Rawson of being too soft on Brookhart; and in February a letter began circulating charging that he had met with Brookhart, Pierce, and several other insurgents and had made a deal with them whereby Rawson would support Brookhart in the primary and Brookhart would support Rawson for committeeman. Shortly thereafter, the standpats published a letter to Rawson from C. B. & Q. President Charles E. Perkins, demanding to know his position on Brookhart.[5]

In private Rawson branded the allegations of an agreement with Brookhart "a lie," charging that the story was the work of Sioux City attorney E. A. Burgess, an old Cummins partisan and irreconcilable standpat.[6] In public, however, he kept his silence. He needed votes from both sides to win at the convention; and while his sympathy was with Brookhart, if for no other reason than he knew no one who could defeat him, he could not say so and risk alienating the standpats.

At the same time Rawson was working to convince the Republican National Committee to hold the 1924 National Convention in Des Moines. He expressed concern that people in the east did not fully understand the conditions in the west. Agriculture had not "come back" like other parts of the country and Rawson hoped that holding the convention in Des Moines would show recognition by the party of the conditions there. Moreover, he said that "certain folks [like Brookhart] have been going around for a year or two claiming that the government is run by the people in the east." Finally, Rawson said the time would come when the party would need the votes of the west, if not in 1924 certainly by 1928. When the vote was taken on the convention site, however, only New Mexico supported the bid by Des Moines. Even Iowa's delegate, National Chairman John T. Adams, voted for the winning city of Cleveland.[7]

The party quarrels in Iowa were also being exacerbated by developments in the U.S. Senate. There Brookhart had been among those voting to deny Cummins the chairmanship of the Committee on Interstate Commerce and give it instead to South Carolina Democrat Ellison Smith. It was an action that had hurt Cummins deeply, leading him in 1924 to reject new efforts to make him chairman. And in Iowa, according to Rawson, it had caused "quite a lot of resentment."[8]

In addition, the progressives had stepped in to deprive Cummins of his usual prerogatives in determining the membership of a special committee to investigate the allegations that Attorney General Harry Daugherty was involved in influence peddling and other illegal activities. As President pro tem of the Senate, Cummins normally chose such committee members. But La Follette and Wheeler had told him that he must agree to appoint Brookhart and four others to the committee. And when Cummins refused, the insurgent-Democratic coalition had changed the resolution to make Brookhart chairman of the special committee. At that time, Cummins said he did not care how the committee was selected. But later he betrayed his indignation over the incident, saying that he would make no "agreement of any kind" with the insurgents, especially one that would put a man of Brookhart's "state of mind" in charge and thus preclude "a fair and impartial investigation." Nor was he mollified when Iowans were reportedly pleased by Brookhart's selection.[9]

Although many were anticipating trouble, the pre-primary convention in early March turned out to be a fairly tame affair. Rawson was elected the national committeeman; the national delegation was instructed to vote for Calvin Coolidge; Cummins was selected as the delegation's leader; and Smith Brookhart was not mentioned. Angered by the "insult" to Brookhart, labor leaders responded by urging Iowans to support the Senator in the primary. But according to Rawson, the Brookhart supporters were actually "tickled to death that nothing was said against him." All in all, Rawson thought, both sides were "happy and satisfied with the convention."[10]

In the primary two familiar issues quickly came forward, one being Brookhart's Republicanism, the other his Americanism. Emphasizing these themes, Burton Sweet's campaign literature said that Iowans should vote for a Republican who advocated Republican principles and policies and who did not impeach the "idealism of America" by comparing the "stability of [the American] government to that of the Russian Soviet."[11]

Brookhart again stressed relief for farmers. But busy in Washington with the Daugherty investigation, he did relatively little campaigning in Iowa. Even on primary election day, he convened yet another session of his investigating committee.[12]

Throughout the campaign, Brookhart remained a strong favorite; and when the votes were counted he had received 55 percent of the total, 199,828 votes to Sweet's 163,413. Carrying seventy-two counties (five fewer than the

1922 primary), he ran strongest in the north central, northwestern, and south central parts of the state.[13]

The Republican National Convention met a week after the primary; and although he was not a delegate, Brookhart was in attendance and, to the undoubted horror of Iowa irreconcilables, received on the second ballot thirty-one votes for vice-president, twenty-five votes coming from Wisconsin and the remaining six from North Dakota.[14] It was Charles G. Dawes, the Chicago banker who had served as the first Director of the Budget, who finally became Coolidge's running mate.

On July 22 Iowa Republicans gathered in Des Moines for the regular state convention. Some were now ready to accept the verdict of the primaries and endorse all Republican candidates for office without specifically naming any. But others wanted a resolution endorsing only those Republican candidates who would endorse Coolidge and Dawes. Asked whether he would support the national ticket, Brookhart had said simply, "I'll do as much for Coolidge as he does for me."[15]

The convention proved to be remarkably calm. It settled upon Lt. Governor John Hammill as the Republican gubernatorial nominee, his selection being necessary because no candidate had received as much as 35 percent of the primary vote. It then proceeded to endorse Coolidge and Dawes, but no other candidates for any office. And in its platform, it catered to both the progressive forces and the anti-Brookhart elements. On the one hand, the platform congratulated Iowa for being second to no other state in passing forward-looking legislation promoting the safety, health, happiness, and prosperity of its citizens. On the other hand it stated:

> Real Republicans have never believed and never will believe that to be progressive they must also be Socialists or Communists or Reds or members of or in sympathy with other like organizations seeking the overthrow of the institutions which made America great and/or our Constitution, which has made the United States the foremost nation of the world.[16]

The speakers included Governor Kendall, John Hammill, State Senator Clem F. Kimball (the nominee for lieutenant governor), and Senator Cummins, who presented the platform. But neither Kendall, who was a Brookhart supporter, nor the other speakers, who were not, mentioned Brookhart by name, apparently for fear that doing so would bring down the fragile structure of unity that they were trying to maintain. The whole time, Brookhart himself sat in silence in the Washington County delegation, making like an Easter Island totem figure who represented either benevolence or malevolence, depending on the outlook of the viewer.[17]

Throughout the primary campaign and into the summer Brookhart faced an issue that would provide fodder for those opposed to him, while at the same time bring significant changes to his family. Smith, his brother, Jim, their wives and Jennie's sister were stockholders in the Farmers' and Merchants' Bank in Washington. Hundreds of banks in Iowa failed under the pressures of the agricultural depression of the 1920s and in April 1924 the Farmers' and Merchants' Bank went under.[18]

Under Iowa law at the time stockholders were liable for an assessment equal to double the value of the stock held. Smith immediately assumed the responsibility for his own stock as well as the stock held by Jennie and her sister. Following the death of his brother two years later, Smith also took over the obligation of Jim and his wife. In all Smith Brookhart was assessed $70,000.[19]

Brookhart was determined to pay all that he owed and by November he had paid half of his original amount. He would spend most of the rest of his life paying the remainder by giving speeches and writing articles for magazines. He insisted, however, that the arrangement be kept private. In future elections his opponents would attack him on the issue of the bank failure and the fees he would collect from speeches and articles. His own pride, his sense of responsibility to the depositors, and his respect for their privacy, would cost him a great deal but he would never waver from his commitment to pay the full amount.[20]

The financial impact on his family was immediate. Two sons, Smith and John, were at Iowa State and had to leave school. Smith would go to Washington, D.C., and take a job in his father's office. Jennie had to manage the household with much less income and made good use of the orchard and garden to supplement the family income. But in the summer of 1924, Senator Brookhart tried to put the family financial troubles out of his mind and concentrate on his race for reelection.[21]

In mid-August E. H. Cunningham wrote Rawson asking whether rumors then current in Washington were true that some Iowa Republicans were working to defeat Brookhart. Calling such a possibility "political chicanery," Cunningham told Rawson:

> Mr. Brookhart has been overwhelmingly nominated. He has been able to carry the Republican Primaries of Iowa through two very bitter fights and the least I think that the opposition can now do is to at least submit to the will of the people and put all of their strength and support back of that Republican ticket.[22]

Cunningham and Rawson represented the attitude of many "common sense" Republicans determined to make the best of a situation they did not like. Others, however, took a different tack and in so doing contributed to two of the most confusing years in Iowa political history. An earlier Rawson correspondent had indicated the course these irreconcilables would take. Writing on February 8, James J. Lenihan, formerly of Cedar Rapids and now in the Justice Department, had complained to Rawson that Brookhart had been voting with the Democrats in the Senate and had spoken favorably of the just deceased Woodrow Wilson. Lenihan then asked Rawson that if Brookhart was "making such a good Democrat on the Republican ticket, why a Democrat might not be made a good Republican on the Democratic ticket."[23] Rawson did not respond to Lenihan's suggestion, but other Republicans were thinking along similar lines and, even before the June primary, were beginning a movement to support Democrat Dan Steck of Ottumwa for senator.

If Smith Brookhart was the rugged individualist, Daniel Frederick Steck was very much the team player. Born in Ottumwa, Iowa, in 1881, he was the son of Albert Steck, a graduate of Michigan University Law School and an active figure in Democratic politics. In 1900 the elder Steck had run for Congress but without success. Except for three years when he was General Counsel for the Colorado Coal and Iron Company in Pueblo, he spent his life practicing law in Ottumwa.[24]

When it came time for Dan Steck to pursue a life's work, he too chose the law. In 1906 he took an LL.B. from the University of Iowa, and while there joined Sigma Nu social fraternity and Phi Delta Phi professional fraternity. Also active in sports, he was both singles and doubles sculls champion.

Returning to Ottumwa, Steck practiced law with his father, served from 1912 to 1916 as County Attorney of Wapello County, and in 1917 enlisted in the Iowa National Guard. Shortly thereafter, he was commissioned by the governor to raise a signal company, and as captain of the 109th Field Signal Battery he saw service in France. After discharge in May 1919, he returned home to his law practice. Like many veterans, he joined the American Legion.

By that time, too, the American Legion was already becoming an important feature not only of Dan Steck's life but of the Iowa scene. By the time the Iowa Department held its second annual convention, on September 2-3, 1920, it had come to consist of 542 posts with 37,299 members. At this convention Hanford MacNider of Mason City had been elected state commander, and Dan Steck had become national committeeman from Iowa.[25]

At the third state convention, held in September 1921, Steck was elected state commander and also a delegate to the national convention later that fall.

While there he placed the name of MacNider before the convention as national commander, and the convention responded with the election of MacNider by acclamation. A month after the convention MacNider wrote to Steck: "I have great faith in you and what you are doing for the Legion in Iowa. We look to you and your Department for inspiration to carry throughout the nation, and we offer you and Iowa all that is within the powers of National Headquarters."[26]

Nor was MacNider the only friend that Steck was to make through the Legion. Linked with him in the chain of command were men like Charles B. Robbins of Cedar Rapids and Bert L. Halligan of Davenport, and throughout the ranks of Iowa legionnaires Steck became widely known. As national committeeman, he was also prominent at the national level, and had appeared with Hanford MacNider to testify in behalf of the Fordney Bill, a veteran's benefit act. All of these ties were to be helpful when Dan Steck decided to run for the United States Senate.[27]

As with similar groups in other nations, the Legion was in theory a social and service organization, stressing the ideal of war-born comradeship kept alive in continuing bonds of "mutual helpfulness," service to "community, state, and nation," and dedication to correct social principles. According to its constitution, it was to be "absolutely non-partisan" and was not to engage in the dissemination of partisan literature or advocate any political candidacy. Yet in June 1924, shortly after the Republican National Convention, Hanford MacNider of Mason City and Theodore Roosevelt, Jr. had organized the Republican Service League, an organization that was to be independent of the Republican Party yet cooperate with it. The goal was to assure that the Republican Party would not "atrophy," to rally "the younger element who are more plastic," and to make them "active participaters" (sic) in party affairs. As MacNider explained it to B. B. Burnquist, Chairman of the Iowa State Republican Party, the men involved were "engaged in organizing inside the Republican Party the serviceman generation to sell them the national ticket and to put them actively at work inside the party for the good of all concerned."[28]

Once formed the Service League had grown rapidly. MacNider took over the leadership of the national organization and through it set out to establish an organization in each state. On September 5 he wrote to Roosevelt, giving him a state-by-state progress report which showed thirteen states with complete organizations and most other states with at least a chairman. On October 16 MacNider reported that "We are actually organized now in forty states, thirty of which have real and intensive organizations. Of course this does not include the hopelessly Democratic south, nor the three or four northern commonwealths, which are so infested with Klan troubles that it seems best to defer our organization until after the election."[29]

Although technically the Republican Service League was a separate organization, it was always closely allied with the American Legion and quickly formed an alliance with the Republican Party. In July Roosevelt met with President Coolidge, who thought the League a "very excellent idea." At the same time, MacNider was meeting with William M. Butler, Chairman of the Republican Party, to solicit his support, and from Butler he received assurances that the organization would be taken care of when it established its headquarters in Chicago. From July on MacNider and Roosevelt were in almost daily contact, particularly about funding or, as MacNider put it, the need to "finance liberally the headquarters in those states which are considered unstable."[30] By election day the Republican National Committee had paid almost $2,500 for the League's office and travel and had advanced it another $15,000 for other uses.[31]

Throughout this period the League was also stretching the Legion's so-called nonpartisanship to the limit. MacNider and Roosevelt, after all, were prominent legionnaires, MacNider a past National Commander and Roosevelt the founder of the Legion. They were also the co-founders of the League; and however much they protested to the contrary, the League was in essence "an organization of Legionnaires who temporarily stepped out of that role into the protective nomenclature of the League in order to rally the Legion vote."[32]

This was a political force, moreover, that would soon be turned against the man who had won the Republican Party's nomination for United States Senator from Iowa. Curiously, the Republican Service League would be used to elect a Democrat, partly because the Republican incumbent was Smith Brookhart, and partly because the Democrat was a legionnaire with ties to the League's leaders, none of whom could abide what they perceived as Brookhart's pro-Russian sympathies.

It is not clear who made the suggestion to Dan Steck that he run for United States Senator. But on March 21, 1924, he wrote to MacNider about the suggestion and asked for his "frank, open reaction." MacNider was not optimistic. The chances were not good, he thought, of getting "many people in such a solid Republican state to wander across the column." But he acknowledged the problems that he and the regular Republicans were having and encouraged Steck to seek the Democratic nomination "if you intend to stay with that party."[33]

Steck left no doubt concerning where his loyalties were. On March 25 he wrote to MacNider: "I am not a party man in the ordinary sense of the term, and am ready to become a MacNider Republican any time you see fit to step forth."[34]

On April 5, following the Democratic State Convention, Steck announced his candidacy and sent notice to Frank Miles, the temporary chairman of the convention and editor of the *Iowa Legionnaire*. Six days later MacNider invited Steck to a large American Legion post meeting in Mason City. "The boys," he thought, "would be tremendously interested in seeing and hearing" from him.[35]

In the resulting contest, Steck won the nomination with 38 percent of the 54,694 votes cast. MacNider was pleased. Writing to Steck on June 6, he expressed the belief that "if the proper organization was built up and enough money could be raised for publicity that you could give old man Brookhart a race for his life."[36]

On September 18 Louis Fay, publisher of *Fay's Democrat*, Clinton, Iowa, reported that he had never seen "party lines . . . more loosely drawn than they are this season." The next month the *New York Times* said that:

> Politics in Iowa is what Hugh Latimer and Mayor Gatnor would call "mishmash." Senator Brookhart, renominated in the Republican primary, is going up and down the state denouncing Mr. Coolidge as the candidate of the "Wall Street bloc." Members of the Old Guard are supporting the Democratic nominee for senator whom, for various reasons, considerable numbers of Democrats reject. Mr. Brookhart is a thorough La Follettian but technically a regular Republican. He called for the withdrawal of General Dawes from the Republican ticket. The Republican State Committee, whose thunder seems to make the Iowans laugh, "read him out of the party." Things looked very bad to the Republicans.[37]

Speculation that Brookhart might join La Follette, who with his running mate Senator Burton Wheeler was a Progressive Party candidate for President, had been strongly denied. Roy Rankin had called it "an absolute lie made out of the whole cloth," and Brookhart had denied that a rumored meeting on a third party had ever taken place. But Iowa Republicans remained unconvinced, some feeling certain that Brookhart would at least endorse the La Follette candidacy.[38]

As the summer ended, however, Brookhart had refused to endorse either La Follette or Coolidge, preferring, as the *New York Times* commented, to stay on the fence "until the drear days of November come." In outlook, the *New York Times* noted, he seemed more "La Follettian" than La Follette himself. And, as Rawson noted, many Brookhart supporters were pro-La Follette and "the kind of speeches [Brookhart] is making are similar to those La Follette makes." But, as Rawson also put it, the senator was "pretty sure of re-election" and remaining atop the political fence seemed to be a winning strategy.[39]

It took Luther Brewer, a long-time Republican newspaper publisher from

Cedar Rapids, to knock Brookhart off the fence. On September 24 Brewer announced his candidacy for the United States Senate and in the announcement declared: "I am a Republican who believes in President Coolidge . . . a Republican who believes in the preservation of the Constitution, a Republican who has faith in Iowa and her people."[40]

Brewer's announcement took Burnquist and Rawson by surprise. They had not been consulted prior to the announcement, and neither thought that the state committee would endorse Brewer. Standpat Republicans were also caught by surprise. Henry C. Wallace said he thought that Brewer's candidacy was "not helpful." And James Lenihan wrote that the candidacy was "unpardonable." It made an issue which would not have existed, he wrote, "and gave an excuse to an all-too-willing Brookhart to jump the fence."[41]

Lenihan's worst fears were realized when Brookhart came home from Ohio, where he had been attending the annual rifle-shooting matches, and proceeded to abandon his lack of comment on the national ticket. Jumping off the fence, he landed with one foot squarely on Charles G. Dawes, calling him an "agent of international banking powers" and demanding his resignation from the ticket. Dawes, he said, "started out like a bold-faced plutogog but his discourtesy and ungentlemanly language quickly reduced him, in his own vocabulary, to a peewit plutogog." The attack produced what the *New York Times* called a "sensation." "The La Follette people," it reported, "were joyous. The Democrats were watching. The Republicans were silent."[42]

All were waiting for the other foot to land, with most expecting it to come down with an open endorsement of La Follette and Wheeler and an open attack on Coolidge. They were only half right. In Emmetsburg, Iowa, on October 3, Brookhart openly attacked the President and his policies, ticking off a litany of issues upon which they differed. "I belong to the farm bloc," he declared. "The President belongs to the Wall Street bloc."[43]

The expected endorsement of La Follette, however, did not come. Instead, Brookhart declared that he had "never thought of leaving the party," that his whole soul was "wrapped up in the principles of Lincoln, Roosevelt, and Kenyon." He also restated his convention promise to "do as much for Coolidge as he would do for me."[44]

Nevertheless, the Republican State Committee wasted no time in declaring that Brookhart had "bolted" from the party. His speech, it said, constituted an attempt to take over the party machinery and become the dictator of Iowa politics. Formal support was now withdrawn, which in practical terms meant little. But the speech and the developments following it did provide a rallying point for Brookhart's diverse opponents. The regular Republicans, the Republican Service League, and the Democrats each tried to capitalize on the incident.

In the crowd at Emmetsburg, Ray Shoemaker, a lawyer from Rolfe, Iowa, managed to take a transcript of the speech and dispatch it to MacNider in Chicago. "I had a damn hard time taking it," Shoemaker told MacNider, "as I had to stand up all the time, several feet from the speaker, with a bunch of clodhoppers jostling me and yelling in my ear from time to time." The text was given to the speakers' bureau of the League, and two days later MacNider reported that he had also given it to Chairman Butler, who had it "firmly clenched in his hand when I left."[45]

In Iowa the Republican Service League also came up with a strategy that would prove important in defeating Brookhart. Many Republicans, it felt, would vote for Steck if they could be broken of their habit of voting a straight Republican ticket. And to educate them, it proposed using sample ballots that showed an "X" in the circle at the top of the Republican column and an "X" in the square beside Dan Steck's name on the Democratic ticket. The idea came initially from Harry F. Lee, a friend of MacNider's in Mason City. Writing on October 24, he expressed the belief that "if this sample ballot marked as I have marked it and with simple instructions is broadcasted over Iowa through the press to those who cannot read or write but do vote and those who read and write but possess an unacknowledged ignorance, it will do the trick."[46]

Lee's sample ballot was disseminated by the League throughout Iowa. *The Evening Gazette* in Cedar Rapids ran it on the front page on October 27, and again on November 1 and 3. It was also used as a poster and appeared wherever Republicans might gather. MacNider wrote Lee, "It is a splendid idea and I hope it does the trick."[47]

Meanwhile, on October 10, Luther Brewer had withdrawn. His campaign had consisted almost entirely of the speech announcing his candidacy. But he had done what he set out to do. Brookhart had been pushed off the fence, and in Brewer's withdrawal statement Iowa Republicans had been urged to vote for Steck.

Luther Brewer's withdrawal statement seems to have taken on two forms. One was very formal and had wide distribution throughout the state. The other was reprinted in the *Journal* and seems to have been tailored for Brookhart's hometown audience:

> I could not as a loyal Republican stand by while a political "coon" was menacing our party. When I saw that nobody else would do anything about it, I announced my candidacy in order to smoke the "coon" out where all good political dogs could see him as I saw him. Nobody told me to do it, and nobody asked me to do it. Now the radical who runs with La Follette to undermine our courts and bring about business stagnation by government

ownership of railroads, like the coon dog down among the trees in the swamp, has been smoked out. Every Republican in Iowa today knows that Brookhart is the same political varmint that I have said he was, and we Republicans of Iowa stand united, like the hounds, in our desire to rid our premises of his presence. Therefore, I ask my Republican friends all over the state to "sic 'em Steck."[48]

Brewer's role in the campaign was summed up by Jim Farquhar, who had purchased the *Cedar Rapids Republican* from Brewer two years earlier:

From a campaign marked by complete stagnation insofar as anti-Brookhart sentiment was concerned, to a militant fighting opposition, was the aftermath of Brewer's entry into the fracas. . . . Brookhart's smoldering resentment burst forth in his ultimatum demanding the withdrawal of Vice Presidential Candidate Dawes and his attack on Coolidge.[49]

As for Steck, he campaigned hard. Again and again he linked La Follette and Brookhart. At the same time, he questioned Brookhart's patriotism, and referring to Brookhart and the Republican Party he labeled the senator a traitor. Democrats, he urged, should seize this rare opportunity to win in Iowa.

Still, on November 2 the *Des Moines Register*'s political analyst, C. C. Clifton, wrote: "There is little doubt Senator Brookhart will be re-elected." And while Brookhart seemed "hoarse and tired" from the hard campaigning of the past month, he was also exuding confidence. His wife, to be sure, seemed to have some doubts. Writing her son on October 22, she had said that the Senator's job was probably safe, "until March 4, at any rate." But doubt was hardly the mood among those at the campaign final event, an election eve rally at the Graham Theater.[50]

For several days it was unclear as to who had the lead. On the morning of November 6, two days after the election, the *Register* proclaimed that Steck had won by 4,000 votes. Brookhart conceded defeat, and Steck then issued a victory statement declaring that he owed the election to "loyal Democrats, Republicans who place ideals above party fealty, and service men of all parties." Subsequent returns, however, changed the count, and the next morning the *Register* had Brookhart with a 1,116 vote lead.[51]

Since it was apparent that there would be a recount, Clyde L. Herring, Democratic National Committeeman, moved quickly to ensure that ballots and machines would not be tampered with. He also called a strategy meeting in his office, bringing together George Huffman, state Democratic organizer, Claude R. Porter, whom Cummins had defeated in 1920, and Edwin T. Meredith, former Secretary of Agriculture. Others, too, were concerned, and before the meeting ended a "peculiar drama was enacted." Into the group, "arm in arm," walked the Polk County Republican and Democratic Chairmen, "both pulling for the election of Steck and both anxious to have all ballots safeguarded in Steck's interest."⁵²

As the recount progressed the state and country were kept apprised of the results: November 8, "Brookhart Faces Contest"; November 11, "Brookhart's Lead Now 743"; November 12, "Brookhart's Majority Cut to 649"; November 13, "Brookhart's Lead Rises to 650." On November 24 the recount ended, with Brookhart now leading Steck by 755 votes out of almost 900,000 cast. Accordingly, Brookhart was declared the winner and awarded a certificate of election by the State of Iowa.⁵³

In all, Brookhart had carried sixty-one counties but had received only 50.04 percent of the vote. He had done well in the northwestern and north central sections of the state, his two traditional strong areas, and fairly well in the south central counties. But he had lost almost all of the eastern third of the state, including all of the First District; and of the major urban counties, he had carried only Polk and Woodbury. He had even lost in Washington County by over 600 votes. "Daddy surely got a jolt for his bolt," said Jennie, "lost this county bad, a sadder but a wiser man. . . . I think the Colonel has learned a lesson about being *so certain*."⁵⁴

Another Washingtonian, Brookhart's old adversary Charles J. Wilson, rejoiced in Brookhart's situation. Writing to congratulate the newly elected Second District Congressman F. Dickinson Letts, Wilson noted that Brookhart lost the city and the county. Wilson said that "the whole senatorial situation can be summed up in the statement that Brookhart's perfidy has met with a very appropriate rebuke."⁵⁵

What had happened to Brookhart's big majority? The simple truth was that he had talked himself out of it. The voters of Iowa, especially the farm voters, were willing to put up with a lot. But attacking the President of the United States in the way Brookhart had done was too much. As C. C. Clifton wrote in the *Register*, Republican voters were inclined to "rise up in indignation against a defamer." And years later Cyrenus Cole wrote: "If Senator Brookhart had not made his speech at Emmetsburg, he would have led the ticket."⁵⁶

In addition, some voters seemed to resent his efforts to be both a Republican and a La Follette Progressive. As Louis H. Cook, Brookhart's friend and confidant, put it:

> There are all kinds of Republicans in Iowa, and a candidate is perfectly safe as long as he can be classified as any one of them. Up to this time, Brookhart had been nominally a Republican. He had tweaked the elephant's tail, dropped cigarette stubs into his ears, and wielded a wicked goad. When, however, he sought to straddle the G.O.P. elephant and the new

progressive hybrid, he took a bad fall.[57]

As the senators began gathering in Washington for the second session of the Sixty-Eighth Congress, speculation was rife about whether Brookhart and the other progressives who had supported the La Follette presidential candidacy would be allowed to take their places in the Senate Republican Conference and retain their committee assignments. One Iowan told Cummins that he hoped the Senate kept Brookhart out of the Conference. But Cummins thought that it made little difference since Brookhart had "never attended anyway."[58]

On November 28 some thirty-four Republican senators (seventeen were absent, including Brookhart) met to decide the question. Heading the efforts at exclusion was Senator David Reed of Pennsylvania, who offered a motion that "it is the sense of the conference that Senators La Follette, Ladd, Brookhart and Frazier be not invited to future Republican Conferences, and be not named to fill any Republican vacancies of Senate Committees." Senator Richard Ernst of Kentucky tried to get this softened. Under his proposed amendment, the senators in question would forfeit "all claims or rights to recognition" as Republicans, "all priority" as Republican members of committees on which they were currently serving, and any "future assignments to any committees of the Senate." But his amendment was defeated. And after an effort to strike the names of Brookhart, Ladd, and Frazier was also defeated, the Reed motion was divided into two parts and each was carried.[59]

In practice the ouster probably did not affect Brookhart very much. He had little seniority in the Senate (at the beginning of the session he was seventy-fourth in seniority), and none of his committee assignments were on major committees. He was, moreover, not a committee man and made no effort to work through the committee structure. And as for the conference, he had, as Cummins noted, never attended. It met thirty-four times during his eleven years in the senate. But not once was he in attendance. Only Senators Robert La Follette, Senior and Junior, equalled that record.[60]

The Republicans also had one other "punishment" for Brookhart, and that was implemented when President Coolidge announced that he would no longer consult the senator for patronage recommendations. Here again, though, the action meant little since it had been rare for either Coolidge or Harding to consult Brookhart anyway. They had worked instead through Cummins or through one of the Iowa House members.[61]

Even before Brookhart had been issued his certificate of election, preparations were underway to contest the results in the Senate. On November 11, W. T. Cozad, a Shenandoah banker and Page County Chairman of the Republican Service League, wrote to MacNider arguing that it was the League's "duty" to assist Steck "out in the open." He would, he said, help to raise money in his district. Two days later MacNider indicated that he was willing to work for Steck "in any way possible." And by November 15, C. B. Robbins, State Chairman of the League, could declare that, "we are going slam-bang in the Steck-Brookhart contest which is going to take a lot of money."[62]

Money in fact was critical, since Steck was not wealthy and had been campaigning for six months during which he had given little attention to his law practice. In January 1925 he wrote to MacNider, asking for $500 to finance his attorney's trip to Washington, D.C. Subsequently, the attorney, James Parsons, wrote to say that $20,000 would be needed to complete the contest successfully. And by November Steck was again asking for money. At Hanford MacNider's invitation, he wrote C. H. McNider, Hanford's father, asking for another $750.[63]

Just how much the Republican Service League contributed is difficult to ascertain. But it must not have been as great as MacNider had hoped. On June 10, he wrote Steck that he was having difficulty getting funds in Iowa and would have to go to Chicago. There he had previously succeeded in obtaining a $1,000 donation from Ralph Van Vechten, Vice-President of the Continental and Commercial National Bank, and Steck himself had some successful solicitations. He had called on W. W. Baldwin, General Solicitor of the Chicago, Burlington, and Quincy Railroad, had been warmly received, and had been assured that Baldwin and others would like to contribute.[64]

Meanwhile, the Senate Committee on Privileges and Elections had created a special subcommittee to consider the Brookhart-Steck contest. Chaired by Senator Richard P. Ernst (Republican, Kentucky), it also included Senators James E. Watson (Republican, Indiana), Walter F. George (Democrat, Georgia), and Thaddeus H. Caraway (Democrat, Arkansas). All were present at its first meeting on July 20, 1925, but the meeting lasted only long enough to order that a recount be taken of all the ballots. "Many ballots," the subcommittee decided, "were rejected . . . on the illegal and fraudulent pretext that they bore distinguishing marks." And prominent among these were the so-called "arrow ballots," created when numerous voters had literally reproduced the arrows that some of the newspapers had drawn from the Republican side of sample ballots to Steck's name. During the official canvass in Iowa these ballots had not been allowed, the Attorney General having ruled that Iowa law forbade any identification mark on the ballot.[65]

The counters then examined each of the 900,000 ballots cast, seeking, as instructed by the committee, to ascertain the intent of the voter. This meant that they ignored the Iowa law about distinguishing marks. The "arrow ballots" were now counted for Steck since that was what the voters had intended.

In its report to the full Senate the committee claimed that it had "arrived at a decision on each ballot without any reference whatever to the total." It had not invoked any "technical rule" and had waived "every irregularity seeking only to give effect to the voter's intent." The result was:

	Brookhart	Steck
Agreed good votes (supervisors and attorneys)	443,831	449,107
Votes ruled good by committee	4,918	1,062
Total	448,749	450,169
Steck Plurality		1,420[66]

Thus, the committee declared that Smith W. Brookhart was not elected in 1924 and that Daniel F. Steck was elected and was therefore entitled to a seat in the United States Senate from Iowa.

While the counters and the committee had spent the summer and fall doing their job, Hanford MacNider had been busy pleading Steck's case. As early as February, he had been in Washington calling on senators. And following his appointment as Assistant Secretary of War in the fall of 1925, he had acquired a privileged platform from which to operate. In early September he wrote Steck, "Those closest to the President know what kind of a fellow you are because I have made it a point to see that they did."[67]

This seems to have been particularly true of Everett Sanders, Coolidge's Secretary, and of Senator William M. Butler, who had been Coolidge's primary campaign manager and had later been tapped by the President to be Republican Party Chairman. From the beginning Butler and MacNider had worked well together, the latter considering it a "privilege to serve with Chairman Butler." And this continued to be the case. When Butler was appointed to the Senate in November 1924, filling the vacancy created by the death of Henry Cabot Lodge and becoming, in the words of William Allen White, the President's "vice-gerent," Steck and MacNider were concerned that he would continue to be a valuable ally. "It is my opinion," MacNider wrote Steck, "that if it comes to a contest on the floor of the Senate, that the administration's wishes will prevail, and that Senator Butler speaks for the administration."[68]

At the same time, the Republican Service League was working on Senator Cummins, responding in particular to Steck's calls for letters from Iowa. Writing to the Senator in December 1925, Charles B. Robbins indicated that the 100,000 men and women of the Republican Service League in Iowa wanted Steck seated and would "resent" any political expediency in favor of Brookhart. And in February 1926, following MacNider's request for a "barrage" from Iowa, the campaign was stepped up. Robbins wrote on behalf of the Republican Service League of the Second District. Cozad wrote from Shenandoah. Other letters arrived from various parts of the state.[69]

Cummins, though, was in a delicate situation. He was up for re-election in the June 1926 primary, and it was well known that if Brookhart was unseated he would be a candidate in the primary. Hence, a vote to seat would appear as an effort to avoid facing Brookhart. A vote to unseat, on the other hand, could be interpreted as vindictive. Nor could Cummins, as some suggested, allow the matter to be delayed in the Senate beyond the filing date for the primary. This, too, would appear as though Cummins were afraid to face Brookhart.

To Cummins neutrality seemed the best course to follow. As early as February 1925 he had taken the position that the contest was a judicial question requiring a determination based on the facts, and time and again he was forced to explain this position. As he told *Gazette* editor Verne Marshall, in January 1926, he was having trouble making either friends or enemies believe that he was "a reasonable, honest man." Still, he thought, the matter ought to be settled according to the facts, whatever the consequences. He intended, at least, to have the approval of his "own conscience."[70]

Cummins also replied in a similar vein to the February barrage of letters that Steck had arranged. And on April 11, 1926, the day before the final vote, he reiterated his position to Ed Kelly, a Des Moines lawyer and longtime Cummins confidant. So far, he declared, he had not exerted any influence on any senator, and he did not intend to do so. He had concluded that he "could not pursue any other course without losing my self-respect and that is infinitely more important to me than anything else."[71]

While Steck needed Republican votes if he was to unseat Brookhart (when Congress opened in January 1926 there were 56 Republicans, 39 Democrats, and 1 Farmer-Labor), he could not appear to be too Republican or he would lose the Democrats. Nor could the possibility of Brookhart's winning Democratic support be ruled out. Many of the Democrats, so MacNider noted, would have been only "too happy to leave Brookhart as a thorn in the side of the Republican majority."[72]

Accordingly, Steck tried to protect his Democratic flank with Edwin T. Meredith, a Des Moines businessman and publisher of *Successful Farming*, who had served as Wilson's Secretary of Agriculture and who regarded himself as a "Democrat, a progressive, and a supporter of prohibition." In March, Steck wrote to Meredith asking him to contact Senators Thomas J. Walsh (Democrat, Montana), William H. King (Democrat, Utah), Matthew M. Neely (Democrat, West Virginia), Ellison DuRant Smith (Democrat, South Carolina), and Huburt D. Stephens (Democrat, Mississippi). All but Walsh were members of the Committee on Privileges and Elections. And Walsh, he felt, should be contacted because he had been critical of Steck, intimating that he was not a good Democrat. This had been a problem ever since Steck, in a speech given at Burlington, Iowa, had criticized Brookhart's handling of the investigation of Attorney General Harry Daugherty and had thereby seemed to Walsh and other Democrats to be showing too much sympathy for the Republicans.[73]

Meredith responded to Steck's request in two parts. On March 19 he sent telegrams to the senators that Steck had named, except for Walsh, and also to Senators Joseph T. Robinson (Democrat, Arkansas), Pat Harrison (Democrat, Mississippi), Claude A. Swanson (Democrat, Virginia), Andrieus Aristieus Jones (Democrat, New Mexico), and Furnifold McLendel Simmons (Democrat, North Carolina). Steck, he assured his correspondents, would be a credit to Iowa and to the Democratic Party. At the same time, he sent a long letter to Walsh praising Steck and trying to explain the latter's remarks concerning the Daugherty investigation. In the end Stephens and Walsh voted for Brookhart; the others voted against him.[74]

On March 27 the Committee on Privileges and Elections reported out the resolution, and on April 5 the Senate began floor debate. "We are going to have a smashing couple of weeks here," Progressive Republican Senator Hiram Johnson (California) wrote his son in late March, "First, we'll have the Brookhart election contest, in which I have the suspicion. . . . that a combination of old line Republicans and partisan Democrats is jobbing Brookhart." Johnson thought that Brookhart had been "so independent of the Republican powers that they would be very glad to be rid of him."[75]

But the seating of Steck by the full Senate was by no means certain, especially since Senator Butler and the regular Republicans were fearful that seating Steck would lead Brookhart to enter the Iowa primary, where he might well defeat Cummins and bring about a replay of 1924. If he were nominated, the regular Republicans would then align themselves with the Democrats and elect another Democrat from Iowa.

The debate revolved around the question of the intent of the voters versus the Iowa election laws. Senators Ernst and Caraway, speaking for the majority of the committee, argued that a majority of voters in Iowa clearly wanted Steck. As Ernst put it, their intention was evident, and therefore Iowa law about spoiled ballots ought to be set aside. Senator Stephens, on the other hand, argued for the right of a state to govern itself. This was also the view taken by Senator Coleman L. Blease (Democrat, South Carolina). He was concerned, he said, about setting a "dangerous precedent."⁷⁶

Meanwhile, Hanford MacNider was busy lobbying for Steck, building, as he said, "little bonfires wherever possible." In late March, he had been "as nervous as a witch about the outcome." MacNider's anxiety increased as the days passed. Writing Robbins on April 1 he said, "Dan's case comes before the Senate today and I am shivering like a dog full of fish hooks." Then later that day when it was delayed again he added, "Tomorrow they say now—perhaps Monday—Damn 'em."⁷⁷

MacNider had decided to concentrate particularly on Senator Butler. Arrangements were made for "numerous" telegrams, and by Wednesday, April 7, Butler was beginning to waver in his support of Brookhart. His weakening stance, when coupled with MacNider's activities as a member of the administration, lent considerable credence to the rumors that the President himself wanted Brookhart unseated.⁷⁸

During most of the week of the debate, MacNider was out of Washington. But returning on April 9, he quickly went to Capitol Hill and proceeded to light more "bonfires." He spent Saturday, April 10, in the Senate lobby talking with senators and urging them to vote for Steck. It was known he talked with Senators David A. Reed (Republican, Pennsylvania), George H. Moses (Republican, New Hampshire), Porter H. Dale (Republican, Vermont), Frank B. Willis (Republican, Ohio), Simeon D. Fess (Republican, Ohio), as well as Butler. By this time the Iowa Democratic and Republican organizations had also come out for Steck. So had the Ku Klux Klan. It is unlikely, however, that Steck welcomed the Klan's endorsement. The previous summer when they had offered to finance the contest, he turned them down.⁷⁹

Under the rules adopted, the Senate was to close debate and vote at 5:00 P.M. on Monday, April 12, and by mid afternoon of that day the galleries were filled. Among the Iowans present were Hanford MacNider, his wife, and E. J. Feuling, Iowa Democratic State Chairman. The action was frantic. As MacNider later described it to Verne Marshall: "At 3 o'clock we were two down; at 3:30 one up; at 4:00 one down and, just before the vote, we thought we were two up. Three men changed their vote on the floor, from what they had told us in advance. We nearly all had heart failure before it was over."⁸⁰

The final vote was 45 for Steck, 41 for Brookhart. Sixteen Republicans, including Butler, Ernst, and Watson, joined twenty-nine Democrats to vote for Steck. Brookhart had thirty-one Republicans, nine Democrats, and the one Farmer-Laborite, Henrik Shipstead of Minnesota. Neither Brookhart nor Cummins participated in the debate, and neither voted.

Hiram Johnson had been correct in his assessment about the old line Republicans. Writing his son after the vote Johnson said that a "very remarkable combination" of "the Republican National Committee, the Democratic organization and the Ku Klux Klan" unseated Brookhart. Johnson continued with his account of the last hours before the vote:

> In spite of Butler, Chairman of the National Committee, [Colorado Republican Lawrence C.] Phipps, the Chairman of the Senatorial National Committee, the Republican members of the Elections Committee, which had rendered a decision against him, we had thirty-one Republican votes in his favor, but, at the last moment, two, who had promised him, and two Democrats who had promised him, were taken from us, with the result of seating his opponent. I think it was unjust and an unfair decision.

As for the future Johnson was not clear whether Brookhart was "dead politically" or "whether the wrong done him will arouse the resentment of his people."[81]

Steck was waiting close by, and almost immediately after the vote he was escorted down the aisle by Senator Cummins and sworn in by Vice-President Dawes. Within the hour Robbins telegraphed MacNider, "Three rousing cheers. News just came. You are the man who put it over." Others were equally enthusiastic, with MacNider being credited for a "truly wonderful victory." He was thanked and congratulated on his efforts "to retire Mr. Brookhart from the Senate." And from E. J. Feuling came the most effusive letter: "I appreciate . . . the most effective help you gave to the cause. . . . May I say, Jack, that I love you, and I am for you all over, yes 100 percent . . . in fact you are the salt of the earth." MacNider assured Feuling that he would "gladly do the whole thing over again . . . for old man Steck."[82]

Other observers echoed the opinion of MacNider's correspondents about his role in the contest. Ed Kelly wrote Cummins that the Legion in Iowa was "pretty loud in its protest" against Brookhart's being seated; and Butler and the Republican National Committee, he noted, had encouraged the Legion's opposition and "actually furnished the money." Similarly, in its explanation of what had happened, the *Register* concluded "that the President was reached effectively from Iowa, under the leadership of Hanford MacNider, and he being convinced that Brookhart ought not to be seated, the New England group led by Butler joined the Steck forces."[83]

There is no doubt that Smith Brookhart won the election in 1924. The first count of the vote showed that he did, and this was reaffirmed by the official canvass following the election. Brookhart received a certificate of election from the state of Iowa, and for most electees this would have been enough.

Why, then, did the United States Senate vote to unseat Brookhart? The answer lies almost solely in the efforts of Hanford MacNider, the American Legion, and the Republican Service League. For the record the Legion maintained its position of non-partisanship. In an editorial following the vote, the *Iowa Legionnaire*, the official publication of the Iowa Department, took exception to an International News Service story that attributed Steck's success to three causes, one being MacNider and his ability "to bring American Legion pressure against the Iowa insurgent." The editorial went on to restate that political activity was prohibited by the constitution of the American Legion. It argued further that one Legion post had supported Brookhart thus proving that the Legion was not mobilized against him.[84]

These denials aside, it is clear that the American Legion posts throughout the country played a role in lobbying for the defeat of Brookhart. Two Brookhart supporters, George Norris (Republican, Nebraska) and Hubert D. Stephens (Democrat, Mississippi), later agreed it was a "matter of general knowledge in the Senate" that legionnaires in many states were contacting their senators to vote against Brookhart. According to later reports from the Senate, two senators, "convinced by the reports and the debate that Brookhart" had "been elected and should [have been] seated," bowed to the pressure from American Legion officials in their states and voted for Steck.[85] There were other groups who wanted Brookhart out, and both political parties in Iowa joined in an effort to oust him. But the guiding force was MacNider. As has been shown, the leaders of the League of Iowa—Robbins, Halligan, Cozad, and others—did little without informing MacNider or first checking it with him. It was MacNider who raised money, and it was MacNider who kept the White House informed.

In Washington MacNider dealt frequently with Senator Butler, and in all probability it was these dealings that explain Butler's change of mind during the senatorial debate. The sequence of relationships between MacNider, Coolidge, and Butler cannot be completely documented, but enough is known to arrive at some preliminary conclusions. Clearly, Brookhart's continuing presence in the Senate was a source of irritation for the President. Even before the Emmetsburg speech there had been little empathy between the two men, and despite the President's pose of disdain about such things, he was, as one biographer put it, "no innocent" when it came to playing the political game. He was undoubtedly receptive when MacNider used his position in the administration to press the case for Steck, and preceding Butler's change of position there were talks between the President and his "spokesman in the Senate." As would be expected, both men subsequently issued statements denying presidential interference. But circumstantial evidence clearly indicates White House intervention with Butler and a role for MacNider in bringing this about.[86]

MacNider had scored only a Pyrrhic victory, however, because Smith Brookhart was down but far from out. The "mish-mash" of 1924 had now become even more confused, and the twisted path of Iowa politics took still another turn as former Senator Brookhart packed his bags to return to Iowa and run in the June primary against Albert Cummins.

First law office in Washington, Iowa, with partner Jackson Roberts outside, c. 1895. This is the base from which Brookhart first ran for public office as county attorney. *Courtesy, John Yount.*

Brookhart with his political aide, Byron Allen (*right*) outside his law office, c. 1930. *Courtesy, John Yount*

Brookhart with his valued, if not always listened-to, campaign manager Frank Lund, in Webster City.

Smith goes to Washington, on the Capitol steps, 1922. *Courtesy, John Yount.*

"Iowa is yours," says Fighting Bob. "I return the compliment," says the Colonel. Senator Brookhart met Bob La Follette in Des Moines, October 15, 1924. *Des Moines Register* photograph. *Courtesy, State Historical Society of Iowa.*

Senator Brookhart welcomes presidential nominee Herbert Hoover at Hoover's West Branch birthplace, Aug. 21, 1928. *Des Moines Register* photograph. *Courtesy, John Yount.*

Although his clenched-teeth style made Brookhart a poor public speaker, he was an early advocate of radio for political campaigns, c. 1928. *Courtesy, John Yount.*

"Impossible Interviews," Senator Smith W. Brookhart vs. Marlene Dietrich, from *Vanity Fair*, September 1932. Senator Brookhart had urged a Senate investigation of the morals of the movie industry. *Courtesy, Harry Ranson, Humanities Research Center, The University of Texas at Austin.*

How To Vote a "Scratched" Ballot

⊠ **Republican**   ◯ **Democratic**

Republican	Democratic
☐ FOR PRESIDENT CALVIN COOLIDGE of Massachusetts	☐ FOR PRESIDENT JOHN W. DAVIS of New York
☐ FOR VICE PRESIDENT CHARLES G. DAWES of Illinois	☐ FOR VICE PRESIDENT CHARLES W. BRYAN of Nebraska
☐ FOR UNITED STATES SENATOR SMITH W. BROOKHART of Washington, Washington County	☒ FOR UNITED STATES SENATOR DANIEL F. STECK of Ottumwa, Wapello County
☐ FOR GOVERNOR JOHN HAMMILL of Britt, Hancock County	☐ FOR GOVERNOR JAMES C. MURTAGH of Waterloo, Black Hawk County
☐ FOR LIEUTENANT GOVERNOR CLEM F. KIMBALL Council Bluffs, Pottawattamie Co.	☐ FOR LIEUTENANT GOVERNOR L. W. HOUSEL of Humboldt, Humboldt County
☐ FOR SECRETARY OF STATE WALTER C. RAMSAY of Belmond, Wright County	☐ FOR SECRETARY OF STATE MAUDE LAUDERDALE of Ft. Dodge, Webster County
☐ FOR AUDITOR OF STATE J. C. McCLUNE of Oskaloosa, Mahaska County	☐ FOR AUDITOR OF STATE E. T. LIKES of Des Moines, Polk County
☐ FOR TREASURER OF STATE RAY E. JOHNSON of Muscatine, Muscatine County	☐ FOR TREASURER OF STATE EDWARD MacDONALD of Coon Rapids, Carroll County
☐ FOR ATTORNEY GENERAL BEN J. GIBSON of Corning, Adams County	☐ FOR ATTORNEY GENERAL M. F. DONEGAN of Davenport, Scott County
☐ FOR SECRETARY OF AGRICULTURE MARK G. THORNBURG of Emmetsburg, Palo Alto County	FOR SECRETARY OF AGRICULTURE
☐ FOR RAILROAD COMMISSIONER B. M. RICHARDSON of Cedar Rapids, Linn County	☐ FOR RAILROAD COMMISSIONER B. B. BURCHETT of Bloomfield, Davis County
FOR JUDGE OF SUPREME COURT (To fill vacancy) ☐ C. W. VERMILION of Centerville, Appanoose County	FOR JUDGE OF SUPREME COURT (To fill vacancy) ☐ EDWIN C. WEBER of Ft. Madison, Lee County
FOR JUDGE OF SUPREME COURT (Vote for Two) ☐ B. G. ALBERT	FOR JUDGE OF SUPREME COURT (Vote for Two) ☐ DAN W. HAMILTON

Des Moines Register October 9, 1924

"Scratched" ballot circulated by the Republican Service League to show Iowans how to vote for Republican candiates, except Smith Brookhart. When the votes were counted, Brookhart won by 755 votes. A challenge was filed with the U.S. Senate, who ultimately overode Iowa law and counted the "arrow" ballots. The Senate then voted to unseat Brookhart.

Smith Wildman Brookhart, portrait taken for Edgar Harlan in 1923 for a bust that was never executed. The photo was part of a series that showed all sides of Brookhart's head.
Courtesy, State Historical Society of Iowa, Des Moines.

Portrait by Boston artist C. Arnold Slade, 1930, shows a resigned Brookhart after his disillusionment with Hoover. The paper in his right hand proclaims "Cooperation." *Courtesy, State Historical Society of Iowa, Des Moines.*

Smith Brookhart leaving the A.A.A. ready to fight for American farmers. Washington, D.C.
Courtesy, State Historical Society of Iowa.

11

The Disrupter Victorious

In Washington, Iowa, the *Journal* expressed "keen" disappointment over the unseating of Smith Brookhart, yet it saw no reason for "commiseration," since he had always been a man to map his own course. From his brief Senate experience, it thought, he would come "smiling and ready for the next battle," with "no disposition to admit that he was in the 'has been' class yet."[1]

Indeed not! After his loss in 1910 Brookhart had assured Senator Dolliver that he was grinding his axe for the next battle. Now he was back at the grindstone preparing for the coming primary election.

In Washington, D.C., Brookhart remained only long enough to pack a suitcase and catch a train home. Arriving at 12:30 on the morning of April 15, 1926, he was given an "enthusiastic welcome" by over 400 people. "Iowa," he told them, "has no senator now. Wall Street has one and Daugherty and MacNider have the other. If Iowa wants a senator I am willing to run for nomination."[2]

After a short night's rest Brookhart went to his office to read through the many telegrams of support and to look over nomination petitions that his Washington County supporters had already filled out. Late the same day he left for Des Moines. But before leaving he announced that he would open his campaign with a speech at the Graham Theater on April 17.

Two days later, then, a good-sized crowd gathered at the Graham, where Brookhart was introduced by the Rev. Carl W. Klein and the theme for the campaign was set. The primary, Klein said, would determine whether senators from Iowa would be "chosen under state laws or in an arbitrary way by the Senate." Brookhart agreed and went on to discuss the continuing discrimination against agriculture, particularly in regard to railroad rates, credit, and tariffs. He also talked again about a farmer-controlled cooperative system. And closing his remarks by charging that Iowa newspapers had not told the truth about the farm situation, he insisted that "it always pays to tell the truth, even if you are kicked out of the United States Senate for it."[3]

On May 1 Brookhart set out on a speaking tour that would take him from Clear Lake to Red Oak to Keosauqua to Badger and many points between. But the one speech that created the most interest was on April 30, when he returned to Emmetsburg, the site of the disastrous 1924 speech attacking Coolidge. Speaking from the courthouse steps before a crowd estimated to number 10,000 people, Brookhart gave the same speech he had been giving elsewhere, thus disappointing those who had come expecting a stem-winder similar to what they had heard two years before. Knowing full well that he had talked himself out of office before, he had now moderated his rhetoric and was keeping to two main themes: the "combinations" against agriculture, and the right of Iowans to choose their own senator. What vitriol he expressed was occasionally directed at Cummins, but most of the time at MacNider.[4]

Cummins probably would not have run for reelection in 1926 if circumstances had been different. Writing to various correspondents in 1924, he had expressed concerns about his health and age, saying that he was determined not to spend the years of his "decadence, either physical or mental, in public office." And in August 1925, a visitor had reported the seventy-five-year-old Senator to be "feeble" and highly unlikely to "live out another term." Had he announced early on that he would not be a candidate, no one would have thought anything of it. But once the Brookhart matter had come to a head, he felt obligated, although "not very keen," to "make the fight." By mid-March he had decided to run and was soon trying to convince others that he was up to it. "I am very well," he told Charles J. Wilson on April 4, "better than I have been for a long time"; and he would not, he thought, need to go to Iowa. He felt "sure that my friends can do more than I could do for myself."[5]

As Cummins prepared for the campaign, Hanford MacNider renewed his attack on Brookhart. Invited by Senator Butler to speak in Boston, he used the occasion to call the man from Washington, Iowa, a "wild . . . ambitious gentleman . . . taking advantage of the drastic upheaval in the economic condition" to mouth nonsense about Russia and grossly exaggerate farm difficulties. Iowans, he said, should be grateful for the "strong, virile, unafraid" leadership that Butler had provided nationally. Thanks to him they could "hold up [their] heads again" as party members.[6]

MacNider, so Brookhart said the next day, was the son of the "greatest enemy" that Iowa agriculture had ever had. His father, C. H. McNider, had been a participant in the "secret meeting" in 1920 that had brought on the farm depression. He had been a member of a small group exercising more power than any comparable group in Russia. And Brookhart wondered if in sending Hanford to Boston, Cummins was endorsing what the elder McNider had done to deflate credit and farm prices.[7]

MacNider's response was to write a letter to the *Register* defending his father and saying that anyone who knew both him and Brookhart could judge who was better qualified to talk about agriculture and banking. Brookhart's move outside the Washington city limits, he added, had not made him the "God-chosen representative of all agriculture." It had been primarily for the purpose of escaping city taxes. And once again, he challenged Brookhart's Americanism, ending with a ringing endorsement of Cummins.[8]

Having seen the letter before it was published, Cummins had been dubious about it. It would have been better, he later confessed to Ed Kelly, not to have brought MacNider's father into the campaign. But, he added, "I could not suggest to him even remotely not to come to the defense of his father." Writing to MacNider two weeks after the letter's publication, he said it was the "best thing" in the campaign yet and hoped for "some more aggressive material."[9]

On May 5 Brookhart's campaign manager, Frank Lund, accused MacNider of trying to scare the public with the Russian bogey. He then challenged him to return to Iowa for a series of debates with Brookhart, something others had also been suggesting. But MacNider refused to do so, citing his desire, as a member of the administration to avoid an open breach of the President's refusal "to meddle in pre-primary affairs." At stake, he thought, was the future of the Republican Party in Iowa. But he wanted to avoid trouble with the administration so long as others could carry the campaign forward.[10]

Even if he could do no more publicly, MacNider was pleased with what he had already done, especially the letter defending his father. Its tone indicated the kind of response Brookhart had been eliciting throughout his career. It was also expressive of the frustrations MacNider and many others felt in the face of Brookhart's successes. And if he was blocked from making more public statements, he continued to have his say in private. Responding to a note congratulating him on his letter to the *Register*, he told insurance executive Frederick Hubbell:

> This business of Brookhart's continued cracking at my old man has gone as long as I could stand it. It has always been my father's feeling that he wasn't worth an answer, but [the *Register*] gave me a chance to slap him in the mouth and the opportunity was gladly embraced.[11]

Such activity, in fact, led some Republicans to suspect that MacNider himself had political ambitions and hoped, in particular, to become Cummins' successor as leader of the Iowa Republicans. Indeed, as some saw it, his success in unseating Brookhart had made him a natural for the role, especially if he could also engineer Brookhart's defeat in the primary.[12]

Other opponents of Brookhart resurrected the failure of the Farmers and Merchants Bank. In May a few disgruntled depositors published a pamphlet that alleged that Brookhart had received favored treatment by state banking authorities. They sent a copy to MacNider in the hope that it would become a campaign issue. Apparently MacNider ignored the letter and the bank was not an issue in the campaign of 1926.[13]

A copy was also sent to the "Sons of Smith Brookhart." Brookhart wrote a letter to the sender attempting to set the record straight. He said that the pamphlet had been prepared by a "malicious attorney for certain interests in Iowa" that fought him and that it was "false in every charge." In discussing the settlement that had been made with the depositors, Brookhart said that many had already been paid and that "others would be paid eventually." As far as is known this is the only time Brookhart ever spoke about the repayment of the depositors.[14]

Brookhart, in the meantime, continued his speaking tour across the state and continued to receive strong labor support. Iowa labor, said J. C. Lewis, was engaged in a last ditch effort to return Brookhart to the Senate; and again the periodical *Labor* published a special Brookhart issue. Events in Washington, D.C., also seemed to help him. There, Attorney General Harry Daugherty had been indicted, vindicating, so it seemed, Brookhart's work as chairman of the special investigating committee. There, too, the administration was doing its best to defeat a farm relief bill. And in the eyes of many Iowans, MacNider had become an instrument of presidential intervention in state and local affairs. Once denounced for his attack on Calvin Coolidge, Brookhart now became an instrument for those who would let the administration know of their discontent. As Mark Sullivan put it: "To those who are disgruntled Brookhart is not mere Brookhart, but is the symbol of the disgruntled to let the east know what Iowa thinks of it. . . . It is a fight of the Corn Belt against New England."[15]

Brookhart, though, had now lost one of his most prominent supporters. In 1924 Dante Pierce had continued to support him, perhaps out of respect for the ties between Brookhart and his father. But in January 1925, Pierce had written Cummins requesting an autographed picture for his office wall, and later in the year he had approached Charles Rawson for letters of introduction to prominent Republicans, including Senator William M. Butler. Pierce was now opposed to the McNary-Haugen Farm Relief Bill, and Rawson thought he would be "a real asset" for the Republican Party in the future. Writing to oil executive W. G. Skelly, he suggested that the *Homestead* be given some advertising business.[16]

Another Brookhart supporter, Warren S. Stone, was also gone now, having died the year before, and with him had gone one of Brookhart's principal sources of financial support. This last, however, was compensated for by money from the so-called Wheeler Defense Fund, originally set up to pay for the defense of Senator Wheeler when Daugherty's Justice Department charged him with improprieties in regard to Montana oil leases. When Wheeler was cleared, what remained of the fund (some 22 percent of that contributed) was returned to the donors. But along with the refunds had gone letters from Wheeler suggesting that the checks be endorsed to Brookhart's campaign. The Iowan, he said, was a poor but honest and courageous man whom the administration had helped to unseat as punishment for his part in the Daugherty investigation. In all, Brookhart told Mercer Johnston after the primary, the money received from this source had amounted to "nearly $2,000" and the letters from its donors had been the "heartiest" he had received.[17]

Throughout the campaign Cummins stayed in Washington, his only speech being delivered over a statewide radio hook-up. In it he attacked Brookhart by name, charging that his legislative record was nil and that his criticism of the Transportation Act was misinformed and unjustified. It was also permeated with an uneasy nervousness, indicating that Cummins did not like or trust the new medium. Apparently he found it difficult to believe he could speak in Washington, D.C., and actually be heard in Iowa. Moreover, the speech followed one by Brookhart, allowing listeners to note the sharp contrast between Cummins' feebleness and Brookhart's vigor.[18]

Cummins' performance in the primary prompted one of his old political foes, standpatter Arthur Francis Allen, to bemoan the passing of a political era. Writing to Judson Welliver, Allen reminisced about the days when "politics was interesting" and "nearly everyone was interested." Once, he recalled, the newspaper "seethed with politics," having it for "breakfast, lunch and dinner." But now the subject elicited little general interest and the newspapers had ceased being "political burden bearers." Although Brookhart was speaking all across the state, the newspapers were ignoring him, and no one seemed to "care even a little what [would] happen at the primary."[19]

Over 400,000 Iowans, however, cared enough to go to the polls on primary day, and almost half of them (49.46 percent) voted for Brookhart. Cummins received 32.52 percent, and three other candidates split the rest. Brookhart won in eighty-three counties; and except for the loss of Pottawattamie, Mills, and Fremont in extreme southwestern Iowa, he carried the entire western two-thirds of the state. As in previous primaries, he lost the east central counties.[20]

As the *Register* saw it, the voters were "blind with rage" over the farm relief issue and as a result had looked for the "biggest and hardest brick they could throw," finding it in the person of Smith Brookhart. A poll of thirty newspapers by the *Literary Digest* also showed that all but two believed that the major factors had been rural discontent and the resentment over Brookhart's unseating. Expressing the feeling of many Iowans, one Polk County farmer commented that "we sent Brookhart to Washington and we're going to send him back. We'll show the Senate that when we have sent a man down there we'll see to calling him home when we want him."[21]

Republican leaders tried to console Cummins. Writing to him, Rawson said, "I don't think any of us realized how sore the people were." And state chairman Burnquist tried to assure him that the "late unpleasantness in Iowa" was not a vote against him but rather a protest against the administration. Cummins knew very well what it was. Arriving in Des Moines in mid-July he said that the "farmer had a kick coming . . . and my defeat was the best way he could register that kick."[22]

In May, MacNider had written that he felt sorry for Cummins, describing him as a "bad example to any young American who wants to make public life his profession—unhappy, feeling that he had been unappreciated and almost penniless." But once the election was over the old senator seemed almost serene. "For myself a great load has fallen from my shoulders," he telegraphed his close friends, "and while I regret defeat, I am happier than I have been for weeks." He was "entirely ready to leave public life," he assured his grandson, and was "longing for a period . . . of peace and quiet" with his family.[23]

Brookhart spent the day after the election sorting through the "bushel or two" of telegrams that he had received. He was also in receipt of many speaking invitations. But these, he said, would have to wait. He was going to be out of town for several weeks. He then went to Des Moines to confer with his political associates, traveled on to Mason City for a speech, and left from there for Washington, D.C.[24]

Back in the nation's capital, Brookhart exercised the privilege of a former senator and sat in a desk on the senate floor. He was greeted warmly by many senators. But Albert Cummins, sitting just four desks away, refused to look at him. Displaying a wide grin, Brookhart told friends that "fighting in a good cause" was a "great tonic," adding that he had gained about ten pounds during the campaign. Soon he was back in Iowa, where Iowa Republicans were using the remaining weeks of June and the first weeks of July as a respite before gathering in Des Moines for the state convention.[25]

In June the Iowa Republican state committee had met to set the date for the convention but had decided to do nothing in regard to the fall campaign. The committee members were to go out of office at the convention; and since most of them were anti-Brookhart, they decided to do nothing and leave him to his own devices. Most were also convinced that he intended to take over the party. The announcement by Frank Lund that Brookhart only wanted a committee friendly to him and had no desire to control it did little to allay this concern.[26]

As delegates gathered in Des Moines, the Brookhart forces made no organized move to take over, although understandably some of his supporters were seeking seats on the state central committee. In their search for harmony, the Brookhart men also decided to leave the platform without a farm plank and thus avoid a choice between the McNary-Haugen Bill and the Coolidge administration's plan. Thinking perhaps of the future, both sides now seemed determined to avoid more rancor. If old hatchets were not buried, said *Register* political reporter C. C. Clifton, their "sharply tempered edges" were "for the time being . . . sheathed."[27]

In the end, it was difficult to tell which side won on the questions of the central committee and the platform. Fourteen of the twenty-two members of the new committee had served on the previous committee, and thirteen of them had signed the resolution initiating the Senate contest that cost Brookhart his seat. But all were now pledged to work for Brookhart in the fall election, and thus it could be said that Brookhart had won a slim victory. On the platform, however, his opponents seemed to come out slightly ahead. They gave up any mention of un-American radicalism. But the platform did endorse the Coolidge administration for its "wise and efficient conduct of the government in accordance with Republican principles."[28]

The most celebrated event at the convention was the keynote address, delivered by Dan Turner of Corning, a former state legislator and future governor. In it he attacked the administration for its failure to provide relief to agriculture, singling out Secretary of Agriculture William Jardine for particular censure. "We have been betrayed," he said, "in the house of our friends." Then, in what was clearly the most electric moment of the speech, Turner announced that he had no reservation about supporting Smith Brookhart for the Senate. "To defeat him now," he declared, "would be interpreted by the statesmen of the Atlantic seaboard as evidence of a division in Iowa on the vital question of stabilization of America's greatest industry."[29]

Having declared his support for Brookhart, Turner then went on to say that Iowans must stop begging and begin fighting. This was the theme of a ringing peroration:

When in this conflict, the call to surrender comes from New England, once the cradle of liberty, now sitting selfish and self-satisfied in the midst of her looms and her factories; when the call to surrender comes from New York and New Jersey and Delaware, once the tenting ground of the immortal continental armies, now sitting insolent and indifferent in the midst of their money bags; when the call to surrender comes from Pennsylvania, where center sacred memories of Independence Hall, of Valley Forge and Gettysburg, now sitting arrogant and ungrateful in the midst of her protected industries; when the call to surrender comes from those protected regions of our common country, Iowa answers—the middle west answers—"We have just begun to fight."[30]

It was a fighting speech and expressed the mood of most delegates far better than the platform did. Many delegates, in fact, said they would print the platform in the *Iowa Official Register* and run on Turner's speech.

This was certainly the attitude of Smith Brookhart, who was seated at the rear of the platform but not scheduled to speak. When he was finally persuaded to say a few words, he announced that he felt no need to give a speech since Turner had already delivered the one he would make. Besides, he said, he had come to conventions for six years with a prepared speech that he had never been allowed to give.

Six years ago I was defeated for Senator, and I couldn't even get inside the convention. Four years ago I was successful, and I was allowed in the last row on the floor. Two years ago I won out again, and was allowed to sit with my county convention that time. This year I won again, and here I am, up square on the platform—positive evidence of the slow but sure advance of civilization.[31]

As Brookhart concluded his remarks, Anita, Iowa, newspaperman Sherman Myers, described by the *Union Advocate* as a "standpatter of the pattiest type," shouted that there were "a few things the Republicans would like to know." The delegates, however, shouted Myers down, whereupon he stormed out of the hall yelling "damned anarchist!" over his shoulder as he left.[32]

Everything considered, the convention was a remarkable display of unity and probably marked the high point of Brookhart's "regular Republicanism." About the only statewide Republican leader not seen shaking his hand was Cummins, who did not attend the convention at all. Even the recently "regularized" Dante Pierce was forced to admit that the support of Brookhart by the convention marked the "termination of the party split . . . evident since Colonel Brookhart's first candidacy in 1920."[33]

Seemingly, Cummins' loss and absence from the convention freed delegates to put aside old quarrels and look ahead to the need for unified action in 1928. And if they were not all happy with Brookhart (Sherman Myers was not alone), most felt that barring another Emmetsburg, which no one honestly expected, they were going to have Brookhart for six years. Resigned to that fact, they went home feeling that everything was settled.

Then, on July 30, Albert Baird Cummins died; and with tributes pouring in, Iowa's political leaders gathered in Des Moines for the funeral. Brookhart attended and had earlier issued a statement about Cummins. "The greater part of my political life," he said, "was spent fighting side by side with Senator Cummins . . . [the] later disagreement between us will never wipe out the memories of those days. His picture hangs by the picture of Lincoln in my office where it has hung since the beginning of our acquaintance."[34]

Cummins' term still had seven months to go, and immediately there was talk of who would be selected to serve out the term. Under Iowa law the governor could appoint someone to serve until the next regular election, which in this case was only three months away. But the remaining four months, the "short term," as it came to be known, were to be served by an electee, which meant that the Republicans would have to hold another convention and nominate another senatorial candidate. Initially, there was confusion about whether the delegates who had already convened could do so again or whether new ones had to be elected. But this was cleared up when the attorney general ruled that the old delegates could sit.

Brookhart considered seeking the short-term nomination, but realized that the pro-Brookhart sentiments at the earlier convention were no guarantee that he could get a majority of the delegates to support such a bid. He also realized that making the bid and losing might well imperil his chances at the full term in the general election. Accordingly, he decided not to take a chance with a convention he knew to be filled with Cummins men, who, it seemed possible, might reject him in order to honor the memory of their dead hero.

Still, it was reported that friends of Brookhart planned to place his name in nomination. And while Brookhart refused to say anything about the matter, Frank Lund noted that Brookhart had a "plain mandate" to "get into the fight for farm relief as soon as possible." His chances also received a boost when Illinois Senator Charles S. Deneen of the Senate Campaign Committee and Senator Charles Curtis of Kansas, the Republican floor leader, came to Des Moines for Cummins' funeral, expressed concern that the Republicans might lose control of the Senate, and said that Brookhart should receive the short-term nomination. Deneen's vote against Brookhart in the Privileges and Elections Committee put special emphasis on his endorsement.[35]

On the other side, former Cummins confidant Ed Kelly said that to select Brookhart would be a "treason to the memory" of the late Senator. Even if

Republicans were no longer quarrelling with Brookhart, he thought it would be far better to choose someone that Cummins would have liked and supported. And there were several in that category, among them Rawson, Kenyon, Kendall, former Supreme Court Justice Scott Ladd, Henry A. Wallace, and Charles E. Hearst. For a time the most talked about candidate, by virtue of the support of Ed Kelly, was First District Committeewoman Martha McClure of Mt. Pleasant, described by a neighbor as a "woman among women [who] stands very high wherever she is." McClure, though, professed surprise at the possibility. "A telephone call last night was the first I knew about it," she said. And in the end, she was not among those whose names were formally considered by the convention.[36]

Meeting on August 6, the convention opened with an emotional tribute to Cummins, delivered by James B. Weaver, Jr. It then got down to the business at hand. Ten names were placed in nomination; and after the first ballot Smith Brookhart led with 368 votes, followed by Des Moines Judge Charles S. Bradshaw, a Cummins man, with 316, Burton Sweet with 249, and Sioux City attorney David W. Stewart with 213. By the third ballot Brookhart had gained seventeen votes, but many of Bradshaw's votes and most of Sweet's had switched to Stewart, giving him enough to emerge victorious.[37]

Stewart appeared to be the perfect compromise candidate. Although he had never run for office before and prior to arriving in Des Moines had never considered doing so, he had credentials appealing to both sides. He was among those in the American Legion who had supported Brookhart in 1924 and was therefore not regarded by Brookhart as a reactionary. And by party regulars he was seen as a young man (age thirty-nine) who could contribute to the party's future, especially with the added credential of a few months in the Senate. The day after the convention, Governor Hammill appointed him to serve out the time until the election; and if his election for the short term had ever been in doubt, it was no longer so when the Democrats decided not to field a candidate against him.[38]

The choice of Stewart received praise from all quarters. In MacNider's view, it was a "very happy solution," which could mean "a new deal for the immediate future"; in the eyes of fellow townsman A. F. Allen, Stewart was "an engaging young man" who would do well. Allen also noted, however, that "being young and inexperienced, he is not only modest but diffident, . . . embarrassed in trying to make a public address," and "rather dazed by the honor so unexpectedly thrust upon him." And as if to prove the point about inexperience, Stewart wrote to Rock Rapids editor John W. Carey telling him how gratifying it was to know that the nomination had come "without any scheming or trading, but merely as a spontaneous action of the convention."[39]

Against Brookhart the Democrats ran perennial candidate Claude R. Porter, who, as Steck had done earlier, attacked Brookhart for his radicalism. In his speech to the Democratic convention, he had declared that "America, the people, will solve every problem and conquer every foe, and it will not be necessary for us to model our economic life after the example of any European country or take lessons in government from Russia." Despite such rhetoric, however, Porter's campaign never really took hold, and most Iowa politicians would have agreed with A. F. Allen's observation in late August that the issue of farm relief made it "practically certain" that Brookhart would win.[40]

One incident that the Democrats did try to exploit was a charge by Brookhart that former Secretary of Agriculture Edwin T. Meredith had been present at the Federal Reserve meeting responsible for deflating agricultural credit. This Meredith denied, and Brookhart was finally forced to admit that he had his facts wrong. Still, he thought, Meredith should have done a better job of protecting farmers from such action; and he was convinced, he said, that Meredith was an enemy of Iowa farmers, second only to C. H. McNider. The MacNiders had one senator "all kissed, caressed and canned," and Meredith, who had Porter on his payroll, was now trying to acquire the other one. As an issue, the incident was soon over and forgotten by almost everyone but Meredith. He continued throughout the campaign to produce articles and pamphlets about it. But even he realized that the effort was not having much effect. Brookhart, he complained to Steck, seemed to have the election "by default."[41]

In early October Porter tried to put some life into his faltering campaign by challenging Brookhart to a debate. The hope, as Democratic State Chairman Ray Fites admitted, was to get Brookhart out of "the bushes" and the "safety zone" where he might be forced into making another error similar to his Emmetsburg speech. Brookhart, however, refused to rise to the bait. The only time the two candidates met was when, by chance, they happened to take the same train to Waterloo. Brookhart, Porter commented later, was a "cool traveling companion," and his refusal to debate, Porter also thought, had "hurt his chances" and improved those of the Democrats.[42]

Brookhart's decision not to debate was the result in part of an earlier meeting between him and the Republican State Committee, at which it had been agreed that the committee would schedule his speeches and he would take no speaking dates on his own. It was apparently understood, too, that he would stick essentially to the same set speech on agricultural distress and the perfidy of the Federal Reserve Board. At least he worked hard not to stray from it and thus to avoid what had happened to him in 1924.[43]

Brookhart had also received some pointed advice about moderating his speech from his old friend Edgar Harlan. Writing right after the June 1926 primary Harlan opened his letter by asking, "Dare I presume on our lifelong friendship with this letter?" He then proceeded to presume on their friendship by relating a story about President John Adams and his failure to receive a second term as president. Once, when Adams and John Randolph of Roanoke were traveling through Baltimore they came to an inn where "Mr. Adams, walking up to a portrait of Washington, and placing his fingers on his lips, exclaimed, 'If I had kept my lips as close as that man, I should now be the President of the United States.'"[44]

The chances that Brookhart would say too much were also lessened by an illness that led him to cancel his speaking engagements for the period from September 9 to September 30. He became ill while visiting Clermont, was forced to return home, and on doctor's orders stayed there to rest for the next three weeks. According to Jennie, the problem was caused by a kidney stone but was not serious enough to require surgery.[45]

Resuming his speaking tour with a speech in Burlington on September 30, Brookhart then went to Oskaloosa on October 2 and in the next two weeks traveled from Des Moines to Oto, Le Mars, Storm Lake, Atlantic, Norwood, Marengo, Newton, back to Clermont, and then to Decorah. From there he was once again forced to return to Washington because of illness, this time that of his brother, State Senator James L. Brookhart, who had been ill for a number of weeks and took a turn for the worse on October 20. Hurrying home, Smith decided to cancel all further campaign appearances, thus, for all intents and purposes, ending the campaign two weeks before the election.[46]

Nothing in the interval, however, changed the contours of voter opinion, and on election day Brookhart was an easy victor. He carried eighty-one counties and received 56.6 percent of the total vote. In the upper four tiers of counties he lost only Dubuque. In the east central region, he ran behind Porter only in Jones, Linn, Benton, Johnson, and Scott Counties, and in southeastern Iowa, only six counties (Lee, Des Moines, Jefferson, Wapello, Davis, and Appanoose) were not in the Brookhart column. Two of these, moreover, Wapello and Jefferson, came very close to being so.[47]

The *Register* called Brookhart's election a "celebration of his reunion with the Party." Republican Chairman Willis Stern hailed it as marking the end of the "factional strife" that had enabled the Democrats to gain a foothold in the Senate two years before. And Brookhart's associates used the occasion to promise that he would continue working for party unity. They could not resist pointing out, however, that while Brookhart had won a decisive victory, Senator William M. Butler had been defeated in Massachusetts and Privilege and Elections Committee Chairman Richard Ernst had been defeated in Kentucky.[48]

Brookhart was naturally pleased, although the edge was taken off the celebrations by the continuing illness of his brother Jim, who finally died on November 11. He was anxious, he told his son, to get back to work; and with the campaign now over and his political situation in Iowa the best it had ever been, he thought that something "constructive" could be accomplished. He might, he added, come to Washington to help Iowa farm groups seek relief in the congressional session beginning in December, and he wondered if he should decide to do so whether an appropriate office could be secured.[49]

By the end of 1926, then, the "mish-mash" of the last two years had been replaced by the closest thing to party unity that the Iowa Republicans had known for years. Although it could be seen as more facade than substance, unity had become the hope of those bruised by years of internecine war, and anxious to put such battles behind them. It was the hope around which plans for 1928 were being built, and those involved could take heart from the fact Smith Brookhart would not be on a ballot for another six years.

Brookhart had acted boldly but foolishly when he had run against Cummins in 1920. His message of economic exploitation had fallen on deaf ears, and his losing effort had only served to earn him the opposition of regular members of the Republican Party. But by 1922 the times had caught up with Brookhart's message. Because of agricultural disasters, he now had an audience ready to listen, and at first he had tried to play the game by the accepted rules, working hard to line up the support of such groups as the Farm Bureau Federation. When that had failed, however, he had become embittered, had charged betrayal on the part of organizational and party leaders, had determined to go directly to the people, and in doing so, had won.

Consequently, in the 1924 to 1926 period, those in charge of the established political machinery had united to defeat Brookhart. In part they acted out of fear for his program, some really believing that it would lead to socialism or worse. In part they feared that he intended to remake the Republican Party in his own image, a charge he repeatedly denied and one that most thoughtful politicians knew to be unfounded since he had never bothered to build the kind of county-by-county organizations necessary for such a move. In addition, they were upset that he had won without them and had thus shown that the political party as the vehicle for election was no longer necessary.[50]

As Brookhart saw it, on the other hand, Iowa's Republican Party had ceased to be the popular institution and advocate that it should be. It had been born, as he said in 1910, to fight a slave-holding oligarchy, and it was to help return the party to its roots that he had joined the insurgency of

Albert Baird Cummins and applauded when the latter had declared that duty to good government and one's own conscience was "more sacred" than duty to party. Like Cummins, he had believed that "we cannot hope to perpetuate the Republican Party so long as a Republican in one part of the country has ten times as much influence in the party as a Republican in another part. And writing for the *Press* in 1913, he had hailed the appearance of a new citizenship in which voters were reexamining their organizational loyalties, demanding that "every party live for the public interest alone," and visiting a "blighting wrath" upon any party that failed to serve the public.[51]

The irony of Iowa politics in the 1920s was that Brookhart had learned these lessons too well and had then turned them back onto the teacher, accusing Cummins of having failed the people of Iowa and later extending this indictment to the Republican Party as a whole. His intent was not to control the party but instead, like a revival preacher, to call it back to its true home. And in trying to do so, he served as the medium for disaffected voters to express themselves.[52]

Still, one must ask, why Brookhart? Were there no others capable of filling the role he assumed or at least challenging him for it in the political arena? The answer seems to be that, by and large, there were not. On the Democratic side, the leading figures tended to go with appeals to anti-Brookhart Republicans rather than popular discontent. This was true of Clyde Herring, Dan Steck, and Claude Porter, even though it proved to be a winning strategy only when Brookhart was counted out in the United States Senate. It was also true of Edwin T. Meredith, who was perhaps the most prominent Iowa Democrat of the period. And even more important in Meredith's case was his preoccupation with the battles over prohibition and other ethno-cultural issues within the Democratic Party. Concerned with these, busy with his burgeoning publishing business, and plagued by chronic ill health, he never emerged as a real Democratic contender for Brookhart's role.[53]

On the Republican side, there was also a dearth of figures capable of speaking to and winning support from the constituencies that Brookhart mobilized. One possibility might have been Fourth District Congressman Gilbert N. Haugen, the chairman of the House Agriculture Committee, and co-sponsor of the McNary-Haugen Farm Relief Bill. But for Haugen a freshman senatorship had little attraction compared to the seniority he had built up since being elected to the House in 1899.

Another figure who might have been able to defeat Brookhart had he chosen to run against him was Hanford MacNider. But this would have had to come through his alliance with the Legion and other veteran's groups and their political allies, not through his ability to provide leadership and direction to the forces of agrarian discontent. There was, in fact, no evidence that he ever understood such discontent. Writing to *Iowa Legionnaire* editor Frank Miles after the 1926 primary, he had confessed that he could not fathom what was in the minds of those who had voted for Brookhart. "I presume, however," he wrote, "that this is some sort of a protest."[54]

Some sort of protest, indeed! That was precisely the point and precisely the issue that Smith Brookhart rode to election victory. MacNider's statement was indicative of the fact that for seven elections those opposed to Brookhart had been running against his personality and record of dissent from party regularity, rather than responding to the conditions of economic distress that had given him an audience. Opponents like MacNider or Meredith may have narrowed Brookhart's margin of victory. But given their failure to address the issues that Brookhart raised, they could not deprive him of a winning majority.

Smith Brookhart would return to the Senate in 1927 as the unchallengeable winner of the election. He would go also as the chosen voice of agrarian protest. And he would again be on trial when he returned to Washington, although this time the issue would not be the possession of his seat. It would be whether he could take the opportunity given him and become an effective advocate for those who had elected him.

12

The Regular Republican and the Fight for Farm Relief

By 1927 Smith Brookhart's analysis of the farm situation had become familiar to most Iowans and many Americans. The problem, he said, was credit, and it stemmed from the May 1920 Federal Reserve Board decision to demand that farmers pay their loans off early. This had produced a continuing farm depression in the midst of an otherwise booming economy. America's much-vaunted prosperity had meant "sheriff's sales for the farmer," for not only had crop prices dropped but land values had decreased and banks had closed across the Midwest—nineteen in Iowa in one week of 1926. "The Wall Street boom," he said, "increased the prices the farmers had to pay for what they buy and decreased the prices they received for their products."[1]

According to Brookhart there were also ample precedents for having the federal government play a role in the recovery of agriculture. The government, after all, had assisted other sectors of the economy. It had, to be specific, created a commercial bank system that had not served agriculture well, had further compounded this with a Federal Reserve system that had been the principal cause of the depression, and following the war had subsidized the railroads in ways that had required farmers to pay higher freight rates.[2]

In addition, Brookhart pointed out that the farmer had contributed huge sums of money to various government corporations. The wartime grain corporation had an accumulated profit of $58 million but this had not been available for farm relief. The Federal Reserve system had a surplus of $218 million in 1924, much of it at least indirectly the result of farmer deposits, yet the farmer had no voice in the use of that surplus. The War Finance Corporation had accrued an undetermined amount of interest through funds deposited in the Federal Treasury, which interest "rightly" belonged to the farmers of the United States.³ The government, Brookhart argued, was not only unwilling to provide new farm relief but unwilling to use possible sources of relief already at its disposal.

In other ways, too, Brookhart insisted, the government had already subsidized almost every interest except agriculture. The wartime fleet built at taxpayer expense was now being sold by the Shipping Board to private shippers at a fraction of the original cost. The power dam at Muscle Shoals, also built at taxpayer expense, was, if the President had his way, to be disposed of in a similar fashion. And Congress had continued to establish tariff schedules that forced the farmer to buy at protected prices while selling on the open market. Farmers, Brookhart said, were "entitled to some consideration at the hands of the government."⁴

The kind of consideration that Brookhart had in mind was policies that would allow farmers to form national marketing cooperatives, assist them in recouping their cost of production plus a reasonable profit, and provide special funds to cover any losses incurred in implementing such guarantees. His bill, he said, would do these things; it would give agriculture the same economic chance that other businesses and industries had enjoyed under the "laws enacted by our government."⁵

Although Brookhart had introduced his farm bill a number of times, he had never been able to get much of a hearing for it. Part of the problem was that it challenged basic assumptions about the American business system. Another part was that it was Smith Brookhart's program, and his reputation as an outsider and a legislative loner was such that it seemed to preclude serious consideration of his program. For example, writing in May 1927, the widow of Robert M. La Follette told him that an article on cooperation and agriculture that he had written for *La Follette's Magazine* was "very able" and well "within the grasp of the everyday reader." But Basil Manly, the 1920 progressive conference organizer, told the younger Senator La Follette that while Brookhart had a "big idea" in the article, it was a "pity that somebody cannot take it and put it into practical form and map out a feasible program for it development."⁶

The farm relief bill that dominated debate during the 1920s was the McNary-Haugen Bill, introduced in Congress by Senator Charles McNary of Oregon and Representative Gilbert Haugen of Iowa and generally regarded as the brainchild of farm implement manufacturer George Peek.⁷ In essence, the bill called for a government corporation that would protect farm commodity prices on the domestic market while selling surpluses on the foreign market. Any losses on such transactions would be covered by assessing an "equalization fee" against the farmers.

McNary-Haugenism had strong supporters that included Agriculture Secretary Henry C. Wallace, the American Farm Bureau Federation, and many business leaders. It also had potent enemies, not least of whom were President Calvin Coolidge and Secretary of Commerce Herbert Hoover. Coolidge objected to the plan on several scores, including his belief that it was price fixing, an improper taxation, and the potential creator of a huge government bureaucracy. During his presidency, Congress passed two versions of the bill, but he vetoed both of them.

Hoover's objections included the fear that McNary-Haugenism would stimulate over-production, benefit large farmers far more than small, and become the precedent whereby other industries could ask for similar government assistance. The result, according to historian Joan Hoff Wilson, would be the "politicizing of the American economy," with Congress becoming a partner in American business and with the time eventually coming when government officials would be concerned less with the "promotion of justice and equal opportunity" than with "barter in the markets." Hoover argued instead for developing marketing cooperatives that could make marketing operations more efficient, enhance the bargaining power of farmers, and help to balance production with demand, thereby ending ruinous overproduction and the consequent huge surpluses.[8]

Although he preferred his own bill, Brookhart decided early on that there were enough positive features in the McNary-Haugen Bills to warrant his support. He liked their cooperative features and wished only that they had been carried further. Local cooperatives, he thought, should be allowed to buy stock in the government corporation and after a few years to take over its management. He also liked the fact that the bills recognized and would deal with an emergency situation and wished only that they contained something more to prevent a future reoccurrence of the problem.[9]

The earliest version of the McNary-Haugen Bill had been defeated in the House of Representatives in June 1924. A slightly revised version had then reached the Senate on the last day of the session in March 1925, being offered at that time as an amendment to a naval bill. It was defeated by a vote of 69 to 17, with Brookhart joining other progressive senators in voting for it. By the time another version was ready for a vote, Brookhart had been unseated. He missed voting on the so-called third McNary-Haugen Bill of 1926 and on the fourth bill that passed Congress and was vetoed by the President in 1927.[10]

By then, however, Brookhart's position was well-known. Again and again, he had noted the special assistance already being given to other groups in the economy, groups that were now arguing against help for farmers; recalled that reformers who had sought to break the chains of slaves or correct oppressive labor conditions had been accused of advancing an economically unsound position; and insisted that farmers were "entitled to a system of laws that will raise agriculture to the same artificial level as all these other great industries." It was "insidious propaganda" by business interests that had defeated the McNary-Haugen Bills, and farmers must learn to reject such propaganda and help to elect congressmen who would "fight the conspiracy of special interests to the finish."[11]

In Iowa, the political battles in which Brookhart had been involved had convinced a number of observers that the state was "thoroughly against the Coolidge administration" and that Iowa Republicans would be receptive to the nomination of a western man in 1928. As early as 1924 one of Brookhart's fellow townsmen had warned Secretary of Agriculture Henry C. Wallace that "no political party need expect much from Iowa" if it failed to "offer some permanent relief for agriculture." And two years later Muscatine banker George M. Titus had told Secretary of the Treasury Andrew Mellon that he was afraid that the President did not realize the real situation in the middle west. He had warned Hoover, he said, that failure to pass farm relief legislation would insure a victory for Brookhart in the primary; and now that Brookhart had won by over 71,000 votes, the administration must take heed. Further rejection of the McNary-Haugen Bill would mean the "gradual disintegration of the Republican Party."[12]

The "western man" that many Iowans had in mind for 1928 was former Illinois Governor Frank O. Lowden, who had tried for the nomination in 1920 and had refused the vice presidential spot in 1924. He was now besieged with letters urging his candidacy, but in Iowa two questions about his prospects remained to be answered. Who would Brookhart support? And could the Iowa Republican Party unite behind anyone?

Beginning in the summer of 1926, Lowden's Iowa correspondents kept him informed about the progress of his candidacy and tried to paint as optimistic a picture as possible concerning the broad base of his support. Old Brookhart foe LeRoy Rader, who wrote to remind Lowden of his support in 1920, told him that "both the Cummins and Brookhart factions meet on a common ground" where he was concerned. And later that year, Harvey Ingham informed him that his recent speech in St. Louis had been praised in the "very highest terms" by both Brookhart and Henry A. Wallace.[13]

Frank Lund, Brookhart's former campaign manager, was the first to contact Lowden regarding an Iowa organization. Writing at the end of February 1927, he pointed out that the Brookhart for Senator Committee was no longer active but that it could be put to work if Lowden intended to become a candidate. Lowden said only that he would keep in touch.[14] Nevertheless, by early April Lund reported to the prospective candidate that an official organization was now in the field.[15]

From the beginning, however, the new organization was haunted by the spectre of the absent Smith Brookhart. Given Lund's past connections to Brookhart, the "old regulars" felt that he could not be trusted. H. O. Weaver worried that the incipient organization had already fallen into the hands of the followers of Brookhart. Vinton attorney M. J. Tobin said it was a "menace" to the Lowden efforts to have the Lund-Brookhart influence in control.[16] But even though Brookhart had not yet declared himself, it was no secret that his preferred candidate was George Norris.

Public and private pressures were exerted on Brookhart to convince him that his support of Norris would be futile. In an April 11 editorial the *Register* said that while Senator Norris was one of the most valuable men in the Senate, he was no La Follette and was ill-suited to lead any successful movement for agricultural relief. The first priority, said the *Register*, was farm relief; and Brookhart's program for financial reorganization, however meritorious, would necessarily have to be put off until the issue of farm relief had been "disposed of." In the *Register*'s view, Lowden could win the nomination and as president secure agriculture relief.[17]

At the same time John D. Denison, a Democrat who had supported Brookhart in 1926, wrote the senator-elect to express his concern about his apparent efforts to organize the state for Norris. Reminding Brookhart of his widespread support in 1925 and telling him that he was making new friends from his old opponents, Denison urged Brookhart not to squander his growing strength in Iowa with an ill-considered Norris campaign.[18]

Throughout June and July, Brookhart continued to haunt the efforts of the Lund organization and make them a far cry from the aggressive campaign that such correspondents as Harvey Ingham were reporting to Lowden. The regulars still wanted to strengthen their influence on a committee that some saw as having been captured by the La Follette-Brookhart "agrarians and other extremists." And on the sidelines, Coolidge supporters under the leadership of former Senators Charles Rawson and David Stewart waited, hoping to pick up regulars who had become dissatisfied with the whole process.[19]

Then from an unexpected quarter the political picture suddenly changed. On August 2 President Coolidge issued a laconic message declaring his intention not to run in 1928. The withdrawal, Brookhart said, was the "greatest political victory the farmers . . . have ever won"; and recommending that farmers get behind a candidate who would fight for economic issues, he declared that in his opinion George Norris was the best man for the job. With this declaration for Norris, Brookhart had finally said in public what had been rumored for months. It brought a final break with Lund and seemed to clear the air among the state's Lowden supporters.[20]

Meanwhile, Brookhart kept busy pushing for farm relief. During the short session of the Sixty-Ninth Congress, which convened on December 6, 1926, he had no official role. David Stewart had been elected to serve out the remainder of Cummins' term. But refusing to let a constitutional technicality stand in his way, he decided to go to Washington, D.C., to see what he could do for farm relief. And as indicated by a speech in Chicago on the way to Washington, he was clearly aware that when he officially took office in December 1927 he would have an important role to play in the organization of the Senate. With forty-eight Republicans and forty-seven Democrats in the next Senate, he believed that his vote would "constitute a balance of power."[21]

Once in Washington, Brookhart quickly joined in the efforts to get the McNary-Haugen Bill out of Congress. He also urged that a special session of Congress be called to begin after March 4. This would be the first session of the new Seventieth Congress, and given the turnover of membership as the result of the November elections, it was felt by many, including Brookhart, that farm relief would have a better chance of passage.[22]

Through January of 1927 the farm bill competed for attention with a banking bill, and behind the scenes Brookhart and his allies worked with Vice-President Charles G. Dawes to effect a compromise that would allow both bills to be brought to the floor. In this they were successful; and once brought up for debate, the farm bill passed both houses of Congress. For the first time, the McNary-Haugen Bill reached the President's desk.[23]

Coolidge's objections were well-known, and on February 25 he sent a long, pointed veto message to Congress, one in which he found nothing good about the bill and said so in no uncertain terms. The Coolidge veto, said Brookhart, was "a veto of the Republican platform, a veto of the rights of the farmer to economic equality, a veto of the West and the South with an underwriting of Wall Street speculation."[24]

While working in Washington, Brookhart also took advantage of opportunities to speak elsewhere, one such engagement being an address before the Open Forum in Baltimore. There he observed that the State Department was currently concerned with communist confiscation of American property in Nicaragua. Yet at home the bolshevik steel trust, Wall Street communists, and socialist New York bankers had confiscated the profits of American farmers and the State Department had paid little attention. Perhaps, he suggested, the Department should "land a few Marines over in the Department of Agriculture and stir things up at home."[25]

Following Congress's adjournment on March 3, Brookhart returned to Iowa, where he spoke before a joint session of the Iowa General Assembly and again set forth his explanation of the farm depression. At the time the legislature was debating a bill to establish cooperative banks in Iowa, a long-time Brookhart goal, and in his address he spoke with more enthusiasm than usual about the necessity of creating cooperative banks. Later in the spring, he would congratulate the legislature and farm and labor organizations for passing the bill, predict that many cooperative banks would be organized in Iowa, and maintain that this "good start in Iowa" would give him the support he would need to get a similar bill passed in Congress.[26]

Prior to the ratification of the Twentieth Amendment to the Constitution in 1933, Congress usually adjourned in March and did not reconvene until December. This long recess allowed Brookhart to spend summers in Washington with his family as well as to travel throughout the state to keep in touch with his constituents. During May he would usually speak at high school commencements. Mid-summer would find him at the Republican Convention. He maintained his interest in rifle-shooting and rarely missed the state and national matches.

He usually traveled around the state alone but occasionally Jennie would go with him. Not surprisingly Smith wanted to get from one place to the next as quickly as possible. But when Jennie was along she liked to stop and visit friends and family along the way. On one occasion as they set off he told her, "Now Jennie, we're not going to have time to stop and visit everybody you would like to visit so just don't plan on it." To which Jennie replied, "Well, Smith, then maybe I should send a card to all these folks and tell them approximately what time we will be through their town and they can stand out on the porch and wave at us as we go by." That apparently settled the matter and they stopped wherever Jennie wanted.[27]

Nevertheless, when Smith traveled he tried to have dinner with family or friends whenever possible. This not only allowed him to keep in touch with people but also made it possible to save money, a continuing necessity after the bank failure. Dinners were an occasion for lively political discussions and Brookhart did not moderate his views to please his hosts. After one heated debate with Morton Mumma, Mumma told him, "Smith Brookhart, you are a God damned radical!" On another occasion Brookhart's brother, Odes, asked him how he could possibly have voted against a particular bill. Smith replied, "Well, Odes, because I wanted to be able to look in the mirror and not be ashamed of the person that I saw there the next morning."[28]

For the host family Brookhart's visits became memorable occasions, especially for the children. In one home, the senator took time to give one of the sons shooting lessons. He frequently dined with his old rifle shooting friend, Morton Mumma and Mumma's daughter remembered being fascinated that Brookhart ate his peas with a knife. One niece recalled that her uncle's visit meant they would have cornbread. She also recalled that once her uncle asked her, "Well, Violet, what are you doing? Are you enjoying life?" She told him about her job and church work. He urged her to "take time to have a little fun." Later, her mother said that Smith spoke with "the voice of inexperience."[29]

Time off for Brookhart usually meant doing other kinds of work. He had no interest in the usual forms of recreation. He did not play golf and had no interest in sports, either as a participant or spectator. His children complained that as soon as they would get a good game going he would call them to do some chores on the farm. When his son John went out for football and came home with an injury, his father asked, "Well, are you satisfied now?" When another son was to go out of town for a game, the senator went to the station and took him off the train because he had not done his chores.[30]

Activities had to be productive and for the senator sports seemed to have no purpose. Rifle shooting was sport, but the real purpose was to train sharp shooters for war. The only recreation the senator allowed himself was fishing. But even then after a couple of days he quickly tired of the activity and returned to more "useful" endeavors.

Brookhart's usual recreation was the useful activity of improving the farm. In the spring of 1925 Jennie reported to her son, Smith, Jr., that "Papa bought himself a garden plow and is going to keep things right. He has worked more here than for years. He and the children have set out 600 strawberries here near the house." Later, after the family had moved to Maryland, a reporter found the senator tending to his trees and commented that "tree surgery is to Brookhart what golf and fishing are to others."[31]

The orchard occupied most of his time. He regularly pruned the older trees and planted new varieties. When it came time to pick the apples Smith insisted that they be picked by hand and carefully wrapped in paper for storage in baskets. Following the bank failure the farm became a source of income for the family and this was Jennie's domain. The hand-picked apples brought a good price and even the wind fall apples could bring one dollar a bushel. She also raised chickens and ducks for sale. All of this took a great deal of her time but she was proud that she could contribute to the family's livelihood.[32]

In addition to all the usual summer activities, throughout the summer of 1927 Brookhart helped his family pack for the move to Washington, D.C. During his earlier sojourn there, they had remained in the "brick house" on the east edge of Washington. But now, with a six-year term certain, he had decided that it was time to take his wife and three younger children east with him.

The move from Washington was not an easy one for the Brookharts. Smith had lived there for thirty-five years and had brought his young bride there thirty years before. Together they had designed and built the brick house, and in it they had raised their children. Both had been active in community affairs, and Jennie had increased her involvement in church and civic affairs in the years Smith had been in the Senate. The prospect of reuniting the family in the east was no doubt a pleasant one for them, and the prospect of living in the nation's capital was no doubt exciting for the younger children. But it was with sadness that they left Iowa.

The *Journal* noted the regret felt by the Washington community at the loss of the family for the "next six years, at least." It admitted, however, that the move would be beneficial for all and wished the family "health, happiness, prosperity and lives of increasing usefulness." At the time the Brookharts believed they would be back. Rather than sell the brick house, they leased it to a neighbor, keeping one room for Smith's use during his visits to the state. But, like many other politicians, Brookhart would find the attraction of the city on the Potomac too great. The family would never return to live in Iowa.[33]

The Brookharts left Washington early on the morning of August 10, having decided to make a vacation of the trip. Their first stop was in Duluth, Minnesota, where they visited their son John and where Smith announced that he would be offering a bill in Congress to establish a Federated Cooperative Corporation as the agency for dealing with the farm surplus. They then drove to Waupaca, Wisconsin, to visit Senator George Norris at his summer home; and subsequently, at Stoughton, Wisconsin, Brookhart told a Harvest Festival crowd that Norris was the only man able to take the place of their former senator, the late Robert M. La Follette, as the leader of the liberals.[34]

Continuing their journey, the Brookharts stopped in Chicago and Detroit and then drove through Canada to Niagara Falls. From there they traveled down the Susquehana Trail to Washington, D.C.[35]

Their new house was a two-story frame house with a big front porch that he had purchased in Hyattsville, Maryland, a house that, if not the "brick house," was at least similar to the houses that could be seen in countless Iowa towns. In Iowa, however, the Senator's new home was reported to be a mansion. To settle questions about it, the *Register* finally ran a picture of the house and asked its readers to decide for themselves. "Discussion of the senator's home," it commented, "ought now to be dismissed." It had no "bearing on his political representation of Iowa," and Iowans would do well to concentrate on other matters, particularly on efforts "to capitalize his individualism, his resistance to influence" and on impressing him with "the breadth of the Iowa liberalism which he seeks to represent." Still, the

Register found room a few days later for a picture of the overall-clad Brookhart up on a ladder "doctoring" the trees at his new home, a seeming assurance that he had not "gone eastern."[36]

The move to Washington, D.C., opened new worlds for the Brookharts, especially the children. The senator now began to attend social functions. Sometimes Jennie went with him but his usual companion was his daughter Edith, then in high school. She accompanied him to White House receptions and they occasionally attended parties at the Soviet embassy. The favorite family activity was a Sunday afternoon visit to the Washington Zoo.[37]

The older daughter, Florence, explored the "crannies and passages and harbors" of the Capitol building. When she was told that the Senate still kept snuff boxes for its members, she managed to get on the floor to see them. They "smelled like the dickens," she said. The congressional subway amused her, "everyone likes to ride on them because it feels so silly." She said one of the "funniest sights [was] a load of pompous senators, coat-tails and ties flying in the wind, . . . riding in on the 'dinky.'" Although Washington, D.C., was a great place she said it would be nice to once more go around the square in Washington, Iowa, and to hear the "corn rustle." When they were asked where was the best place in the world, Florence Brookhart said it was "still spelled with four letters [I-O-W-A]."[38]

Jennie rarely went out socially but she did enjoy her membership in the senate wives' club. They met regularly to socialize and to roll bandages for the Red Cross. She also served as a tour guide for visitors from home. But for the most part the famous and powerful in the nation's capital did not impress her much. One exception was shortly before World War II when King George VI and Queen Elizabeth came to visit the White House. On that occasion she took the streetcar in to see the queen. "Queens are getting mighty scarce," she said. For Jennie the highlight of the move to Maryland was that her family was under one roof again.[39]

Once in the capital, Brookhart joined other progressive senators to develop an agenda for the coming Congress. He worked in particular with William Borah of Idaho, Gerald Nye and Lynn Frazier of North Dakota, George Norris and Robert Howell of Nebraska, Henrik Shipstead of Minnesota, and the two Wisconsin senators, John J. Blaine and Robert La Follette, Jr. Not all of the group, however, were always involved in the several meetings. Nor would they all agree on policies and tactics, a fact that had crippled the progressive bloc in the past and would continue to do so in the new Seventieth Congress.

The agenda that emerged by mid-September included the McNary-Haugen Bill, flood control in the Mississippi Valley, and opposition to tax reduction. The last was tied directly to the other two, the argument being that whatever surplus that accrued through existing levies should be used to pay for farm relief and flood control. Immediately following the announcement of these legislative goals, Brookhart left town for a western tour, during which he urged farmers to demand "full government aid" for their "desperate condition."[40]

Returning to Washington in October, Brookhart announced that he and his progressive allies would soon offer concrete recommendations for farm relief. Calling the search for the causes of the farm depression the "highest duty of statesmanship," he declared that it was the "duty of Congress" to provide real relief and not settle for a "decoy bill" based on the "specious plan that it has a chance."[41]

The details of what the progressive group considered to be real relief came in a statement it issued on November 20. It called for the formation of an export corporation with enough capital to market the "entire exportable surplus," thus going well beyond the McNary-Haugen scheme's focus on particular commodities. It also called for farmers to be paid the cost of production plus 5 percent, a price level, Brookhart, said, that would protect farmers in the same way manufactured goods were currently protected. In addition, the export corporation would in time become a national farmers' cooperative.[42]

As Brookhart conceded in his statement, however, the progressives could not agree on how much funding would be necessary and how these funds would be provided. Brookhart himself thought that the corporation would need about $1.5 billion to do its job; and he acknowledged that while some of the group wanted to raise the money through a McNary-Haugen-like equalization fee, others believed such a fee to be unconstitutional. A direct government appropriation, he implied, would have the support of all and was probably the way to go.[43]

The difficulty the insurgent group had in agreeing on a farm program was typical of the history of farm relief. Farmer groups had never been able to agree on a single plan, and this had always made farm relief legislation difficult. President Coolidge, moreover, was able to use this history of indecision to argue that the farm groups themselves were to blame for what had happened. The inability to agree, he hinted in early November, made the possibility of any future farm relief unlikely.[44]

Although Coolidge did not criticize Brookhart by name, Senator Steck did. Steck noted Brookhart's opposition to McNary-Haugenism and to the candidacy of Frank Lowden, and noting that Iowans were in favor of McNary-Haugenism and Frank Lowden, he said that the impasse on farm relief could be laid directly on the doorstep of Brookhart and the progressives. Brookhart, however, brushed aside such criticism and reminded the

President that even if the farm groups could not agree on a plan, this did not excuse him from the "pledge of his party to extend farm relief."[45]

In announcing the farm program, Brookhart had been careful to indicate that he was speaking in the name of the other progressives. But in the public mind the relief plan quickly became identified as his and was in fact essentially the same plan he had announced the previous August. The *Register* referred to it specifically as "Brookhart's plan" and went on to call it "vague" and "revolutionary" and to argue that putting farming in the hands of the government would result in a "complete change in the relations of the government to business." It would be better, the *Register* said, to stick with the McNary-Haugen Bill, which was known, was fairly broadly supported, and would pay for itself.[46]

That Brookhart was now acting as a spokesman for the progressive group was a new development, due in part to his big electoral margin in 1926. Farm relief had been the issue then; the voters had spoken; and Brookhart had thus become the logical choice to act as spokesman on that question. Other factors that helped make Brookhart the spokesman included the disarray in the progressive ranks reflected particularly in the inability of Robert M. La Follette, Jr. to fill the gap left by the death of his father, George Norris' confusing signals about his interest in the presidential nomination, and William Borah's preoccupation with whom he would support for the nomination. In a sense, it was more or less by default that Brookhart spoke for the progressives on farm relief.[47]

In the meantime, the progressive senators had also decided that they did not want and could not support Lowden in 1928. Norris was their preference; and while initially he had shown reluctance to have his name put forward, he would eventually acquiesce to their combined request. The problem was timing of the announced support, a delicate matter since doing it too early might create diversions that would jeopardize farm relief action while doing it too late would reduce the likelihood that Norris could head off Lowden.[48]

Again Brookhart seemed to lead the way in such action as was taken. He spent the fall trying to organize the progressive group to come out for Norris, and in a secret meeting held in his office on November 2 the group laid plans for Muscatine radio station owner Norman Baker to build a high power radio station in Washington, the broadcasts of which would be picked up by Muscatine station KTNT and sent throughout the Midwest. This was to be the voice of progressivism. But it was a scheme that could not be implemented and seemed about as unrealistic as did the prospect of the Norris candidacy.[49]

The Seventieth Congress convened on December 5, 1927, and at last Smith Brookhart's thirteen-month tenure as senator-elect was over. By custom he should have been escorted down the aisle of the Senate chamber by his Iowa colleague Daniel Steck. In 1922 Cummins had performed this courtesy. But Steck now refused to do so.[50]

The new Senate consisted of forty-eight Republicans, forty-seven Democrats, and one Farmer-Laborite, which meant that the insurgent bloc of Norris, Frazier, Nye, Blaine, La Follette, Shipstead, and Brookhart was in a position to influence key legislative decisions. Although they would vote with the Republicans to organize the Senate, they had no qualms about crossing party lines on specific issues.

Brookhart was reassigned to two committees he had served on before, Interoceanic Canals and Military Affairs. His new committees included Banking and Currency, Civil Service, Post Office, and Claims. In spite of his deep interest in the subject, however, he did not serve on the agriculture committee.

As Congress convened, the *New York Times* listed ten issues with which it would have to deal, among them flood control, prohibition, various water projects, public utilities, ship building, and agricultural relief. But as far as Senator Brookhart was concerned, agricultural relief was the only issue that mattered. And while formal debate over this question would not take place until April, the line between what Calvin Coolidge would accept and what Brookhart and many in the Congress had hoped for was drawn early. In his annual message to Congress, the President, while noting that some progress had been made in the farm economy, acknowledged that farmers still needed help. But any governmental price-fixing scheme, he said, would be "unsound and bound to result in disaster." And any subsidy plan (like that Brookhart proposed) would "work out the same way." He proposed instead to establish a marketing board with a revolving fund from which loans could be made to farm groups at modest interest rates.[51]

Brookhart called Coolidge's farm message the worst that had ever been sent to Congress on the subject. It left no possible avenue for relief, he said, and if this became the position of the Republican Party in the coming election, the West and South would "end the career of the Republican Party."[52]

Such hyperbole might be overlooked in most cases. But Brookhart meant it. He believed, perhaps naively, that the platform promises of a party were important and ought to be kept. Four years earlier, he said, the party had promised agricultural equality and had failed to deliver that promise, and it wanted to make the same pledge in another election, thus getting the farmer vote again. But if it would not keep its pledges, it deserved to be defeated. The great issue, he declared, was equality:

> Equality is the basic principle of Americanism; it was written into the Declaration of Independence in the beginning; but it has been nullified by selfish interests throughout our history. The time has come when inequality has grown so great against agriculture that it stands out today as the greatest problem of our Republic save and except the problem of human slavery.[53]

The McNary-Haugen Bill, in a redrafted version, was again introduced on March 7, 1928. Its proponents insisted that it contain the controversial equalization fee, and they let it be known that they would not compromise on that issue. But other changes had been made from earlier versions. It now applied to all crops but offered protected prices only on a limited amount of the goods produced, thus providing an incentive for production control. In addition, it now gave more encouragement to cooperatives. The McNary-Haugenites hoped that the changes would enhance the prospects of getting the President to accept the equalization fee.[54]

In late March, Brookhart introduced his own bill, which rather than seeking to curb production would simply hold the surpluses off the market so as to guarantee farmers cost of production plus a reasonable profit. According to Brookhart's calculations, this would cost $600 million, and again he argued that a similar subsidy had been paid to the railroads under the Esch-Cummins Act and that it was only "comparative justice" to do the same for farmers. He also rejected the contention that his bill was a subsidy while the McNary-Haugen Bill was not. Both were subsidies, he said, and his acknowledgment of this would make it easier for him to endorse the McNary-Haugen Bill as it moved toward passage.[55]

In fact, by April 12, the day the Senate vote on McNary-Haugen was scheduled to take place, he was ready to support it. His only objection was that it did not provide enough of a subsidy. As for the equalization fee, Brookhart believed that it was within the limits of constitutionality. But it was one reason Coolidge had vetoed the previous bill, and Brookhart now wondered if "good common horse sense" did not dictate removing the fee from the bill "at this time."[56]

In the debate, Brookhart still urged senators to vote for his own bill, this despite a concession that the President would surely veto it. The result, South Dakota Senator William McMaster implied, would be only a "protest in the name of agriculture" that would "accomplish nothing definite" for the farmer. But Brookhart replied that "if we vote for the [McNary-Haugen Bill], we do just the same thing, only we do not protest . . . as strong."[57]

As debate on the McNary-Haugen Bill neared an end, Brookhart offered two amendments. The first would raise the level of subsidy support, theoretically, to the same level as the subsidy of his own bill. The second would have added his cost of production plus 5 percent profit scheme. Both amendments were defeated on a voice vote. He then offered his own bill as a substitute for the McNary-Haugen Bill and tried to depict it as a reasonable synthesis of various other proposals. It was, he said, really the bill of Senator Robert Howell, since many parts of Howell's bill could be found in it. And it had antecedents in the original McNary Bill. He also claimed that it was not "my bill," but rather "a bill expressing what I think to be the rights of the farmer"; and if it was vetoed, he wanted to go back to Iowa and say to farmers that he had fought for all they were "entitled to have."[58]

A roll call vote was demanded for Brookhart's substitute, and when it was over sixty-four senators, including most of the progressives, had voted against it. Only Borah, Republican John Blaine of Wisconsin, and Democrats Thomas F. Bayard of Delaware and Coleman Blease of South Carolina joined Brookhart. A few minutes later Brookhart joined the majority of fifty-three senators to pass the McNary-Haugen Bill. Three weeks later the House also voted for the bill, and after some adjustments by a House-Senate Conference Committee the bill was sent to the President.[59]

Meanwhile, in Iowa, Brookhart's vocal support of his own bill had initially led many to believe that he was totally opposed to McNary-Haugen, and before the vote Charles Hearst had wired him that Iowa farmers would hold him responsible if his "amendments and interference" defeated the bill. Brookhart's response had been to charge that Peek and Charles G. Dawes were hoping that the bill would be vetoed "to keep it alive as a political football for boosting Dawes into the Presidency." Peek, he said, had even discussed a possible Dawes candidacy with him. Hearst then wrote to Peek, who denied the charges and said that he had personally intervened with Senator McNary for a speedy passage of the bill and had quit talking to Brookhart in the spring of 1927 after the senator had refused to give open support to McNary-Haugenism. Quoting Brookhart's statement in the *Congressional Record* that he knew the President would not sign the bill, Peek also told Hearst that he could only conclude that the senator did not want the farm subject "fairly disposed of" but preferred "agitation, regardless of the plight of the farmer."[60]

Also in Iowa, two old foes of Brookhart expressed bewilderment and chagrin at his vote for McNary-Haugen. Hanford MacNider wrote his father that despite Brookhart's "loud talk" he did not have enough "nerve" to vote against the bill, and in reply the elder McNider wrote that farmers in the Mason City area were damning Brookhart for his vote. "Notwithstanding that he voted for it," the elder McNider said, "they think he is against it."[61]

The MacNiders' feelings were understandable. Smith Brookhart had done the unexpected and compromised, however slightly, on an issue. If Iowans were uneasy, as McNider reported, it was because they were unaccustomed to his settling for less than a full loaf. Later, during the fall campaign, the *Register* would note that he had voted for the McNary-Haugen Bill "very reluctantly" and then only after "vigorously" pushing his own bill.[62]

Even before final passage of the bill, efforts were underway to persuade Coolidge to sign it. In early May a delegation that included Peek, McNary, and Hearst told the President that they had made every effort to amend the bill to meet his objections. As for the equalization fee, they regarded it as absolutely essential. Without it the plan would fail.[63]

At about the same time, another and more curious series of meetings may have taken place. According to Brookhart's story anyway, Secretary of Commerce Herbert Hoover sent Louis Crossette, one of his aides, to summon Brookhart to a clandestine meeting in a local hotel. Hoover, Brookhart was told, wanted to discuss the farm situation. And at the subsequent meeting, he was assured that his and Hoover's ideas were alike on farm relief and that a solution might be found if he would go to Coolidge and persuade him to allow the McNary-Haugen Bill to become law without his signature.[64]

Following the meeting, Brookhart said he went to the White House, where he told the President that the 1926 election and the passage of the McNary-Haugen Bill for two successive years amounted to mandates for agricultural relief and argued that by allowing the bill to become law without his signature he could conscientiously acquiesce in the wishes of the electorate. Coolidge told Brookhart that his argument seemed "persuasive" but then quickly deflected the conversation to show the old marksman a new rifle he had been sent.[65]

That Hoover actually did what Brookhart said seems questionable, given his long-standing opposition to McNary-Haugenism. But one should also note that Hoover did want to be president, and that his stand on the farm question seemed to be hurting his candidacy in the farm states. As Lowden operative Herman Steen wrote to *Wallaces' Farmer* editor Donald Murphy in March 1928, those in the Hoover organization were "greatly discouraged." They needed the middle west to elect Republicans yet their efforts to woo farmers had fallen flat. And as of May, Vinton attorney Michael J. Tobin was telling Secretary of the Treasury Andrew Mellon about the deep-seated opposition to Hoover's candidacy in the corn belt. Political success seemed to require a strengthening of Hoover's hand in the farm states, and no one knew this better than Hoover's chief political operative George Akerson. In early March Akerson had written Dante Pierce that the main fight against Hoover would be that he could not carry the farm states; and even earlier he had begun to marshal forces that would help Hoover with farmers. In particular he had persuaded American Farm Bureau Federation President James R. Howard to revise a pamphlet detailing Hoover's record of support for agriculture and make it available for use. As rewritten, the pamphlet would be widely circulated during the campaign.[66]

Hoover's weakness in the farm states had also become even more evident as the delegate selection process began. Seventeen states, including the farm states of Illinois, Nebraska, and Indiana, selected their delegates by primary election; and in all three of these farm states Hoover lost to strong favorite son candidates. Nor did he do much better in the convention states having large farm populations.[67]

In Iowa, for example, Lund and his committee had done their work well, the result being that when the Republicans had met in early March there was little doubt that a delegation instructed to vote for Lowden would go to the national convention. There was still a fight, however, over the language of the resolution to be adopted by the convention; and in the end a text condemning the administration and declaring "irrevocable opposition to the candidacy of Herbert Hoover" had been defeated. In its place the party had passed a resolution declaring that the best hope for agriculture was the McNary-Haugen Bill and the candidacy of Frank Lowden. Hoover received only two delegates from Iowa.[68]

At the June national convention, of course, Hoover would receive the nomination on the first ballot. But he would receive only thirty-seven of the 283 delegates from the ten midwestern states. And on the eve of the convention, Hoover confidant Edgar Rickard would be writing in his diary that "hard-boiled politicians" were lining up against Hoover and that the farm question was the "crux of the situation."[69]

For these reasons, something like the meeting described by Brookhart may have occurred. Brookhart had the potential to be a powerful foe, not only before the convention but also during the fall campaign. He had, as columnist Mark Sullivan put it, "probably received a larger proportion of farmer votes than any other man who ever ran in any state." This potential could be reduced if Hoover could make him believe that their views on farm relief were essentially the same. And one way of doing this would be to send Brookhart to Coolidge with the impression that Hoover, like Brookhart, was a reluctant supporter of McNary-Haugen. This could be done, moreover, in the secure knowledge that the bill would be vetoed anyway. Given Coolidge's position, there was no chance he would sign it. Under these circumstances, a meeting in which Hoover suggested the errand to Coolidge, and left Brookhart to infer that he desired it to be successful, seems within the range of possibilities.[70]

In the past, moreover, Brookhart had tended to see Hoover as having at least some progressive-mindedness. Although Hoover had once told Hanford MacNider that two Democratic senators from Iowa would be better than returning Brookhart, this was not known to the senator. On the contrary, he had believed Hoover to be friendly and helpful during the 1923 European trip, and on various occasions he had praised Hoover's wartime role as food administrator, even going so far as to suggest it as a model for what the government could do in the current farm crisis. He had also characterized recent anti-Hoover speeches in the Senate as the "most unreasonable" statements "ever printed in the *Congressional Record.*"[71]

In any event, Brookhart seemed to have the impression now that a Hoover farm policy would differ in major ways from the one Coolidge had been pursuing, and this proved to be another step toward "regularity." As we shall see, his identification with the mainline Republicans would become complete with his controversial support of Hoover in the fall campaign, and one feature of that support would be his defense of Hoover's activities on behalf of farm relief.

On May 23, 1928, Coolidge vetoed the McNary-Haugen Bill. The current version, he acknowledged, was less objectionable than the bill of the previous year, but it still contained the equalization fee, which in his view was an unjust tax. He also said that the bill would fix prices, create an extensive bureaucracy, and stimulate overproduction.[72]

Reaction to the veto in Iowa was swift and bitter. *Wallaces' Farmer* editor, Henry A. Wallace, saw it as a clear indication that those responsible were committed to the "industrializing" of America. Charles Hearst sent a telegram to Brookhart, deploring the veto and urging efforts to override it. "The fate of agriculture," he said, "depends on this action." And claiming that the veto had been the "greatest mistake" of Coolidge's career, Brookhart took to the senate floor to give a point-by-point rebuttal of the veto message.[73]

The veto also thrust the agricultural issue into the forefront of the presidential campaign and gave Lowden supporters renewed hope for his nomination. As H. O. Weaver put it, Coolidge's action had "placed the Lowden stock above par in Iowa" and had aroused hope that the same would be true all over the country.[74]

Such hopes, however, were not to be realized. It was already, as the convention would soon make clear, too late for Lowden. Nor were his supporters able to influence the Republican platform as they had still had hopes of doing when the convention met. The agricultural plank endorsed Hoover's scheme for a federal farm board to assist in developing a system of farmer owned and controlled associations. It did not mention McNary-Haugen.[75]

For some the alternative was to support the Democratic candidate, Al Smith. And in Iowa, reported *Register* editor Harvey Ingham, when pictures of Smith came on the movie screen, "there was no mistaking the applause . . . it was spontaneous and enthusiastic." One of Hoover's correspondents also reported that a great many farmers felt that the Republican Party had ignored their wishes.[76]

One group of farm leaders generally ready to support Smith was the Corn Belt Committee, which met in Des Moines on July 16. There it followed the lead of George Peek, who had called Hoover the "arch enemy of agriculture," and proceeded to pass a resolution endorsing the Democratic platform. At least fifty of the committee's sixty-two members also declared their intentions to vote for Smith. Brookhart, even though he was an honorary member of the committee, was not in attendance. He had received no notice, he said, of the last few meetings, and anyway, his obligation was to "the farmers and not to these men."[77]

Indeed, by this time Brookhart was moving closer to a public declaration of his support for Hoover. Although the alleged May meeting between the two remained secret, this was not the case with a meeting that took place immediately prior to Brookhart's return to Iowa, and in late June he told Iowa reporters that Hoover seemed to him likely to go further than the Republican platform on farm relief. He also had a talk with *Homestead* editor Frank Moorhead, who reported to Akerson that the Senator was "quite friendly" to Hoover.[78]

Brookhart decided, however, to delay any formal announcement until after the Democratic convention. He wanted to see what the Democrats would do; and they did pledge relief in a plank that endorsed McNary-Haugenism without specifically mentioning it by name. As Brookhart saw it, though, the plank was an "interminable and unthinkable document" showing "profound ignorance" of the agricultural situation. And not only that, the Democrats insisted upon taking credit for the Federal Reserve System, the very agency that had done more damage to agriculture than everything else put together. The Democratic action seemed to firm up Brookhart's decision to announce his support for Hoover.[79]

Brookhart's opinion about the Democrats was apparently based solely on their agricultural plank. The old prohibitionist made no mention of the fact that the Democratic candidate, New York Governor Al Smith, was a wet as well as a Roman Catholic. Although these two issues would figure prominently in the coming campaign, Brookhart would ignore them.

The announcement finally came at the Polk County convention meeting in Des Moines on June 30. There Brookhart told the Republicans that Hoover had given him assurances that as president he would work for real agricultural relief; and furthermore, he had expressed general agreement with the plans for a government-sponsored export corporation. Brookhart's announcement, said the *Homestead*, was likely to make him the "storm center in Iowa politics."[80]

In the wake of the announcement, moreover, a number of former Brookhart supporters did begin expressing their displeasure. Milo Reno, for example, now president of the Iowa Farmers' Union, excoriated Brookhart for supporting those whom he had formerly accused of betraying agriculture and thus associating himself with the MacNiders. Politics, he conceded, made for "queer bedfellows," but he hoped that Brookhart would not follow the "distressful example of Senator Cummins' gradual transition from a progressive defender of the plain people to a reactionary supporter of the vested interests." And two weeks later, a member of the Corn Belt Committee predicted that if Brookhart had "flopped over to the camp of McNider, Coolidge, [Secretary of Agriculture] Jardine and the rest," he would surely lose the support of the "common folk of Iowa."[81]

As Republicans gathered in Des Moines in mid-July, Smith Brookhart was in the unusual position of being among the "regulars" and of having his picture displayed alongside those of other "prominent" Republicans arriving in the city. The party, it seemed, was more united than at any time since 1920. Its insurgents, who had caused it so much grief in the past, were either gone or, like Brookhart, were supporting Hoover. As one old insurgent put it, "The extreme left in Iowa has frittered out." And as if to show how much things had changed, the man scheduled to address the convention in support of Herbert Hoover was Smith Brookhart.[82]

The only real controversy at the convention was over the agricultural plank of the platform. Brookhart presented his plan of a government subsidy, which was, so the *Register* reported, "amicably received" but voted down. Frank Lund then presented a resolution specifically endorsing the McNary-Haugen Bill, but that too was voted down. What the convention finally settled on was a plank professing "supreme confidence" in the "word, integrity and ability" of Hoover and calling for the formation of a federal farm board that would be "financially self-sustaining by the use of an equalization fee" or some other similar method. In the latter respect, the plank clearly went further than Hoover had been willing to go.[83]

Brookhart's appearance before the convention marked the first time he had been asked to give a formal address since he had chaired the meeting of 1912, and he began his speech by pointedly remarking on his lack of support from convention delegates in past years. Then, moving to the question of farm relief, he outlined his early support of Norris and his subsequent decision to support Hoover. The latter, he said, had agreed with him that cooperative marketing was "*a* solution of the farm situation." And while he seemed insufficiently aware of the need for emergency action, he offered the best available prospect for securing effective relief. Politically, Brookhart's own program had been rejected by national and state Republicans, and what the Democrats were offering was wholly unacceptable. Besides, Brookhart said, Hoover was the "greatest administrator" in the country, with a strong record of accomplishments in the past, and the Republican plank was "good, if it was interpreted rightly."[84]

Later in the campaign Brookhart would put aside whatever ambivalence he may have felt in July and support Hoover more enthusiastically, this despite the fact that the two men did not really agree on anything but the general ideal of cooperative marketing. His stance would result in still friendlier relations with and more praise from the regular Republicans and a further estrangement from Milo Reno and the Iowa Farmers' Union.

In the Iowa farm papers, there was a division of opinion as to what had happened at the convention. The *Homestead* called it the most harmonious convention in years and noted with some satisfaction that Brookhart had been an important factor in the deliberations. *Wallaces' Farmer* thought that Brookhart's argument for Hoover support would have had more credence if he had "stood firmly for the McNary-Haugen Bill" instead of his own. It also thought that farmers would like a strong statement from Hoover. And in the *Iowa Union Farmer*, the focus was on Brookhart's assertion in his convention speech that Milo Reno had double-crossed Iowa farmers by working with George Peek rather than Brookhart. In a long response, Reno defended his support of McNary-Haugenism and charged that it was Brookhart who had gone over to the camp of the enemy. His "natural egotism" had been "flattered" by those who wanted him to "pull their chestnuts out of the fire," leading him to expand the late German Kaiser's "me and Gott" to "me, Hoover, and Gott." And he had ended up abandoning the progressive principles he had once espoused and associating himself with the "reactionary group of the Republican party."[85]

Other Farmers' Union members also expressed their displeasure at what Brookhart had done. On July 23 John E. Bremmer, secretary of the Monona County Farmers' Union, had invited Brookhart to speak at a meeting in Mapleton. But following his endorsement of Hoover the invitation was withdrawn. Brookhart's response to such snubs was to intensify his attacks on George Peek, charging that the latter had gone over to the Democrats, and to lament the fact that Bremmer and the Farmers' Union had now "fallen into the hands of Tammany Al Smith boosters."[86]

Brookhart was also pleased when N. C. Gray, another Monona County man, invited him to speak at the Million Dollar Wheat Harvest Festival to be held in Blencoe. As the Festival chairman, Gray said, he wanted to prove that Monona County was not dominated by a "bunch" of Farmers' Union radicals like Bremmer. He assured Brookhart that amplifiers would be set up so that several thousand could hear him.[87]

In his Blencoe address on August 16, Brookhart again attacked Peek as a self-seeking politician hoping to advance his own interests at the expense of farmers. He also told of his own efforts to secure farm relief over the past eight years, blamed the failure of these efforts on the lack of support from established political organizations, and offered more praise of Hoover. Following the speech, the President of the Monona County Farmers' Union, Andrew Johnson, shook Brookhart's hand. "I am still with you," Johnson said, adding that he had been "mislead" about Hoover and was glad to have the matter cleared up.[88]

Following the Blencoe address, the county's Farmers' Union also decided to repudiate Bremmer's action and join with the local American Legion Post in inviting Brookhart to speak in Mapleton. There he appeared on September 13, speaking for two hours under threatening skies and telling the seven hundred in attendance that he appreciated the fairmindedness of the Farmers' Union in inviting him and realized that not all members had joined in the "discourtesy" of the previous month. He then praised Hoover's record while attacking the Democratic candidate, Al Smith. He was aware, he said, that there were Smith supporters in the audience and he wanted them to know the New York Governor's record on farm relief. In a 400-page critical study of Smith by the noted biographer Henry F. Pringle, he had been forced to read all the way to page 375 before finding the "first and last" word on farm relief. Smith, he had concluded, offered farmers nothing.[89]

The denouement of what one Iowan called the "Reno-Brookhart wild west show" came at the Farmers' Union state convention in September. Reno had invited Brookhart following the Republican convention in July, declaring that he wanted to give the senator an opportunity to explain his remarks about "double-crosses." Brookhart had accepted, and as he stepped up to the platform he quickly realized that, despite the applause, many of the 1,500 members in attendance were hostile. Consequently, he began by observing that he had heard of wagers being made that he would not appear. "Well, here I am," he said, "and you can pay off those bets."[90]

Then in a slow and deliberate manner, Brookhart proceeded to defend the record of Hoover and to answer the charges that George Peek and others had made about the candidate. He defended Hoover's position on the McNary-Haugen Bill and told the delegates of the visit to Coolidge at Hoover's request. He also attacked the record of Al Smith as unsympathetic to agriculture, finishing his recitation of Smith's deeds with the question "what do you think of that?" One voice on the balcony responded: "I guess we try him anyway."[91]

During the speech Brookhart was interrupted frequently by catcalls and hecklers, and at one point these became so strident that Reno had to call for order. The catcalls also continued as he left the podium and took a seat at the back of the hall. Finally, in an acknowledgment of his new status, he left the room with the Polk County Republican Party Chairman on one arm and the Secretary of the Des Moines Chamber of Commerce on the other.[92]

The catcalls, however, changed to cheers when Reno rose to speak, proceeded to blame Hoover and Coolidge for the low farm prices of the past eight years, and called for the passage of a resolution condemning the Republican party for turning a "deaf ear to the pleas for justice for agriculture." The resolution passed by acclamation, whereupon Reno led the delegates in singing Al Smith's campaign song "The Sidewalks of New York." Then to the accompaniment of more cheering, Reno removed his coat, rolled up his sleeves, and launched into an attack on Brookhart. The senator, he said, seemed to be suffering from a "severe attack of Peekitis"; and while he would not question Brookhart's integrity, "I just don't think sometimes he's smart." Brookhart, he said, had become a standpatter, and the audience, he thought, should be charitable because the life of such a person was "going to be hard enough." He himself was sad about what had happened to a former ally.

> When I see a man fall for blandishments and evil influence; when I see a man a victim of his own colossal egotism, I feel sorry for him. It's a pathetic thing. If Senator Brookhart can't deliver his new friends, they'll throw him out like an old rag.[93]

Brookhart's reputation was clearly hurt by the imbroglio with the Farmers' Union. Its members had been among his most loyal supporters, and now they hooted him out of the hall. In reporting the incident, the *New York Times* sympathized with his suffering but said that in time he would recover from his wounds.[94]

To a degree, moreover, this would prove prophetic. The next fall, after he had broken with Hoover over the President's betrayal of his campaign promises to agriculture, Brookhart would again appear before the Farmers' Union convention, would admit his disappointment with Hoover, and would be greeted with a rousing ovation, a better reception, he would admit wryly, than the one he had had the year before. Still, he would never again have the whole-hearted support of the Farmers' Union.[95]

Meanwhile, in the weeks following the Des Moines convention, Brookhart had also been basking in the glow of his newfound prominence. One of the first words of congratulations came in a telegram from Senator Borah, who told him that his work for Hoover had been received with "general satisfaction" in the West. He also reminded Brookhart of the opportunity this presented for agriculture, and Brookhart in reply said that a great deal would depend on Hoover's coming speech on agriculture, scheduled to take place at a homecoming rally in West Branch. There, at Hoover's birthplace, his campaign managers hoped to enhance his appeal for farmers, and to help do so campaign manager James W. Good had arranged for a two-day conference of agricultural leaders, Republican congressmen, and Republican Party workers. The conference was to be held in conjunction with the Hoover visit, and during it Good hoped to have the conferees meet with the candidate to dispel any doubts "as to the sincere and sympathetic attitude of Mr. Hoover toward this basic industry."[96]

Hoover, though, did not wait until he got to West Branch to speak out on farm relief. In his acceptance address at Palo Alto, California, on August 11, he took up the question and acknowledged the "urgent economic problem" facing the nation's farmers. Relief, he said, could be achieved through tariff revision and through the establishment of a farm board to aid in the stabilization of farm markets.[97]

In Iowa the major farm publications gave Hoover's remarks a cautious endorsement. Farm leaders were also cautious, many saying that they wanted to hear more when Hoover came to West Branch. Brookhart, though, was enthusiastic. Declaring that the speech displayed a "real knowledge" of the problem, he predicted that under Hoover's "construction of the platform" it would be easy to write an effective farm relief bill.[98]

The homecoming at West Branch took on the atmosphere of part-carnival, part-family picnic, and part Republican unity-fest as thousands wandered about the village and packed the big tent to listen to political speeches. Republicans from all factions of the Iowa party joined to praise the virtues of the native son; and as Brookhart rose to speak, he was given a rousing reception. In his address, he urged his listeners to "choose this native son because he best understands your present problems and accurately sensed the precarious position of the farmer during the deflation period." The speech was interrupted by applause a number of times, none more loudly than when he declared: "You have always known where I stand on the farm question. If Herbert Hoover were not for farm relief, I wouldn't be for him, if I got kicked out of the Senate half a dozen times."[99]

The main attraction was Hoover's speech that evening. In it the candidate began with a paean to his boyhood in West Branch. He then went on to contrast the Iowa of that period with the current situation; nowhere, he observed, was the change more obvious than in agriculture. He also admitted a "sentimental regret" for the "passing of old-time conditions." But it was necessary, he said, to recognize that change was inevitable and that because of it the farmer was now selling his goods as one of thousands of producers and therefore had "become enmeshed in powerful, and yet delicate, economic forces" that were working "to his disadvantage."[100]

Hoover then reiterated the farm relief proposals from his Palo Alto speech. His goal, he said, was a "more economic and stable marketing system" for farmers to be achieved through a Federal Farm Board and large-scale farmer cooperatives. He was not in favor of putting government in control of agriculture or of subsidizing farm prices. Rather, he hoped that with "governmental assistance and an initial advance of capital," the agricultural industry would "reach a stature of modern business operations by which the farmer" would attain independence.[101]

At West Branch, Hoover spent the night on a nearby farm, and the next morning he and his family went on to Iowa City for a brief visit with University of Iowa President Walter Jessup. From there, they journeyed to Cedar Rapids, where Hoover held a series of meetings. These included lunch with thirty agricultural journal publishers, a meeting with Hanford MacNider and a delegation of veterans, a talk with a delegation of state farm leaders, and a reception for a group of farm state senators and congressmen, including Brookhart.[102]

On the afternoon of August 22 Hoover left Cedar Rapids, and on that evening the Iowa Republican Party held a rally officially opening the campaign in the state. State chairman Willis Stern had asked Brookhart to preside at the rally and to introduce the principal speaker, Indiana Senator James E. Watson; and as Brookhart rose to speak, he was greeted with prolonged applause. "What's the matter with you?" he asked with a broad grin on his face, "The last time I stood on a platform in Cedar Rapids you yelled for Dan Steck." This was followed by further raillery at the "Cedar Rapids gang." And declaring that anywhere else in Iowa it would not be necessary to say anything about the farm problem, Brookhart then took an hour to explain the situation to the partisan and friendly crowd.[103]

Over the next three months Brookhart would criss-cross the Upper Midwest speaking for Hoover. Immediately after the rally in Cedar Rapids, he went to Crown Point, Indiana, for a major address at the Lake County Fair. There he called the Republican candidate "able, courageous, efficient, and successful," and again he defended Hoover's wartime food administration record and said that he could do the same to bring farm relief. Again, too, he attacked Peek, noting that during the same period, Peek had been serving as chairman of the Commerce Department's Industrial Board, a position in which he had worked to lower food prices and thus the prices farmers received for their products. Peek's service on this board, said Brookhart, had "stabbed Hoover in the back and the American farmer at the same time."[104]

In addition, Brookhart claimed that once the farm depression began,

Hoover had supported the original Norris farm relief bill, which if passed would have given the farmer cost of production plus a reasonable profit. Secretary of Agriculture Wallace, however, had given his support to the McNary-Haugen Bill, and it was Wallace who had won the support of Harding. Hoover, so Brookhart said, was returning to the original Norris program, and "upon this theory," it was possible to write a farm bill "that will give equality to agriculture."[105]

The Crown Point speech became Brookhart's standard campaign statement for Hoover. It was reprinted by the Republican National Committee in pamphlet form and was then widely distributed throughout the farm states. As critics saw it, Brookhart had moved capriciously from his own program to McNary-Haugenism to support Hoover. But some commentators, the *Register* among them, concluded that his enthusiasm for Hoover was not an "overnight affair." He had been a long-time supporter of the cost-of-production program that Hoover now seemed to embrace.[106]

Following the Indiana speech, Brookhart returned to Washington, Iowa, where he spoke at the annual Dutch Creek Fair. There well over six hundred people, the largest crowd ever at the rural neighborhood event, heard him give a "clear and convincing exposition of the issues." He then left for Chicago, where he spoke at a Republican Labor Day rally, and from there continued east for a strategy meeting with Hoover and other Republican leaders.[107]

During a day-long meeting with Hoover, Brookhart discussed the farm situation at length and he emerged from the meeting declaring his "wholehearted" agreement with Hoover. He said that he told Hoover that he had recently visited Iowa, Illinois, Indiana, Ohio, Nebraska, and Missouri, and that farmers in those states were "satisfied" with Hoover's farm proposals. He had also been in the South and told reporters that this normally Democratic stronghold, especially Georgia, Louisiana, and Tennessee, was worthy of the "serious attention of the Republicans."[108]

At the strategy meeting, Brookhart coordinated his speaking schedule with the Hoover campaign plans, the result being that he was kept on the move all over the Midwest. In one fifteen-day stretch in mid-September he gave forty-three speeches in Iowa, almost always to large and friendly crowds. At Winterset, for example, he spoke to upwards of three thousand people; at Atlantic he filled the city hall; at Manning he held the "close attention of those present and no heckling was done"; and at Fort Dodge, where he was introduced by the Tenth District Committeewoman, Gladys W. Griffith, who called his campaign for the farmer "courageous," the crowd was so large that public address speakers were set up to accommodate those forced to remain outside.[109]

During the first two weeks of October, Brookhart campaigned in North

Dakota and Nebraska, where he also attracted large and enthusiastic audiences. On October 9, for instance, he spoke before a crowd of over seven hundred Republicans at Fremont, Nebraska. He then swung back through Iowa and moved into Missouri, delivering a speech in Sedalia and following this with a sentimental return to his birthplace, Memphis. There before an overflow crowd of friends and relatives, he was introduced with understandable hometown hyperbole. "His eloquent tongue," said the master of ceremonies, "[is] ever ready in debate and his voice [is] always raised in denunciation of wrong." As the introduction ended, the band began playing the "Iowa Corn Song" and the crowd cheered wildly. Brookhart had trouble choking back his emotion. But with tears in his eyes he acknowledged the welcome. He then launched into his usual campaign speech and ended by predicting a sweeping victory for the Republican ticket.[110]

Although Brookhart was generally well received as he moved across the Midwest, the *Register* reported that some of his old supporters in northwest Iowa were no longer with him. This area of the state had been La Follette's stronghold in 1924, and it was the part of the state with the most radical Farmers' Union membership. In appearances there, he decided to confront the Farmers' Union opposition head on. Following the ordeal at the Farmers' Union convention, he routinely began his speeches to such audiences by asserting that Milo Reno thought he ought to desert Hoover but that he thought differently. His reply was a defiant "I won't do it."[111]

Such experiences were evidence of a changed status, and so in a different way was his appearance before the Des Moines Chamber of Commerce on September 21. Earlier in the day he had been shouted down at the Farmers' Union convention. But before the Chamber of Commerce he was cordially received and his standard message was greeted with polite, if not wholly enthusiastic, applause. Being Brookhart, however, he could not resist commenting on how slow those in the audience had been to recognize the farm problem. A few years before, he reminded them, they had ignored him; two years before they had tolerated him; now they had given him a royal welcome. "Two years hence," he said, "you may even pay some attention to what I say."[112]

Meanwhile, opponents of Hoover were hoping that Brookhart would make political mistakes that would aid their cause. Senator Steck, for example, tried to prod him into an exchange by noting his past irregularity and questioning the basis of his support for Hoover. Smith supporter Frank Murphy of Minnesota tried to lure him into another Emmetsburg-like mistake by challenging him to a debate about who was double-crossing the farmer, a challenge that Brookhart did not accept. And when the Senator told the story of how Hoover had sent him to Coolidge, Steck was quick to question his veracity. Why, he wanted to know, had Hoover not gone to Coolidge himself or at least made his role in the affair public? To this, Brookhart replied that Hoover had gone to Coolidge. He had, he said, been told of such action by six Congressmen, including William Hull of Illinois.[113]

When questioned about the matter, Congressman Hull told reporters that Brookhart's account was "substantially correct." He had met with Hoover in July and had learned that Hoover was "anxious to help agriculture" and seemed to agree that the McNary-Haugen Bill was "the only opportunity." He came away with the impression that Hoover had wanted to give the bill a chance to work and had so indicated to Coolidge. George Akerson was then questioned and, after allegedly discussing the question with Hoover, issued a carefully worded nondenial statement: "I do not have any idea in the world that Mr. Hoover ever did such a thing, or that Mr. Brookhart said any such thing."[114]

The revelation, said the *Register*, had changed the "complexion" of the campaign in the Midwest, where many farmers had remained leery of Hoover and his position on McNary-Haugenism. In early August, Edwin N. Hopkins, an Iowa supporter who worked for the Meredith Publishing Company, had warned Hoover that eastern Republicans should not "make light" of the equalization fee feature of the bill because "a lot of people out this way believe in it." And on September 11, writing to Hoover again, Hopkins was still worried that "thousands of farmers" believed that Hoover would carry out Coolidge's "unfriendly" farm policies. "Everything possible must be done," Hopkins told Hoover, "to convince the farmers that you will support their cause." According to the *Register*, Brookhart had rendered Hoover this most important service.[115]

To the Smith people in Iowa, the discrepancy between Hoover's public opposition to McNary-Haugen and his alleged private support of it seemed to be just the issue needed to embarrass him. Peek wrote to General Hugh S. Johnson at the Democratic National Committee campaign office saying that Akerson's denial of Brookhart's claim should be widely used. And on October 3, J. I. Myerly of the Iowa Agricultural Equality League, a group funded by the national Smith Independent Organizations Committee headed by George Peek, sent a telegram to Hoover asking about the apparent contradiction between Brookhart's statements and Akerson's comment in the *New York Times*. Iowa farmers, the wire said, were "entitled to know" the truth, and Hoover owed them a "personal and public" explanation. Akerson sent the telegram to Hoover with a note saying that it was apparently an attempt to drag him into a controversy with Brookhart and advising him to "forget" the matter.[116]

Myerly kept up the pressure. Speaking on October 11, he charged that Hoover knew the best way to get a veto of the McNary-Haugen Bill would be to send Brookhart to Coolidge to ask the President not to do it. He added that he still had had no response to his telegram to Hoover.[117]

On October 16 Myerly sent another telegram, which prompted Akerson to wire Dante Pierce asking with some irritation just who Myerly was and what lay behind his ploy of sending telegrams in the hope of getting "damaging replies." Pierce replied that Myerly was head of the Smith campaign in Iowa, was working at Peek's directions, and was being paid by Peek.[118]

Milo Reno also wanted to keep the question alive. In a long pre-election article, he traced the history of the McNary-Haugen Bill and of Hoover's opposition to it, referred to Brookhart as Hoover's "minister plenipotentiary" to Iowa farmers and an "errand boy" between Hoover and Coolidge, and wondered why Hoover had not contacted the President himself. Brookhart's statement, he said, "may be" true, but if so, Hoover should clear the air by pledging to sign a future McNary-Haugen Bill.[119]

There was no reason, however, for Hoover to say anything about McNary-Haugen. In a *Register* straw poll published on September 30, 61 percent of those participating favored the election of Hoover. He ignored the demands for a statement, and Brookhart did not mention the incident again.[120]

In the last days of the campaign, Brookhart was constantly on the move. In Ottumwa on October 25 he was asked to comment on a report that George Norris had endorsed Al Smith and said that he would not believe it until he had heard it from Norris. When the endorsement was finally confirmed, he labeled it a "mistake" and said that he hoped Norris would realize this "in due time."[121]

On October 26 Brookhart was in Chicago, where he was joined by Congressman Gilbert Haugen and New York Agriculture Commissioner Clarence S. Wilson for a nationwide radio broadcast. He then went to Wisconsin for speeches in Sparta and LaCrosse and from there to Springfield, Illinois, and then back to Milwaukee. On the Saturday night before the election, he returned to Washington, but on Sunday evening left for Waterloo, where he was scheduled to give a radio address the following noon. It had been a long campaign, and by the time it was over Brookhart was showing the strain of his busy schedule. Still, he was enthusiastic and predicted as a conservative estimate that Hoover would carry Iowa by a margin of at least 100,000 votes. The Iowa farmer, he told a reporter, was a "pretty sensible man" who had not been "led astray by the extravagant promises of Al Smith and the Democratic party." His last speech was in

Clinton on Monday evening, after which he returned to Washington to spend election day.[122]

When the votes were counted, Hoover carried Iowa by 244,259 votes and swept to a decisive victory nationwide. To a degree the outcome was a vindication for Brookhart, who had staked his reputation and hard-won "regularity" on Hoover and could now, as the *Register* noted, share in the "triumph." There were some, moreover, who believed that his work for Hoover had changed votes. Writing to the *Register* just before the election, a Monona County doctor said that although he had never supported Brookhart before he would now take his advice and vote for Hoover. And later a Sioux City real estate man and former mayor told Hoover that while he had not been a Brookhart supporter in the past, he had seen the senator turn the votes of "thousands" of farmers away from Al Smith.[123]

For all his work, Brookhart was curiously quiet about claiming the spoils of victory. He issued no statement regarding the election, preferring, so it seemed, to stand on the assumption that Hoover knew what he had done for him. His post-election views, however, could be inferred from his last campaign statement:

> Herbert Hoover is the one man who stands before the American people in this campaign with a record of achievement in behalf of the agricultural interests of the country. He is in accord with the views which I have continually expressed that agriculture is entitled to an absolute equality with other industries. I believe that his election will bring about such equality.[124]

The second session of the Seventieth Congress convened on December 3. But it was a lame duck session with many of its members either defeated or retiring from office, with Coolidge in the last months of his presidency, and with the attention of most people focused on the president-elect. Farm interest groups were waiting to hear what Hoover would propose for farm relief and who would be selected as his Secretary of Agriculture.

Under these circumstances, farm leaders, congressmen, and administration officials were generally agreed that serious farm relief legislation would have to wait for the Seventy-first Congress. Brookhart was openly opposed to trying to do anything in the lame duck session. There would, he said, be no time to discuss any bill intelligently; and given the outcome of the election, the bill discussed would have to be something other than McNary-Haugen. Realistically, moreover, nothing could be started without word from Hoover, and until January 6 he would be out of the country on his Latin American tour.[125]

One major item of speculation during the period was that concerning who would become Hoover's Secretary of Agriculture. The first rumors suggested that he would keep William Jardine, but Brookhart told the *Register* that he had learned from a "high source" that this was not the case. He was urging the appointment of Dante Pierce. But, Hoover had decided early that none of the "farm papers" had cabinet material, thus ruling out not only Pierce but Henry A. Wallace, the son of Hoover's old cabinet adversary.[126]

The name most frequently mentioned for the nomination was Thomas D. Campbell, a Montana wheat farmer, who had recently been to Russia where he had advised the government about agriculture. Campbell had the backing of many in the party, especially banking and financial interests. But because of the latter, Brookhart was not in favor of his appointment and advised Hoover against it.[127]

Hoover finally appointed Arthur M. Hyde, a former reform governor of Missouri, noted for giving the state an efficient and business-like administration. This was a quality that especially appealed to Hoover. Brookhart said only that Hyde was a "good selection."[128]

It is difficult to tell whether Brookhart had any influence on Hoover's decisions. But he did confer with the president-elect a number of times in January and February, and the public perception was that he had become a regular party leader and something of an administration insider. Favorable comments about him began to appear much more frequently than before in eastern conservative newspapers; and the *Register*, referring to a Senate speech he had made, said that he was "becoming a remarkably effective public speaker."[129]

Other Iowa newspapers also joined in this praise of Brookhart. The *Oelwein Register* admired his willingness to take the lead on issues. The *Afton Star-Enterprise* and the *Madrid Register News* commented favorably on his farm program. And the *Manchester Press* expected him to follow the path taken by Senator Cummins and become a "pronounced conservative" before the end of his term. The *Decorah Journal*, however, doubted that the Brookhart of 1928 was any more Republican than he had been in 1924. In the interim he had simply beaten the "old gang" and would now proceed to "make them like it."[130]

Still, in spite of such public perceptions, there is no evidence to suggest that Brookhart had any role in Hoover's choice of a Secretary of Agriculture. On the contrary, his uncharacteristically lackluster response to the selection of Hyde suggests that the new Secretary did not have Brookhart's support. And if this was the case, what did it bode for his ability to influence policy making on other issues? Could it be dismissed as unimportant, or did it mean that his hopes of shaping the new administration's farm relief program were ill founded? Brookhart was inclined to believe the former. But his "regularity" in the party and his optimistic perceptions of the man he had helped to elect and upon whom he had staked his reputation would be sorely tested.

Brookhart unveiled his farm relief plan in mid-March. As usual his chief concern was market operations to raise farm income and to that end he proposed a $1.5 billion stabilization fund that would allow farmers to be paid the cost of production plus a profit of 5 percent. He presented the plan to Secretary Hyde and reported that Hyde had accepted it "in principle."[131]

When the plan was presented to Hoover he remained noncommittal, saying only that his position on agriculture was clear and could be found in his campaign speeches. Still Brookhart was optimistic. He thought that Hoover and Hyde wanted to solve the farm problem and if they remained in that frame of mind he could work with them.[132]

On March 25 the Senate Agriculture Committee began hearings on farm relief legislation. Since the administration had no plan to present as yet, Brookhart appeared as the first witness and presented his own bill. Everyone present was familiar with its contents and with his long-held arguments for equality for agriculture. Consequently, some of the liveliest questioning concerned Hoover's position on it, particularly since Brookhart had been introduced to the committee with the claim that no one was closer to Hoover than he was.[133]

Would the President, Senator Thaddeus Caraway wanted to know, sign the bill if Congress passed it? Had Brookhart discussed this with him? And in reply, Brookhart had to admit that he had not. All Hoover had done was to say he would sign "any effective bill" that would give farmers relief. But, Brookhart continued, he would not bring a bill before the committee if he did not expect it to be signed into law. His bill, he felt, was consistent with the promises Hoover had made in the campaign and was also consistent with the Republican platform.[134]

The sharpest questions about Hoover's intentions came from Brookhart's old ally, Senator George Norris. Couching his remarks in the stilted language of senatorial courtesy, Norris challenged Brookhart's assurance that Hoover would sign a bill. He recalled that agricultural relief had been before Congress for years and that previous presidents had either vetoed the legislation or worked for its defeat. Why, he wondered, would Hoover be any different? Moreover, said Norris, Hoover had not disclosed a detailed plan in the campaign nor had he done so since. The "promises of a political platform . . . [were] 90 percent buncombe," and he wondered if Brookhart wanted to go over the "ground again after we have been over it dozens of times unless we know in advance that we are going to have the bill approved."[135]

Brookhart agreed that all platforms (excepting Norris') were "buncombe" but he took exception to Norris' claim that Hoover's plan was unknown. It had been explained in "200 speeches" during the campaign, and that was not buncombe. Nor did he intend, Brookhart added, "to quit plowing the ground for agricultural relief until we get some results."[136]

There was, however, little more that Brookhart could say. For all of his "closeness" to Hoover, he still did not know what the President's farm program would be and had little more to go on than whatever assurances Hoover had given him the previous summer and in the months following the election. Within weeks he would learn that his faith in Hoover had been misplaced.

The details of the administration's farm plan began to emerge in early April and were not to Brookhart's liking. The plan would create a federal farm board to administer a loan program to local cooperatives, which in turn would loan money to members; and to finance this Secretary Hyde proposed an appropriation of only three hundred million dollars. In Brookhart's view this was far from enough, and he promised a fight on the Senate floor to increase the appropriation. He also disliked the feature of the plan that would make the board a part of the Agriculture Department. It should, Brookhart believed, be an independent agency; and he told reporters that he would take both questions as well as the size of the appropriation to Hoover.[137]

Congress convened on April 16, and the next day the president sent his long-awaited plan for farm relief to Capitol Hill. The only difference between it and the Hyde proposal of two weeks before was that the appropriation for the farm board had been raised to a half billion dollars. The surplus problem, Hoover made it clear, was to be handled by local cooperatives organized by commodity, and the government would in no way be involved with the buying and selling of commodities or with fixing their prices.[138]

With one notable exception most Republicans praised the bill. Brookhart's initial reaction was that the bill was "inconsistent" with the positions Hoover had taken in the campaign, and shortly thereafter he took to the floor of the Senate where he spelled out the inconsistencies in a two and one-half hour speech. As always he insisted that the goal was attaining equality for agriculture, and again he went over the reasons for the lack of equality. He then undertook a comparison between Hoover's statements during the campaign and the contents of the bill and of the message to Congress that had accompanied it.[139]

During the campaign, Brookhart noted, Hoover had said that the agricultural problem must be solved; that cooperatives were a part of a solution but not a complete solution; and that part of the solution must be to "secure greater stability in prices." But now he had taken positions "inconsistent" with those earlier pledges. Instead of saying that the problem must be solved, he was claiming that it could not be cured in a day and that such problems "can not be cured by legislation; they can not be cured by the Federal Government alone." Somehow nots and can nots had gotten into his program, indicating that he was moving away from those who had come into the current session of Congress expecting that his "pledges that 'It must be solved' would be kept." Similarly, even though he had admitted during the campaign that the "traditional cooperative is often not a complete solution," he was now going to rely solely on government loans to cooperatives. And finally, even though he had said that there needed to be a "greater stability in prices" and given the impression that this meant government intervention in the marketing system of the sort once undertaken by the wartime Wheat Administration, he was now rejecting this course of action and saying that "no governmental agency should engage in the buying and selling and price fixing of products."[140]

At bottom, Brookhart felt that he had been betrayed. At considerable political risk he had supported Hoover in 1928, had been a tireless campaigner, and by his own count had made over two hundred speeches for Hoover in which he had told midwestern farmers that he and they could work with him to produce meaningful farm relief. Now, he told the Senate:

> it was upon these speeches and those pledges that I presented the farm problem to the farmers of a dozen states in the Union. It was upon those pledges together with the pledges of the platform itself, that I believed we could get a bill under this administration that would be adequate and that would solve at least the farm-marketing problem. This bill does not keep those pledges; this bill hardly even purports to keep those pledges. . . . We were called in extraordinary session, with agricultural relief as the special purpose and are to go back to the farmers with this kind of a gesture and say, "This is all we can do for you." No; there will be a hereafter about all this. . . . I want to say to the Senate that I am here to fight and to fight to a finish, and the farmers are not going to be double-crossed with my consent.[141]

The April 24 speech became a "declaration of war on the administration." It was also a "declaration of independence" for Brookhart, who now broke with the regular Republicans and realigned himself with the insurgents. The move, however, provoked surprisingly little comment from Iowans. Most had apparently expected that he would break with Hoover sooner or later, and very few were willing to comment for the record. One exception was Milo Reno, who, immediately after Hoover had presented his plan, had said that he would laugh at Brookhart's support of Hoover if it were not so "pathetic." Expressing sorrow now for the "extravagant statements" Brookhart had made during the campaign, Reno nevertheless said that he admired his courage and hoped that a good farm bill would be passed.[142]

True to his word, Brookhart fought an unsuccessful battle to amend the farm bill and make it more like his own. But when it came time for the final vote on the bill, he went along with the farm state senators who voted for it. As passed, the bill provided for loans to cooperatives to help them form national marketing associations for each major commodity. In addition, the new Farm Board could establish government stabilization corporations to assist in emergencies through special loans or open market operations.

It was not all that Brookhart wanted. But the year before he had voted for the attainable McNary-Haugen Bill even though he did not like it, and now he did the same thing with the Hoover Bill. He still did not think that the bill went far enough; later he would call it a "toy bill." But it was all farmers were going to get, and he had no choice but to support it.[143]

Since 1921 Smith Brookhart had been fighting for relief for Iowa farmers. He had tried unsuccessfully to secure his own version of a farm bill, based on the cooperative marketing of agricultural products. When that effort failed, he supported the prevailing farm relief bill only to have that rebuffed by a president of his own party.

As 1928 approached he looked for a candidate and a farm relief plan that he believed was correct as well as one that could be passed and signed into law. He found his candidate in Herbert Hoover. As the wartime director of Food Administration, Hoover had advocated the kind of price supports Brookhart believed were now necessary. Moreover, Hoover supported the idea of marketing cooperatives as a means of more efficiently and profitably handling the huge agricultural surplus. Thus Hoover and Brookhart appeared to be in general agreement on a farm program.

But all was not what it seemed to be. The Hoover-Brookhart alliance was doomed from the start because of fundamental differences between the two men. Hoover's view of a government loan to private cooperatives was consistent with the kind of volunteerism and business associationalism he had advocated as Secretary of Commerce. But that was very different from the large-scale government-sponsored market cooperative advocated by Brookhart. Furthermore, by 1928 Hoover had long since rejected the idea of government price-fixing. He believed by that time that the artificial price supports of the Wheat Corporation had contributed to the farm depression he was trying to alleviate.[144]

In their conversations during the campaign, Hoover had either convinced Brookhart that they were in agreement or Brookhart had convinced himself. Either one is possible. By 1928 Hoover had become a master of the political "game," and as his biographer, George Nash observed, Hoover was "expert at tailoring his arguments to his audience." Brookhart had labored so long on the fringe that to hear someone of Hoover's stature agree with him must have been a heady experience. Moreover, he was probably blinded by the adulation that came with his newfound "regularity." But he should have remembered his own words. In 1910 he had said he would rather be "right than be regular." Being "right" had served him well for almost twenty years. In 1928 being "regular" seriously damaged his credibility and would be one factor that would lead to his eventual defeat.[145]

Berryman in the *Washington Star,* from the *Sioux City Journal,* October 7, 1924. *Courtesy, State Historical Society of Iowa.*

RULED OUT! Bransbaun in the *San Francisco Chronicle*, from the *Sioux City Journal*, October 10, 1924. Courtesy, State Historical Society of Iowa.

BORING FROM WITHIN. Harper in the Birmingham *Age-Herald*, from the *Literary Digest*, October 18, 1924. *Courtesy, State Historical Society of Iowa.*

"WHAT D'YA MEAN, YOU'LL NOT DESERT ME?" James in the *St. Louis Star,* from the *Literary Digest,* October 18, 1924. *Courtesy, State Historical Society of Iowa.*

BOLT OR NUT? Pease in the *Newark News,* from the *Literary Digest,*
October 18, 1924. *Courtesy, State Historical Society of Iowa.*

THE BACK TO NATURE MOVEMENT IN IOWA. J. N. Ding Darling in the *Des Moines Register*, June 2, 1926. *Courtesy, University of Iowa Libraries (Iowa City)*.

THE LAST DAY OF THE ROUNDUP. J. N. Ding Darling in the *Des Moines Register,* June 6, 1932. *Courtesy, University of Iowa Libraries (Iowa City).*

13

The Populist Becomes a Democrat

In 1928 Smith Brookhart sat for a portrait by artist Allen Philbrick. It was an election year and Brookhart had thrown his lot in with candidate Herbert Hoover in the hope that he would at last have real influence on agricultural policy. The artist portrayed a vigorous Brookhart, standing up, even appearing to lean out of the frame, his suit and tie slightly disheveled, staring directly at the viewer, ready for any assault on his program.

Two years later Brookhart sat for another portrait. Painted by Boston artist C. Arnold Slade, this shows a dignified, seated Brookhart, a man in repose. In his right hand he offers the viewer a paper with "cooperation" written on it. The Slade portrait shows Brookhart after his disillusionment with Hoover and at a time when opponents and Iowa Republican leaders were already looking ahead to the election of 1932 when Brookhart would be on the ballot. He seems to say that he still held to his fundamental beliefs, and continued to offer them as a solution to the problems that faced the nation.

Jennie, the family, and even the subject liked the Slade portrait better. But Brookhart's old friend, Edgar Harlan, preferred the first. "It is Brookhart in action," he told him, "if it has a certain crudeness it is a crudeness of the physical fearlessness of the champion and advocate. It is of the ruggedness of character and not the distortions of grotesqueness which go with aimlessness or weakness."[1] By the time the portraits were painted Smith Brookhart had spent his years in and out of the Senate concerning himself almost exclusively with the issue of agricultural relief. But with the passage of the Hoover farm program, Brookhart's remaining years as a senator became less focused and other issues and interests came to the fore. The major element of continuity was his continued application of a populist critique. As boom gave way to depression, he continued to blame Wall Street speculators, the concentration of credit, and the growth of corporate monopolies for the basic inequalities in the American economy, and he continued to offer remedies that called for the redistribution of wealth and power, the creation of new employment opportunities, and special relief to veterans.

As has been shown, Brookhart had a populist's faith in the notion of equality. He took the Declaration of Independence and Constitution literally as documents that enshrined equality of opportunity as the very foundation of Americanism, and he saw the Jeffersonian world of yeomen farmers as the best example of how this equality was to be achieved. Thus, when Brookhart fought for equality for agriculture, he meant not only parity in the market place and the political arena but also the preservation of the small individual farmer on his own land. Writing in 1927, he had declared that he was "unalterably opposed to corporation ownership of land." What he would later term the "chain farm" was opposed to the very nature of Americanism.[2]

Brookhart applied a similar argument in critiquing the growth of chain stores. In his mind, the small independent businessman stood alongside his neighbor, the small farmer, as a co-heir of the Jeffersonian ideal. Yet, increasingly in the 1920s, the small, independent, locally owned store found itself competing with units of a statewide or nationwide mercantile chain. Acting on the idea that consolidated management and purchasing functions could reduce costs and raise profits, developers of such chains had become especially active after World War I. In Iowa, by 1928, there were some 142 retail firms with headquarters in other states and about 475 firms with headquarters in the state and branch stores throughout it.[3]

As early as 1922, Brookhart had urged small businessmen to organize lest the "chain-store idea" force them onto the "rocks of disaster." As he saw it, the chain store was an evil monopoly, similar to the other monopolies that he had long fought. Like them, it had taken advantage of the "vicious system of corporation laws" and was now in the process of taking business away from the local merchant and destroying the "civic life of the small communities."[4]

As a defense against chain stores, Brookhart urged that local merchants form cooperatives similar to the cooperatives he had long urged for farmers. They might do so as "home defense leagues" or "community builders," and he noted that some had already been established. In Des Moines, for example, about seven hundred independent grocers were engaged in cooperative purchasing that was helping them to compete with chain grocers.[5]

In May 1928 Brookhart had offered a Senate resolution calling on the Federal Trade Commission to investigate the chain store system. Under it, the FTC was to determine whether the growth of chains violated anti-trust laws, whether the chains could be regulated under current law, and what, if any, changes in the law were needed. The resolution was adopted by a unanimous consent motion, but it would be four years before the FTC issued a report. By then it was too late for Brookhart to make use of the information.[6]

Brookhart also supported the Capper-Kelly bill, a measure that had first been introduced in 1926, and continued to be introduced in succeeding Congresses. It would allow manufacturers to establish retail prices for branded products and would thus establish a fair trade price that would prevent chain stores from using their volume-buying capacity to undersell independent competitors. Brookhart said that Capper-Kelly would give to small manufacturers, wholesalers, and retailers the same ability to fix prices that large corporations possessed and was therefore necessary to prevent the consolidation of the "production and distribution of the necessities and luxuries of life" in the "hands of a few."[7]

Another group of small businessmen that Brookhart sought to assist was the independent motion picture theater owners. Their enemy at the time was the large motion picture companies who had consolidated the production end of the rapidly growing industry and were trying to establish control over the exhibition end, partly by opening their own theaters but also through a block-booking system that forced independent exhibitors to take all or much of a studio's output in order to obtain the pictures that they wanted to exhibit. This had both economic ramifications and a social or moral dimension.

Economically, it meant that exhibitors had to pay to lease movies that they could not or would not show, or that they knew would not be patronized in their communities, while morally it was said to encourage the showing of movies that helped to undermine the community's moral structure. It was another example, Brookhart believed, of the evil exercise of monopoly power.

Brookhart had first offered an anti-block-booking bill in December 1927. He had also testified on behalf of it before the Senate Committee on Interstate Commerce, arguing there that its purpose was to prevent abuses that had a monopolistic tendency and prevented a free choice by independent exhibitors. The movie, he said, was an important part of the "economic, family, and social life" of the community, and it was therefore a matter of "grave public concern" when local exhibitors had no local control over what was shown in their theaters. The Committee heard a number of witnesses testify about the bill, but the Seventieth Congress had adjourned without taking action.[8]

Brookhart reintroduced the bill in 1929; and speaking for it on the floor of the Senate, he argued that it was necessary to "preserve for the American people the remaining vestige of competition" in what was becoming an increasingly monopolistic industry. He also argued that it would give the theater owner the "right of selection" of the films his public would want their children to see. And from this point on he tended to put increasing stress on the community standards aspect of the issue. Speaking in 1930 before a convention of Michigan theater owners, he stressed the potential of the movies not only to entertain, but to advance culture and propagate ideas. They were comparable to the schools in these regards, and "no government worthy of the name," he noted, had failed to retain "some measure of control" over education. It followed that control should be extended to the movies.[9]

As an advocate of government control, Brookhart also rejected the view that the industry had developed an effective system of self-regulation. In the face of sensational scandals, it had hired former Postmaster General and Republican National Chairman Will H. Hays to set standards for its output. But within a short time, Brookhart charged, Hays' real job had become one of protecting the industry from government reform or regulation and paving the way for further "monopolization."[10]

In Iowa, Brookhart received some support for his efforts to change the practice of the movie industry. The *Des Moines Register*, for example, commented that the movie industry could indeed become a "burdensome monopoly," and it expressed gratitude that Brookhart had forced the matter into the open. As might be expected, he also received high praise from the organizations of independent exhibitors. Speaking darkly about the "super-government" that controlled the industry and used the movie screens for "political purposes," the national secretary of one group told Brookhart that his investigations should be continued. So far, he said, they had only given a "glimpse" of what was going on. And the editor of a newsletter for exhibitors was even more effusive. In a letter to Brookhart, which he published in his newsletter, P. S. Harrison told him that:

> To break this monopoly is the wish of every independent theatre owner, and they look to you, my dear Senator Brookhart, to save them. Please do not be discouraged by the machinations of the Hays crowd, who put many obstacles in your way. Go forward, resting assured that the heart of every independent theatre owner is with you.[11]

The Brookhart Bill, however, did not pass in the Seventy-first Congress; and in February 1932 the senator introduced still another version of it. Like its predecessors, the third bill was aimed at preventing "restraint upon free competition" through the practice of block-booking. But in the Senate speech with which he introduced the bill, Brookhart stressed even more strongly the social and moral aspects of block-booking. The movies, he said, were second only to the homes, schools, and churches in their influence for good or evil on the "culture, habits, and morals of the public." Actors and actresses were "the idols of the young," yet often their off-screen lives were even more degrading than those they portrayed on the screen. And because their lives were "chronicled in countless publications," the average boy or girl knew more about these actors than about those who run the government.[12]

Concluding his remarks on the bill, Brookhart urged the Senate to continue its inquiry into the industry, and to that end he introduced a resolution to accompany the bill calling on the Committee on Interstate Commerce to reopen hearings on the matter. His goal, he said, was threefold, that those under investigation:

> see that competition in the business is kept decent and is not conducted in violation of the anti-trust laws, that they will see the wisdom of dissolving their chains of theaters and leaving the field of exhibition to the independent operators with their knowledge of public tastes and their local good will, and that they will restore prosperity to the great producing organizations by restricting them to their legitimate function of making wholesome pictures for the entertainment of the people.

Referred to the committee in February 1932, the bill languished there until December. It was then brought to the floor and passed over for any further consideration.[13]

Brookhart's economic argument about block-booking was consistent with his other economic arguments. But his argument about the on-screen roles and off-screen lives of movie stars came largely from hearsay evidence. In fact he was as innocent of movie stars as the "average boy or girl" was about politicians. Once he came home and told his family, "You know, I saw Alice Roosevelt Longworth in the elevator today and she was with some acting lady." His family learned from the newspaper that the acting lady was Ethel Barrymore, one of the great actresses of the day.[14]

On another occasion *Vanity Fair* magazine published a caricature of an imaginary interview between Brookhart and Marlene Dietrich. This was part of a series of such interviews drawn by Miguel Covarrubias and other subjects included interviews between John D. Rockefeller and Joseph Stalin, Eugene O'Neill and Jimmy Durante and Al Capone and Chief Justice Charles Evans Hughes. Each drawing was accompanied by a dialogue between the two people pictured. The Brookhart-Dietrich interview had Dietrich protesting that the immorality Brookhart ascribed to Hollywood did not exist. He said he made it his business to find it and then asked her to show him around the town. When the magazine appeared on the newsstand his son took a copy home and the family made much of it. The next day as his son drove the senator to the office, Brookhart asked, "Who is Marlene Dietrich?"[15]

The fight to preserve small farmers and small businessmen was just one manifestation of Brookhart's abiding populism. It had as its general theme that economic opportunity ought to be a universal characteristic; or, put another way, that each individual ought to be in control of his or her own life. And as a corollary of this, it held that sovereignty lay in the people and was to be exercised through their elected representatives. As James B. Weaver had put it in 1892, elective control was the "only safeguard of liberty." And representatives of the people should therefore work to bring institutions like the Senate, the Executive, and especially the Supreme Court under this kind of popular control. The latter, according to Weaver, had acquired a power that the founding fathers had never intended it to have, the power of judicial review; it had used this power to shield and protect such enemies of democracy as the slave power and big business corporations; and the way to advance democracy was to return to the intent of the founders, make the legislature the "supreme power," and put the judiciary back in a "subordinate" role.[16]

With this analysis, Brookhart agreed. In 1912 he had written a series of editorials on the issue of judicial recall, in which he had echoed Weaver and had said that the courts were the "last refuge of the big interests and the jackpotters." Their power to set aside legislative actions was in his view a "great menace" to liberty. And as a remedy, he had advocated the recall of judges by election. This, he had written, was "merely re-clothing the ballot box with the power it extended to the judiciary in the first instance. There is no power, in a republican form of government, that should be higher than the ballot box as a last resort on any question."[17]

It was not surprising, then, that the Brookhart of 1930 should use the occasion of the nomination of Charles Evans Hughes to be Chief Justice for a renewed attack on the Supreme Court. The court, he noted, contained some progressives willing to put human rights ahead of property rights. But historically, it had served the latter and helped to produce a government engaged in unequal treatment of its citizens, and Hughes' background as a corporation lawyer was such that confirming him would add one more justice to the court who would maintain the status quo.[18]

In conjunction with this attack, Brookhart also revived his projects for making the judicial system more responsive to the will of the people. He again advocated judicial election and recall, and he introduced a Senate resolution in favor of requiring a unanimous decision for the Supreme Court to declare a law unconstitutional. If anyone was to decide the constitutionality of a law, he thought, it should be the people's openly elected representatives, who were "just as honest" as any court and just as capable of following the Constitution. They had been elected by people who were competent to govern themselves and select representatives who would follow the Constitution.

Hence, the basic principle should be that "the Constitution made by the people should be construed by the representatives of the people."[19]

His fights against chain stores, movie moguls, and the Supreme Court were logical extensions of Brookhart's populist critique. But these new targets had not made him forget his earlier original foes, Wall Street and the Federal Reserve system. In July 1929, in an article entitled "Has the Federal Reserve Act Failed?," he had warned that unchecked speculation in the stock market could produce "one of the gravest economic crises" in American history. And in October, once the crash had occurred, he quickly concluded that the Federal Reserve system had been a disastrous regulatory failure. It had allowed credit to collect in the large New York banks and to be used by them to fuel the speculative fervor, an activity that was little more than gambling with the money that should have been available to farmers for credit. And now, not just the farmers but the entire nation had reaped the whirlwind. With a vehemence that was strong even for him, Brookhart declared that Congress "ought to kill this gambling business. . . . I mean kill it; I do not mean compromise or regulate it or anything of the kind."[20]

As might be expected, Brookhart also found the answer in the kind of cooperative banking system that he had advocated. Back in February 1928, he had introduced a bill to establish federal cooperative banks and a cooperative reserve system, a bill that Secretary of the Treasury Andrew Mellon had said would "impose upon the banking structure of the country a confusing duplication of functions and machinery" at "variance with the fundamental purposes of the Federal Reserve Act." And in January 1930 he offered the bill again, found that Mellon was still opposed, and took to bemoaning the fact that the United States was "the only civilized country which prohibits the farmer and labor from organizing their own savings into a cooperative credit system under their own control." The bill died in the Senate Banking committee, and with it died Brookhart's hope of cooperation as the answer to farm credit needs and speculative excess.[21]

In 1931 Brookhart also returned to his populist roots with criticisms of the gold standard reminiscent of those once made by the Greenbackers, the Populist Party, and the William Jennings Bryan wing of the Democratic Party. The gold system, Brookhart argued, should be ended, and in December 1931 he introduced a bill to bring this about. The system, he said, was not the sole or even primary cause of the depression. But a better system more capable of preventing depressions could be developed. And he could see no reason why the country should continue to "cling to this fetish" of gold. Its proponents had promised eternal prosperity, but instead the country had got a depression every few years.[22]

The traditional Populist remedy of bimetalism, Brookhart thought, would be an improvement over the existing system. But the real answer, he finally decided, was a dollar based on the value of all commodities rather than precious metals alone and a supply of dollars that would grow at a steady rate rather than being determined by the Federal Reserve Board. He proposed to calculate the aggregate value of all 550 commodities that entered into the Department of Labor's calculation of the consumer price index and to keep the value of the dollar at a fixed fraction of this aggregate value. And the money supply he would increase by 4 percent a year, a figure that represented the long-term average annual increase in net national income. In effect, he would combine the commodity dollar plan advanced by various other monetary reformers at the time with the kind of fixed monetary growth rule advocated by both populist and conservative critics of the Federal Reserve system.[23]

Brookhart hoped that this scheme would stabilize the value of the dollar and keep enough dollars in circulation in a way that the gold standard could not. He proposed it in 1932, but few people bothered to comment since by that time, he was, for all practical purposes, a lame duck senator.

Meanwhile, Brookhart kept busy outside the Senate as a popular speaker on the Chautauqua circuit. In the summer of 1930 he traveled throughout the South, East, and Northeast delivering approximately seventy lectures and reportedly receiving as much as $500 plus expenses for each speech. One Iowa paper reported that he was making $26,000 a year from his speaking dates, which when added to his $10,000 Senate salary gave him a gross income of $36,000. These figures are probably exaggerated. In January 1930 he signed a contract to give ten or more Chautauqua speeches for $100 per speech. Yet even if the lower figure is correct, it would still seem an enormous sum to Iowans suffering from the depression.[24]

What Brookhart would not say, of course, is that he needed the money to pay off the bank debt. His reticence on the issue made him appear somewhat greedy and left him open to criticism. In Iowa several newspapermen soon began to take notice of Brookhart's "double salary." The *Rock Valley Bee*, for example, criticized him for collecting a Senate salary while "working for his health" on the Chautauqua circuit. And the whole issue was further magnified when the Senate was called into a special session in July 1930 to debate the London Naval Treaty. Although Brookhart favored the treaty, he saw no reason to interrupt his schedule and return to the Capitol for the debate.[25]

Arriving in Des Moines on July 15 for the Republican State Convention, Brookhart defended his absence from the Senate. His speaking dates, he said, were close to Washington, which meant that he could get back for a vote if necessary. He had also been given to understand that no vote was scheduled while he was in Des Moines.²⁶

After leaving Des Moines, Brookhart did make an appearance in the Senate, arriving there on July 21 just in time to vote for the treaty. His appearance on the last day of the special session enabled him to collect his salary for the entire session. Nor did this escape notice in Iowa, where the *Register* had put a box on page one indicating the number of days that the Senate had been in session and the number of days that Brookhart and Steck had been absent. The absentees, the *Register* said, "should be reminded by their constituents that neglect of duty at this critical time is indignantly disapproved."²⁷

Whether Brookhart's attendance record was worse than other senators is doubtful. At the time lax attendance was common. But his absences while keeping lucrative speaking dates would give his opponents an issue to use against him in the 1932 campaign. They could depict him as being cavalier about his Senate responsibilities, although in fact he took them quite seriously.²⁸

On the Chautauqua circuit, Brookhart had a number of speeches that he used again and again. There were speeches on cooperative economics, the farm problem, Wall Street, and his trip to Europe. But most often he talked about the first issue of his political life, prohibition. This, although a life-long dry, he had never turned into a moral crusade. His emphasis instead had been on what it could contribute to healthy and productive living and to national efficiency. But he remained a strong supporter of the Eighteenth Amendment, regarding it as the "greatest victory for civilization" to come out of World War I. And while he had not felt it necessary to say much about it in the 1920s, even in campaigning for Hoover against Smith, he was now ready to challenge the repeal movement and its arguments that the "noble experiment" had failed.²⁹

As Brookhart saw it, national prohibition had not failed; rather it had never really been tried, because from the beginning enforcement had been lax. It had been put under the aegis of the Treasury Department, which, so said Brookhart, had "not been in sympathy with the prohibition law" and had "not cared to enforce it." In January 1930 he demanded the removal of Secretary Mellon and several other department officials for failure to enforce the law.³⁰

To illustrate his point about lack of enforcement, Brookhart also revealed that liquor had been served openly at a dinner attended by a number of senators. He was then called before a grand jury to testify about the matter, but no action was taken. The revelation created a national sensation. But most commentators would probably have agreed with *Commonweal*'s observation that while it was good to know the truth there was no excuse for Brookhart's "gross lapse in good taste."[31]

The furor over this revelation had barely died down when Brookhart made another that again put him in the headlines. Charging that the problem of prohibition enforcement was due to the attitude of high society, he told about the New York Century Club and the "Fish House rum punch" served at its annual dinner. This was another example, he said, of a small elite group which thought that it was above the law. There was, he conceded, a small "crowd of intellectual people" who wanted repeal. But this was small "in comparison with the whole number" of Americans.[32]

In addition, Brookhart was ready to take on repeal advocates in public debate. In February 1930, he and New York Congressman Fiorello La Guardia went to Cleveland to debate the issue: "Resolved, that prohibition can be enforced." It was a lively debate, but the only real winner was the audience who packed the hall to enjoy the show.[33]

The next month Brookhart traveled to New York City to challenge attorney Clarence Darrow in a debate moderated by syndicated columnist Heywood Broun. The liberal Darrow said that people ought to be allowed to do what they wanted regarding liquor. Brookhart replied that Darrow was preaching "anarchy," since it was the "duty of every man . . . to obey the will of the majority." Later Darrow said of Brookhart: "He is sincere; it's too bad he is uncivilized."[34]

The liquor controversy followed him even when he left the country. In March 1931 Smith and Jennie joined two other senators and their wives for a trip to the Panama Canal Zone. He had kept the household stirred up for weeks in preparation for the trip and had even made a "huge concession" to Jennie when he agreed to buy a new lightweight suit, some new shoes, and six new shirts! They sailed aboard the *Ancon* on March 17 and arrived in Panama on the 23rd.[35]

Brookhart did a great deal of fishing and was very proud when after catching many small fish he reeled in a forty-pound red snapper. Brookhart and the other senators toured American facilities in the Canal Zone and spoke at high schools and military installations. But a controversy arose when he was invited to speak at the Panama Club, a club for Americans who lived in the Canal Zone. The Club served liquor and Brookhart refused to attend a wet party. The matter received wide attention in the newspapers and, it was reported, strained relations with the Republic of Panama. Brookhart said that he would introduce a resolution to prohibit members of the American Armed Forces in Panama from patronizing any establishment that served alcohol.[36]

A week after Brookhart left Panama the American entertainer Will Rogers appeared in Panama. The American Ambassador Roy T. Davis told

Rogers of the furor Brookhart had created and asked him to say something about it. Appearing that night Rogers told the audience, "I read what our Senator said about your 'wallowing in sin.' . . . Just as soon as I read that I hopped in a plane and flew to Panama. . . . I thought if you was 'wallowing in sin,' why I'd ask you to move over and I'd wallow with you."[37]

Brookhart would later oppose the Twenty-First Amendment. But by then he would be like King Canute trying to hold back the tide. The tide had even turned in Iowa. In February 1932 the *Register* conducted a straw poll on the question of prohibition. In it 38,061 Iowans said that they were in favor of the repeal of the prohibition amendment and 28,419 said they were against repeal.[38]

In his stand for prohibition, he remained consistent throughout his career. But his revelations and debates on the question made him seem more foolish than principled. In the midst of a senate debate on the issue Senator David I. Walsh of Massachusetts put a bit of doggerel in the *Congressional Record*:

> I come from way out in Iowa
> The home of corn and many an art,
> Where bootleggin's so bad
> It makes all of us sad
> That everyone knows it but Brookhart.[39]

In the face of changing attitudes in the country and state, his stance gave Iowans one more reason to question whether he should continue to represent them.

Despite the fact that Brookhart was often in the headlines, Iowans still had difficulty in assessing him. One who tried was Sioux City editor Arthur F. Allen, who said that Brookhart was "not lacking in courage" and was more "respected" than before but was often "reckless" and still "personally disliked." As for his program, Allen thought it was not constructive and that he was too much of a lone wolf to achieve it. Still, Allen concluded with some surprise that he thought that Brookhart's hold upon the state was "as strong as ever."[40]

Another assessment came from Iowa Falls editor I. A. Nichols, who wrote that while Brookhart gave the state progressive leadership he was either "too far out of line with the tribe or too far ahead of the tribe to be effective." One of Brookhart's Senate colleagues agreed. His views on economics were "honest," but they were too "fantastic" to be implemented.[41]

Still another assessment came from a sometime Brookhart ally, Louis Cook. Writing in *North American Review*, Cook said:

Senator Brookhart . . . wins because the people believe he is sincere and because he voices a lot of protests which touch a sympathetic spot in the hearts of Mr. Common Citizen. Brookhart is unquestionably a demagogue, in the old and original Greek sense of the word. He is a leader of the people, voicing the views of the masses of citizenship as against the views of the men who represent the oligarchies of business and partisan politics. Leaders of this type are seldom popular with the so-called vested interests, but they do get a lot of votes. . . . Brookhart will be up for reelection in Iowa again in 1932. . . . He has no organization, many of his former strong supporters are either opposed to him or are no longer active. . . . That noise you hear in Iowa is not the wind rustling in the corn. It is the boys who are supposed to run things politically whetting their snickersnees upon their boot soles.[42]

While the editors offered assessments, the politicians in Iowa seemed equally ambivalent and as early as 1930 were already looking ahead to 1932. Writing shortly after the June 1930 primary, one statehouse politician urged the new gubernatorial nominee, Dan Turner, to run against Brookhart. And following Brookhart's departure from the 1930 Republican State Convention, ostensibly to vote on the Naval Treaty, Iowa Congressman Cyrenus Cole wrote the President that Iowa farm conditions had created animosity toward the Senate as a whole and that Brookhart "seemed to sense the changed conditions" and "slipped out of town."[43]

The coming election remained an object of speculation throughout the winter of 1930-1931. Former Sioux City Mayor William S. Gilman wrote Hoover to report that although the eleventh district was united on other matters, there was "considerable difference of opinion" regarding Brookhart. And another northwest Iowa man told Henry A. Wallace that opinion seemed to be that Brookhart was so strong that he could not be beaten. Wallace's correspondent, however, reminded him of the story of David and Goliath.[44]

If Republicans were beginning to sense the possibility of a Brookhart defeat, the Democrats were even more optimistic. The economy was sinking even deeper into depression; farm foreclosures were on the rise; and dissatisfaction with all officeholders was growing. Democrats began to think that their time had come and were encouraged by the fact that while Steck had lost in 1930, they had elected their first Congressman since 1914. They felt that their chances of defeating Brookhart were now better than they had been in 1924.[45]

Brookhart knew that he was vulnerable, and in May 1931 he came back to Iowa to begin repairing fences. He had always done his best when campaigning personally and he now hoped to see as many Iowans as possible. He found, however, that both parties were gearing up to unseat him and that he had not yet regained the strong support that the Farmers' Union had given him prior to 1928. In addition, his administrative assistant and chief political operative, Roy Rankin, was ill. He died of cancer in the late fall of 1931 and had to be replaced by the senator's son, Smith, Jr. Just out of law school, the younger Brookhart had none of the political savvy and knowledge of the state that Rankin had possessed and so could not adequately fill his shoes.[46]

Nevertheless, Brookhart remained as optimistic and pugnacious as ever as he criss-crossed Iowa in search of votes. In Floyd County he spoke before 2,000 farmers gathered at a picnic of cooperative associations, giving a speech that might have been given in 1922. In it he blamed Wall Street, the 1920 Federal Reserve Board decision, and the Transportation Act of 1920 for the ills of farmers; offered a federal cooperative bank system as the remedy; and claimed that while the newspapers would call him a "bolshevik" and an "anarchist," he was actually bringing out truths that the papers were trying to conceal. Although the speech was billed as the opening of his reelection campaign, the only reference to the coming election was his statement that he had been fighting farmers' battles for years and that if they wanted him to continue he would "be glad to carry on."[47]

The big political event of the summer came in September when politicians gathered for the opening day of the Iowa State Fair. It was important to be seen there, and no politician facing reelection would miss the opportunity to shake hands with thousands of Iowa farmers. Brookhart had been campaigning all summer and seemed more confident than ever on opening day when he was pictured with Iowa's other senator, L. J. Dickinson, who had defeated Dan Steck in 1930, the first time in years that both senators had attended the fair on the same day.[48]

Republican unity, however, was only superficial. Two Republicans, Louis E. Eickelberg of Waterloo and Lars J. Skromme of Roland, had already announced that they were candidates against Brookhart. In addition, several other Republicans were being mentioned as possible candidates. Included in this group were former Governor John Hammill, former opponent Howard Clark, and former senator David Stewart. The most prominently mentioned Democrat was former senator Dan Steck.[49]

Brookhart's weakness in Iowa was revealed dramatically by a *Register* straw poll taken in early 1932, the first results of which indicated that 59 percent of those polled were against his reelection. Brookhart's response was to write the paper, saying that he was amazed at the conclusions reached by comparing the results of a poll taken before the primary with vote totals from his last general election. Pointing out correctly that he had never done as well in a primary as in a general election, he said that those who voted for him in the straw poll would do so in the primary and that they would be joined by many others in the general election. In reality, he claimed, Republicans had not "cooled off" toward him but had "warmed up" considerably.[50]

Obviously, though, Brookhart was trying to put the best face possible on a bad situation. The final results, published in early March, indicated that he had received only 41 percent of the nearly 78,000 ballots tabulated; and even more troubling was the fact that of the 38,189 Iowans who said they had voted for him in 1926, only 29,913 said they would vote for him in 1932. The underlying problem was perhaps best pointed out by Jennie. Writing her son Ned in mid-February, she had said that:

> They are having a straw vote in Iowa—the senator will not get all, perhaps enough—there's much bitterness about present conditions—no sale for farm products—high taxes, etc. So much money tied up in the banks that are closed—they must blame someone.

One month later she wrote Ned, "He thinks he will win easily but I'm not so sure—time will tell."[51]

Two nationally known Iowans were mentioned as possible Brookhart opponents. In the summer of 1931 a number of Iowans suggested that *Register* cartoonist Ding Darling oppose Brookhart. The possibility of a Darling candidacy remained current throughout the fall and winter. Darling finally put an end to the talk in January 1932 when he published a letter in the paper stating that he declined to run. Darling had never made a secret of his opposition to Brookhart and he told Iowans, "No, I don't want to be a senator; but I'd be very grateful for a chance to vote for a good one."[52]

Henry A. Wallace had also been urged by friends to run. But in the end he too declined. When an astrologer had suggested to Wallace that the stars were right for a candidacy, the editor told a friend:

> Fate may decide that I run against him but it will not be my decision. Neither do I know whether I would run against him in Republican primaries, Democratic primaries, or as an independent. Still I hope I will not have to run at all—although it now appears I could get a lot of influential support.[53]

If Darling and Wallace were unwilling to take on Brookhart nine other Iowa Republicans announced an intention to run against him in the primary election. Four, however, decided to drop out before the ballot was printed. This left the senator with five challengers.

One was Louis Eickelberg, who had entered the race the previous fall and was now offering a scheme to restore "perpetual prosperity" by keeping all the factors of the economic system in balance. He would receive only about 8,500 votes and would attribute this to the fact that his idea was "too deep for the people" to understand.[54]

The second candidate was former attorney general George Cosson, who favored cutbacks in government expenditures and a reduction in taxes. He was also especially effective with a series of questions in which he asked Brookhart what he had done to raise any farm price by 1 percent, or to provide one additional job, or to aid business. The questions helped to paint the picture of Brookhart as an ineffective senator who, for all his talk, had accomplished nothing. Cosson would take 29,687 votes from Brookhart.[55]

Brookhart's third opponent was Glenn C. Haynes, a former state auditor who had also been Commander of the Iowa American Legion. In his platform, Haynes attacked Brookhart's absenteeism by promising "the devotion of my full time" to the duties of the Senate. He also proclaimed that he would enter the "Republican primary as a Republican," and would work to "restore the good name of Iowa and enhance the prestige" of the Iowa delegation in Congress. He would receive 43,050 votes.[56]

The Cosson and Haynes candidacies were especially damaging to Brookhart since they were able to mobilize those who felt that his ten years of demanding action on the farm question had only left farmers in worse shape than ever. They also appealed to those who no longer took pride in Brookhart's vaunted social and political independence and saw him instead as being unproductively eccentric.

The fourth candidate was Brookhart's former campaign manager, Louis H. Cook, a writer and editor for several newspapers and the author of several national magazine articles about Brookhart. He would finish next to last, with only about 12,000 votes, but he was the candidate who, in October 1931, had raised the most damaging issue of all. Brookhart, he had charged, was guilty of nepotism in that he had employed four of his children, one following the other, at government salaries ranging from $1,500 to $3,000. He also alleged that Brookhart had collected travel expenses to attend an official funeral in Iowa at a time he had already been in the state.[57]

Brookhart was not the only senator with family members on the payroll. An article in the *Atlantic Monthly* listed twenty-four senators who employed members of their families. Nor was the practice illegal, a fact that Cook was careful to point out. But still, the idea that the children of a senator could get jobs at a time when the children of many other Americans could not hurt Brookhart. In addition, the charge was damaging to his portrayal of himself as an anti-establishment, anti-organization politician. He now seemed just like all the other politicians, out to take care of himself and his family first. It was an issue that would not go away, that probably affected the results in the

Register poll, and that Brookhart would have to spend much of his time trying to answer.[58]

The fifth challenger, Shenandoah nurseryman and radio personality Henry Field, came into the race as party leaders sought to prevent a repetition of what had happened in 1922 when the opponents had so split the anti-Brookhart vote that Brookhart won. Cook had early warned about this, suggesting that all other candidates get behind him; and in early April, minor candidate William Galloway had withdrawn because he feared that party professionals were trying to so split the vote that no one would receive 35 percent and the choice would be left to the convention. At this stage, another minor candidate who later withdrew, Vernon Haig, also suggested a meeting to settle on one candidate. But nothing came of this. By this time party leaders believed they had found someone to play the role that Clifford Thorne had sought to play ten years earlier, someone, in other words, who would be well known to farmers, sympathetic to their situation, moderately progressive on other issues, and therefore able to lure away some of Brookhart's expected constituency. Field, it was believed, could do this. His seed catalogs were to be found in most Iowa homes; and his radio program, featuring farm news, household hints, gardening tips, and a folksy "It's Henry himself speaking," had made him a familiar and comfortable member of farm families all over the Midwest.[59]

Party leaders had come to Field to urge him to run for the Senate. But suspecting that they only wanted him on the ballot to split the vote so that Brookhart would not win, he had initially declined. Some of his townsmen had then organized a Henry Field for Senator Club under the leadership of A. N. Ahlgren. They had asked him to reconsider; and when he did not rule out the possibility, the club had sent a letter to party members across the state asking them to indicate their support. At the state convention in Des Moines on March 22, Field was met by a constant stream of people urging him to run, and late that afternoon he made his announcement and declared that he would run on the slogan: "From Iowa and Proud of It." Iowa, he said, was the "best state in the union," and he wanted the rest of the country to know it. "If I don't win," he added, "I'll have a lot of fun. I'm not going to abuse anybody; just strive to win the nomination as a businessman and farmer."[60]

Field had not wanted to run as the candidate of the bosses and had come in only after the Ahlgren group had generated a groundswell of support. But one *Register* correspondent said that it was "self-evident" that the bosses, who cared "nothing for Henry Field," had injected him into the Senate race to defeat Brookhart. Senator George Norris also wrote to Field, defending Brookhart's record in the Senate and saying that it would be a "serious blow to the Progressive cause" if he were defeated. He then reminded Field that if no one got 35 percent and the nomination went to a convention, no progressive could expect to win, and it had come to him confidentially, he said, that the "machine politicians" had flooded the ticket to defeat Brookhart and that Field's role was to divide the farm vote.[61]

In reply, Field told Norris of his high personal regard for Brookhart but said that the senator could not get reelected. He then said:

> I don't believe you down at Washington know the real grass-root situation here in Iowa, as well as some of we people out here do, and I don't think you realize the drift there has been away from Senator Brookhart in the last two years. Not that he hasn't been true to the interests of the people, as he has generally been headed in the right direction. But the complaint is that he has accomplished nothing whatever with his legislative proposals. They admire you because you have really accomplished something, but Senator Brookhart hasn't seemed to put his proposals over.[62]

In Field's view, if Norris wanted a progressive senator from Iowa it would have to be him.

Field hoped for a campaign "conducted on a high plane of courtesy and good fellowship." He invited Brookhart to speak over his radio station and to "eat chicken stew with Mrs. Field and myself at the cottage." But Brookhart would have none of it. He said that Field's entry into the race had been engineered by the same men who had "stabbed [him] in the back" before and because of that their former relationship had changed. He wrote Field:

> I would be glad to meet you again and sit with you and your good wife at dinner in the little doll house and look you straight in the eye and say that Henry Field is my good friend; that he refused to be deceived by a vicious gang of politicians and withdrew from the race to aid in the fight for the farmers, the laboring people, and the common people of Iowa.[63]

Meanwhile, Brookhart had left Iowa the day before the March convention. Byron Allen, his campaign manager, had told reporters that the press of Senate business would make it impossible for him to attend. And not until May, despite the fact that the field of contenders kept growing and changing so that Brookhart's principal concern was to get 35 percent of the vote, would he return to Iowa to begin his own campaign.[64]

Arriving in Washington, Iowa, on May 2, Brookhart seemed to relish the prospect of another battle. He was in high spirits and said that he was confident that the people would return him for another term in the Senate.

That night he opened his campaign with a speech in the gymnasium of the YMCA.[65]

The speech was vintage Brookhart and would become his standard campaign speech. It began with a brief nod to his early hero Theodore Roosevelt, whose death in 1919 had allegedly changed history. The Rooseveltian era, Brookhart said, had been characterized by government involvement in business. But the year following Roosevelt's death Warren G. Harding had run on the slogan of "less government in business and more business in government," and there had followed a decade of business in government that had brought the Transportation Act, massive ship subsidies, currency deflation, chain stores, and all the other familiar Brookhart targets. Its culmination had been the Great Depression.[66]

During this era of "business in government," Brookhart said, business had succeeded in making "extortionate" profits. But it had failed to provide general prosperity for the American people or create the jobs needed for full employment. And since business had failed in this "duty of civilization," it was up to government to provide jobs. He had no doubt, moreover, that government could do so. Citing such successful examples of government in business as the public schools, the national highway system, the post office, and the Panama Canal, he said that Congress must now determine how to restore prosperity.[67]

Brookhart acknowledged, however, that such action by Congress would take time to bring about. And in the meantime, he told his audience, there were two immediate problems that demanded attention. The first was the agricultural relief issue, the need there being for a government corporation to handle the marketable surplus. The other was unemployment relief, which he would provide through public works projects and through prompt passage of the veterans bonus bill calling for immediate face-value redemption of the World War bonus insurance certificates scheduled to mature in 1945.[68]

In addition, Brookhart argued that any long-term remedy must involve redistribution of wealth. He had calculated that the average economic growth rate was 4 percent. Yet, many large businesses had profit rates greater than 4 percent; and those that did so, he thought, should be heavily taxed. He would also tax any resale of stock that took place within sixty days of the initial purchase, which, as he saw it, would help both to curb big business and to prevent the kind of stock speculation that had denied credit to farmers and brought on the depression.[69]

Brookhart's 1932 campaign speech was a reaffirmation of his populist belief that all Americans should share equally in the economic rewards of society. It was also a reflection of the progressive's use of the government to regulate society where inequalities existed. The *Register* called it a "Bold and Candid Speech" that pulled no punches, declaring that it was "in his analysis of the economic problem and in his statement of a remedial program that the senator swings the sledge." It then went on to agree with Brookhart about the cupidity of big business, but to raise some serious objections to his plan for redistributing wealth.[70]

This was not the first time that Brookhart had offered a serious alternative to business as usual in the United States. His earlier proposals of government ownership of the railroads had brought him the label of communist. His system of cooperative economics had been met with similar charges. But Iowans in general had not seemed to take those accusations seriously. On the contrary, they had seemed to appreciate their senator on the attack.

In this campaign, however, Brookhart was no longer on the attack. He was now on the defensive, not in regard to his program but in regard to charges of personal misbehavior, of nepotism and inattention to duty. As Louis Cook observed, the "gaunt wild-eyed and apostolic" Brookhart of 1922 had become "sleek, somewhat portly and well-satisfied."[71]

Throughout the campaign the issue of nepotism would not go away. On May 30 *Time* magazine ran a story listing five members of the Brookhart family who were receiving government salaries. One son, it noted, was his father's secretary; a daughter was a senate office clerk; another son was a commercial attache in Bangkok; one brother was a federal court bankruptcy referee; and another brother was federal court bailiff. Their combined salaries were $14,750.[72]

Both before and after the *Time* story, Brookhart defended the members of his family, pointing out correctly that no one had criticized them for not doing their jobs. At one point in the campaign, he also claimed that two of them were Civil Service appointments. But when Field learned from the Civil Service Commissioner that this was not the case, Brookhart dropped this defense. Like the other candidates, Field was careful to point out that what Brookhart had done was common practice in the Senate. But, Field said, Brookhart's attempt to claim Civil Service status for those appointments ran counter to his reputation for sincerity.[73]

Increasingly, moreover, Iowans seemed to agree with Henry Field. The *Register* reprinted editorials representing opinion from Atlantic to Wall Lake, and most essentially agreed with the editor of the *Victor Record*. Writing that Field had "pulled the wool off the Iowa voters' eyes," the editor said that the voters would demand an "explanation of [Brookhart's] family affairs in Washington politics, more interest in Iowa affairs, and less howling about Wall Street."[74]

As the June primary date approached, Field emerged as Brookhart's principal attacker. Speaking in response to the Senator's campaign opener, he criticized the record of achievement: "He's been down there at home plate for 10 years trying to hit home runs but so far he's hit nothing but foul balls." And while attacking Brookhart's plan for government intervention, Field was also able to raise the nepotism issue. He charged that Brookhart's plan for recovery must mean government jobs for everyone, a specialty that seemed to "run in the Brookhart family."[75]

As it progressed, moreover, the Field campaign took on the trappings of a circus. He traveled around the state with a covered wagon, brass band, and steam calliope, offering chicken stew dinners where Mrs. Field handed out her recipe and assuring Iowans that even though he had eleven children, he would, if elected, be the "only Field in Washington." Brookhart said that if Iowans wanted chicken stew, they should send Henry Field to Washington, to which Field responded that if they wanted the "same old boloney," they should send Brookhart. There was little discussion of Brookhart's economic program.[76]

Meanwhile, Brookhart traveled around the state exuding optimism. In the first two weeks of May, he gave two and sometimes three speeches a day in towns ranging from Sioux City to Shenandoah to Keosauqua. And on May 15 he felt confident enough to leave off campaigning and return to Washington, D.C., for ten days. Predicting that he would get 50 percent of the vote, he claimed that this was the "easiest battle" he had ever been in.[77]

Glenn Haynes, however, said that Brookhart's optimism amounted to "whistling in the graveyard" and was as "bare of facts" as his record was "barren of accomplishment." And George Cosson accused Brookhart of "hiding behind a smokescreen of self-pity." Haynes and Cosson were correct in saying that Brookhart's optimism was misplaced. By mid-May the momentum had clearly swung to Field. The thirty editorials that the *Register* reprinted on May 22 were all favorable to Field.[78]

Meanwhile, five Democrats, including former Senator Steck, were also vying for their party's nomination and commenting on the Republican race. Charles F. Lytle, a former Republican state legislator who had left the party in disgust, thought the Republicans had a choice between the "futile Brookhart" and a "machine-made candidate who will jump through the hoop when the party bosses crack the whip." And speaking in Clear Lake, Democratic candidate Nelson Kraschel told his audience to "enjoy the Republican senatorial clowns in the parade" of the primary because none would "appear in the main show."[79]

The presence of five Democrats on the primary ballot was unusual. In recent elections for senator, the Democrats had always settled on one candidate. But there was a feeling now that the political wind was changing, and the pressure of a real Democratic race spelled trouble for Brookhart. In past elections, he had been able to count on some Democrats to cross-over in the primary; but now, with a real Democratic chance at a Senate seat and with Democrats running strong races up and down the ballot, there would be little of this and especially little of it in such strong labor towns as Clinton and Waterloo. In the latter, one estimate was that Brookhart would lose as many as 1,500 Democrats who had voted for him in the past.[80]

In late May, Brookhart returned to Iowa and resumed his two-a-day speaking schedule. He also brought in other progressives in an attempt to shore up his sagging campaign. In Des Moines, for example, his old debating opponent, Congressman Fiorello La Guardia, spoke to the large Italian community. In Waterloo, Senator Robert La Follette was featured, and from South Dakota Senator Peter Norbeck came in to give speeches at Waterloo and Decorah. Senator William Borah also sent a statement of support, and efforts were made to get Senator Norris to come into the state and help repair a "dangerous situation." Norris, however, said that it would be "impossible" for him to comply with the request.[81]

As Brookhart toured northeast and eastern Iowa during the last days of the campaign, he continued to press his economic program and to draw large audiences. But clearly, he was losing ground to Henry Field. The *Register* political writer, C. C. Clifton, made his own 1,500 mile tour of the state and reported in a series of articles that Brookhart was losing strength in every congressional district and that in most districts it was Field who was picking up the former Brookhart voters. In the last article of the series, Clifton said that given the widespread dissatisfaction with Brookhart and the defection of Brookhart's former Democratic supporters, Field would receive the nomination. Most other Iowa political observers also agreed with this assessment, as did the editors of many Iowa newspapers.[82]

Field ended the campaign with a radio address entitled "Debunking Brookhart, or Knockout the Flapdoodle and Poppycock." In response, Brookhart decried the "slander and misrepresentation" of his opponents. Claiming that Iowans would not be deceived by such tactics, he said that he was still confident of victory.[83]

On June 7 Jennie wrote to Ned that "the smoke has cleared away and S. W. is 2nd in the race." That understated the situation. On election day, Iowans had turned out in record numbers to defeat Brookhart. Henry Field received 47 percent of the vote while Brookhart got only 35 percent. He carried only twenty-seven counties, down from eighty-three in the 1926 primary. And of the twenty-three counties he had never lost, he carried only eight. He had asked the people to choose, and they had.[84]

The *Journal* said that Brookhart's defeat was the price he had paid for being outspoken. It regretted the "cheap, unworthy" attacks on his family and reaffirmed the pride that Washingtonians felt for the Brookharts. It even hinted that this might not have been his last campaign. But the senator had no comment. As he left for the capitol, he responded to questions with a wave and a smile.[85]

Reaction around the state and nation was what could be expected. President Hoover was said to have received the news of Brookhart's defeat with "great pleasure." Frank Lowden expressed "great surprise" at the result. And a Hoover correspondent probably expressed the feelings of most organization Republicans when he told the President that the state had "breathed a sigh of relief" at the Brookhart defeat. One long-time Brookhart supporter, on the other hand, told the senator that "they kind of had the cards stacked against" him. He promised continued support in the future.[86]

Brookhart had lost the election because Iowans had tired of him. When farmers had been a beleaguered minority in a prosperous nation, Brookhart had been their outspoken advocate. But he had done nothing more than speak out. The nepotism and absenteeism issues had also made him seem like a typical politician, lining his own nest.[87]

Moreover, Iowa farmers, especially Farmers' Union members, never really forgave Brookhart for his support of Hoover in 1928. In that election Senator George Norris and Farmers' Union President Milo Reno had supported the Democrat Al Smith. Reno's biographer has written that if Brookhart had "followed the lead" of Norris and Reno "the stigma of being officially Republican might not have hurt him so much in 1932." H. R. Gross, who was on the staff of the *Iowa Union Farmer*, and later served in Congress, concurs in that opinion. Writing in 1981 Gross said that Brookhart's failure to follow the lead of Norris and Reno "cost him later his strongest base of support."[88]

In past elections, too, Brookhart had been the underdog, fighting not only Wall Street but an Iowa Republican Party that he claimed was controlled by Wall Street and was depicting him erroneously as a dangerous radical. Iowans did not see him as such a radical, and he won sympathy when the party stole the 1924 election from him, seemingly because he was a threat to the position held by regular party leaders. Henry Field, however, was not perceived as being a part of the party apparatus that Brookhart had condemned for its undemocratic practices. He was an outsider, both in this sense and in the sense that he had no connection with the politicians who had failed to solve the depression. Moreover, he did not treat Brookhart as a dangerous threat, but rather as being phony and ridiculous. Rather than label his opponent's program as communistic or Bolshevik, he said that it was the same old boloney. And while farmers might not recognize a communist or a bolshevik, they knew when someone was full of boloney. In 1932 that was what they thought Brookhart to be.[89]

The day after returning to Washington, Brookhart spoke on the floor of the Senate in favor of the unemployment relief bill under consideration. And in the remaining five weeks of the session, he would take an active role in Senate business. He was especially concerned with the worsening situation of agriculture and spoke often on the subject. He was also much interested in the presidential politics of that summer.[90]

In 1931 Brookhart and other progressives had begun to look for an alternative to Hoover and to consider the chances particularly of Norris and La Follette. They had also talked about the possibility of another Bull Moose Party. Brookhart, for example, had thought that "the voters are more prepared for discarding old party ideals now than in 1912. . . . Today party ties are not so strong and the feeling of revolt is ripe for a Progressive movement in the Republican party." This, however, had come to nothing, and one commentator had noted that the progressives would "have to sneak back into the reservation."[91]

Still, with Brookhart, one could never be sure. Probably, if the Republicans had written an agricultural plank that he could support, he would have given the party's nominee at least tacit support. But at the Republican National Convention in mid-June, the party adopted a plank stressing what the Hoover administration had done to bring agricultural relief, and with this Brookhart was completely unsatisfied. He undertook a point-by-point refutation of its claims, insisted that the efforts of the previous four years had been too little, too late, and declared that the convention had run "away from the Republican platform of four years" before. Agriculture had been "kicked out the back door and told to go hence for its relief and for its rights."[92]

Brookhart objected especially to the part of the plank that said "control of production" was the "fundamental problem of American agriculture." Like many agricultural spokesmen before the New Deal, he had opposed production controls and seemed to have an almost mystical feeling that God had given land to farmers to use. To take it out of production, he believed, would be to run counter to the proper order of creation. And given the vagaries of weather, the only way one could have effective production control was to enter into a "contract with the Almighty, and he will not sign up."[93]

Instead, Brookhart favored full production with some of the surplus of good years set aside for use in the lean ones. Relief would come through domestic price supports and the selling abroad of that not used here or put aside. This had been the basis of his own farm bills as well as of most other farm bills throughout the 1920s. It was what the Republicans had previously advocated, and it was also, he said, the solution of Joseph and the Pharoah in the Old Testament.[94]

The day after the 1932 Republican platform was adopted, Brookhart sat down at his Senate desk and wrote an agricultural plank that reflected his views. He then took it across the aisle to Democratic Senator Cordell Hull, who was a member of the platform committee for the Democratic convention scheduled to convene within the week. Handing the plank to Hull, Brookhart said, "If the Democrats want to carry the agricultural states I think this platform will do it." Hull read what he had written and told him, "I agree with every proposition." He promised, so Brookhart said, to try to get it in the platform.[95]

Whatever Brookhart's influence may have been, the Democratic plank did advocate extension of farm cooperatives, control of surpluses on the domestic market, and action to guarantee prices to farmers. It also condemned the Republican view that production should be restricted to the "demands of the domestic market." Brookhart was now ready to support the Democratic platform. But he was still not sure about the Democratic nominee, Franklin Delano Roosevelt.[96]

Brookhart and Roosevelt had first met in August 1929, when the senator had paid a call on the New York Governor. They had talked about prohibition, and Roosevelt had agreed with Brookhart that a national referendum on the subject would result in keeping the Eighteenth Amendment. They had also discussed the farm situation, and after the meeting Brookhart had said that Roosevelt possessed a "keen grasp of agricultural problems."[97]

In the intervening years, their contacts had been casual; and as long as there was a possibility that he would be the Republican nominee for senator, Brookhart had refused to take a position on a possible Roosevelt candidacy. His defeat in the primary, however, seemed to free him from whatever loyalty to the Republican Party that may have remained. He would finally decide not only to give Roosevelt his open endorsement but to endorse Roosevelt's criticism of the Hoover administration.[98]

The Senate adjourned on July 25, and the Brookharts left to visit their son John and his family in Duluth, Minnesota. It was one of Smith's rare vacations and during it he slept late every morning, went fishing, and seemed in general to enjoy himself. Still, future plans were not far from his mind. He was considering an offer from a Chicago concern to be its legal counsel, and he continued to think about politics.[99]

Since June there had been rumors that Brookhart would run as an independent in the Senate race. He had refused to comment. But, the speculation continued, and he was receiving numerous letters urging him to run. Those closest to him, including Jennie, urged him not to. She told him that there were not enough votes to "swing it." Yet, she knew that ultimately he would keep his own counsel. He was looking over the situation and as of mid-August had still not made a decision.[100]

Bryon Allen, meanwhile, had begun a quiet campaign to get Brookhart into the race. On September 10, he sent a letter to leaders of past Brookhart campaigns and was told by eleven of the twelve who responded that Brookhart should run. He then chaired a meeting to plan a third party convention that would nominate Brookhart. This was to be held in late September in Washington, Iowa; but before a definite date was set, Allen wanted further meetings to be sure there was adequate support.[101]

It now seemed almost certain that Brookhart would run, and some expected him to state his intentions on September 21 at a Farmers' Holiday Association meeting in Moville, Iowa. The Holiday Association was a new outgrowth from the Farmers' Union. It was now attempting to raise farm prices by having the farmers take a "holiday" and hold farm products off the market, and the Moville meeting was supposed to plan strategy on how best to carry the Association's message to the Capitol. Brookhart's invitation had expressed hope that he might fill that role.[102]

At Moville, three thousand farmers stood in the rain to hear Brookhart give essentially the same speech that he had used during the primary campaign. He expressed pride that the Farm Holiday movement had begun in Iowa; and referring to a query in his invitation about whether he had the guts to speak before the group, he told the audience that he had had the "'guts' for ten long years" but that this was the "first time any group with any 'guts'" had got behind him. Contrary to expectations, however, he did not reveal whether he intended to run as an independent. The closest he came was to remind the farmers that once before he had been defeated and they had sent him back to the Senate.[103]

Still, it was common knowledge that Brookhart would run. The day before the Moville speech, Frank Lund had issued an invitation for those interested in a Brookhart candidacy to come to the convention in Washington on September 26. A form letter was also sent soliciting money and support. And while this said that Brookhart had not yet agreed to run and needed a show of enthusiasm to persuade him, it seems unlikely that the convention would have been arranged without the candidate's consent.[104]

The convention met at the place where Brookhart had begun almost all of his other campaigns, the Graham Opera House. It was now a movie house and had been renamed the State Theater. And it was there that nearly three hundred people gathered, filing in under a marquee that advertised a movie aptly entitled "A Successful Calamity." Most of the audience consisted of local people, but there were several delegations from around Iowa, especially from northwest Iowa where Brookhart had spoken the week before.[105]

The convention had the usual round of speeches and resolutions. Former Sioux City Mayor Wallace M. Short introduced a resolution to name the new party the Progressive Party of Iowa. Brookhart's old friend, the Reverend Carl W. Klein, nominated him for senator. And in a seconding speech, Mrs. T. H. Jones of Boone extolled Brookhart's service to the common people of Iowa. His candidacy, she said, was "Iowa's opportunity to save" homes, businesses, farms, and institutions.[106]

In his acceptance speech, Brookhart said little that was new. He urged President Hoover to call a special session of Congress before the election in order to deal with the farm problem, establish a public works program, and increase the money supply. If Hoover did this, Brookhart said, he would be reelected. He also reiterated his belief that the country owed a job to "every man who will work," and he urged the payment of the soldiers' bonus. In addition, he said that the "final and permanent remedy for all these evils" would require a "new deal, a re-organization of American business throughout, upon cooperative principles." In concluding his formal address, he told the crowd, "I'm going into this fight to win, not to achieve a personal victory, but for the people of this state. . . . If you people are ready to . . . fight for your rights, I'll stay with you."[107]

No one was quite sure what effect Brookhart's candidacy would have on the race. Field commented that it was a "free country" and that Brookhart could run if he wanted to. He doubted, he said, that Iowans wanted him "no matter how bad he wants the job." But he conceded that Brookhart would take votes away from him.[108]

Gubernatorial candidate Dan Turner's correspondents were divided on the effect that Brookhart's candidacy would have. A few thought that Brookhart would win; others thought that he had some support but did not know who would win; and still others conceded his strength but thought that Field or Democratic candidate Louis Murphy would win. Among Democrats in general, the early view was that Brookhart would split the Republican vote. But as the race progressed, they became fearful that he would take more votes away from Murphy than from Field.[109]

A weary Jennie summed up the situation. Writing to Ned on September 30, she said:

> You read the *Register* so you know Daddy has announced himself as an

Independent candidate. I said all I could to stop him. He got hundreds and thousands of letters urging him to run—but I think there will not be enough. He likes to listen to what he wants to hear. The farm strike in the middle west must be considered. I shall be glad when election is over. So much radio stuff is political—so rabid—fortunately we don't have to listen.[110]

Brookhart campaigned where he could. On October 1 he was in Cherokee, the next week in Jones County, and on October 8 back west in Pottawattamie County. Five days later, he was in Waterloo, where he conferred with supporters but refused to release a schedule of future speaking dates. He would only say that there would be "plenty happening shortly." The invitations were not coming in as before.[111]

Indeed, Brookhart did not even receive support from his home town. There the *Journal* printed a ballot in its issue of October 17 and 437 readers marked it and sent it in. The results showed Brookhart a distant second to Henry Field and only two votes ahead of Democrat Louis Murphy. The *Journal*'s editor took no stand. In every election, he said, there were winners and there were losers and it "behooves us all to keep cool, calm and collected."[112]

Brookhart lost badly. He finished third in every county in the state and received only 4.4 percent of the total vote. Murphy won with 54.8 percent of the total while Field received 40.7 percent. Brookhart did not comment on the results of his own election but did send a telegram to presidential winner Franklin Roosevelt. "Congratulations upon your tremendous victory," he told Roosevelt, "Hope your career equals Andrew Jackson."[113]

In Iowa the hopes of the Democrats were realized to a greater degree than anybody could have imagined; they elected a president, a senator, and they swept the statehouse. Included in this last group was Mrs. Alex Miller, the widow of Brookhart's old publishing rival at the *Washington Democrat*, who was elected Secretary of State, the first woman elected to a state executive office. The House delegation also changed dramatically. It had consisted of ten Republicans and one Democrat; following the census of 1930 the state lost two seats in Congress and would now have three Republicans and six Democrats, including Edward Eicher of Washington. Writing to Ned after the election, Jennie said: "This is the *day after*. We listened until midnight—everything gone Democratic. The biggest slide I've ever seen. The Col. 'also ran' not even as much as I expected. They thought me quite pessimistic."[114]

Brookhart left Washington on November 10, traveling first to St. Louis and then to Chicago to visit friends. While there, he fell ill with pneumonia and was told by the doctor that he was too ill to be moved to a hospital. One of his sisters, a nurse, came to care for him, and after a few weeks he was able to go east to his home in Maryland. The week before Christmas, however, he suffered a relapse and was sent to Walter Reed Hospital. It would be mid-January before he would be able to return to the Senate.[115]

Meanwhile, Brookhart had returned to the Senate with the intention of making good use of the time that remained. On January 26 he introduced Senator-elect Murphy around the chamber and helped him to get established. He also spoke on a number of issues and continued his fight against the repeal of prohibition. His last action in the Senate was to threaten to filibuster a bill relating to the prescription of medicinal liquors. He told the Senate that "the first vote we had when we came into session in this Congress was on a booze bill, and the last vote shall not be on a booze bill if I can prevent it."[116]

Brookhart might have been speaking about his career as an elected official. Forty years before, his first action as the new County Attorney had been to prosecute violators of Iowa's prohibition law. Now his last action was to continue his efforts to prevent the sale of liquor. In the first instance, he had been on the prevailing "dry" side of the issue. Now that position was rapidly losing ground. Times had changed; but on this issue, Smith Brookhart had not.

14

The Republican New Dealer

When Franklin Delano Roosevelt took the oath of office to begin his term as President on a gray, rainy March 4, 1933, Smith Brookhart finished his term in the Senate. The *Register* commented that "one of the picturesque figures" of the senate had returned to private life. The paper noted that he intended to keep his Iowa residence so that should he choose to run for office again, he could. Although Brookhart professed no plans to do so, and the paper thought that based on "political probabilities" he would not, nevertheless, it said, "one never knows. These are stormy and stressful times, and the colonel has always thrived in war rather than in peace."[1]

The political life of Smith Brookhart began in the late nineteenth century and spanned the first four decades of the twentieth. First elected to political office in the Gilded Age, he was defeated in his bid for re-election on the eve of the New Deal. His journey from Republican County Attorney to progressive senator in the 1920s to defeat in 1932 parallels the journey of one form of American liberal politics from populism to progressivism to New Deal Democracy.

Brookhart's ideology came from the populism of James B. Weaver in 1892. But his first elective office in 1894 was as a regular Republican, and he was proud to be a member of the party that had been founded to rid the nation of a great evil: slavery. His first elective office was also won by championing one of the most controversial reforms of nineteenth-century political life: prohibition.

In the next decade his study of railroad rates led him into the reformist progressive wing of the party and he never lost the reformist orientation of his Progressive Republicanism. He had become convinced that progressivism was the true heir to the reformist beginnings of the party of Lincoln.

He first ran for the Senate, however, when it became clear to him that the Republican Party had deserted its legacy of reform and that his own political goals were becoming more incompatible with the party's goals. Nevertheless, he remained a Republican; and following the death of Cummins in 1926 and his own subsequent election to a full term, he worked within the party to try to achieve agricultural relief.

Brookhart had a well-delineated plan to bring relief to those sectors of the economy that were in trouble during the 1920s. Because the prevailing economic system had failed farmers, he proposed that they should join together in Rochdale cooperatives and take control of their own destinies. But cooperatives had not been successful for nineteenth-century agrarian reformers, even where they had been tried, allegedly because they did not have access to ready credit. And to remedy this, Brookhart suggested the most radical part of his program: that cooperative banks be established to free farmers from the control of the established banking system and thus allow them to control all phases of their economic lives. In addition, he demanded that the federal government give to farmers the same kinds of favors it had granted to other sectors of the economy. Industry was booming, he thought, because the government had passed laws and tariffs that favored business expansion. Hence, it should regulate the economy to insure that farmers had the same opportunities.

In a sense, Brookhart had placed himself in an untenable position. He was calling for a radical change in society at the same time that he was trying to proclaim his allegiance to it and work within its rules. His opponents called him a communist, a Bolshevik, an anarchist, or a socialist. But he was none of these; he was not a threat to the country. He was, however, a threat to American business practices. When President Calvin Coolidge said that "the business of American is business," most Americans nodded in assent and considered Brookhart's attack on one as an attack on the other.

Despite all this, Brookhart argued for his plan constantly and passionately throughout his years in the Senate. Whether fighting for enforcement of prohibition laws, better equipment and training for soldiers, or relief for farmers, his passion was his greatest strength and his greatest weakness. It was because of it that he often spoke intemperately, causing his opponents to misinterpret him and giving them opportunities to fight him. But those for whom he spoke responded to him. He spoke their language and understood their problems, and in the 1920s, Iowa farmers rallied to him in great numbers. He became their spokesman in Washington.

Brookhart's passion also led to a single-mindedness that hampered his effort to secure agricultural relief. He was unable to compromise and accept something less than he started out to attain; and the few times he did compromise, the vote for the McNary-Haugen Bill in 1928 being one example, he was perceived as insincere. Compromise was accepted as a norm in other politicians, but in Brookhart it seemed to be a fault.

Another reason that Brookhart was unable to get his reform program implemented was his lack of political skills. He cared little about the day-to-day operation of a political office, preferring to leave such details to aides. And curiously, for a politician, he was an introverted man, oftentimes lost in thought and unaware of those around him. He was not able to participate in the back-slapping give-and-take so characteristic of politicians, and he found it difficult to build the kinds of coalitions necessary to get bills passed.

During the 1932 campaign, Brookhart's opponents pointed out with great effect that he had not accomplished anything during his years in the Senate; and measured in terms of legislation passed, their charge was true. No major law bore his name, and his own plan for farm relief seldom received a serious hearing. In part, this was because his ideas challenged the basis upon which the economy was organized; in part, it was because many politicians were put off by the passion of his rhetoric; and in part, it was because he lacked the skills necessary to bring it about. For all these reasons, Brookhart's program for assisting farmers to control their own destinies through cooperatives was the "road not taken."

Brookhart, however, did have an impact on Iowa politics. The remarkable series of seven Brookhart elections from 1920-1926 was an extension of the twenty-year struggle between the two wings of the Iowa Republican Party, with Brookhart picking up the progressive cudgel that he thought Cummins had dropped. Yet it was also a period during which Brookhart went his own way, drawing votes of agrarian protest from large numbers of Iowans of both parties. By opposing him the regular Republicans were able to repair the long-standing party rift and achieve dominance in the party apparatus.

The period of Brookhart's party "regularity" from 1928 through 1929 was an aberration and probably his one great mistake. Since he had fought party leaders for years, there was no solid basis for unity, and their acceptance of him in 1928 was reluctant at best. The break that occurred in 1929 was inevitable, and the episode was damaging both to the party and to Brookhart. For years he had labeled the party as an agent of those who had brought on the agricultural depression and blocked agricultural relief; and in 1932, when all were suffering from the Great Depression, Iowans were ready to look elsewhere for relief and leadership. Brookhart had paved the way.

It is interesting to speculate what might have happened if Brookhart had broken with the Republican Party after his break with Hoover in 1929. He would have had three years to prepare Iowans and himself for a Democratic Smith Brookhart running for re-election, and by 1932 the Democratic Brookhart and his long-held views would have been in at least one current of what became the New Deal. But doing this would have required the cooperation of the Iowa Democratic Party, which would have been difficult to secure. And more than that, it would have required a political daring and skill that Brookhart did not possess and a prescience that few possessed in 1929.

Once Brookhart had made his commitment to progressivism and acknowledged his debt to Weaver's populism, he did not change. At first he had insisted that his views of government involvement were consistent with traditional Republicanism and he tried to call his party back to its reformist legacy. Indeed, he would always maintain that he did not desert the party but that the party had deserted its roots. But by 1932 he had come to realize that his views and those of the Republican Party were moving farther apart and that there was no longer any chance of their being reconciled. By 1932 the Democratic Party had picked up the reformist legacy of Brookhart's Republican-populist-progressivism.

In 1933 Brookhart still identified himself as a Progressive Republican. Writing to President Roosevelt to recommend someone for a federal appointment, Brookhart assured the president that the candidate was a "Progressive Republican like myself" who could be depended upon in the New Deal. The next year Brookhart wrote Roosevelt again to tell him that the president had the opportunity for the first "realignment of political issues since Lincoln." Brookhart said Roosevelt's program met the demands of "every Progressive Republican, as well as the rank and file of the Democrats." Finally, Brookhart said he thought that it would take three terms to finish the job and urged Franklin Roosevelt not to "make the mistake of Theodore Roosevelt who at first declined to run for the third term."[2]

Brookhart had become a progressive in large part because of Theodore Roosevelt. Now, with the second President Roosevelt, except for the name, he had become a New Deal Democrat. Speaking in 1981, Otha Wearin, a former New Deal Congressman from Iowa, said of Brookhart: "He should have been [a Democrat]. He thought like a Democrat." When told of Wearin's comment, Smith W. Brookhart, Jr. said: "Well, I think others have said the same and often said that he was way ahead of his time. He was a New Dealer before we had a New Deal." And finally, former New Deal Senator Claude Pepper of Florida expressed admiration for Brookhart because he was "a stalwart liberal and an able advocate primarily of the firm interest of the country. He was regarded, at least by liberal Democrats, as a man of character, ability, deep conviction and courage."[3]

Even before Brookhart left office there was speculation about what he would do next. He rented an office at 744 Jackson Place in Washington, but as to what he had in mind, not even his family was sure. In a Christmas letter, John told his brother Ned that he did not know what their father would do. There had been talk of a "good thing" in Chicago, but he knew nothing definite. The previous September, Brookhart had said that he had several offers but had mentioned nothing specific.[4]

In January 1933 the press carried a report that he would be named Governor of the Canal Zone; and while he refused to comment, Jennie was reported to be delighted at the prospect of avoiding another Iowa winter. Brookhart denied a report that he would represent the interests of the Soviet Union in Washington, and during the same period an Iowan suggested to Roosevelt that Brookhart be his Attorney General.[5]

Writing Milo Reno shortly after he left office, Brookhart said he wanted to discuss the future with Reno. He was particularly interested in the nature of the farm program the new administration would formulate. "If it is not adequate," he told Reno, "the fault [would be] with the farm leaders as the president is willing to go through." He claimed that the new Secretary of Agriculture, Henry A. Wallace, had promised that the program would include his ideas about marketing programs for the surplus as well as a cost of production payment. But, Brookhart told Reno, "We will see."[6]

At the end of April the *Register* reported that there was a "persistent rumor" that Brookhart would be appointed to a "fairly responsible" position in the Department of Agriculture. One month later Brookhart was appointed a special advisor for Russian trade in the newly created Agricultural Adjustment Administration. The Roosevelt administration hoped that one way to spur the Depression economy would be to enter into trade agreements abroad. Many felt that the Soviet Union, which had a great need for agricultural products, would be a fertile area for trade. One stumbling block to increased trade with the Soviets, however, was the fact that the United States had never recognized the Soviet government. Thus the trade issue was seen by many as a wedge to open the whole question of diplomatic recognition by the United States.[7]

Brookhart's solution for the farm crisis had always been to develop markets for the farm surplus. Since his trip to the Soviet Union in 1923 he had come to believe that it could be a valuable trading partner. Now he had the opportunity to influence American policy and begin to see his long-held beliefs put into practice. In a statement at the time of the appointment Brookhart said that, "Russia's ability to absorb this country's surplus carryover at this time is practically unlimited . . . and there's no reason why that market can't be developed."[8]

Brookhart did not intend to limit trade possibilities to agricultural products; he thought that the Soviet Union could also be a market for American industrial goods. In his appointment statement he said he had already received a proposal involving a "large industrial project," and that he was "in touch with Amtorg Trading Corporation, which is the Russian government's trade representative in the country." He said he expected "some important results within a short time."[9]

Brookhart's boss at the AAA was George Peek. Peek was the originator of the ideas that became McNary-Haugenism and he and Brookhart were usually on opposite sides of the agricultural relief issue. Peek acted quickly to set some public limits on Brookhart's role with the AAA. Peek said Brookhart was to provide "purely factual studies" as a service to American businessmen and potential trading partners. Brookhart would work for the AAA and his job there would have no "bearing upon the United States government regulations with any foreign country." That, Peek said, was within the purview of the State Department. Moreover, there was an agreement that Brookhart would work behind the scenes and not make speeches and he would not talk to the press without first consulting Peek. If Peek hoped that such an arrangement would muzzle his outspoken trade advisor, he would soon learn how difficult that would be.[10]

The relationship between Peek and Brookhart at the AAA was strained from the beginning. Not only did they differ on agricultural policy, but Peek did not really want Brookhart in the first place. Most people considered the appointment a political payoff for Brookhart's work in the 1932 campaign. The belief was that Brookhart had entered the general election the previous year to split the Republican vote and elect the Democrat, Louis Murphy, to the Senate. But writing in response to a letter from A. J. Gary, from Denison, Iowa who objected to the Brookhart appointment, Murphy denied playing any role in the appointment. The responsibility for the appointment rested with President Roosevelt, Murphy said, who "felt that Senator Brookhart, in his campaign against Mr. Hoover in Iowa, had rendered the party a service that should be rewarded."[11]

Other Iowans agreed with Gary. Porter Eckerman, a Democrat from Ottumwa (Dan Steck's hometown), said the Brookhart job was "little less than a laughing matter." The only thing Brookhart had done for Iowa was to "make it a laughing stock among states." A Cedar Rapids Republican said he had hoped that his vote against Brookhart the previous year "would help to sound a death knell" for Brookhart and all his relatives.[12]

But there was also support for the Brookhart appointment. In a letter to the *Register*, J. R. Winslow challenged Porter Eckerman's charges about Brookhart. Brookhart's warnings about Wall Street had been true and he had been right about prohibition enforcement. Now, whatever Brookhart received from the administration "he deserves." One Roosevelt correspondent told the

President that during a midwestern speaking tour he had found widespread support for Brookhart. "In his appointment you not only picked a popular man, who gave you his best support—but you also selected a very able man."[13]

The most significant show of support came from Milo Reno. Writing Brookhart shortly after the appointment, Reno said that "your selection for assisting Peek has done much to reconcile me to the many things that have been done and some of the things that have not been done by the present administration." Reno felt that Wallace was too close to the "Farm Bureau Crowd," and he thought that Peek and Brookhart could counteract their influence on the Secretary of Agriculture. Reno said he had recently been at a meeting in Salina, Kansas, and told Brookhart that the sentiment he found there insured "the plain people of the United States of, at least, one defender."[14]

His initial salary was $6,500 which was later cut to $5,000 when there was a general scaling back of government salaries. The money was welcome since he was still paying off the bank debts. Jennie reported all the details to the children and assured them that he was "quite busy." "Father brings us melons every day, musk melons, 7 for a quarter, so we eat plenty. . . . There is talk of big sales in Russia—motor trucks, cotton, etc. . . . I think he will not go to Russia in the near future—but things happen right fast."[15]

Brookhart liked being back in the center of things. He was given an office in the Department of Agriculture building which quickly filled with stacks of reports on trade and economic figures. Although he dealt with other nations, one day, for example, the Minister of Greece came to talk about buying wheat, his principal focus remained Russia. Newspapermen who had believed that the job was merely a political sinecure, came away impressed.[16]

Brookhart worked on two problems that had to be solved for trade to take place between the United States and the Soviet Union. The first was that in order for any potential trading relationship to fully develop, the United States would have to grant diplomatic recognition to the Soviet Union. Brookhart had advocated recognition for ten years. The other problem was that the Soviet Union had little to offer in exchange and little cash to buy American products. Brookhart favored a barter arrangement but announced that he was not opposed to the extension of credit to the Soviet Union by the United States.

During the remainder of 1933 Brookhart worked to convince American firms that trade with Russia was viable. In August, for example, he convened a group of representatives from agricultural and industrial companies to "consider methods of credit and financing for the export of American products to the U.S.S.R." But he was fighting an uphill battle. Although American goods were available, the Russians had no money with which to purchase them and American institutions were reluctant to grant credit. Nevertheless, Brookhart continued to maintain that the Russian market was huge (in November he said it was as much as $520 million, a figure others said was too high) and that Russia was a good credit risk.[17]

Meanwhile, Brookhart also tried to convince opponents of recognition of the benefits it would bring to the United States. Many Americans opposed recognition on religious grounds. In the fall of 1933 Brookhart carried on an extended correspondence with the Rev. John Henry Hopkins, the retired Episcopal Rector of the Church of the Redeemer in Chicago. Hopkins wrote Brookhart in August to protest recognition of a country "openly antagonistic toward nearly every Article in our National Constitution." Hopkins said that never in history had there been such an "atheistic set of fanatical murderers, liars and savages, as these deluded men." Moreover, Brookhart's argument that it would be financially advantageous for the United States was the same argument Judas Iscariot had used 2,000 years before. Finally, he said he was "ashamed" of Brookhart for "advising such a contemptible and disloyal act on the part of our Government for mere money." In a subsequent letter Hopkins apologized for the "discourteous" tone of his letter, but he did not apologize for his strong feelings about recognition.[18]

In the following weeks the two exchanged long letters. Brookhart denied he wanted "Russian gold, as Judas wanted silver; I want to sell our farm products and industrial materials." He then reiterated his long-standing position on the Soviet Union and the United States. Both are revolutionary. The United States government runs the school system, post office, utilities, health programs and public roads, all of which are similar to the Soviet Union. Moreover, the people were good people:

> created by the same God that created you. . . . They have succeeded. They have doubtless committed many things that are wrong. . . . [But] is it not the part of a good Christian spirit, instead of condemning and denouncing these people and their leaders to recognize them, treat them as human beings, and join with them for the peace of the whole world, which they desire and which we desire above everything else?[19]

Brookhart admitted that he disagreed with their religious attitudes but he added that religion should play no part in government relations. He said he had seen "hundreds" of churches "open and free" when he visited in 1923. Furthermore, the United States recognized "every other pagan and infidel" nation in the world and under the First Amendment granted atheists the same rights as Christians. Finally, no churchman could object to communism in the light of the passage in Acts 4:34-35 ("nor was there anyone needy among them, for all who owned property or houses sold them and donated the proceeds. They used to lay them at the feet of the apostles to be distributed to everyone according to his need"). Hopkins remained unconvinced, however, and in his last letter to Brookhart said, "I hope and pray that until they abandon their Anti-God and Anti-Home attitude, we will never recognize them as a government, no matter how many tractors and electric plants they may build."[20]

Brookhart had been advancing his arguments for recognition for ten years and they seemed proper and logical to him. The United States had a surplus of farm products and the Soviet Union needed them. The sale of industrial goods to Russia would create manufacturing jobs in the United States. He could, and did, argue those points at length with anyone who objected. But Hopkins' religious arguments, and his passion, did not yield to logic and it seems odd to see Brookhart resorting to religious argumentation. He never did so about liquor or the movies and organized religion was not an important part of his life. Still, his cause was important so Brookhart was willing to go onto his opponent's turf to try and convince him of the correctness of his cause.

In the larger debate, however, Hopkins was not an important player. At the same time as Brookhart was corresponding with Hopkins he was also meeting with the Rev. Edmund A. Walsh, S.J. Fr. Walsh had founded the Georgetown School of Foreign Service in 1919 and in 1922 had served as head of a papal relief mission to Russia. Walsh was one of the most vocal leaders of the Roman Catholic opposition to recognition.[21]

Walsh and Brookhart had been introduced by mutual friends and the two had a series of meetings on the question of recognition. At the same time Walsh was meeting with the president. Walsh objected to recognition based on Russia's goal of worldwide revolution, its official atheism, and continued religious persecution. Walsh expressed his reservations to Brookhart and a synopsis of their talks found its way to officials in Moscow. In return they asked Walsh to "specify who is in prison on account of religion and where." Walsh told Roosevelt that he was compiling a list of those in prison and he seemed encouraged by the Soviet willingness to consider religious questions as part of the conditions for recognition.[22]

Negotiations about recognition began in early November between Roosevelt and the Soviet delegate, Maxim Litvinov. In the meantime Brookhart stepped up his public relations effort. On November 8 he published a newspaper article explaining what recognition meant for America. He said the two great nations were far enough apart that they had no real conflicting interests; in fact cooperation between the two would further insure peace. There were also benefits of trade with the United States, which also meant jobs. Credit would have to be extended and Brookhart had urged that for months, and he said their experience of paying off debts was good. Finally, Brookhart said that the risks would pay huge rewards for America, "I have faith that it will take our agricultural surpluses and employ several hundred thousand of American labor."[23]

Roosevelt and Litvinov completed their talks on November 16 and announced that differences had been worked out and an agreement had been reached. In exchange for recognition the Soviets agreed to scale down their claims of worldwide revolution by subversive means, and, to Walsh's delight, they promised that American citizens in Russia would have free exercise of religion. Both sides also agreed to put off until later a settlement of long-standing debts. Brookhart said that recognition "means more to the peace of the world than almost any event at this time." And if "adequate credit" could be arranged, the United States could make sales in the "near future."[24]

Jennie wrote Ned that "Daddy is much pleased over the affairs of the last few days." In the meantime some of Brookhart's friends asked Roosevelt to consider him for the post of ambassador. Senator George Norris wrote the president to intercede on his behalf, and Senator Murphy said Brookhart's nomination would be supported by "Norris, Johnson and others." Brookhart wanted the position, and probably asked Norris, Murphy and the others to suggest his name to Roosevelt.[25]

When the president named William C. Bullitt to the post, Brookhart was deeply disappointed. He likely felt that at age sixty-four, this was his last chance for a larger role in government. As always Jennie was more realistic: "I think [Roosevelt] knew Bullitt is a better fit—speaks several languages, is a rich man, has spent much time in Europe." Years later their daughter, Edith, agreed with her mother, "He would have been . . . inappropriate."[26]

Brookhart soon put his disappointment aside and worked to reach trade agreements. But the extension of credit to the Soviet Union remained a problem. In March, Senator Joseph T. Robinson (Democrat, Arkansas), the majority leader of the Senate, asked Brookhart for a statement about the problem. Brookhart told Robinson that there was great potential for trade and that currently fourteen other nations had extended credit so "they certainly seem to be a good credit risk." The only potential problem would be war, but Brookhart thought that risk was small.[27]

The next month Brookhart found himself in the middle of a growing dispute between Peek and Henry Wallace. Some conservatives thought that the Department of Agriculture and the AAA advocated too much central planning. Secretary of Agriculture Henry A. Wallace had recently published a pamphlet called *America Must Choose* which seemed to call for increased government control.

Peek agreed with these critics of the department, which had led to his leaving the AAA at the President's request on December 15, 1933. Roosevelt, however, wanted to keep Peek within the government, the better to keep him from criticizing New Deal programs. Therefore, Roosevelt appointed Peek as a special advisor to the President on foreign trade. Chester C. Davis, a long-time Peek associate, was appointed to replace him as the head of the AAA.[28]

Peek's appointment as a presidential advisor on trade began immediately following his resignation from the AAA. Later, Peek was appointed head of the new Export-Import Bank and in March 1934 Roosevelt created the Office of Special Assistant on Foreign Trade as part of the National Recovery Administration. Peek's work at the White House and then the NRA overlapped Brookhart's work at the AAA. It is doubtful that Roosevelt intended this but the result was a weakening of Brookhart's position as Peek assumed a larger role in the trade question. Peek's appointment was the beginning of the end for Brookhart as trade advisor to the AAA.[29]

On February 2, 1934, Brookhart observed his sixty-fifth birthday. Jennie said that not many were "so well at that age. He sleeps and eats like a youngster." But if his health was secure at age sixty-five, his position at the AAA was further weakened following a set of speeches he made in March. Speaking on March 16 to the New School of Social Research Brookhart described his tour of collective farms in the Soviet Union in 1923. He said that the United States had made a mistake when it gave public lands to the railroads and homesteaders in the nineteenth century. If the government had kept the land and developed it on a communal system, Brookhart speculated that "many of the hardships of pioneering would have been avoided and likewise most of the failures . . . and the horrors of our skyscraper civilization [could have been] prevented."[30]

Among the critics of Brookhart for this speech was Iowa Senator Lester J. Dickinson. Writing to a local newspaper, Dickinson criticized Brookhart for his statements about the government land programs and his advocacy of cooperative farming. He also did not like Brookhart's "utterances favorable to certain aspects of the Russian system."[31]

In a published response Brookhart reminded Dickinson of their earlier alliance on agricultural issues and of his support of Dickinson in the senatorial primary election. But following the election Dickinson had "double-crossed" Brookhart and the people of Iowa and "jumped clear into the Wall Street financial autocracy." Brookhart denied that his ideas were treasonable but said that treasonable ideas came from those who condemned the government when it attempted "to do anything for the country at large." As for cooperative farms, Brookhart reminded Dickinson that the Amana Colonies in Iowa had been pure communism until their recent change to capitalism, and they had been very successful. "You bark and snarl" at everything the administration had tried, "without suggesting a single constructive idea." The only idea Dickinson had, Brookhart said was "to turn us back to the bankruptcy and chaos of the Hoovers, the Mellons and the Morgans."[32]

Then on March 29 Brookhart spoke at a private dinner at Washington's Shoreham Hotel given for Thomas McInerney, President of the National Dairy Products Company and a resident of Dubuque. In this speech Brookhart outlined yet again his views about the Soviet constitution and the rights he said it gave the people. According to Brookhart they had the right of a lifetime job, free education, free medical service, disability and old age insurance. He said nothing in the speech that he had not been saying for over ten years. At the end of the evening Senator Josiah W. Bailey (Democrat, North Carolina) accused Brookhart of advocating the overthrow of the American government to set up a Soviet regime. Bailey called Brookhart the "ambassador of Russia," to which Brookhart replied, "playfully" according to the newspaper, that Bailey was the "ambassador from hell."[33]

Reports of the speech and Brookhart's encounter with Bailey floated around the Capitol through the weekend and on Monday evening a full account appeared in the newspapers. Brookhart denied that he advocated a change in the American form of government. He did reiterate his view, however, that the United States "could well adopt some of Russia's advancements" and that this could be done under the present American constitution. "I have confidence in our flag," he said. "But I am not like those who sit back and bark that it can't be done. I am the one who is loyal, not they. And if that is treason, make the most of it."[34]

This speech and the publicity surrounding it fueled the rumors that Brookhart's days at the AAA were numbered. The relationship between Brookhart and the AAA had never been good and now he had broken the agreement to make no speeches. One rumor had him returning to Iowa to run for governor. But Brookhart said that he would stay out of that race and support former Governor Dan Turner who had announced his candidacy to reclaim the office. Brookhart said he had heard nothing about another rumor that he would run for Congress. Still another rumor said he would join the new Export-Import Bank Peek was forming. He said that an appointment had not been decided upon but it seems unlikely that Peek would appoint Brookhart to any position.[35]

The furor over the speech soon died down and Brookhart continued to try to find manufacturers willing to extend credit to the Soviet Union. As if to emphasize that he was still on the job, the *Register* published a photograph of Brookhart at his desk holding a paper referring to the Soviet Union. Jennie told Ned that "Father is sitting tight, holding his job, hoping they will have more active trading with the Soviets." He kept Peek informed of his progress on a regular basis. But it is clear that neither Davis nor Peek thought that he was accomplishing anything.[36]

On September 11 Davis called Peek to ask about a proposed Brookhart trip to New York and Philadelphia to talk with companies about exports to the Soviet Union. Davis admitted that he did not keep in close touch with Brookhart and asked Peek what he was doing. Peek replied that he did not think Brookhart was "doing much good." Davis expressed concern about whether Brookhart would "gum things up" for projects Peek was working on and suggested that perhaps Brookhart should move back under Peek's jurisdiction. Peek resisted the suggestion but told Davis he had no objection to Brookhart's travel plans. Davis said he would authorize the travel and "pray he does no harm."[37]

Davis apparently did not pray hard enough. While in Philadelphia Brookhart made a speech that again emphasized his radicalism. He talked about the Soviet Union, and said that the Soviet and American constitutions were similar except for the religious clause. He said that the American post office, schools, dams, the Tennessee Valley Authority, and other examples of government programs were what he called "entirely communistic." He then advocated cooperatives and cooperative banking and charged: "If this be Communism let my critics make the most of it." Some observers conceded his points about many of these government programs, but he always seemed to include an inflammatory statement that made them part company with him. For example, following his usual speech in October, a questioner asked if the country could be changed and he replied that a revolution might be necessary: "When you consider that only twenty-six hundred were killed during the Soviet Revolution and it benefited one hundred and sixty million it is worthwhile to consider."[38]

Brookhart's days at the AAA were clearly numbered. Chester Davis was already nervous about the perceived liberal leanings of the AAA. In fact, following Peek's resignation, and the appointment of Davis, some liberal members were "purged." Brookhart's rhetoric could only cast further suspicion on the AAA.

On his part Brookhart must have been frustrated. The continuing problem of arranging credit was not going well so the "deals" were not taking place. With Peek at the White House dealing with trade issues, there was less for Brookhart to do. He kept busy, but did not do much.

But there was a deeper source of frustration, namely, that the entire premise of the AAA was production control. Like most American farmers,

Brookhart had always opposed production controls. This was based on the deeply held belief that only God should control production. Instead, as we have seen, the focus of his agricultural plan throughout the 1920s was to create new markets.

Brookhart always claimed that he had written the agricultural plank of the 1932 Democratic platform which advocated a fixed price above production costs. It was on that basis that he campaigned for Roosevelt. Moreover, his position as trade advisor presumed that he would be finding markets for farm products. But when the Agricultural Adjustment Administration was finally created and put into operation, it called for control of production. Production quotas, called domestic allotments, for each crop and kind of livestock were determined and land was to be taken out of production to achieve those quotas. Crops already planted in the spring of 1933 had been plowed under and newly born livestock was destroyed. The plan was controversial from the beginning and went against everything Brookhart believed.

Brookhart charged that the AAA program had been taken from the Republican platform and he felt betrayed. He had supported Herbert Hoover in 1928 and did not get the kind of farm relief he wanted. He had supported the Democrats and the appointment of Wallace in 1933 and again did not get what he believed was needed. Years later he said, "Hoover double-crossed me and then Wallace double-crossed me."[39]

Brookhart left the AAA on January 15, 1935. It is not surprising that he left, what is surprising is that he stayed so long. He neither resigned nor was he directly fired. Rather Chester Davis eliminated the position of trade advisor and all of Brookhart's responsibilities were assumed by Peek. Jennie told Ned that his "job with the AAA 'folded up,'" but that he already had "something better—so he says."[40]

A few weeks later Florence Brookhart wrote her brother, Ned, that he would "find Dad and Mother older, with less energy—quite willing to take life easier. Both seem well except for that." Smith Brookhart was now sixty-six and Jennie was sixty-five. It had been nearly thirty-eight years since Smith brought his bride to their new home in Washington, Iowa. They had seven children, mostly raised by Jennie because of Smith's long periods of time away for the military and politics. She had also been active in various community activities. His life in those thirty-eight years had been full of shooting trips and political campaigns.[41]

The previous two years since his defeat had been more settled than they had known since they were first married. He maintained a busy pace, and as Jennie said, had "done so much . . . talking." But he traveled less and they had more time together. When they went out socially it was often with Democratic Congressman Edward Eicher and his wife. The Eichers were from Washington, Iowa, and hometown ties brought them together in the capital. Florence Brookhart could not be faulted for thinking that he would be willing to take life easier. But even she underestimated her father.[42]

Shortly after his resignation, the *Des Moines Register* published a photograph of a smiling Brookhart, carrying an umbrella and briefcase, and tipping his hat. Many no doubt hoped that the tip of the hat meant good-bye, I am leaving the arena. But the brief article that accompanied the picture indicated otherwise. Calling Brookhart, "Iowa's most colorful politician," it said he was still in Washington, "one eye on lobbying for cost of production, the other on the 1936 senatorial race."[43]

The "lobbying" eye focused on a bill recently introduced by Congressman Eicher and Senator William Gibbs McAdoo (Democrat, California). Their bill guaranteed the farmer the cost of production and then had a scheme to sell surpluses on the foreign market. It was essentially the same bill Brookhart had advocated for ten years and he called Eicher's Bill "the best farm bill ever produced." Meanwhile to support himself he opened an office to find export markets for American firms.[44]

The other eye looked back to Iowa. Smith and Jennie had never lost interest in what was happening in their home state. They continued to vote there, usually, but not always, for Republican candidates. In 1932 and 1934, for example, they voted for the Republican, Dan Turner, for Governor. They probably also voted for Ed Eicher for Congress. Although a Democrat, Eicher was a friend and a dry running against a wet candidate. When prohibition had ended with the Twenty-First Amendment, Iowa passed laws to control liquor as much as possible. The state created state liquor stores which was the only source for the purchase of alcohol. Jennie noted that there were "many liquor stores in Iowa . . . [which] will restore prosperity—*so we hear*."[45]

Meanwhile, Brookhart's speeches and activities had attracted the attention of the Federal Bureau of Investigation. Charges that Brookhart was a communist dated back to his first campaigns for the senate. These charges had been intensified following the trip to the Soviet Union in 1923. Most Iowans, however, seemed to consider such charges as little more than political rhetoric and only his most ardent opponents took them seriously. Still, it was an easy charge to make and the suspicion followed him through the 1920s.

In 1932, for example, former Attorney General Harry M. Daugherty published an emotional book to clear his name. Daugherty wrote that the Brookhart committee, which had investigated his activities while Attorney General, had begun its work following a "state call" on Brookhart and Senator Burton Wheeler by "the Communist leaders in their Russian Capitol." He said they had been "received in the inner Soviet circles as 'comrades,' and came back to the United States to praise their teachers."[46]

Daugherty's charges initiated an FBI review of its files on Brookhart. It found evidence of the "radical beliefs" of Brookhart and Wheeler but there was no evidence of any connection between Brookhart and Wheeler and Soviet officials regarding the Daugherty matter. In a holograph note on the memo FBI Director J. Edgar Hoover wrote, "This confirms my impression that the statement in the Daugherty book is without foundation in so far as factual data is concerned."[47]

Nevertheless, throughout the 1930s the FBI maintained surveillance of Brookhart and kept a record of the meetings he attended and the speeches he made. It reported, for example, that in 1934 Congressman Hamilton Fish (Republican, New York) said that Brookhart might be a member of the American Civil Liberties Union. His 1935 speech before the Open Forum and speeches and appearances at meetings of such groups as the National Youth Congress, Friends of the Soviet Union, the Scottsboro Committee, and the National Right to Work Congress were all duly noted. Often a comment was added that many known communists were present.

The theme of most of these speeches was similar to the controversial speech he had made in April 1934, and the speech later that year in Philadelphia. But other speeches attacked the American military and military expenditures. On April 23, 1936, for example, he spoke at a peace rally at the University of Iowa. He advocated a civilian army, and said that a professional army would create a "social caste of officers" and "lead the United States into every world war." Moreover, he said he would participate in a "war of defense but not [of] aggression." But he had been saying that since World War I. He said he was against the World Court and the League of Nations unless it was accompanied by a world-wide cooperative economic system, ideas dating back to the 1920s. Finally, he urged a reduction in appropriations for the Navy. Although he knew the "war profiteers" wanted more battleships built, he said he did not think that a battleship was "any longer a defensive armament" and he had "serious doubts as to its value for any purpose." Later when a reporter asked about one student anti-war group, the Veterans of Future Wars, Brookhart said, "They're having fun, and I'm not against fun."[48]

The FBI, however, did not have a sense of humor. A memorandum of

February 10, 1941, asked whether further investigation should be done to determine if Brookhart should be placed on a list of subjects for "custodial detention" in the event of a national emergency. Apparently such detention would take place only if Brookhart tried to leave the country in wartime. In September, J. Edgar Hoover said Brookhart should be considered for detention and on December 8, 1941, Hoover issued the detention card. But in July 1943 the Attorney General wrote Hoover that he could find no basis in law for the custodial detention classification, that it was "unreliable" and it was a "mistake." Brookhart's classification was not cancelled, however, until July 1945, seven months after his death.[49]

In March 1936 President Roosevelt asked an aide to find out if Brookhart intended to run in the Republican primary election against Senator Lester Dickinson. Dickinson was a persistent and very outspoken critic of the New Deal and Roosevelt would not have been unhappy if he were defeated. The aide returned with the information that Brookhart was expected to enter the race. Furthermore, other Iowa congressmen thought he would do fairly well since Dickinson was perceived as weak. But Brookhart was also perceived as somewhat discredited so no one was sure just what would happen. The common wisdom was that in order to win the nomination Brookhart would have to appeal to the followers of Dr. Francis Townsend who had a scheme for old age pensions, and other radical groups that had sprung up in recent months. The best Brookhart could do, Roosevelt was told, was to split the vote so much that the Republican convention would choose the nominee, in which case Dickinson would win.[50]

Ever since he left the AAA Brookhart had been an unknown factor in Iowa politics and Roosevelt was not alone in wondering what he would do. Roosevelt may have hoped that Brookhart could unseat the New Deal critic, Dickinson. Republicans may have feared that the always unpredictable Brookhart could do the same. And the recently formed Farmer-Labor Party worried about what a Brookhart candidacy would do to its fragile coalition of various dissident groups.

The Farmer-Labor Party began to form in late 1933 from groups who felt that the New Deal did not adequately serve the needs of farmers. Following organizational meetings in 1934, the new party ran candidates in two state senate districts and twenty-four house districts and former Sioux City Mayor Wallace M. Short ran for governor. None of these candidates won but they did succeed in winning 2 percent of the vote which gave the party legal status and meant its candidates could appear on primary election ballots.[51]

On May 20, 1935, Howard Y. Williams, national organizer for the

Farmer-Laborites, sent a letter to a number of Iowans to solicit information about Brookhart. It stated that he could not win in the Iowa Republican primary because his supporters there had moved to the new Farmer-Labor Party. It suggested instead, that he might have a better chance by running as the Farmer-Labor candidate for governor. Archie Carter, the editor of the *Dubuque Leader*, a labor newspaper, said that the Brookhart letter was "raising a hell of a mess." There seemed to be very little support for a Brookhart senate candidacy but many agreed that he should run for governor.[52]

It was unlikely, however, that he would accept a third-party candidacy. For thirty years he had maintained that true Republicanism was progressive and he had refused to leave the party. In 1912 he had supported Theodore Roosevelt's Bull Moose Party while at the same time presiding over the Republican State Convention. In 1924 he had refused to leave the party to join La Follette's Progressive Party. In 1932, to be sure, he did run on the Progressive Party ticket, but as we have seen that was a deliberate strategy to pull votes away from Henry Field and elect the Democrat Louis Murphy. And after 1932, when he had come to believe that progressive goals were being advanced by the New Deal Democratic Party, he still refused to leave the Republicans.

On April 6 Brookhart joined four other Republicans in the race against Lester Dickinson. In his announcement statement he said that the field was "wide open for a candidate with a definite record and a definite program." Roosevelt and Wallace had "good intentions" with their programs for agriculture, but Brookhart said his program was better. Brookhart charged that Dickinson had originally supported the New Deal, then recanted his support. Now, Brookhart said, Dickinson offered only "glittering generalities."[53]

Unlike all his previous Senate campaigns Brookhart did not begin with a rally in Washington, Iowa. Instead he accepted the invitation of the Emmetsburg Chamber of Commerce to "fire [the] opening shot" of the campaign in the town where he had made his ill-fated speech in 1924. Appearing in Emmetsburg on April 23 Brookhart made reference to his appearance there twelve years before. The speech then was both an "analysis and a prophecy" of economic conditions and political leadership that had largely come true. At the time people said it had been a mistake that cost him his seat. Admitting that the speech was controversial, however, he said he lost his seat because of a "framed up contest."[54]

The remainder of the speech covered very familiar ground for Iowans who had followed his career. He blamed Wall Street speculators for the Depression, explained business cycles, called for a farm program that dealt with the marketing of surpluses and not production controls. He said the

"Old Deal" had been "competitive economics"; the New Deal was "experimental economics." Brookhart called the "Republican party to a rebirth in the oldest, most conservative, soundest, most stable, most humane and most successful business system ever devised by the mind of man. I call it cooperative economics."[55]

Reaction to his candidacy was not enthusiastic. One columnist said he had entered the race not as the prodigal son but as the prodigal's father, ready to save his party from dissolute living. Brookhart's old adversary, Verne Marshall of the *Cedar Rapids Gazette*, called it a bomb burst on the Iowa political scene. Marshall also questioned Brookhart's residency as did another Iowan who referred to him as "formerly of Iowa, late of the Soviet [Union] and now of Maryland." Still another writer asked, "Are we going to be subjected to this Brookhart affliction, after such a hard winter?" And *Time* magazine said simply: "Again, Brookhart."[56]

Even before the Emmetsburg speech Brookhart had to react to charges that he had been paid by private companies to arrange deals with the War Department for the sale of surplus military supplies. Writing to Congressman John McSwain of the House Military Affairs Committee, Brookhart said that following his departure from the AAA "several American firms" employed him to sell their products abroad. Among them was the company against which the charges had been leveled. He denied making any contacts while still a government official and his dealings afterward were between the company and the Soviet government and the trading agency Amtorg. Neither Brookhart, nor those with whom he consulted, including Senator George Norris, thought there was any conflict of interest. The incident played little part in the campaign. Perhaps Iowans were used to controversy about Brookhart and so thought nothing of it. Or maybe they did not take his latest candidacy seriously enough that it mattered.[57]

In mid-May *Register* reporter C. C. Clifton surveyed the political climate in the nine congressional districts of Iowa. Only in the Eighth District, north central Iowa, did he find any significant support for Brookhart. Even in the Ninth District in northwest Iowa, where the Farmers' Union and later the Farmers' Holiday Association had been the strongest, Clifton could find very little support for Brookhart. In contrast, in the 1932 primary, 26 percent of Brookhart's vote had come from these two districts. Still, Clifton reported that Brookhart was enough of an unknown factor that Republican leaders expected him "to get quite a vote."[58]

Brookhart said that the "professional prognosticator" of the *Register* would get a surprise. He had visited eighty-eight counties and as usual had campaigned without funds, a manager, or advertising. He stayed in private homes and had his supporters drive him around. He said he had support from farm and labor organizations, Spanish-American and other war veterans, and independent merchants. He also claimed the support of Father Charles E. Coughlin, a vocal critic of the New Deal and the Townsend Old Age Pension clubs. In all he said he would receive 45 to 50 percent of the vote.[59]

On May 28 Brookhart was in Washington, Iowa visiting his brother Thompson when he received word that his three-year-old grandson was dead. The son of Smith Brookhart, Jr. and his wife, Betty, William Brookhart had run into the street and was struck by a car and killed. Brookhart immediately cancelled all further campaign appearances and returned to Washington, D.C., to be with his family.[60]

On election day Brookhart lost badly! Dickinson received 41 percent of the vote (105,416 votes) and Brookhart received 22 percent (58,129), 13 percent less than in 1932. Brookhart carried only five counties, four in north central and northwest Iowa where the "prognosticator" had suggested he could win, plus Washington County. The new Farmer-Labor Party had nominated George Buresh who received 72 percent of the Farmer-Labor vote, but his 1,199 votes represented only a small fraction of the total votes cast.[61]

With the primaries over, the Iowa Senate race was settled. Lester Dickinson for the Republicans, former governor Clyde L. Herring for the Democrats, and George F. Buresh the Farmer-Labor candidate. Brookhart tried to put politics behind him as he gathered with his family in Washington, Iowa, for the June 22 wedding of Florence Brookhart and Clarence E. Yount of Prescott, Arizona. Both bride and groom were graduates of the George Washington University College of Medicine and would practice medicine together in Prescott.

The wedding took place at noon in front of the fireplace of the brick house whose renters kindly vacated the house for the day so that the Brookharts could go "home." It was a small wedding with only family and close friends present. While the society page reported what the bride and her attendant wore, the father of the bride also elicited comment. Dressed in white trousers and a blue coat, the *Register* said it gave an "impression of formality for the man who wore sack suits to the White House."[62]

The afternoon of the wedding the Brookharts held an open house for their many friends in Washington. It was a time to renew friendships and relay the latest family news. It was only three weeks since his primary defeat and so everyone also wanted to know what he would do next. Brookhart apparently told some people he would return to Iowa in a few weeks to practice law. But he said that he had no interest in a third party candidacy for the senate as some newspapers had reported.[63]

Fate soon thrust Brookhart back into senatorial politics when on July 16, Senator Louis Murphy was killed in an automobile accident. Twice before in Brookhart's political career death had upset what was presumed to be a settled senate race. In 1908 William B. Allison had died shortly after defeating Brookhart's political mentor, Albert B. Cummins, in the preferential primary thus giving Cummins another opportunity for the senate. In 1926 Cummins himself had died following his defeat by Brookhart in the primary. Now Murphy's death revived the talk that Brookhart would enter the race to serve out the remaining two years of Murphy's term.[64]

Both the Farmer-Labor Party and the Republican Party convened on July 25 to select their nominee to serve the remainder of Murphy's term in the senate. The Farmer-Labor convention nominated Brookhart for the senate with 125 votes to only twenty-seven votes for the second candidate and five for the third. Although Wallace Short said he was "confident" Brookhart would accept the nomination, Brookhart said "I don't know what it all means. I will have to look at it." Admitting that he was in sympathy with the general ideals of the party, after all, he said, "we are all progressives," nevertheless he refused to make a commitment to run. At the Republican convention Brookhart received no votes and when the chairman announced that Brookhart had been nominated by the Farmer-Labor Party the crowd booed. Jennie said, "the political pot is boiling . . . and of course it will be more and more until November."[65]

Two factors seemed to weigh on Brookhart as he considered whether to accept the nomination. The first was the endorsement by the Iowa Farmer-Labor Party of the presidential candidacy of North Dakota Congressman William Lemke on the Union Party ticket. Formed in June the Union Party brought together the followers of Father Charles Coughlin's National Union for Social Justice, Dr. Francis Townsend's Old Age Pension Plan, and the late Louisiana Senator Huey Long's Share Our Wealth scheme now headed by Gerald L. K. Smith. Although each had a different program they were united in their criticism of Roosevelt and the New Deal. Short was the leader of the effort to endorse the Lemke candidacy and following several weeks of maneuvering he succeeded in getting the endorsement at the same convention that nominated Brookhart.

The second factor influencing Brookhart was related to the first. Although Brookhart had urged the president to sign the Frazier-Lemke Act which provided for government refinancing of farm mortgages, he thought Lemke was too critical of Roosevelt. While Brookhart himself had been critical of Roosevelt's agricultural program, he thought Roosevelt was still closer to his own views than Lemke or the Republican Party candidate for president, Governor Alf Landon of Kansas.[66]

Rumors began to circulate that Brookhart would not only support

Roosevelt in the coming election, but would also actively campaign for him. On August 6 Brookhart met with Iowa Governor Clyde Herring, currently the Democratic candidate for the full-term Senate seat. Although it is not known what they talked about, it is reasonable to assume that one item of discussion would have been the fact that Roosevelt was running behind in Iowa, an impression confirmed a few days later with the publication of the Gallup Poll. The thinking apparently was the Brookhart "controlled" some 40,000 votes in Iowa, which was not an unreasonable number since he had received over 59,000 in the recent primary. If Brookhart could deliver those votes to Roosevelt it could make a difference in a close race. Moreover, it could not have been lost on Herring that the more votes Roosevelt received, the better his own chance to defeat Dickinson. Following the meeting with Herring Brookhart issued a statement that only served to further confuse the issue:

> There have been a lot of complications since my nomination by the Farmer-Labor Party. I haven't yet decided this thing in my own way. A number of things have happened since the nomination which have a bearing on what I will do in the campaign. No, I do not want to say what they are. Yes, it does sound mysterious; some of the things were a mystery to me.[67]

One week later he announced that he would not accept the Farmer-Labor nomination. Writing to Mrs. Minnie Duval, the secretary of the Iowa party, he reminded her that he did not ask for the nomination nor was he consulted about it. Identifying himself as a "progressive Republican," he said he was in sympathy with the movement but could not support their endorsement of Lemke. He said he would join with the Farmer-Labor leaders in Minnesota and Wisconsin, who had not endorsed Lemke, and work for the election of Roosevelt. "Farmers will be a unit for Roosevelt," he said. "In the election it looks like we will get enough farmers and working people and independent merchants . . . to carry [Iowa]."[68]

He threw himself into the campaign with the kind of vigor that seemed to have been lacking from his own campaign in the spring. In September he attended a conference in Chicago called to unite progressives around Roosevelt. He spoke throughout Wisconsin and Minnesota, including a major address before a Farmer-Labor group in Mankato. The last two weeks of October he spent in Iowa where Roosevelt continued to trail Landon in the polls. The *New York Times* said on October 23 that Landon would carry more states than the six Hoover had carried in 1932. Writing two days before the election *Register* political columnist C. C. Clifton said the election in Iowa was still close.[69]

Franklin Roosevelt swept to the largest victory since 1820 and carried all but two states: Maine and Vermont. In Iowa he received 55 percent of the votes down from 59 percent in 1932. But in 1936 he had two opponents in Iowa, Landon received 43 percent and Lemke received 3 percent.

It is difficult to know just how effective Brookhart's efforts were. In early August the view had been that Brookhart "controlled" 40,000 votes in Iowa. Roosevelt led Landon in Iowa by nearly 24,000 votes, a much closer margin than Roosevelt had over Hoover in 1932. Moreover, Lemke received over 29,000 votes in Iowa. It would seem, then, that the "anti-Roosevelt" vote in Iowa was greater in 1936 and Brookhart could have held enough votes for Roosevelt to make a difference. One who thought so was George L. Berry, long-time President of the International Pressmen and Assistants' Union. Brookhart had worked under Berry's direction during the campaign and following the election Berry told Roosevelt that Brookhart's contribution had been of "great value."[70]

Following the election Brookhart's friends worked to get him a position on the Interstate Commerce Commission. Writing to Ned on January 12, Jennie said she had hoped there would be news about the appointment but apparently "red tape" had held it up. Nevertheless she said Brookhart felt sure something would come that would "give us security." In March the appointment still had not been made and four of Iowa's Democratic Congressmen wrote Roosevelt to urge that he do so soon. Senators Wheeler and Norris also intervened on his behalf but the appointment did not come.[71]

Through the summer friends of Brookhart continued to press the president to give Brookhart a job. Most notable of these was George Berry, now a United States Senator from Tennessee. Writing Roosevelt in July, Berry reminded the president of Brookhart's "generous and effective assistance" during the campaign and also recalled Roosevelt's comment that Brookhart would be given "some appointment." Berry said Brookhart was in a "distressing position due to the long period of unemployment" and urged a quick response.[72]

Berry wrote Roosevelt again in September and said that Brookhart was really "very needy." Roosevelt directed his secretary, Marvin McIntyre to ask Henry Wallace to do something for Brookhart because "I really would like to have him taken care of." Wallace was reluctant, however, to take on Brookhart. He told McIntyre he could give Brookhart a small position but there would have to be a clear understanding that Brookhart was to engage in no political activity. Once again, no job was forthcoming.[73]

In November Brookhart suggested to McIntyre that he would like a position on the Securities and Exchange Commission. He reminded McIntyre of his record of criticism of Wall Street both in and out of Congress. Once again Roosevelt tried and asked McIntyre to speak with Securities and Exchange Chairman William O. Douglas. But once again, there was no job for Brookhart. One year later he was still trying for a job. Writing Roosevelt directly, Congressman Eicher said Brookhart thought that Iowa's senators had "become dilatory in pressing his claims." But this appeal, like all the others, was unsuccessful.[74]

Smith and Jennie were now alone in the house in Hyattsville, Maryland. The children were all grown and gone but their son Smith and his family lived in the area so they could enjoy their grandchildren. They also traveled to see their children across the country. The garden continued to be important. One summer Jennie reported they were growing figs, peaches, grapes, and of course, apples. But they also began to show the effects of age. One Iowan recalled meeting Brookhart in 1938 when he gave him a tour of the area. His recollection was that Brookhart "seemed tired and not very well. He was not a young man any more."[75]

Meanwhile, Smith continued to work for the causes that had been so important during his political career. For example, he was executive counsel for the Little Business Men's League of America and often represented the League in Congressional hearings. The League advocated regional government controlled banks to insure that small businesses could obtain loans. To discourage monopoly and insure the survival of privately owned small businesses, it wanted higher taxes on chain stores. And it advocated price controls to insure fair competition.[76]

In February 1937 he was elected to the executive committee of the newly formed National Lawyers Guild. The Lawyers Guild brought together liberal lawyers who believed that the legal profession all too often represented the interests of property rather than the interests of the people. Members believed that the legal profession should not "stand as an obstacle . . . of every social and economic reform." At its initial meeting the Guild supported President Roosevelt's recent plan to expand the size of the Supreme Court and advocated two constitutional amendments. The first would prohibit the Supreme Court from ruling on the constitutionality of state laws. The second would require a vote of the people to amend the Constitution. In later years the Guild would advocate civil liberties for aliens, an end to the poll tax, strengthening of the National Labor Relations Board, the disbanding of the Dies Committee formed by the House of Representatives to investigate un-American activities, appropriation of funds for the extension of legal services, and a national health program.[77]

The Lawyers Guild was the latest means for Brookhart to express a long-held idea: that the people should rule. He had advocated judicial recall and opposed the world court because there was no legislative feature to it. Now in the 1930s he circulated a brief opposing judicial review by the Supreme Court. The constitution gave limited powers to the Supreme Court, he argued, but gave the Congress (the peoples' branch) the right to "regulate" the appellate jurisdiction of the court. In the 1803 decision, Marbury v. Madison, the court took upon itself limited powers of review, but subsequent courts had expanded those powers. He said it was "better to trust the Congress and the people who elect it, than the courts, who because of their life tenure get beyond the control of the people." For Congress to give review jurisdiction to the courts was to "pass the buck" and he urged Congress to reassert its own powers.[78]

He also maintained his interest in politics. He continued to be critical of the administration's agricultural policy and Secretary of Agriculture Henry Wallace. There had been no appreciable improvement in the condition of farmers and he said that farmers would speak loudly at the polls. Brookhart blamed Wallace and called for his resignation. In an attempt to blunt Brookhart's criticism, in December 1938 Roosevelt suggested to Wallace that he give Brookhart a job. Wallace knew better and when the criticisms continued he told Roosevelt:

> I really don't think Brookhart should get much attention. He certainly has no national influence, and his following in Iowa today is insignificant. He has a one-track mind, and considerable persistence, but I don't believe much else to contribute to the present-day discussions.[79]

Wallace's assessment was in a large measure correct. Brookhart had little new to say. In the late 1930s he worked on the manuscript for a book on cooperative economics. Entitled "Cooperative Economics or Illiterate Facts vs. Intellectual Fiction," it is a compilation of all the arguments he had been advancing for over thirty years. Whether he ever intended to have it published is not clear. What is clear is that it is unlikely that anyone would have published it.[80]

Nevertheless he continued to advance his case. He made the rounds of the offices of friendly congressmen. Iowa Congressman Otha Wearin recalled that he would visit Wearin's office every three or four weeks to talk about the farm bill, politics, or whatever was in the news. He rarely stayed more than half an hour and Wearin said Brookhart was always interested in his viewpoint. The visits, Wearin thought, were "just to feel the pulse of Congress," to be, even in that small way, a part of events.[81]

His income in those years came from his small law practice. He mainly represented companies who wanted to do business overseas. He did some traveling, often to New York, but Jennie's letters through 1940 indicate that although he was "busy," there was not much result. "Daddy has lots doing," she wrote Ned early in 1941, "much of it a mirage (you see it, you don't.)" Still he brought some income and in early June, 1942, he realized a long-standing goal when he paid off the last of the debt from the bank failure.[82]

In August 1942 the years caught up with him and he entered a hospital. His office first said it was only for a rest, but it was soon known that he had suffered a major stroke. Jennie told Ned, "It's old Father Time . . . 73 is past the allotted time—but we never thought of him as old."[83]

His left side was paralyzed and he was unable to grip a crutch well enough to walk. He took physical therapy but was not able to make much progress. Edith came to read to him and feed him his meals. He also began the long process of coming to terms with his life and letting go. He told Edith about his childhood and his regrets that he did not do a better job of providing for his family. Other times he would be very upbeat; one day he told his family that all he needed was a Grimes apple every day.[84]

After the first of the year Brookhart was moved to a veterans hospital near St. Petersburg, Florida. The change seemed to do him good. He wanted to get into the bay to swim but he was much too weak for that. On his seventy-fourth birthday he told Jennie that when their youngest son, Joe, got out of the service, the two of them would "get a jeep and drive over the new highway to Alaska."[85]

Except for the paralysis his health was good and he maintained an interest in politics. In April he issued a statement advocating the candidacy of Supreme Court Justice William O. Douglas for president: "I hope the Democrats nominate Justice Douglas in 1944. But no matter who nominates him, I'd be for him. I know him. I am certain he would make the best postwar president we could have." But for the most part he grew increasingly frustrated. One day he told Jennie, "I will not spend the rest of my life in hospitals because I have a *bum leg.*"[86]

That summer Jennie took him to Duluth, Minnesota, to be with their son, John, and his family. Although he was bedfast he enjoyed the company of his grandchildren. But he was making no progress toward recovery, in fact he was in a gradual decline. In August he finally accepted the use of a wheel chair.[87]

That fall Smith and Jennie moved to Prescott, Arizona. Smith went into a veterans hospital and Jennie moved in with their daughter, Florence. He seemed contented with this arrangement but he was declining further. John said he was "duller" and did not "handle himself as well." Nevertheless, Brookhart said that Florence would have him up and walking, but John said his father was "chasing rainbows."[88]

He tried to read the papers to keep up with the world but reading was difficult. He had a man come to shave him and take him for exercise. He would talk with anyone who would listen and he regaled them with his ideas and plans. Jennie and Florence and her son, John, visited him as much as possible and he enjoyed having young John around.[89]

Jennie died suddenly on December 30, 1943, of heart failure. It had been a long time since that Epworth League dinner in Bloomfield when Smith noticed Jennie serving giblet gravy. They had been married forty-seven years. She watched him move from small-town attorney to become a state and national figure. Their marriage was marked by long separations while he pursued his interests and she stayed home to raise the family. Writing shortly after her death, Ralph Shannon, the editor of the *Washington Evening Journal* said of her:

> Mrs. Brookhart looked after the "home department" in those earlier years. She was the court of appeals, the chief justice, the final arbitrator. Her authority and influence were wielded quietly, and no one ever saw her flustered, even when youthful spirits threatened to shake the house off its foundations. The Brookhart boys and girls were not noted for their placid tranquility. . . . [Now] all are contributing to the general welfare.[90]

But she was also involved in Smith's political life. Her letters reveal her as an astute observer of the scene and probably his best advisor. Had he listened to her more he might have avoided some of his self-created problems. It is also clear that what she really wanted was to have her husband at home with the family. Years later their son Smith said of his parents' marriage, "They apparently loved each other very much. I think the only time she talked about romance in their marriage to me, she said, 'Well, there's never been anyone else.'"[91]

Smith declined rapidly following Jennie's death. He was less alert and when he talked it tended to be about his childhood. A few old friends from Iowa wrote letters about politics and the war, but he was not able to sustain much interest in anything.

On November 15, 1944, Smith Brookhart died. He was taken back to Washington, Iowa to be buried next to Jennie and their son, Sam. The Reverend Carl Klein said of his long-time friend, that he was a "friend of the common man . . . [who was] uncompromising in his attitude toward wrong, whether it be in private or in public." The editor of the *Journal* also mentioned his firm beliefs. "Once he decided he was right the arguments ended . . . and from that moment on there was action." The *Journal* also commended his "honesty, his tenacity, his complete indifference to the conventions. He was a non-conformist of the first magnitude, a rugged individual, a man to be reckoned with." C. C. Clifton wrote in the *Register* that Brookhart had been born in Missouri, "the commonwealth of curiosity," and when he used his curiosity and found something wrong "he flew at it like a rooster and stayed against it like a bulldog." In military training and politics, Clifton said Brookhart was a "straight shooter."[92]

Smith Wildman Brookhart was born four years after the Civil War, a war fought with muzzleloading muskets, and he died a few months before the end of World War II, a war fought with weapons of gruesome efficiency, including the atomic bomb. In his career in rifle shooting he helped advance the progress of military weaponry and he continued to give his expertise on new weaponry until shortly before his stroke.

As a progressive politician, however, he represented that earlier time. A politician in the age when "modern" campaigning by use of the airplane and radio came into its own, he was most at ease simply talking issues with farmers around the kitchen table. He knew and understood their world which was still largely rooted in the nineteenth century.

He was one of the last exponents of the nineteenth century view that farmers should produce and then find ways to market their crops. Although he was never able to achieve his goal of government sponsored marketing cooperatives, he continued to try and influence agricultural policy. But when the New Deal agricultural policy went in the direction of production controls, Brookhart and his nineteenth century views were cut adrift from mainstream policy.

He was also a last link to earlier agricultural protests that distrusted centralizing financial power and demanded that farmers be allowed to control their own destiny. Many of his sponsors when he first ran for political office had their roots in the Anti-Monopoly Party and the Grange of the 1870s. He knew James Baird Weaver at the height of populism in the 1890s and came to revere his views. As a Progressive, he advocated reforms that made greater citizen participation possible and attempted to free the government from the influence of business powers that denied power to the people. His heroes in that fight had preceded him in death: La Follette twenty years before, Cummins two years later, and George Norris only two months before.

He often criticized the system and was branded as disloyal, a communist, a socialist, or worse. Yet he remained a very loyal American. He never really wanted to replace the American system with something different, he just wanted the system to be altered to allow everyone an equal opportunity to benefit from what America offered.

Throughout his career people made fun of his simple lifestyle. He grew his own food, he refused to allow his fame to change his habits of simple dress, and he showed little interest in much of what was considered "modern" and "progressive" in the 1920s. Whether he was in the corridors of power in the Capitol, or the streets of Moscow, or on the target range, or on an Iowa back road seeking a voter, Smith Brookhart never forgot his roots in rural America. As his sister said of him shortly before his death, "He was just a good honest sturdy country boy."[93]

NOTES

INTRODUCTION

1. Jerry Alvin Neprash, *The Brookhart Campaigns in Iowa, 1920-1926* (New York: Columbia University Press, 1932).
2. George H. Mayer, *The Republican Party, 1854-1966* (New York: Oxford University Press, 1967), p. 385.
3. Malcolm Moos, *The Republicans, A History Of Their Party* (New York: Random House, 1956), p. 329. I found very few examples of the use of quotation marks with his name.
4. See Ellis W. Hawley, *The Great War and the Search for a Modern Order, A History of the American People and Their Institutions, 1917-1933* (New York: St. Martin's Press, 1979).

1. FARMER'S SON

1. *Washington County Press*, March 25, 1910 (hereinafter cited as *Press*).
2. *Press*, February 4, 1910.
3. *Press*, March 25, 1910.
4. *Press*, January 28, 1910. *Mount Pleasant Journal* quoted in *Keokuk Daily Gate City*, May 4, 1910; *Keokuk Daily Gate City*, May 4, 1910.
5. *Iowa Official Register, 1911-1912* (Des Moines: Iowa State Printer), p. 561; Brookhart to Dolliver, June 16, 1910, Jonathan Prentiss Dolliver Papers, State Historical Society of Iowa Library, Iowa City, Box 56, Folder 7.
6. The biographical material about Smith Brookhart was taken from a number of sources. *Biographical Directory of the American Congress, 1774-1949* (Washington, D.C., 1950), p. 894; "Smith Wildman Brookhart," address to the State University of Iowa Political Science Club, February, 1932, (*Congressional Record*, 72 Cong., 1 Sess., pp. 6236-6239.) Also used were comments made in various periodical articles and newspaper accounts as cited in the bibliography. Unpublished biographical sources include interviews and correspondence with Smith W. Brookhart, Jr., Florence Brookhart Yount, Edith Brookhart Millard, and Mabel Wildman Rice. Particularly helpful were two sets of notes taken by his daughters during the senator's last illness. These will be cited as "Notes Taken by Edith" and "Notes Taken by Florence." These notes are in the possession of Florence Brookhart Yount. These and other things in her possession will be cited as FBY Collection.

The only full biography is Ray S. Johnston's unpublished thesis, "Smith Wildman Brookhart: Iowa's Last Populist" (M.A. Thesis, State College of Iowa, 1964). Johnston's work, however, has been superseded in part as more manuscript collections have become available.

Other theses about Brookhart include: Corwin D. Cornell, "Smith W. Brookhart and Agrarian Discontent in Iowa" (M.A. Thesis, University of Iowa, 1949); Barry A. Russell, "The Changing Concept of Iowa Progressivism: Smith W. Brookhart vs. Albert B. Cummins, 1920-1926" (M.A. Thesis, University of North Carolina, 1973); Cornelius Holland Bull, III, "Smith Wildman Brookhart—Neither God Nor Little Fish" (Senior Thesis, Department of History, Princeton University, 1950); George William McDaniel, "Smith Wildman Brookhart: Agrarian Radical in New Era America" (Ph.D. Dissertation, University of Iowa, 1985). For Brookhart's first years see the Memphis (Missouri) *Conservative* and *Reveille,* 1869-1874.

7. *Western Progress,* Spring Valley, Minnesota, January 26, 1876; July 28, 1875; July 26, 1876; Odes E. Brookhart to Edgar Harlan, November 28, 1926, Edgar R. Harlan Correspondence, State Historical Society of Iowa, Des Moines, File 62B, Part 5, Group 7.

8. *Western Progress,* Spring Valley, Minnesota, August 30, 1876. See also the issues of August 6, September 13, and October 25.

9. Interview, Violet Brookhart Gunn, August 24, 1981.

10. "Notes Taken by Edith," FBY Collection. By 1890 the family of Abram and Cynthia Brookhart had grown to ten children. Smith W. Brookhart to John Henry Hopkins, September 16, 1933, Franklin Delano Roosevelt Papers, Franklin Delano Roosevelt Presidential Library, Official File, 220a, Box 2.

11. This was probably part of a series of histories written by Joel Dorman Steele and published by A. S. Barnes and Company throughout the 1880s and 1890s.

12. *Legal Tender Greenback,* Bloomfield, Iowa, April 29, 1886; May 6, 1886; *Davis County Republican,* May 6, 1886.

13. *Legal Tender Greenback,* Bloomfield, Iowa, January 10, 1889; February 11, 1889; April 18, 1889. See the same paper, 1888, 1889 *passim,* for Brookhart's continuing involvement in the society.

14. *Legal Tender Greenback,* April 18, 1889; June 20, 1889. In the fall the same newspaper reported that Brookhart left to attend the University of Iowa. There is no record, however, that he ever enrolled and within a few months his name appears in the paper in connection with activities in Bloomfield. [October 3, 1889].

15. Interview, Mabel Wildman Rice, August 7, 1981; Violet Brookhart Gunn, August 24, 1981.

16. *Legal Tender Greenback,* June 5, 1890; June 12, 1890; *Davis County Republican,* June 18, 1891.

17. *Davis County Republican,* July 30, 1891.

18. *Davis County Republican,* June 11, 1891.

19. Mildred Throne, "Iowans in Congress, 1847-1953," *Iowa Journal of History* 51 (October, 1953): 341.

20. *Press,* February 15, 1912.

21. *Congressional Record,* 67 Cong., 4 Sess., (January, 1923), pp. 2129ff; *Portrait and Biographical Album of Jefferson and Van Buren Counties, Iowa* (Chicago: Lake City Publishing Company, 1890), pp. 482-484; *Washington* (D.C.) *Star,* April 29, 1923.

2. ESTABLISHMENT COUNTY ATTORNEY

1. *The Washington Gazette,* December 9, 1892 (hereinafter cited as *Gazette*). *The Washington Evening Journal,* November 23, 1926 (hereinafter cited as *Journal*). Large portions of this chapter have been previously published as "Prohibition Debate in Washington County, 1890-1894: Smith Wildman Brookhart's Introduction to Politics," *The Annals of Iowa,* (Winter, 1981): 519-536.

2. *Census of Iowa for the Year 1895* (Des Moines: F.R. Conaway, State Printer, 1896), p. 271; Lewis Atherton, *Main Street on the Middle Border* (Bloomington: Indiana University Press, 1954).

3. *Journal*, September 17, 1895.

4. *Journal*, February 10, 14, 1898.

5. *N. W. Ayer and Son's American Newspaper Annual, 1890* (Philadelphia: N. W. Ayer and Son, 1890), p. 228; Ibid., 1899, p. 268. For a brief history of newspapers in Washington, see Hugh H. McCleery, *Newspapers and Other Publications of Washington, Iowa: A Brief History* (Washington: *Washington Evening Journal*, 1944). Washington also had a Democratic paper, the *Washington Democrat*, and a politically independent paper, the *Daily Hustler* (later the *Evening Journal*). For the complexities of the ideological basis of partisanship in late nineteenth century Iowa, see Richard Jensen, *The Winning of the Midwest, Social and Political Conflict, 1888-1896* (Chicago: The University of Chicago Press, 1971).

6. *Gazette*, August 11, 1893.

7. Dan Elbert Clark, "The History of Liquor Legislation in Iowa, 1878-1908," *Iowa Journal of History and Politics* 6 (October 1908): 591-592. For the story of liquor legislation before 1878, see the same author's "The Beginnings of Liquor Legislation in Iowa," loc. cit. 5 (April 1907); "The History of Liquor Legislation in Iowa, 1846-1861," loc. cit. 6 (January 1908); "The History of Liquor Legislation in Iowa, 1861-1878," loc. cit. 6 (July 1908).

8. *Gazette*, August 18, 1893; *Press*, August 23, 1893.

9. *Press*, October 18, 1893; October 25, 1893.

10. Clark, "History of Liquor Legislation, 1878-1908," p. 598; *Gazette*, March 30, 1894.

11. Kathy Fisher, *In the Beginning There Was Land: A History of Washington County, Iowa* (Washington: Washington County Historical Society, 1978), pp. 313-323; S. N. Fellows, *History of Prohibition in Iowa* (Des Moines: Iowa Anti-Saloon League, 1905), p. 11; Clark, "History of Liquor Legislation, 1878-1908," pp. 560, 568; *Press*, April 18, 1894.

12. *Gazette*, August 3, 1894; *Press*, August 15, 1894.

13. *Press*, December 12, 1912; Ibid., January 2, 1913. In 1911, Brookhart and three others bought the *Press*; the editor and manager was H. H. Walter.

14. *Press*, January 2, 1913; biographical information from various sources including: Howard A. Burrell, *History of Washington County, Iowa, From the First White Settlements to 1908*, 2 vols. (Chicago: S. J. Clarke Publishing Company, 1909); *Portrait and Biographical Album of Washington County, Iowa* (Chicago: Acme Publishing Company, 1887). There is no biographical information on D. H. Logan or Dr. Sheafe.

15. *Press*, June 11, 1879; *Gazette*, March 30, 1894; *Iowa State Register*, June 24, 1894.

16. *Press*, August 29, 1894; (Two others also received votes at the county convention; a Mr. Meacham got 13, Mrs. Meacham got 1); *Gazette*, August 31, 1894; *Press*, October 31, 1894; November 14, 1894.

17. Shambaugh, *Messages and Proclamations*, 7:50, "Biennial Report of the Auditor of State," *Iowa Documents, 1900*, 7 vols. (Des Moines: F. R. Conaway, State Printer, 1900), 1:194; William R. Boyd, "Liquor and Common Sense in Iowa," *Harper's Weekly* 53 (June 19, 1909): 13.

18. *Journal*, December 10, 1894.

19. *Journal*, December 19, 1895. For accounts of typical liquor cases, see the *Journal*, March 12, 1895; April 19, 1895; July 22, 1896; December 9, 1898; December 29, 1898; August 1, 1899; August 14, 1899.

20. U.S. Congress, Senate, Committee on the Judiciary, *Hearing on S. 1392, A Bill to Reorganize the Judicial Branch*, 75th Cong., 1st Sess., April 16, 1937, p. 1599; U.S. Congress, Senate, Committee on Civil Service, *Hearing on S. 1995*, 70th Cong., 1st Sess., March 20, 1928, p. 40; *Press*, May 22, 1896.

21. *Press*, August 26, 1896; *Gazette*, October 30, 1896.
22. Brookhart's account book shows an income growth from $362.92 in 1894 to $1,222.79 the next year. Over the next few years his income from his practice ranged as high as $1,958.27. In 1902 he would make over $2,000 and by 1907 his income was over $3,000. Account book in Smith Wildman Brookhart Papers, State Historical Society of Iowa, Des Moines. *Journal*, March 13, 1895; July 13, 1895; April 3, 1897.
23. *Journal*, November 11, 1926; *Annals of Iowa* 15 (April 1927): 637.
24. *Journal*, January 21, 1902; June 28, 1911. Two Brookhart sisters also would graduate from the Academy and the brothers eventually moved their parents to Washington.
25. Iowa National Guard, Roll Book, 2nd Regimental Iowa Infantry, State Historical Society of Iowa, Des Moines, pp. 103, 99; Adjutant General of Iowa VI, Iowa National Guard, State Historical Society of Iowa, Des Moines, Iowa National Guard, Box 13, Report Co. D, File 79; *Journal*, February 3, 1897; August 16, 1897. Hereinafter Adjutant General of Iowa will be designated AJT.
26. *Journal*, January 30, 1897; June 24, 1897.
27. *Tulsa* (Oklahoma) *Tribune*, March 20, 1923; "Notes Taken by Edith," FBY Collection.
28. *Journal*, July 8, 1897; July 9, 1897.
29. *Journal*, November 1, 1897; December 2, 1897. Brookhart's account book indicates that he built the house for $2,838.24. (Brookhart Papers, State Historical Society of Iowa, Des Moines.) *Journal*, December 23, 1897. The *Journal* first reported that the child would be named Dewey, no doubt in honor of the hero of the battle of Manila in the just completed Spanish-American War. Whether that was a serious suggestion is difficult to tell but it is certain that Jennie had a great deal to say about the name since Charles and Edward were the names of her two brothers. (*Journal*, September 14, 1898.)
30. *Journal*, February 25, 1898; December 17, 1898; February 14, 1899; August 11, 1899.
31. Jennie Brookhart to her brothers, March 30, 1899, FBY Collection.

3. SOLDIER AND CITIZEN

1. Large portions of this chapter have been previously published as "Martial Sons of Martial Sires," *The Palimpsest*, Volume 7, Number 1 (Spring, 1989): 32–48.
2. *Journal*, February 21, 1898; March 9, 1898; March 25, 1898; March 14, 1898.
3. *Democrat*, May 11, 1898; *Journal*, April 26, 1898; *Gazette*, April 29, 1898.
4. *Press*, May 4, 1898; *Democrat*, May 4, 1898.
5. *Democrat*, May 25, 1898.
6. *Press*, May 18, 1898; *Democrat*, May 11, 1898.
7. Smith Brookhart to Jennie, June 12, 1898, FBY Collection; *Journal*, July 16, 1898; *Press*, July 20, 1898.
8. *Gazette*, May 27, 1898; *Press*, May 25, 1898.
9. *Gazette*, June 10, 1898.
10. *Gazette*, July 8, 1898; *Journal*, June 1, 1898.
11. *Press*, June 22, 1898; Smith W. Brookhart to Jennie Brookhart, June 6, 1898, FBY Collection.
12. *Gazette*, June 17, 1898; June 24, 1898; July 1, 1898; July 8, 1898; *Democrat*, August 17, 1898.
13. Smith Brookhart to Jennie Brookhart, May 27, 1898; June 3, 1898; June 12, 1898; FBY Collection.
14. *Democrat*, July 13, 1898; *Journal*, July 8, 1898; *Gazette*, July 15, 1898; *Gazette*, July 15, 1898.

15. *Democrat*, September 7, 1898; *Journal*, September 5, 1898; September 1, 1898; *Press*, September 7, 1898; *Gazette*, September 2, 1898.
16. *Gazette*, August 26, 1898; *Democrat*, August 24, 1898; *Press*, July 13, 1898.
17. *Press*, August 24, 1898; *Gazette*, August 26, 1898.
18. *Journal*, August 30, 1898.
19. *Journal*, August 22, 1898; Telegram, Mayor George Ross to Governor Leslie Shaw, August 22, 1898; Governor's Papers, Correspondence Spanish-American War 1898-1899, GII 653-B, File 17, State Historical Society of Iowa, Des Moines.
20. *Journal*, October 14, 1905; August 27, 1898; September 2, 1898.
21. Col. Douglas V. Jackson to Shaw, August 26, 1898, Governor's Papers, Correspondence Spanish-American War 1898, GII 653-A, File 11; Shaw to Jackson, August 27, 1898, Governor's Letter Book, June 6-August 27, 1898, p. 971; Congressman John A. T. Hull to Shaw, August 22, 1898, Governor's Papers, Correspondence Spanish-American War 1898, GII 653-A, File 11; Shaw to Hull, August 26, 1898, Governor's Letter Book, June 6-August 27, 1898, p. 959; Shaw to Senator William Boyd Allison, August 27, 1898, Governor's Letter Book, June 6-August 27, 1898, p. 982; Shaw to Senator John Gear, August 27, 1898, Governor's Letter Book, p. 984; Shaw to R. A. Alger, August 27, 1898, Governor's Letter Book Telegrams, April 19, 1898-January 15, 1902. All at State Historical Society of Iowa, Des Moines.
22. *Democrat*, September 21, 1898; September 28, 1898; *The Florida Times-Union and Citizen*, Jacksonville, Florida, September 20, 1898; *Press*, September 28, 1898; *Journal*, September 14, 1898; September 27, 1898; September 28, 1898.
23. *Journal*, December 1, 1898; December 2, 1898.
24. *Journal*, May 31, 1901.
25. *Journal*, May 31, 1901.
26. *Journal*, November 12, 1919; April 3, 1926.
27. Jennie Brookhart to her brothers, October 30, 1898, FBY Collection.
28. *Press*, September 21, 1898; November 2, 1898; *Journal*, September 19, 1898.
29. *Journal*, October 11, 1900; November 16, 1900; November 17, 1900; November 19, 1900.
30. *Journal*, September 26, 1896.
31. *Journal*, June 14, 1905; June 19, 1905; November 12, 1910.
32. *Journal*, April 28, 1900; May 11, 1900; May 12, 1900; May 15, 1900; May 23, 1900.
33. *Journal*, April 13, 1903; December 16, 1903; December 18, 1903; June 15, 1910; For the general activities of the club, see *Journal* throughout the years.
34. *Journal*, March 2, 1906; March 30, 1906.
35. For the Carris Company, see *Journal*, June 12, 1907; November 7, 1910; For Mills Seed, see *Journal*, June 5, 1907.
36. For the lecture series, *Journal*, September 20, 1905; For the short course, *Journal*, March 25, 1911; April 22, 1911; November-December 1911, *passim*; November-December 1912, *passim*.
37. *Journal*, January 9, 1900; January 9, 1906; January 20, 1913; June 6, 1902.
38. *Journal*, August 20, 1903; 1903 *passim*; January 21, 1904; May 9, 1904; January 20, 1905; January 18, 1906; December 7, 1906.
39. *Journal*, March 5, 1907.
40. *Journal*, January 15, 1908.
41. *Journal*, November 30, 1907.
42. *Journal*, July 14, 1908; September 29, 1908.
43. *Journal*, April 12, 1908; December 30, 1908; October 27, 1908.
44. *Journal*, January 5, 1909; December 24, 1909; January 4, 1910.

45. *Press*, April 14, 1915; April 21, 1915; Interview, Merritt E. McDaniel, May 29, 1982.
46. *Davis County Republican*, June 11, 1891; June 18, 1891; *Journal*, October 25, 1895; December 5, 1908; February 9, 1905.
47. *Journal*, June 2, 1894; August 8, 1905; August 10, 1905.
48. *Journal*, February 14, 1899; August 11, 1899; December 3, 1899; December 22, 1910.
49. *Journal*, February 7, 1906; November 8, 1912; June 16, 1911.
50. *Journal*, April 2, 1909. Interview, Florence Brookhart Yount, October 16, 1980; *Press*, April 30, 1909. Brookhart Account Book, Brookhart Collection, State Historical Society of Iowa, Des Moines.
51. *Journal*, April 11, 1910; September 20, 1910; December 22, 1910.
52. *Journal*, December 15, 1910.

4. SHARPSHOOTER

1. Smith W. Brookhart to Gen. M. H. Byers, December 3, 1898, Iowa National Guard, AJT III, Box 55, Corr ING, 50 Reg, Co A-G, File 459; *Journal*, January 6, 1899; January 25, 1899; January 27, 1899; Portions of this chapter were previously published as "Smith Wildman Brookhart: 'The Man Who Taught the Army How to Shoot.'" *The Palimpsest* 75, No. 1 (Spring, 1994): 30-45.
2. *Journal*, February 10, 1899; February 11, 1899; February 15, 1899; May 19, 1899; May 29, 1899.
3. Osha Gray Davidson, *Under Fire, The NRA and the Battle for Gun Control*, (New York: Henry Holt and Company, 1993), p. 22.
4. Davidson, *Under Fire*, p. 26.
5. *Journal*, October 20, 1894; October 22, 1894; December 14, 1896.
6. *Journal*, September 27, 1894; December 10, 1896; October 12, 1897.
7. Smith W. Brookhart, "Rifle Training in War, Part 5," *Arms and the Man*, LXIV, No. 6, May 4, 1918, p. 111.
8. Smith W. Brookhart, "Rifle and Pistol Practice," *Arms and the Man*, LV, No. 7, November 13, 1913, p. 126; Smith W. Brookhart, "Rifle Training in War, Part 5," *Arms and the Man*, LXIV, No. 6, May 4, 1918, p. 107.
9. Smith W. Brookhart, "Rifle and Pistol Practice," *Arms and the Man*, LV, No. 7, November 13, 1913, p. 126. Brookhart, "Rifle Training in War, Part 5," *Arms and the Man*, LXIV, No. 6, May 4, 1918, p. 107.
10. Smith W. Brookhart, "Rifle and Pistol Practice," *Arms and the Man*, LV, No. 7, November 13, 1913, p. 126.
11. U. S. Congress, Senate, Committee on Military Affairs, "Hearings on S. 3983," May 29, 1940, p. 51.
12. *Journal*, June 7, 1899; Brookhart to Byers, June 7, 1899, Iowa National Guard, AJT III, Box 55, Corr ING, 50 Reg, Co A-G, File 459; *Journal*, May 3, 1901.
13. *Journal*, March 21, 1902; August 10, 1912. On another occasion Brookhart wrote Byers that Company D had voted in favor of a Congressional appropriation to equip the National Guard with "the latest and best arms." (Brookhart to Byers, February 24, 1900, Iowa National Guard, AJT III, Box 55, Corr ING, 50th Reg, Co A-G, File 459.)
14. Iowa National Guard, AJT VIII, Box 113, File 5, Muster Rolls Spanish-American War.
15. *Journal*, June 11, 1900; July 17, 1900; July 18, 1900.
16. *Journal*, August 16, 1899.
17. Brookhart to Byers, October 2, 1899; October 9, 1899, Iowa National Guard, AJT III, Box 55, Corr ING, 50th Inf Reg, Co A-G, File 459, Co D, Brookhart-Wilson.

18. Petition, August 24, 1900; Jasper Neiswanger to Byers, September 12, 1900; George Williams to Byers, September 31, 1900; Endorsement Adjutant-General's Office, September 21, 1900; Iowa National Guard, AJT III, Box 55, Corr ING, 50th Inf Reg, Co A-G, File 459, Co D, Brookhart-Wilson.

19. Brookhart to Byers, March 23, 1901, Iowa National Guard, AJT III, Box 55, Corr ING, 50th Inf Reg, Co A-G, File 459, Co D, Brookhart-Wilson.

20. *Journal*, May 9, 1902. C. J. Wilson to Major John Hume, April 12, 1902; April 28, 1902, Iowa National Guard, AJT VI, Box 14, File 101. F. W. Bishop to Hume, April 30, 1902; Hume to Byers, May 12, 1902, Iowa National Guard, AJT VI, Box 14, File 101. C. J. Wilson to Byers, May 10, 1902; Brookhart to Byers, May 14, 1902, Iowa National Guard, AJT III, Box 55, Corr ING, 50th Reg Inf, Co A-G, File 459, Co D, Brookhart-Wilson. Almost immediately a new Company D was formed.

21. *Journal*, October 11, 1907. The Allison trophy was displayed in the window of the Steck Jewelry Store. (*Journal*, October 15, 1907.)

22. *Journal*, January 16, 1907. In 1909 the Guard was reorganized and Governor Beryl F. Carroll appointed Brookhart Chief Ordnance Officer which included the former role of Chief Inspector of Small Arms Practice. In 1913 Governor George W. Clarke continued the appointment. (*Journal*, May 13, 1909. *Iowa Official Register, 1911-1912*, [Des Moines: State Printer, 1911], p. 283. *Iowa Official Register, 1913-1914*, [Des Moines: State Printer, 1913], p. 847.)

23. James A. Drain, "Rifle Reminiscences," *Arms and the Man*, L, No. 19, August 10, 1911, pp. 431-437. Ibid. L, No. 20, August 17, 1911, pp. 459-463.

24. *Journal*, April 11, 1907; May 11, 1907; October 16, 1907; *Arms and the Man*, XLIII, No. 22, March 5, 1908, p. 535; Davidson, *Under Fire*, p. 27; General Orders No. 61, Office of Adjutant General, April 27, 1903, National Board for the Promotion of Rifle Practice, Board Activities 1903 File. The board is now called the Office of Civilian Marksmanship.

25. Ibid. *Journal*, August 27, 1910; November 1, 1910.

26. Iowa National Guard, AJT VI (124), File 896, Small Arms Practice, 1909 Report, June 22, 1909; *Arms and the Man*, XLVI, No. 15, July 15, 1909; *Arms and the Man*, LXVIII, No. 4, October 1, 1920, p. 9.

27. Frank J. Kahrs, "Winning the 1912 Palma," *Arms and the Man*, LII, No. 26, September 19, 1912, pp. 503-509, 514.

28. *Journal*, June 10, 1912; *Arms and the Man*, LII, No. 11, June 13, 1912, p. 220; *Arms and the Man*, LII, No. 20, August 15, 1912, p. 398.

29. Kahrs, "Winning the 1912 Palma," *Arms and the Man*, LII, No. 25, September 19, 1912, p. 508.

30. Brookhart to William Howard Taft, September 14, 1912, William Howard Taft Papers, Library of Congress, Reel 446; Taft to Brookhart, September 16, 1912, Ibid.

31. *Journal*, September 19, 1912.

32. *Journal*, September 29, 1911.

33. *Journal*, July 6, 1912. Fred S. Hird, another Iowan trained by Brookhart, was also on the Olympic team. (*Arms and the Man*, LII, No. 8, May 23, 1912, p. 152.)

34. *Arms and the Man*, LII, No. 24, September 12, 1912, p. 483; *Arms and the Man*, LXVII, No. 11, January 15, 1921, p. 258.

35. War Department Special Orders No. 289, December 11, 1913, National Archives, Record Group 94, Office of Adjutant General, Box 3375, Item 2104521; Brookhart, "Rifle and Pistol Practice," *Arms and the Man*, LV, No. 7, November 13, 1913, p. 126.

36. Memorandum, Assistant Secretary of War, April 6, 1916, National Archives, Record Group 94, Office of Adjutant General, Box 8091, Item 2391745; Memorandum, Chief of Staff, War Department, April 3, 1916, Office of Adjutant General, Record Group 94, National

Archives, Box 8091, Item 2391745.

37. Brookhart to Baker, April 10, 1916, Record Group 94, Office of Adjutant General, National Archives, Box 8091, Item 2391745; Baker to Brookhart, April 13, 1916, Ibid.

38. Memorandum, Chief of Staff, War Department, June 6, 1916, Office of Adjutant General, Record Group 94, National Archives, Box 8091, Item 2465127.

39. *Press*, December 27, 1916; U. S. Congress, Senate, Committee on Military Affairs, "Hearing on S. 3983," 67 Cong., 3 Sess., May 29, 1940, p. 51.

40. *Press*, December 27, 1916; January 3, 1917.

41. Smith W. Brookhart, Memorandum for the Commandant, December 3, 1918, William Howard Taft Papers, Library of Congress, Reel 201.

42. Brookhart to William Howard Taft, January 1, 1918, William Howard Taft Papers, Library of Congress, Reel 188.

43. Brookhart to Taft, January 1, 1918, William Howard Taft Papers, Library of Congress, Reel 188. Brookhart discussed the issue of rifle shooting on many occasions. Throughout the period of World War I he wrote frequently about it in the *Washington County Press* and *Arms and the Man*. When he was in the Senate he spoke about it whenever the question of War Department appropriations was debated. Still later he testified before Congressional committees about weapons and would refer to the debate about theories of shooting.

44. *Congressional Record*, 72 Cong., 2 Sess., p. 3959; Newspaper clipping, no name, no date. The clipping was enclosed with a letter from Edwin T. Meredith to Joseph P. Tumulty, July 19, 1916, Office of Adjutant General, Record Group 94, National Archives, Box 8276, Item 2439449. Meredith was the publisher of *Successful Farming* in Des Moines and later will be Secretary of Agriculture in the Wilson administration. Tumulty was the principal aid to Wilson.

45. *Congressional Record*, 72 Cong., 2 Sess., p. 3959; *Arms and the Man*, LX, No. 22, August 24, 1916, p. 429; James B. Trefethen, compiler, James E. Serven, editor, *Americans and Their Guns, The National Rifle Association Story through nearly a century of service to the nation*, (Harrisburg, PA: Stackpole Company, for the National Rifle Association, 1967), p. 182.

46. Interview, Edith Brookhart Millard, January 23, 1981.

47. Interview, Edith Brookhart Millard, January 23, 1981; Interview, Smith W. Brookhart, Jr., July 5, 1981.

48. Interview, Florence Brookhart Yount, October 16, 1980; *Journal*, January 31, 1916.

49. *Journal*, January 31, 1916.

50. Interview, Smith W. Brookhart, Jr., July 5, 1981; Interview, Florence Brookhart Yount, July 7, 1981.

51. Pershing to Adjutant General and all Army and National Guard commanders, September 24, 1917, Office of Adjutant General, Record Group 407, Central Decimal File 1917-1925, Box 822, File 353.14; *Congressional Record*, 72 Cong., 2 Sess., p. 3959; Brookhart to Taft, January 1, 1918, William Howard Taft Papers, Library of Congress, Reel 188; Interview, Smith W. Brookhart, Jr., July 3, 1981.

52. "'Ally' Officers to Train U. S. Riflemen," *Arms and the Man*, LXII, No. 269, September 22, 1917, pp. 508–509; "The American Idea at Last," *Arms and the Man*, LXIII, No. 4, October 20, 1917, pp. 68–69.

53. *Congressional Record*, 72 Cong., 2 Sess., p. 3959.

54. *Press*, November 21, 1917. During his first few months in the service Brookhart kept a diary. My account of those months relies heavily on this diary. The diary is now in the possession of Smith W. Brookhart, Jr.; Interview, Smith W. Brookhart, Jr., July 3, 1981.

55. Brookhart, *Diary*; *Press*, December 5, 1917.

56. *Press*, December 5, 1917.

57. Brookhart, *Diary*; *Press*, December 26, 1917; January 30, 1918.

58. Years later Brookhart said that within weeks of his meeting with Baker the generals who had opposed him and his theories were reassigned. Brookhart said that he "presumed" the reason was their opposition and the memorandum. It is not possible, however, to be sure of the precise reason for their reassignment. (*Congressional Record*, 72 Cong., 2 Sess., p. 3960.)

59. Trefethen and Serven, *Americans and Their Guns*, p. 186.

60. Smith W. Brookhart, "Rifle Training in War," *Arms and the Man*, LXIV, No. 2, April 6, 1918, pp. 23ff. The quote is on page 23; The subsequent articles appeared in ibid., April 13, 1918, pp. 45ff; April 20, 1918, pp. 65ff; April 27, 1918, pp. 85ff; May 4, 1918, pp. 107ff; May 11, 1918, pp. 127ff; Maj. S. W. Brookhart, U.S.N.G., *Rifle Training in War* (National Rifle Association of America for the National Board for the Promotion of Rifle Practice, 1918).

61. "Day of Untrained Riflemen Ended in American Army," *Arms and the Man*, LXIV, No. 11, June 8, 1918, p. 207; "'All Ready on the Firing Line' At the Perry Small Arms School," *Arms and the Man*, LXIV, No. 10, June 1, 1918, p. 187.

62. "Day of Untrained Riflemen Ended in American Army," *Arms and the Man*, LXIV, No. 11, June 8, 1918, pp. 207ff; "Notes from the Small Arms School," *Arms and the Man*, LXIV, No. 12, June 15, 1918, pp. 229f; "Camp Perry Officers Celebrate Fourth," *Arms and the Man*, LXIV, No. 16, July 13, 1918, pp. 313f.

63. "Notes from the Small Arms School," *Arms and the Man*, LXIV, No. 19, August 3, 1918, pp. 371-372.

64. "Notes from the Small Arms School," *Arms and the Man*, LXIV, No. 19, August 3, 1918, pp. 367, 371.

65. Minutes of June 24, 1918 meeting National Board for the Promotion of Rifle Practice, Board Archives, 1918 File; "Holding of National Matches Officially Recommended," *Arms and the Man*, LXIV, No. 15, July 6, 1918, pp. 283ff.

66. Kendrick Scofield, "Holding of National Matches Officially Recommended," *Arms and the Man*, LXIV, No. 15, July 6, 1918, p. 285; Trefethen and Serven, *Americans and Their Guns*, p. 189.

67. War Department Annual Reports, 1919, Chief of Staff, p. 314; "Riflemen Meetings Held," *Arms and the Man*, LXIX, No. 12, March 1, 1922, p. 17.

68. *Arms and the Man*, LXV, No. 19, February 1, 1919, pp. 372-373; *Arms and the Man*, LXVI, No. 7, May 10, 1919, p. 125; Interview, Florence Brookhart Yount, October 16, 1980.

69. Kendrick Scofield, "National Board and N.R.A. Prepare for Rifle Shooting Campaign," *Arms and the Man*, LXV, No. 17, January 18, 1919, pp. 323-331.

70. Minutes of Annual Board Meeting, National Board for the Promotion of Rifle Practice, 1920 File; "Annual Rifle Meetings Held," *Arms and the Man*, LXVIII, No. 12, February 1, 1921; "New Instructors Developed at Camp Perry," *Arms and the Man*, LXIX, No. 1, September 15, 1921, pp. 9-10; "The Start at Perry," *The American Rifleman*, LXXI, No. 8, September 15, 1923, p. 11.

71. Trefethen and Serven, *Americans and Their Guns*, p. 216; *The American Rifleman*, LXXV, No. 6, June 1927, p. 11.

72. Trefethen and Serven, *Americans and Their Guns*, p. 221; M. A. Reckord, "National Matches Definitely Secured for Fall of 1928," *The American Rifleman*, LXXVI, No. 4, April 1928, pp. 19, 32; M. A. Reckord, "National Matches Assured Annually," *The American Rifleman*, LXXVI, No. 7, July 1928, p. 14.

73. U. S. Congress, Senate, Subcommittee of the Committee on Appropriations, "Hearings on H. R. 9209," 76th Cong., 3rd Sess., 1940, pp. 334-348; U. S. Congress, Senate, Committee on Military Affairs, "Hearings on S. 3983," 76th Cong., 3rd Sess., 1940, pp. 50-63.

5. THE MAKING OF A PROGRESSIVE

1. John Y. Stone to James S. Clarkson, January 16, 1897, James S. Clarkson Papers, Library of Congress, Washington, D.C., Box 2.

2. Mildred Throne, "Iowans in Congress, 1847-1953," *Iowa Journal of History* 51 (October, 1953): pp. 335-348.

3. Daniel Turner to Thomas Bray, March 20, 1960, Thomas J. Bray Papers, University of Iowa Libraries, Iowa City, Box 1; Edward Lissner, "Iowa's Political War and Its Bearing Upon the Destiny of the Republican Party," *Harper's Weekly* 50, no. 2574 (April 21, 1906): 549.

4. The standard work on Cummins is Ralph Mills Sayre, "Albert Baird Cummins and the Progressive Movement in Iowa" (Ph.D. diss., Columbia University, 1958); Dan Elbert Clark, *History of Senatorial Elections in Iowa* (Iowa City: State Historical Society of Iowa, 1912), pp. 222-234, p. 230.

5. Thomas Richard Ross, *Jonathan Prentiss Dolliver: A Study in Political Integrity and Independence* (Iowa City: State Historical Society of Iowa, 1958), p. 141.

6. Clark, *Senatorial Elections in Iowa*, pp. 239-245.

7. Fleming Fraker, Jr., "The Beginnings of the Progressive Movement in Iowa," *Annals of Iowa* 35, No. 8 (Spring, 1961): 579; *Press*, August 14, 1901.

8. Richard Clarkson to James S. Clarkson, November 17, 1901, Clarkson Papers, Box 2.

9. *Journal*, August 5, 1896; October 31, 1899.

10. *Press*, September 19, 1900.

11. *Journal*, October 31, 1900.

12. George M. Titus, "The Battle for Biennial Elections," *Annals of Iowa* 29, No. 3 (January 1948): 163-175.

13. *Journal*, December 28, 1900.

14. Iowa law held that a proposed amendment had to be passed in identical form by both Houses of two successive General Assemblies. When the proposed amendment was referred from one House to the other and one General Assembly to the next it had to be entered in full in the journal of each house. In this case the Senate had passed the law and entered it in full in its journal. The House also passed it but entered it using only the title and not the full text. The Supreme Court ruled this error rendered the amendment invalid. (State of Iowa v. Brookhart, 113 Iowa 250 [1901]).

15. *Press*, February 6, 1901. Bailey used as a precedent the opinion of the court that ruled the 1882 prohibition amendment invalid because of the same flaw of disagreement between journal entries.

16. *Journal*, August 8, 1901; Smith W. Brookhart, "How Mr. Blythe Ruled Iowa," speech, Campaign Broadside, (n.p., 1908); *Journal*, September 28, 1901.

17. Brookhart to Cummins, January 10, 1902; January 14, 1902, Albert Baird Cummins Papers, State Historical Society of Iowa, Des Moines, Box 3, File 10. Cummins to Brookhart, January 20, 1902, Cummins Papers, Letter Book 1; *Press*, April 9, 1902.

18. *Press*, April 30, 1902; May 7, 1902.

19. *Press*, June 4, 1902; June 11, 1902.

20. *Press*, May 27, 1903. Palmer was a Civil War hero who had risen to the rank of Colonel. After the war he served in the Iowa General Assembly and later was appointed to the railroad commission. He served there by election from 1898 to 1915. Active in the Grand Army of the Republic, Palmer was state commander and served one term as national commander. (*Annals of Iowa* 16 [April, 1929]: 632-33). Brookhart, "How Blythe Ruled Iowa."

21. It is difficult to know the exact chronology of the following events. Brookhart told the story often and I have combined the following six accounts to put together the facts as I believe

them to have occurred: Brookhart, "How Blythe Ruled Iowa," 1908; James L. Wright, "Iowan Now 'Abe' Among Senators," *Cleveland Plain Dealer*, January 12, 1923; James B. Morrow, "A Hunter of Wall Street Devils," *The Nation's Business* (March, 1923): 21-22; a campaign biography probably written by Brookhart's secretary, Roy Rankin, for the campaign of 1926; and Brookhart's account in "Notes Taken by Edith" and "Notes Taken by Florence." In none of these accounts, however, did Brookhart ever attach a specific date to any of the events.

22. Wright, "Iowan Now 'Abe.'"

23. Morrow, "Wall Street Devils"; Brookhart, "How Blythe Ruled Iowa"; Roy Rankin, campaign biography. Years later Grundy Center attorney William G. Kerr recalled sitting across from Brookhart at a banquet in 1908: "I did not know him personally, but he appeared a stalwart and rugged individual, and a long-time supporter of Cummins. He knew that when any citizen was after a position and needed the support of Senator Allison, that before Allison made a decision in the matter he first must consult Mr. Blythe. [Brookhart] rebelled at such a situation." (William G. Kerr, "A Rough Draft of My Recollections of Smith W. Brookhart and Associated Events Attending It," [January 17, 1958], Henry A. Wallace Papers, University of Iowa Libraries, Iowa 51, 890-904.

24. Morrow, "Wall Street Devils," p. 21.

25. *Press*, February 17, 1904. There is no other instance where the *Press* ran a picture to accompany an editorial.

26. *The Washington Democrat*, August 17, 1904; October 26, 1904.

27. Thomas James Bray, "The Cummins Leadership," *Annals of Iowa* 32 (April, 1954): 250.

28. "Notes Taken by Florence," FBY Collection.

29. Cummins to Young, February 17, 1905, Cummins Papers, Letter Book 12.

30. Ibid., March 14, 1905.

31. A general account of the Interstate Commerce Law Convention is found in Robert H. Wiebe, *Businessmen and Reform: A Study of the Progressive Movement* (Chicago: Quadrangle Paperbacks, 1968), pp. 51-54.

32. Ibid., p. 53.

33. Larrabee had been a state legislator during the 1870s and voted against a railroad regulation law because he felt it was not strong enough. Elected governor in 1885, Larrabee was well into his first term when he got into a dispute with C. B. & Q. President Charles E. Perkins over the rates the railroad charged the state to haul coal to the state school at Glenwood. Reelected governor in 1887, Larrabee marshalled his forces in the 1888 legislature and got a bill passed that established the Board of Railroad Commissioners. The railroads attempted to challenge the law in court but the courts ruled against them and the law stood. Unlike most nineteenth century Iowa governors Larrabee was an example of a strong executive, taking an active part in lobbying the legislature to get his bill passed. Historian Leland Sage has noted that Larrabee's advocacy of government regulation of industry makes him "a forerunner of the Progressive Movement." (Leland L. Sage, *A History of Iowa* [Ames: The Iowa State University Press, 1974] pp. 204-208, quotation p. 208).

34. "Address of Ex-Governor William Larrabee, of Iowa," *Amendment of the Interstate Commerce Law* (Washington, D.C., 1904), pp. 9-10.

35. *Chicago Tribune*, October 25, 1905; October 26, 1905.

36. Smith W. Brookhart, "Interstate Commerce Law Convention," *Gazette* [October, 1905], Cummins Papers, Box 32, File 127, Clipping no. 505.

37. Ibid.; *Proceedings of the Interstate Commerce Law Convention Held at Chicago, Illinois, October 26 and 27, 1905*, (n.p.), pp. 4-7.

38. Ibid., pp. 44-47.

39. Ibid., pp. 66-67.

40. Ibid., p. 81.
41. Brookhart, "Interstate Commerce Law Convention."
42. Ibid.
43. Ibid.
44. Brookhart to Cummins, November 4, 1905, Cummins Papers, Box 20, File 77.
45. Cummins was elected to a two-year term in 1901 and reelected in 1903. He would have normally run again in 1905 but the Titus Amendment had been re-submitted and made it to the Constitution unflawed. As a result Cummins' second term was extended one year and he ran in 1906 for a term commencing in January, 1907.
46. Brookhart, "How Blythe Ruled Iowa"; *Journal*, November 6, 1906; Cummins to Brookhart, March 19, 1906, Cummins Papers, Letter Book 15.
47. *Iowa Official Register, 1907-1908*, (Des Moines: Iowa State Printer, 1907), pp. 407-485.
48. *Iowa Official Register, 1907-1908*, (Des Moines: Iowa State Printer, 1907), p. 341. Although the title Colonel as used here was honorary, Brookhart carried it the rest of his life. Even while in the Senate most Iowa newspapers referred to him as Colonel Brookhart rather than Senator Brookhart. When Cummins went to the Senate Brookhart lost his staff position. But the next Governor, Beryl F. Carroll appointed Brookhart to the regular Guard position of Chief Ordinance Officer with the rank of Lieutenant Colonel, and his successor as governor, George W. Clarke, continued the appointment.

On active duty during World War I, Brookhart would eventually receive a commission as a full colonel; *Press*, October 4, 1907. Brookhart had been practicing his riding prior to going to Keokuk. One day someone from the *Press* watched the practice and commented, "He rides well—at least we did not see him slip off, either sideways or straight back over the crupper."

49. *Press*, December 27, 1907; *Journal*, January 18, 1908; *Press*, March 13, 1908; June 26, 1908.
50. *Press*, May 1, 1908; May 22, 1908; Brookhart, "How Blythe Ruled Iowa." Curiously, the *Press*, which had always supported Blythe, ran the full text of this speech along with a picture of Brookhart. The paper balanced this, however, with an editorial attacking the speech. "J. W. Blythe, horned and hoofed, as [Brookhart] paints him," the editor wrote, "is not the J. W. Blythe as we think we know him to be. But then you know we must be rescued from the hands of the oppressors and the country must be saved about every so often." (*Press*, May 8, 1908).
51. *Press*, August 14, 1908; October 16, 1908; October 23, 1908; *Iowa Official Register, 1909-1910*, (Des Moines, Iowa, State Printer, 1909), pp. 598-600; *Press*, November 6, 1909. Brookhart may have done some good during his fall speaking tour around the county. In the June primary Allison defeated Cummins 1276 to 756; in the November primary Lacey lost 15 votes for a total of 1261 while Cummins picked up 126 votes for a total of 882.
52. *Journal*, October 16, 1909; *Press*, October 22, 1909.
53. See Ross, *Dolliver*, pp. 282ff; Samuel G. Blythe, "Implacable Iowa," *The Saturday Evening Post*, April 9, 1910, pp. 8ff; *Press*, January 7, 1910; *Fairfield Ledger*, quoted in *Burlington Gazette*, April 27, 1910; *Brighton Enterprise*, quoted in *Burlington Gazette*, April 23, 1910; *Burlington Gazette*, May 7, 1910.
54. *Keokuk Gate City*, quoted in the *Burlington Gazette*, May 5, 1910; *Donnellson Review*, quoted in *Burlington Gazette*, April 18, 1910; *Burlington Gazette*, May 25, 1910.
55. *Press*, January 21, 1910. Ironically, when a few weeks earlier Kennedy had been in Washington to meet with the Commercial Club members about the new building, Brookhart was a member of the committee; *Burlington Gazette*, April 26, 1910; April 27, 1910; May 13, 1910; *Burlington Hawk-eye*, April 14, 1910.
56. *Burlington Gazette*, May 27, 1910.

57. *Journal*, May 24, 1910.
58. *Press*, June 17, 1910; Clark, *Senatorial Elections in Iowa*, pp. 258-260.
59. Ibid.
60. *Press*, January 27, 1911; July 7, 1911.
61. Brookhart to Robert M. La Follette, July 6, 1911, La Follette Family Papers, Library of Congress, Washington, D. C., Box J-3; Brookhart to Houser, September 15, 1911, Ibid.
62. *Press*, December 7, 1911.
63. *Journal*, November 24, 1911; *Press*, December 1, 1911.
64. *Press*, December 1, 1911.
65. *Press*, March 14, 1912.
66. *Press*, June 27, 1912.
67. *Press*, July 18, 1912.
68. *Press*, January 30, 1913.
69. Brookhart, "How Blythe Ruled Iowa."

6. RAILROAD REFORMER AND SENATORIAL CANDIDATE

1. *Press,* January 2, 1913.
2. *Journal,* November 6, 1906.
3. *Journal,* March 12, 1906; July 11, 1907; November 2, 1911; November 4, 1911; January 11, 1912; January 20, 1912; November 12, 1912; November 19, 1912.
4. Louis W. Koenig, *Bryan, A Political Biography of William Jennings Bryan* (New York: G. P. Putnam's Sons, 1971), pp. 414-415; U. S., Congress, Senate, Joint Committee on Interstate and Foreign Commerce, *Hearing on J. Res. 25*, 64th Cong., 1st Sess., December 9, 1916, p. 583; *Press*, February 13, 1913.
5. Brookhart to Theodore Roosevelt, May 23, 1914, Library of Congress, Washington, D.C., Reel 184.
6. *Press,* April 10, 1913. Brookhart collected ten of the articles together and published them as a pamphlet, *Government Ownership of Railroads,* June, 1913. Quotations used herein will be cited to the dates of their original publication in the *Press*. *Press,* April 10, 1913; May 22, 1913; May 15, 1913; April 24, 1913; May 29, 1913. The following February Brookhart expanded his belief in government ownership to include the telephone lines: "It is needless to say that the federal ownership of wire and wireless communication will be a fact within a few years. The government ownership of railroads will be the next step. With the government owning and conducting these lines of activity in the interest of the owners—the people—service would be enhanced and its cost would be greatly decreased." (*Press,* February 5, 1914.)
7. *Press,* November 5, 1914; February 18, 1915.
8. *Press,* April 28, 1915; H. W. Danforth, Introduction to: Brookhart, *The Invisible Government* (The National Council of Farmers' Co-operative Associations, 1915), p. 5.
9. Walker D. Hines, *War History of American Railroads* (New Haven: Yale University Press, 1928), pp. 5-6; U. S. Congress, Senate, *Hearing on J. Res. 25,* p. 583, 595, 605, 612, 606.
10. *Press,* December 19, 1917; U.S. Congress, Senate, Joint Committee on Interstate and Foreign Commerce, *Hearing on J. Res. 25,* 65th Cong., 2nd Sess., December 14, 1917, p. 2187.
11. *Press,* December 4, 1913. Brookhart said he hoped senators were not often forced into such long talks. In a *Press* editorial, March 6, 1918, Brookhart reported a visit to the Cummins home where the two talked about the railroad bill at length; Sayre, "Cummins," p. 493.
12. *Cedar Rapids Gazette,* January 23, 1919, has a partial text of the speech from which

the quotation is taken. The *Cedar Rapids Republican,* January 24, 1919, reported the reaction of the audience as being attentive but unpersuaded.

13. Iowa, General Assembly, House, *Journal of the House,* 38th General Assembly, March 27, 1919, pp. 1355-1356, 1359, 1361-64.
14. *Press,* June 14, 1916.
15. *Press,* March 6, 1918.
16. Ibid.
17. Jennie Brookhart to Smith Brookhart, September 22, 1919, FBY Collection.
18. Jim Brookhart to Smith Brookhart, September 23, 1919, FBY Collection.
19. *Des Moines Register,* January 5, 1920. (Hereinafter cited as *Register*).
20. Ibid.
21. *Iowa Farm Bureau Messenger,* November 20, 1919.
22. Ibid.
23. *Register,* January 10, 1920.
24. *Register,* January 10, 1920; January 13, 1920.
25. *Iowa Homestead,* January 15, 1920; February 26, 1920. (Hereinafter cited as *Homestead*).
26. L. C. Kurtz to Cummins, February 18, 1920, Cummins Papers, Box 19, Jan-Feb 1920 File; *Register,* February 22, 1920.
27. *Des Moines Capital,* January 21, 1920; R. H. Spence to Cummins, January 22, 1920, Cummins Papers, Box 19, Jan-Feb 1920 File. Cummins to Spence, January 26, 1920, Ibid.
28. Brookhart to Mrs. James M. Pierce, November 8, 1922, Brookhart Papers, Des Moines.
29. *Journal,* March 20, 1920.
30. Ibid.
31. Ibid.
32. Journal, March 31, 1920.
33. A copy of the speech was enclosed in James Pierce to Robert M. La Follette, April 1, 1920, La Follette Family Papers, Library of Congress, Washington, D.C., Box B-86.
34. Ibid.
35. Ibid.
36. *Register,* April 3, 1920.
37. *Homestead,* April 1, 1920; Pierce to La Follette, April 1, 1920, La Follette Family Papers, Box B-86. La Follette to Pierce, April 12, 1920, Ibid., Box B-112.
38. *Homestead,* March 25, 1920.
39. *Wallaces' Farmer,* April 9, 1920; April 30, 1920; May 14, 1920.
40. Ibid., June 4, 1920; May 28, 1920; June 4, 1920.
41. *Locomotive Engineers Journal,* 54, no. 3 (March, 1920): 244.
42. Ibid., 54, no. 6 (June, 1920): 523; Record Group 46, "Records of the United States Senate," Campaign Expense Reports, Smith W. Brookhart, 1920, National Archives. There was one other large contribution, $1,500 from John F. Gay. The amount makes it unlikely that it was a private contribution but I have been unable to discover anything about Mr. Gay or what group he may possibly have represented.
43. *Register,* March 27, 1920; April 19, 1920.
44. Ramseyer to Homer Roth, March 29, 1920, Christian W. Ramseyer Papers, University of Iowa Libraries, Box 1.
45. Waite to Cummins, April 2, 1920; Corey to Cummins, March 27, 1920; Taylor to Cummins, March 26, 1920, Cummins Papers, Box 19, April 1920 File.
46. Copeland to Cummins, January 30, 1920, Cummins Papers, Box 19, Jan-Feb 1920 File; March 26, 1920, Box 19, April 1920 File.
47. Galer to Cummins, March 27, 1920, Cummins Papers, Box 19, April 1920 File.

48. Wilson to Cummins, April 7, 1920, Ibid.
49. Cummins to W. W. Copeland, April 1, 1920, Ibid.
50. Cummins to Cyrenus Cole, April 15, 1920, Cyrenus Cole Papers, State Historical Society of Iowa, Iowa City, Box 2.
51. *The Iowa Magazine* (February 5, 1920): 8. An article in the March issue by Samuel O. Dunn, editor of *Railway Age,* was titled "The Plumb Plan is a Soviet Scheme." The magazine continued with this strident anti-communist content until August, 1920, when, without explanation it returned to its original format and content.
52. Charles Merz, "The Line-Up in Iowa," *The New Republic,* 22, no. 282 (April 28, 1920): 267. The *Muscatine Journal* called the Brookhart campaign "historic in that it marks the first attempt on the part of an Iowan to gain senatorial honors through an attack upon existing trade methods. The success of such a political expedient . . . would seriously challenge the present merchandise distributive process." (*Register,* April 19, 1920).
53. *Register,* April 13, 1920; May 17, 1920; April 14, 1920; April 19, 1920; April 21, 1920.
54. Brookhart, "Why I Am a Candidate," *Homestead,* May 27, 1920.
55. *Register,* March 21, 1920; April 23, 1920.
56. *Homestead,* April 29, 1920.
57. Cummins to George Curtis, April 5, 1920, Cummins Papers, Box 19, April 1920 File; Cummins to Louis Kurtz, May 8, 1920, Cummins Papers, Box 20, May 1920 File.
58. Lou Black to Cummins, May 24, 1920, Cummins Papers, Box 20, June 1920 File; Call to Cummins, May 21, 1920, Cummins Papers, Box 20, May 1920 File.
59. Brookhart, "Col. Brookhart Replies to Senator Cummins," *Locomotive Engineers Journal,* 54, no. 6 (June, 1920): 525-527; Brookhart, "Why I am a Candidate," *Homestead,* May 27, 1920; *The Iowa Union Farmer,* January 28, 1920; May 5, 1920; May 9, 1920.
60. *Register,* May 25, 1920.
61. *Register,* June 7, 1920; May 24, 1920.
62. *Iowa Official Register, 1921-1922,* (Des Moines: Iowa State Printer, 1921), pp. 424-425; *Homestead,* June 17, 1920; *Iowa Official Register, 1915-1916,* (Des Moines: Iowa State Printer, 1915), pp. 650-651.
63. *Register,* June 9, 1920; R. H. Spence to Cummins, June 17, 1920, Cummins Papers, Box 20, June 1920 File.
64. Kenyon to Cummins, June 24, 1920, Ibid.
65. *Homestead,* June 24, 1920.
66. Cummins to Harding, June 18, 1920, Cummins Papers, Box 20, June 1920 File; Cummins to Watson, June 21, 1920, Ibid; Cummins to Kenyon, July 1, 1920, Cummins Papers, Box 20, July 1920 File.
67. Koenig, *Bryan,* p. 74.
68. Howard W. Allen, *Poindexter of Washington, A Study in Progressive Politics* (Carbondale and Edwardsville: Southern Illinois University Press, 1981), pp. 170-199.

7. COOPERATIONIST AND REPUBLICAN INSURGENT

1. James H. Shideler, *Farm Crisis, 1919-1923* (Berkeley and Los Angeles: University of California Press, 1957), p. 46.
2. For the roots of the farm crisis of the 1920s, see Shideler, *Farm Crisis,* pp. 46-75. *Federal Reserve Bulletin* (Washington, D.C.: Government Printing Office, 1920), p. 556. See also George Soule, *Prosperity Decade, From War to Depression: 1917-1929* (New York: Rinehart & Company, Inc., 1947), pp. 96-106.

3. *Register*, November 29, 1920.
4. *Homestead*, December 9, 1920.
5. Ibid.
6. *Congressional Record*, 67 Cong., 4 Sess., p. 2129.
7. James B. Weaver, *A Call to Action* (Des Moines: Iowa Printing Co., 1892), p. 351; Fred Emory Haynes, *James Baird Weaver* (Iowa City, The State Historical Society of Iowa, 1919) p. 334.
8. John L. Thomas, *Alternative America: Henry George, Edward Bellamy, Henry Demarest Lloyd and the Adversary Tradition* (Cambridge, Massachusetts: The Belknap Press of Harvard University Press 1983), p. 365.
9. Weaver, *Call*, p. 183.
10. The People's Party platform is found in George McKenna, ed., *American Populism* (New York: G. P. Putnam's Sons, 1974), pp. 89-94. The quotation is on p. 91.
11. Edward Bellamy, "The Programme of the Nationalists," *The Forum*, 17 (March, 1984): 82; *'If Elected . . .' Unsuccessful Candidates for the Presidency 1796-1968* (Washington, D.C.: Smithsonian Institution Press, 1972), p. 272.
12. Lawrence Goodwyn, *Democratic Promise: The Populist Movement in America* (New York: Oxford University Press, 1976), p. 139, 272.
13. Daniel Joseph Doyle, "Rochdale and the Origin of the Rochdale Society of Equitable Pioneers," (Ph.D. Dissertation, St. John's University, 1972), p. 260; *Congressional Record*, 67 Cong., 4 Sess., p. 2552.
14. Solon Justus Buck, *The Granger Movement: A Study of Agricultural Organization and Its Political, Economic and Social Manifestations 1870-1880* (Cambridge: Harvard University Press, 1913), p. 261; Goodwyn, *Democratic Promise*, pp. 45; 622; Fred E. Haynes, *Third Party Movements Since the Civil War with Special Reference to Iowa: A Study in Social Politics* (Iowa City: The State Historical Society of Iowa, 1916), pp. 253, 255; Smith W. Brookhart, "Cooperative Economics," *The Iowa Liberal*, Vol. I, No. 1 (May, 1925) 4.
15. *Press*, August 21, 1918; Howard A. Burrell, *History of Washington County, Iowa, From the First White Settlements to 1908*, Vol II (Chicago: S. J. Clarke Publishing Company, 1909), p. 559; *Press*, June 25, 1914; January 31, 1917; August 22, 1917.
16. *Iowa Union Farmer*, May 19, 1920.
17. *Congressional Record*, 67 Cong., 4 Sess., p. 2766.
18. *Iowa Union Farmer*, May 19, 1920; Smith W. Brookhart, "Economic and Political Cooperation," speech, 4th Annual Iowa Farm Bureau Federation Convention, January 11-12, 1923, in *Iowa Yearbook of Agriculture* 1922, (Des Moines: State of Iowa) 378-382; speech, Council of Foreign Relations of New York City, January 26, 1923, in *Congressional Record*, 57 Cong., 4 Sess., pp. 2551-2553; speech annual convention, Brotherhood of Locomotive Engineers, June 10, 1924, in *Labor*, June 21, 1924; speech, "Governmental Aid for Cooperative Marketing, Academy of Political Science, January 1, 1924, in *Proceedings of the Academy of Political Science in the City of New York*, Vol. X, No. 4 (New York: Columbia University) 33-44; *Congressional Record*, 70 Cong., 2 Sess., pp. 1007-1008; 71 Cong., 2 Sess., pp. 1045-1050; 72 Cong., 1 Sess., pp. 1001-1001; *Congressional Record*, 67 Cong., 4 Sess., p. 2553.
19. U. S., Congress, Senate, Committee on Interstate Commerce, *Amending Section 10 of Clayton Act*, 66th Cong., 3rd Sess., January 13, 1921, pp. 92-106; U. S., Congress, Senate, Joint Commission of Agricultural Inquiry, *Agricultural Inquiry*, 67th Cong., 1st Sess., July 11, 1921, pp. 9-39; *The Iowa Union Farmer*, June 1, 1921.
20. Lafayette Young to Lafayette Young, Jr., April 30, 1921, Lafayette Young Papers, State Historical Society of Iowa, Des Moines, Box 4, Letters from 1921.
21. *Homestead*, November 3, 1921; *The Iowa Union Farmer*, November 16, 1921; January 11, 1922; *Wallaces' Farmer*, January 13, 1922.

22. *Register*, October 3, 1921; October 5, 1922; October 7, 1922; *New York Times*, October 7, 1922.
23. *Register*, February 2, 1922; Robert K. Murray, *The Harding Era, Warren G. Harding and His Administration* (Minneapolis: University of Minnesota Press, 1969), p. 217.
24. Abraham Hollingsworth to Nathan E. Kendall, February 14, 1922; Kendall to Hollingsworth, February 18, 1922, Nathan E. Kendall Papers, State Historical Society of Iowa, Des Moines, General Correspondence, File 221.
25. *New York Times*, February 1, 1922; *Register*, February 1, 1922.
26. John Denison to Kendall, February 1, 1922; John Ellmaker to Kendall, February 1, 1922; William F. Kopp to Kendall, February 5, 1922; Carle Duekes to Kendall, February 5, 1922, Kendall Papers, General Correspondence, File 200.
27. William D. Boies to Kendall, February 13, 1922, Kendall Papers, General Correspondence, File 220.
28. James D. Glasgow to Kendall, February 10, 1922; Kendall to Glasgow, February 15, 1922, Kendall Papers, General Correspondence, File 552.
29. Albert B. Cummins to Web Byers, February 13, 1922; Cummins to Rawson, February 13, 1922, Cummins Papers, Box 25, Jan–Feb 1920 File.
30. Kendall to Shirley Gilliland, February 9, 1922, Kendall Papers, General Correspondence, File 552.
31. *Register*, February 19, 1922; Nathan E. Kendall to Cyrennus Cole, May 18, 1936, Cyrenus Cole Papers, State Historical Society of Iowa, Iowa City, Box 2.
32. *Register*, February 18, 1922; *Wallaces' Farmer*, February 24, 1922. As a long-time supporter of the Farm Bureau, the *Wallaces' Farmer* probably would have preferred J. R. Howard or E. H. Cunningham; *Register*, February 18, 1922.
33. William H. Johnston, et al. to Mercer G. Johnston, February 4, 1922, Mercer Johnston Papers, Library of Congress, Washington, D.C., Box 47.
34. Gutzon Borglum Papers, Library of Congress, Washington, D.C., Box 83. The standard work on the Conference for Progressive Political Action is Kenneth Campbell MacKay, *The Progressive Movement of 1924* (New York: Columbia University Press, 1947).
35. "Declaration of Principles Adopted by The Conference for Progressive Political Action, February 1922," Mercer Johnston Papers, Box 47.
36. *Register*, September 5, 1922.
37. Stationery letterhead, Conference for Progressive Political Action, March 15, 1922, Mercer Johnston Papers, Box 47.
38. *Journal*, February 21, 1922.
39. *Register*, June 1, 1922; May 16, 1922.
40. *Register*, May 16, 1922.
41. *Register*, May 4, 1922; April 7, 1922.
42. *Register*, February 21, 1922; March 13, 1922.
43. J. R. Howard to Robert M. La Follette, December 29, 1921; La Follette to Howard, January 21, 1922; Howard to La Follette, January 31, 1922; Brookhart to La Follette, February 25, 1922, La Follette Family Papers, Box B-93.
44. Brookhart to La Follette, February 28, 1922, March 1, 1922, ibid.
45. *Journal*, March 15, 1922.
46. J. R. Howard to Brookhart, March 13, 1922 FBY Collection; *Register*, March 19, 1922.
47. *Homestead*, March 16, 1922.
48. Lafayette Young to David J. Palmer, March 17, 1922, Lafayette Young Papers, Box 4, Letters from Jan–Aug 1922.
49. William W. Copeland to Cummins, March 20, 1922; Cummins to Copeland, March 24, 1922, Cummins Papers, Box 25, March 1922 File.

50. David W. Norris to Cummins, March 17, 1922; Cummins to Norris, March 22, 1922, Cummins Papers, Box 25, March 1922 File.
51. *Register*, March 18, 1922; Howard to Brookhart, March 2, 1922, FBY Collection.
52. Howard to C. W. Hunt, March 18, 1922, published in the *Homestead*, May 11, 1922.
53. La Follette to Dante Pierce, March 29, 1922, La Follette Family Papers, Box B-118.
54. Howard to Thorne, April 1, 1922, FBY Collection.
55. Howard to Brookhart, April 4, 1922, FBY Collection, emphasis added.
56. Brookhart to Howard, April 8, 1922, published in the *Homestead*, May 11, 1922.
57. *Register*, April 4, 1922.
58. *Homestead*, April 6, 1922.
59. Coverdale to Don Berry, April 10, 1922, published in the *Homestead*, May 11, 1922; *Register*, April 12, 1922; April 14, 1922.
60. Hugh H. McCleery, *Newspapers and Other Publications of Washington, Iowa: A Brief History* (Washington: *Washington Evening Journal* 1944.); *Register*, February 24, 1822. A reprint of an Alex Miller article in the *Burlington Gazette*; *Register*, April 12, 1922. Reprint of a *Democrat* article.
61. *Journal*, April 15, 1922.
62. *Journal*, April 17, 1922.
63. *Journal*, April 19, 1922.
64. Howard to Brookhart, April 17, 1922, FBY Collection. In a holograph note at the bottom, Howard added that the letter was dictated "before I knew Thorne definitely announced."
65. Brookhart to Howard, April 25, 1922; FBY Collection; Samuel R. Guard to Brookhart, May 5, 1922, FBY Collection.
66. *Journal*, April 15, 1922.
67. *Journal*, April 19, 1922.
68. Ibid.
69. *Journal*, April 21, 1922; April 26, 1922.
70. *Homestead*, April 20, 1922; May 4, 1922; May 11, 1922.
71. *Wallaces' Farmer*, April 21, 1922; May 19, 1922; Young to Mark Sullivan, April 26, 1922, Young Papers, Box 4, Letters from Jan–Aug 1922.
72. Cummins to Byers, April 17, 1922, Cummins Papers, 25, April 1922 File.
73. *Journal*, May 6, 1922.
74. C. F. Shaffer to Thorne, April 23, 1922; J. E. Jackson to Thorne, April 26, 1922, Clifford Thorne Papers, University of Iowa Libraries, Iowa City, Box 37.
75. *Register*, April 22, 1922.
76. Ibid.
77. *Journal*, April 27, 1922; *Register*, April 25, 1922.
78. *Journal*, May 3, 1922.
79. *Register*, April 29, 1922; *Iowa Forum*, May 3, 1922.
80. *Journal*, May 5, 1922; *The Iowa Union Farmer*, May 31, 1922; Robert M. La Follette, "Iowa and The United States Senate," *La Follette's Magazine* (April, 1922): 55.
81. Circular letter, Conference for Progressive Political Action, May 19, 1922, La Follette Family Papers, Box B-195.
82. Dell Glazer to Roy Rankin, May 10, 1922, Charles Rawson Papers, State Historical Society of Iowa, Des Moines, Vol. II, File G. Rankin was Rawson's secretary and maintained political contacts in Iowa for Rawson; Rader to Rawson, May 17, 1922, Rawson Papers, Vol. IV, File R.
83. J. H. McCord to Rawson, May 11, 1922, Rawson Papers, Vol. III, File M; John Sieh to Brookhart, May 9, 1922, FBY Collection.
84. *Register*, June 5, 1922.

85. *Iowa Official Register, 1923-1924*, (Des Moines: The State of Iowa, 1923), pp. 392-393.
86. *New York Times*, June 7, 1922.
87. *New York Times*, June 8, 1922.
88. *Homestead*, June 22, 1922; *The Iowa Union Farmer*, June 11, 1922; *Locomotive Engineers Journal*, 56, (July, 1922): 513.
89. *Wallaces' Farmer*, June 16, 1922.
90. "A New 'Iowa Idea'," *The Literary Digest*, (June 24, 1922): 8; "The Meaning of Brookhart," *The Outlook*, 131, no. 9 (June 28, 1922): 363.
91. *Register*, June 6, 1922; *Chicago Tribune*, June 10, 1922.
92. La Follette to Brookhart, June 12, 1922, La Follette Family Papers, Box B-118; Kenyon to Brookhart, June 17, 1922, FBY Collection.
93. *Journal*, June 6, 1922; *Washington Democrat*, June 14, 1922.
94. *Washington Democrat*, June 14, 1922.
95. Thorne to Brookhart, June 6, 1922, FBY Collection; Thorne to W. F. Hunter, June 27, 1922, Thorne Papers, Box 37; *Davenport Democrat and Leader*, May 2, 1923; Elizabeth Thorne to author, November 29, 1981.
96. *New York Times*, June 13, 1922.
97. Interview, Al Baldridge, July 21, 1981.
98. Weaver, *Call*, p. 351, 394, 443.

8. VICTORY WITH NATIONAL IMPLICATIONS

1. *Register*, June 11, 1922; June 13, 1922.
2. *Register*, June 25, 1922.
3. Rawson to E. H. Cunningham, June 19, 1922, Rawson Papers, Vol. I, File C.
4. *Register*, June 18, 1922.
5. Cummins to Charles Bradshaw, July 13, 1922, Cummins Papers, Box 25, July 1922 File; See also Cummins to Louis Kurtz, July 14, 1922, Cummins Papers, Box 25, July 1922 File.
6. *Register*, June 7, 1922. Another writer the following week expressed the opposite view. Saying he was a Democrat and therefore unable to vote for Brookhart, the writer felt, nevertheless, that the "common people" had won a "notable victory for popular government in the nomination of Brookhart." Noting that Brookhart would have no chance in the convention the writer said "the primary law is dangerous to the political rings." (*Register*, June 15, 1922.); Charles Pickett to Burt J. Thompson, July 3, 1922, Charles Pickett Papers, University of Iowa Libraries, Iowa City, Box 4, Item 2444.
7. *Register*, June 16, 1922; June 17, 1922.
8. *Des Moines Capital*, June 29, 1922.
9. *Register*, August 2, 1922.
10. *Des Moines Capital*, July 28, 1922.
11. *Des Moines Capital*, August 1, 1922; August 2, 1922.
12. *Register*, August 20, 1922.
13. *Iowa Official Register, 1923-1924* (Des Moines: The State of Iowa, 1923), pp. 299-303.
14. *Register*, August 3, 1922; *The Newton Daily News*, September 5, 1922.
15. *Register*, August 4, 1922.
16. *Register*, August 9, 1922.
17. Payne to Cummins, August 6, 1922, Cummins Papers, Box 25, August 3, 1922.

18. *Register*, July 2, 1922; August 3, 1922; *Des Moines Capital*, August 3, 1922.
19. *Marshalltown Times-Republican*, August 24, 1922.
20. *Register*, September 5, 1922.
21. *Journal*, October 4, 1922.
22. "Progress of Socialism in Iowa This Year," (Des Moines: Iowa Anti-Socialist Society, n.d.), Found in Edwin T. Meredith Papers, University of Iowa Libraries, Iowa City, Box 30, Item 17812; *Homestead*, October 12, 1922.
23. *Register*, October 1, 1922; *Journal*, October 14, 1922.
24. *Register*, October 19, 1922. Perry Engle kept the situation in a state of confusion. Returning home following the Burlington meeting he had said that the convention "unqualifiedly endorsed" Brookhart for senator. (*The Newton Daily News*, September 5, 1922).
25. *Register*, October 29, 1922.
26. *Register*, October 8, 1922. The following August Brookhart belatedly thanked poet Corydon Brown and said he appreciated the poem "more than almost anything written in the whole campaign because of your experience and sincerity." (Brookhart to Brown, August 30, 1923, FBY Collection).
27. Cummins to John S. Moore, August 14, 1922, published in *Marshalltown Times-Republican*, August 24, 1922.
28. *Register*, August 27, 1922.
29. Cummins to George Roberts, October 17, 1922, George Roberts Papers, State Historical Society of Iowa, Iowa City, Letters 1920s; *Register*, October 7, 1922.
30. *Journal*, September 16, 1922.
31. *Register*, September 29, 1922.
32. *Register*, September 26, 1922.
33. *Journal*, September 29, 1922; *Register*, October 1, 1922.
34. *Register*, October 2, 1922.
35. *Register*, October 3, 1922.
36. *Register*, October 4, 1922.
37. Ibid.
38. *Register*, October 6, 1922; *Homestead*, October 12, 1922; Pierce to La Follette, October 16, 1922, La Follette Family Papers, Box B-94.
39. Arthur Capper to Pierce, October 12, 1922, La Follette Family Papers, Box B-94; Rankin to Rawson, October 6, 1912, Rawson Papers, Vol. IV, Misc. File; *Register*, October 29, 1922.
40. *Register*, October 18, 1922, October 20, 1922, October 30, 1922, October 29, 1922.
41. *Journal*, November 6, 1922.
42. *Iowa Official Register, 1923-1924* (Des Moines: The State of Iowa, 1923), pp. 495-496.
43. *Iowa Official Register, 1919-1920* (Des Moines: The State of Iowa 1919), pp. 384-407; *Iowa Official Register, 1921-1922* (Des Moines: The State of Iowa, 1921), pp. 459-460.
44. Austin Haines, "Smith W. Brookhart, Dissenter," *The Nation*, Vol. 15, No. 2991 (November 1, 1922): 466.
45. *Register*, November 8, 1922; Brookhart to William Kenyon, November 8, 1922; Brookhart to Mrs. William Larrabee, November 8, 1922; Brookhart to Mrs. James M. Pierce, November 8, 1922, Brookhart Papers, Des Moines.
46. *Register*, November 9, 1922; Rawson to Henry Rose, November 28, 1922, Rawson Papers, Vol. IV, R File.
47. *New York Times*, November 26, 1922, Section IX, p. 1.
48. *Journal*, November 10, 1922.
49. *Journal*, November 17, 1922.

9. IN WASHINGTON AND EUROPE

1. *Journal*, November 9, 1922; Pierce to La Follette, November 14, 1922, La Follette Family Papers, Box B-94; Kopp to Brookhart, June 7, 1922, FBY Collection.
2. *Register*, November 21, 1922; Rawson to P. R. Baldridge, November 29, 1922, Rawson Papers, Vol. I, B File.
3. Iowa General Assembly, Senate, *Journal of the Senate*, 40th General Assembly, January 11, 1923, p. 133.
4. Ibid.; *Cedar Rapids Gazette*, October 30, 1924.
5. *Congressional Record*, 67 Cong., 3 Sess., p. 440. The rose and a note from Brookhart to his family are in the FBY Collection; Brookhart to Mrs. Ingar Hylen, December 2, 1922, Brookhart Papers, Des Moines.
6. *Congressional Record*, 67 Cong., 4 Sess., pp. 25, 2649; Brookhart to Jennie Brookhart, December 11, 1922, FBY Collection; *Washington Democrat*, February 7, 1923.
7. Brookhart to Jennie, December 11, 1922, FBY Collection; Brookhart to E. R. Harlan, February 6, 1923, Brookhart Papers, Des Moines.
8. Brookhart to E. R. Harlan, February 6, 1922, Brookhart Papers, Des Moines.
9. Iowa, General Assembly, Senate, *Journal of the Senate*, 40th General Assembly, January 11, 1923, p. 134. Brookhart's statement about ex-governors refers to the fact that during the campaign six former governors of Iowa came out against him.
10. Belle Case La Follette and Fola La Follette, *Robert M. La Follette, June 14, 1885–June 18, 1925*. (New York: The Macmillan Company, 1953), p. 1026ff.
11. Basil M. Manly, "The Conference of Progressives Held in Washington, D.C., December 1 and 2, 1922, Preliminary Report of Proceedings," *The People's Legislative Service, Special Bulletin*, n.d., in Gutzon Borglum Papers, Library of Congress, Washington, D.C., Box 83; La Follette and La Follette, *La Follette*, pp. 1066-1068.
12. La Follette and La Follette, *La Follette*, pp. 1066-1068; *New York Times*, December 2, 1922, p. 2.
13. Robert K. Murray, *The Harding Era, Warren G. Harding and His Administration* (Minneapolis: University of Minnesota Press, 1969), p. 323; *San Francisco Examiner*, June 18, 1922; *Homestead*, September 21, 1922. A campaign broadside printed a statement by Brookhart on the subject: "I am opposed to ship subsidies for the same reason that I am opposed to railroad guaranties, and I will vote against them in every form." (Brookhart Papers, Des Moines.)
14. James H. Shideler, *Farm Crisis 1919-1923* (Berkeley and Los Angeles: University of California Press, 1957), p. 237.
15. Iowa, General Assembly, Senate, *Journal of the Senate*, 40th General Assembly, January 11, 1923, p. 135; *Register*, December 1922.
16. *New York Times*, December 13, 1922; Brookhart to Jennie Brookhart, December 11, 1922, FBY Collection.
17. *New York Times*, December 19, 1922, p. 4.
18. *Congressional Record*, 67 Cong., 4 Sess., p. 621; Murray, *The Harding Era*, pp. 286-287; *Congressional Record*, 67 Cong., 4 Sess., p. 626.
19. Ibid, p. 625. For the Norris Bill see Richard Lowitt, *George W. Norris, The Persistence of a Progressive 1913-1933* (Urbana: University of Illinois Press, 1971), p. 177.
20. *New York Times*, December 20, 1922, p. 18; *Register*, December 23, 1922.
21. Brookhart to Brainard H. Shearer, January 18, 1923, Brainard Shearer Papers, University of Iowa Libraries, Iowa City, Box 1.
22. Kenneth L. Roberts, "Filibusters," *The Saturday Evening Post*, 195, no. 46, (May 12, 1923): 174; Lowitt, *Norris*, p. 325.
23. *Congressional Record*, 67 Cong., 4 Sess, p. 4745.

24. *Homestead*, February 8, 1923.

25. "President Felton of Great Western Writes Senator Brookhart," *The Iowa Magazine*, March 1, 1923, p. 406; *Railway Review* 72, no. 5 (February 3, 1923): 224–225; "Brookhart-La Follette Bloc Begins Radical Government Ownership Fight," *Railway Review* 72, no. 4 (January 27, 1923): 71; "A Gigantic Program of Confiscation," *Railway Age* 74, no. 5 (February 3, 1923): 316.

26. "Senator Brookhart's Radical Railroad Bill," *Railway Age* 74, no. 9 (March 3, 1923): 503–504.

27. James C. Davis, "New Capital Needed in Fight Against Nationalization," *Railway Review* 72, no. 12 (March 24, 1923): 558–561.

28. "Senator Brookhart's Radical Bill," p. 503; "Brookhart-La Follette Bloc," p. 172; Letterhead, People's Reconstruction League, Mercer Johnston Papers, Box 48.

29. George L. Record to James Couzens, February 20, 1923, James Couzens Papers, Library of Congress, Washington, D.C., Correspondence I, Box 17; Letterhead, National Conference on Valuation of American Railroads (To Conserve the Public Interest), La Follette Family Papers, Box B-201. Iowa's Governor N. E. Kendall was on the Cooperating Group of Governors.

30. *Des Moines Capital*, February 6, 1923; *Washington Post*, March 9, 1923; *Des Moines Capital*, February 6, 1923.

31. *Journal*, March 13, 1923; March 21, 1923.

32. *Register*, January 3, 1923; Clipping, Black Scrapbook, FBY Collection, p. 65. The clipping is unidentified and undated but it is likely from the *Baltimore Sun* in the spring of 1923.

33. Clippings in the Black Scrapbook on the subject of Brookhart's dress include those from the following newspapers: *Boston Herald*, *New York American*, *Indianapolis News*, *New Orleans Times Picayune*, *Rocky Mountain News* (Denver), as well as a number of Iowa newspapers; *Register*, February, 1923; *Journal*, March 21, 1923. Brookhart made one exception to his rule of never appearing in dress clothes. "I will wear a silk hat," he told the *Philadelphia Public Ledger*, "at the inauguration to the Presidency of Judge William S. Kenyon." (*Ledger*, February 20, 1923.)

34. Jennie to Smith Brookhart, Jr., November 23, 1924; November 3, 1925, Charles E. Brookhart Collection.

35. Pierce to La Follette, February 19, 1923, La Follette Family Papers, Box B-96; Brookhart to Herbert Hoover, April 23, 1923, Herbert C. Hoover Papers, Commerce Report, Herbert Hoover Presidential Library, West Branch, Iowa, Box 544.

36. *Davenport Democrat and Leader*, April 23, 1923; Interview, Richard McCleery, July 18, 1981.

37. Circular Letter, April 26, 1923, Record Group 59, "Records of the Department of State," Correspondence, American Consulate at Edinburgh, 1923, Part II, Vol. 166; *Davenport Democrat and Leader*, April 24, 1923.

38. Smith W. Brookhart, "What I Really Saw and Learned in Europe in 1923," *The Saturday Evening Post* 102, no. 37 (March 15, 1930): 23. Brookhart wrote this article in response to an earlier article by Dennis, "The European Education of Senator Brookhart," *The Saturday Evening Post* 202, no. 204, (December 14, 1929). Dennis later included these two articles in a collection of essays, *Gods and Little Fishes* (Indianapolis: The Bobbs-Merrill Company, 1931). In this collection Brookhart added a sub-title to his essay "What I Really Saw and Learned in Europe in 1923, In Contrast with the Scholarly but Provincial Picture of My Friend and Traveling Companion, Dr. Alfred Pearce Dennis."

39. Brookhart, "What I Really Saw," p. 165.

40. Ibid, p. 166.

41. Prince to Secretary of State, June 2, 1923, Record Group 59, "Records of the

Department of State," State Decimal File, 1910–1929, Box 325.

42. David Burner, *Herbert Hoover, A Public Life* (New York: Alfred A. Knopf, 1978), pp. 130–137.

43. Ibid., p. 136. For the complete story of the ARA withdrawal see: Benjamin M. Weissman, *Herbert Hoover and Famine Relief to Soviet Russia 1921–1923* (Stanford, California: Hoover Institution Press, 1974), Chapter 7.

44. Charles Herring to Brookhart, May 29, 1923, Hoover Papers, Commerce Department, Box 134, Folder 02321; D. C. Poole to Secretary of State, May 31, 1923, Record Group 59, "Records of the Department of State," State Decimal File, 1910–1929, M316, Roll 133.

45. John R. Ellingston, "Report on Senator Brookhart's Visit to Russia," *Documents on the American Relief Administration Russian Operations, 1921–1923, Volume III*, pp. 516—531, Herbert Hoover Presidential Library.

46. Interview with Senator Brookhart, *Aurora*, June 25, 1923, enclosed with Peter A. Jay to Secretary of State, June 29, 1923, Record Group 59, "Records of the Department of State," State Decimal File, 1910–1929, M316, Roll 72. There is a certain irony in Brookhart's high opinion of Trotsky, because in some ways they were alike. Historian Edward Carr has written of Trotsky that he "had no political instinct in the narrower sense, no feeling for a situation, no sensitive touch for the levers of power. It was this defect which rendered him blind. . . . But, even more than these personal shortcomings, the evolution of events contributed to his defeat. . . . As a revolutionary to the finger-tips, he was an incongruous figure in an age which seemed (though falsely seemed) to be set on a path of consolidation and stabilization. As an individualist, whose past recalcitrance to party discipline was unforgotten and unforgiven, he was suspect in a party which hymned the praises of collective leadership and was obsessed by the bogy of a Bonaparte. Trotsky was a hero of the revolution. He fell when the heroic age was over." (Edward H. Carr, *A History of Soviet Russia, Socialism in One Country, 1924–1926* [New York: Macmillan Company, 1958] p. 152.)

47. *New York Times*, June 12, 1923, p. 26.

48. *Journal*, June 23, 1923; *Homestead*, July 26, 1923; *New York Times*, June 16, 1923, p. 12; "What Senator Brookhart Saw in Europe," *The Spotlight* VIII, no. 2 (August, 1923): 11.

49. *New York Times*, Junes 16, 1923, p. 12.

50. Edward H. Carr, *A History of Soviet Russia, The Interregnum, 1923–1924* (New York: The Macmillan Company, 1954), pp. 3, 7, 366. A positive picture of Russia in 1923 was also drawn in a letter to Hoover from William C. Garner, Chief of Communications, Russian Unit, A.R.A. Writing Hoover on May 24, 1923, Garner said that the change for the better from the previous year was "enormous." After giving Hoover a detailed report, Garner concluded that "I think that Russia can go steadily upward from 1923 forward without outside aid. Its upward march will be very slow. This march would be terrifically speeded up if the economic policies were sufficiently modified to give outside investors the guaranties they obtain in other countries. I am an optimist on Russia." (Garner to Hoover, May 24, 1923, Hoover Papers, Commerce Department, Russia-General File.)

51. Peter A. Jay to Secretary of State, June 29, 1923, Record Group 59, "Records of the Department of State," State Decimal File, 1910—1929, M316, Roll 72.

52. Dennis, "European Education," p. 189.

53. Journalist Norman Hapgood had written Beneš that "Senator Brookhart is a progressive and influential member of our Senate. When he reaches Prague he will have just returned from Russia." (Hapgood to Beneš, June 5, 1923, Brookhart Papers, Des Moines.)

54. Dennis, "European Education," p. 11.

55. Brookhart to Edgar Harlan, February 6, 1923; Plunkett to Brookhart, January 19, 1923, Brookhart Papers, Des Moines.

56. *New York Times*, July 18, 1923, p. 23; *New York Times*, July 18, 1923, p. 23. "What

Senator Brookhart Saw," p. 11. In addition to a number of newspaper interviews and news stories Brookhart published three first hand reports: "Brookhart Reports to Iowa Farmers," *Homestead*, July 26, 1923; "Russia As I Saw It," *Iowa Legionnaire* 3, no. 13 (September 7, 1923): 14; "Russia—As I Saw It," *The Locomotive Engineers Journal* (October, 1923): 791-792.

57. *Register*, July 19, 1923; Brookhart to Herrick, July 23, 1923, Myron Herrick Papers, The Western Reserve Historical Society, Cleveland, Ohio.

58. *Register*, July 23, 1923.

59. *Register*, July 24, 1923; July 26, 1923.

60. *Register*, July 28, 1923.

61. Landis' "Speech," *Iowa Legionnaire* 3, no. 12 (August 22, 1923): 12.

62. *Register*, August 17, 1923.

63. "If Brookhart Had Answered Landis?" *Iowa Legionnaire* 3, no. 12 (August 22, 1923): 11, 1.

64. "Senator Brookhart and MacNider Don't Hitch," Ibid., p. 11.

65. *Register*, August 19, 1923.

10. DEFEAT OF THE DISRUPTER

1. Pierce to La Follette, March 9, 1923, La Follette Family Papers, Box B-96. Portions of this chapter were previously published as "The Republican Party in Iowa and The Defeat of Smith Wildman Brookhart, 1924-1926," *The Annals of Iowa*, (Winter/Spring 1987): 413-434; *New York Times*, September 17, 1923.

2. Cummins to Ed Kelly, December 3, 1923, Cummins Papers, Box 26; L. J. Dickinson to Ed Kelly, January 29, 1924, Hanford MacNider Papers, Herbert Hoover Presidential Library, West Branch, Iowa, Corr. Gen. 1924-1925 September Kansas-Knotts.

3. D. A. Emery to Cummins, January 24, 1924, Cummins Papers, Box 27; Cummins to G. W. Dawson, February 4, 1924, Cummins Papers, Box 27, January-February File; E. A. Burgess to Cummins, March 8, 1924, Cummins Papers, Box 27, January-February File.

4. *Register*, January 3, 1924; Rankin to Rawson, February 16, 1924, Rawson Papers, Box V, File XXIII.

5. *Cedar Rapids Republican*, February 13, 1924; "Where Does Rawson Stand?" Political Broadside, Cummins Papers, Box 27, March-April File.

6. Rawson to Ray Stewart, February 13, 1924, Rawson Papers, Box V, File XXII; Rawson to Paul Moore, March 1, 1924, Box VI, File XXV.

7. Minutes of the Republican National Committee, Committee on Arrangements, December 11-12, 1923, Box 42, National Archives.

8. Ralph Mills Sayre, "Albert Baird Cummins and The Progressive Movement in Iowa" (Ph.D. diss., Columbia University, 1958), pp. 530-534; Rawson to Cunningham, January 10, 1924, Rawson Papers, Box V, File XX.

9. Cummins to O. M. Brockett, February 25, 1924, Cummins Papers, Box 27, January-February File; Cummins to Don Berry, March 31, 1924, Cummins Papers, Box 27, March-April File; Ed Kelly to Cummins, March 12, 1924, Cummins Papers, Box 27, March-April File. The "breaks" continued to go against the Cummins-standpat forces when on April 30 the *Register* ran an editorial praising the work of the Brookhart committee.

10. *Register*, March 5, 1924; March 6, 1924; Rawson to William S. Kenyon, March 5, 1924, Rawson Papers, Box VI, File XXV.

11. Campaign Pamphlet, President Jessup Papers, University of Iowa Libraries, Iowa City, Folder 69.

12. U.S. Congress, Senate, Select Committee on Investigation of the Attorney General,

"Hearings on S. Res. 157," 68th Cong., 1st Sess., 1924, p. 2965.

13. *Register*, June 2, 1924; *Iowa Official Register, 1925-1926* (Des Moines: Iowa State Printer, 1925), pp. 420-421.

14. *Official Report of the Proceedings of the Eighteenth Republican National Convention* (New York: The Tenny Press, 1924), pp. 185-186.

15. *Register*, June 22, 1924.

16. *Iowa Official Register, 1925-1926* (Des Moines: Iowa State Printer, 1925), p. 308.

17. *Register*, July 23, 1924.

18. Iowa State Banking Department, Bank Inventories, Box 26, State Historical Society of Iowa, Des Moines.

19. Interview, Smith W. Brookhart, Jr., July 3, 1981; Edmund D. Morrison, Jr. to Author, June 26, 1981. Mr. Morrison's father, Edmund D. Morrison, was the attorney for the receivership for the bank; Interview, Florence Brookhart Yount, October 16, 1980.

20. Interview, Edith Brookhart Millard, January 23, 1981; Jennie to Smith Brookhart, Jr., November 14, 1924, Charles E. Brookhart Collection.

21. Interviews, Florence Brookhart Yount, October 16, 1980; Smith W. Brookhart, Jr., July 3, 1981; Edith Brookhart Millard, January 23, 1981.

22. Cunningham to Rawson, August 19, 1924, Rawson Papers, Box V, File XXI.

23. Lenihan to Rawson, February 8, 1924, Rawson Papers, Box V, File XXI.

24. The biographical material available on Steck is slight. The principal sources have been the *Biographical Directory of the American Congress, 1774-1949* (Washington, D.C., 1950 and the *Register*, November 6, 1924.); Edward H. Stiles, *Recollections and Sketches on Notable Lawyers and Public Men in Early Iowa* (Des Moines: The Homestead Publishing Company, 1916), p. 649.

25. Jacob A. Swisher, *The American Legion in Iowa, 1919-1926* (Iowa City: State Historical Society of Iowa, 1929), pp. 70-71, 73.

26. Ibid., p. 139; MacNider to Steck, December 12, 1921, MacNider Papers, Series 2, Box 6.

27. Swisher, *Legion in Iowa*, pp. 248-249, 139.

28. Ibid., p. 8; Theodore Roosevelt, Jr., September 5, 1924, MacNider Papers, Scrapbook 1924, Box 17; MacNider to B. B. Burnquist, September 23, 1924, MacNider Papers, Republican Service League, 1924 State File, Iowa General.

29. MacNider to Roosevelt, September 5, 1924, MacNider Papers, Republican Service League, 1924 General File, Roosevelt, Col. T., Box 88; MacNider to Roosevelt, October 16, 1924, Ibid.

30. Roosevelt to MacNider, July 18, 1924, Ibid.; MacNider to Roosevelt, August 18, 1924, Ibid.; MacNider to Roosevelt, August 31, 1924, Ibid., Box 86.

31. Stubs of Republican National Committee checks in MacNider Papers, Republican Service League, 1924, General File, Expense Vouchers, Box 87. The actual figures are:

Expenses paid by RNC		Advances from RNC	
September 12	$ 290.57		
October 7	636.97	October 7	$10,000
October 16	818.54	October 21	5,000
October 29	678.46		
November 7	72.32	March 22-25, 1925	2,000
	$2,496.86		$17,000

These expense checks were issued in response to statements presented by the Republican Service League. The $2,000 advance in March 1925 was to cover the expenses of a national convention of the League held that month.

32. A typical example of the position they maintained throughout is a telegram from Roosevelt to MacNider: the "Legion as an organization should never engage in partisan politics but every member of the Legion as an individual should engage in partisan politics." (Roosevelt to MacNider, September 10, 1924, MacNider Papers, Republican Service League, 1924 General File, Republican, Col. T., Box 88.); Marcus Duffield, *King Legion* (New York: Jonathan Cape & Harrison Smith, 1931), p. 102.

33. Steck to MacNider, March 21, 1924, MacNider Papers, Steck, Daniel 1924–1925, September, Box 72; MacNider to Steck, March 22, 1924, Ibid.; MacNider to Steck, March 22, 1924, Ibid.

34. Steck to MacNider, March 25, 1924, Ibid.

35. *Register*, April 6, 1924; MacNider to Steck, April 11, 1924, MacNider Papers, Steck, Daniel, 1924–1925, April, Box 72.

36. *Iowa Official Register, 1925–1926* (Des Moines: Iowa State Printer, 1925), pp. 426–427; MacNider to Steck, June 6, 1924, MacNider Papers, Steck, Daniel, 1924–1925, June, Box 72.

37. Fay to Cummins, September 18, 1924, Cummins Papers, Box 28, July-August-September File; *New York Times*, October 31, 1924.

38. *Register*, April 22, 1924; Rankin to Rawson, April 30, 1924, Rawson Papers, Box VI, File XXVIII; *Register*, May 3, 1924; *New York Times*, May 2, 1924.

39. *New York Times*, July 25, 1924; September 29, 1924; Rawson to Reed Lane, September 4, 1924, Rawson Papers, Box VII, File XXXII; Rawson to Ray C. Meyer, August 30, 1924, Rawson Papers, Box VII, File XXXII.

40. *Register*, September 25, 1924.

41. Wallace to Rawson, October 6, 1924, Rawson Papers, Box VII, File XXXIII; Lenihan to Rawson, October 15, 1924, Rawson Papers, Box VII, File XXXIII.

42. *Register*, September 25, 1924; *New York Times*, October 2, 1924.

43. *New York Times*, October 4, 1924.

44. Ibid.

45. Ray Shoemaker to MacNider, October 4, 1924; MacNider to Shoemaker, October 6, 1924, and October 8, 1924, MacNider Papers, Republican Service League, 1924 State File, Iowa, Shoemaker, Ray D.

46. Harry F. Lee to MacNider, October 24, 1924, MacNider Papers, Republican Service League, 1924 State File, Iowa General, Box 89.

47. MacNider to Lee, October 27, 1924, MacNider Papers, Republican Service League, 1924 State File, Iowa General, Box 89.

48. *Journal*, October 10, 1924.

49. *Cedar Rapids Republican*, November 10, 1924.

50. *Register*, November 2, 1924; Jennie Brookhart to Smith Brookhart, Jr., October 16, 1924, Charles E. Brookhart Collection; Jennie Brookhart to Smith Brookhart, Jr., October 22, 1924, Charles E. Brookhart Collection.

51. *Register*, November 6, 1924; November 7, 1924.

52. *Register*, November 7, 1924.

53. *New York Times*, November 8, 1924; November 11, 1924; November 12, 1924; November 13, 1924.

54. *Iowa Official Register, 1925–1926* (Des Moines: Iowa State Printer, 1925), pp. 540–541; Jennie Brookhart to Smith Brookhart, Jr., November 6, 1924, Charles E. Brookhart Collection.

55. Wilson to Letts, November 6, 1924, Letts Papers, University of Iowa Libraries, Iowa City, Box 1.

56. *Register*, November 9, 1924; Cyrenus Cole, *I Remember I Remember* (Iowa City: State Historical Society of Iowa, 1936), p. 465.
57. Louis H. Cook, "Brookhart, Insurgent," *North American Review* 231 (February, 1931): 179-180.
58. George E. Lichty to Cummins, November 18, 1924; Cummins to Licthy, November 22, 1924, Cummins Papers, Box 28, October-December File.
59. Minutes of the Republican Caucus & Republican Conference & Index, April 4, 1911-June 2, 1936, Office, Secretary for the Republican Conference, United States Senate, Washington, D.C.
60. Ibid.
61. *New York Times*, December 23, 1924.
62. Governor Kendall sent the certificate to Cummins, telling the Senator this was done "as required by the rules of the Senate as I interpret them." (Kendall to Cummins, December 8, 1924, Governor Kendall Papers, State Archives of Iowa, General Correspondence, File 249.); Cozad to MacNider, November 11, 1924, MacNider Papers, Republican Service League, 1924 State File, Cozad, W. T., Box 89. Cozad's phrase "out in the open" suggests that the Republican Service League had been financing Steck in a less public way. In fact, Bert Halligan, Second District Chairman of the League, had written MacNider on October 1, 1924, to ask for money. MacNider wired Halligan on October 7: "Father told Dan Sunday that he would make substantial contribution and I shall try to do the same." (Halligan to MacNider, October 1, 1924; MacNider to Halligan, October 7, 1924, MacNider Papers, Republican Service League, 1924 State File, Halligan, Bert L., Box 89.); MacNider to W. T. Cozad, November 13, 1924 MacNider Papers, Republican Service League 1924 State File, Iowa, Cozad, Box 89; C. B. Robbins to MacNider, November 15, 1924, MacNider Papers, Republican Service League, 1924 State File, Iowa, Robbins, Col. C. B., Box 89.
63. Steck to MacNider, January 10, 1925, MacNider Papers, Steck, Daniel F. 1924-1925 September, Box 72; James Parsons to MacNider, April 11, 1925, MacNider Papers, Steck, Daniel F. 1924-1925 April; Steck to McNider, November 24, 1925, MacNider Papers, Steck, Daniel F. 1925 October, 1928, Box 72. Throughout the 1920s the elder McNider spelled his name "Mc" but urged his son to use "Mac" because he thought the form was more correct. The family would later unify the spelling as "Mac." I have retained the style used by father and son during the period.
64. MacNider to Steck, June 10, 1925, MacNider Papers, Steck, Daniel F. 1924-1925 September, Box 72; Ralph Van Vechten to MacNider, January 31, 1925, MacNider Papers, Steck, Daniel F. 1924-1925 September, Box 72; Steck to MacNider, January 10, 1925, MacNider Papers, Steck, Daniel F. 1924-1925 September, Box 72.
65. U.S., Congress, Senate, Subcommittee of the Committee on Privileges and Elections, *Hearings*, 69th Cong., 1st Sess., 1925, pp. 9-10; One newspaper, the *Council Bluff Nonpareil*, printed the sample ballot on page one of its November 2 issue. Beneath the ballot was a caption explaining that here was reproduced "a ballot correctly marked" to scratch a ticket. Many voters no doubt felt that to "correctly mark" their ballots they needed to include the arrows shown on the sample.
66. U.S., Congress, Senate Committee on Privileges and Elections, *Report of the Committee Together With Minority Views*, 69th Cong., 1st Sess., 1926, p. 14. The agreed good votes were those the supervisors and attorneys for Brookhart and Steck had agreed upon as not disputable. The other votes were disputed, and the committee had been called upon to make a ruling.
67. Steck to MacNider, February 18, 1925, MacNider Papers, Steck, Daniel F. 1924-1925 September, Box 72; MacNider to Steck, September 3, 1925, MacNider Papers, Steck, Daniel F. 1924-1925 September, Box 72.
68. MacNider to Calvin Coolidge, November 15, 1927, MacNider Papers, Calvin Coolidge;

William Allen White, *A Puritan in Babylon* (New York: The Macmillan Company, 1938), p. 309; Steck to MacNider, January 13, 1926, MacNider Papers, Steck, Daniel F. 1925 October–1928, Box 72.

69. Steck to MacNider, September 4, 1925, MacNider Papers, Steck, Daniel F. 1924–1925 September, Box 72; Robbins to Cummins, December 29, 1925, Cummins Papers, Box 30. Robbins apparently exaggerated the membership figure for Cummins' benefit. On January 18, 1926, Robbins wrote to MacNider and reported that the "strength of the organization is 45,000 men, plenty of pep, prestige and enthusiasm." Robbins would be more likely to give MacNider an accurate number and to inflate the membership to lobby Cummins. However, 45,000 men, if properly organized would have been a potent force. (Robbins to MacNider, January 18, 1926, General Correspondence, 1926.); MacNider to Steck, February 1, 1926, MacNider Papers, Steck, Daniel F. 1925, October–1928, Box 72; Various writers to Albert B. Cummins, February, 1926, Cummins Papers, Box 31.

70. *Register*, February 6, 1925; Cummins to Verne Marshall, January 31, 1926, Cummins Papers, Box 31, January–February File.

71. Cummins to Kelly, April 11, 1926, Cummins Papers, Box 31, April File.

72. MacNider to Steck, September 3, 1925, MacNider Papers, Steck, Daniel F. 1924–1925 September, Box 72.

73. Peter L. Petersen, "The Reluctant Candidate: Edwin T. Meredith and the 1924 Democratic National Convention," *The Palimpsest* 57 (September/October, 1976): 147; Steck to Meredith, March 18, 1926, Edwin Thomas Meredith Papers, University of Iowa Libraries, Iowa City, Box 32, Folder 115, Item 19506.

74. Meredith to various recipients, March 19, 1926, Meredith Papers, Box 32, Folder 115, Item 19498; Meredith to Senator Walsh, March 19, 1926, Meredith Papers, Box 32, Folder 115, Item 19498.

75. Hiram Johnson to Hiram Johnson, Jr., March 29, 1926, in Robert E. Burke, ed., *The Diary Letters of Hiram Johnson, 1917–1945*, Volume 4, 1922–1928, (New York: Garland Publishing, Inc., 1983) n.p.

76. *Register*, April 11, 1926.

77. MacNider to Steck, March 20, 1926, MacNider Papers, Steck, Daniel F. 1925 October–1928, Box 72; MacNider to Halligan, March 23, 1926, MacNider Papers, Halligan, Bert L., 1925–1928, Box 57; MacNider to Robbins, April 1, 1926, MacNider Papers, Robbins, C. B. 1926 January–June, Box 68.

78. Robbins to MacNider, April 6, 1926, MacNider Papers, Robbins, C. B. 1926 January–June, Box 68.

79. Telegram, May 12, 1926, to *Sioux City Tribune*, MacNider Papers, Kelly, John H.; *Register*, April 11, 1926. Steck to MacNider, June 11, 1925, MacNider Papers, Steck, Daniel F. 1924–1925 September, Box 72.

80. MacNider to Marshall, April 16, 1926, MacNider Papers, Marshall, Verne 1926–195, Box 62.

81. Johnson to Johnson, April 14, 1926, Burke, *The Diary Letters of Hiram Johnson*.

82. Robbins to MacNider, April 12, 1926, MacNider Papers, Robbins, C. B. 1926 January–June, Box 68; W. F. Zumbrunn to MacNider, April 13, 1926, MacNider Papers, Steck, Daniel F. 1295-October–1928, Box 72; William C. McArthur to MacNider, April 14, 1926, MacNider Papers, Campaign 1926 Brookhart-Cummins, Box 44; MacNider to Feuling, May 1, 1926, Ibid.; Ed Feuling to MacNider, April 28, 1926, MacNider Papers, Campaign 1926 Brookhart-Cummins, Box 44; MacNider to Feuling, May 1, 1926, Ibid.

83. Kelly to Cummins, April 15, 1926, Cummins Papers, Box 31, April File; *Register*, April 17, 1926.

84. *Iowa Legionnaire*, April 23, 1926.

85. Telegram, May 12, 1926, to *Sioux City Tribune*, MacNider Papers, Kelly, John H.
86. White, *Puritan in Babylon*, p. 264, 318; *New York Times*, April 8, 1926; April 9, 1926.

11. THE DISRUPTER VICTORIOUS

1. *Journal*, April 13, 1926.
2. *Journal*, April 15, 1926. One Washingtonian not present at the station was Charles J. Wilson. Still fighting the good fight he had begun thirty years before, Wilson told MacNider that Brookhart had not "voted a straight Congressional, State or National ticket in the last twenty-five years. There is not an atom of constructiveness in his entire make-up and his success can only be credited to the discontent and distressing mental attitude of the people following the reconstruction incident to the War. He is an egotist, and an ambitious demagogue, and nothing more."

MacNider was of a similar mind. Writing Wilson on April 26 he said: "You and I feel exactly the same way about your fellow townsman and it seems to me this campaign is a good time to decide whether Iowa wants a half moron and half red or whether they want to stay within the Party." (Wilson to MacNider, April 24, 1926; MacNider to Wilson, April 26, 1926, MacNider Papers, Campaign 1926 Brookhart-Cummins, Box 44.)

3. *Journal*, April 19, 1926.
4. *Register*, May 1, 1926.
5. Cummins to James Blythe (brother of C. B. & Q. General Counsel Joseph W. Blythe), February 28, 1924, Cummins Papers, Box 27, January-February File; Cummins to Bert Keltz, November 28, 1924, Cummins Papers, Box 28, October-December File; Robbins to MacNider, August 28, 1925, MacNider Papers, Robbins, C. B.; Cummins to Burt Thompson, March 1, 1926, Cummins Papers, Box 31, March File; Cummins to Wilson, April 4, 1926, Cummins Papers, Box 31, April File.
6. *Register*, April 23, 1926.
7. *Register*, April 24, 1926.
8. *Register*, May 4, 1926.
9. Cummins to Kelly, April 29, 1926, Cummins Papers, Box 31, April File; Cummins to MacNider, May 15, 1926, MacNider Papers, Cummins, Albert B. 1924-1926.
10. *Register*, May 6, 1926; MacNider to Robbins, May 3, 1926, MacNider Papers, Robbins, Col. C. B.; MacNider to Marshall, April 25, 1926, MacNider Papers, Marshall, Verne 1926-1956, Box 62.
11. MacNider to Hubbell, May 6, 1926, MacNider Papers, Campaign 1926 Brookhart-Cummins.
12. On MacNider's ambitions see Ed Kelly to Cummins, April 24, 1926, Cummins Papers, Box 31, April File.
13. "The Committee" to MacNider, May 10, 1926, MacNider Papers, General Correspondence, Bacon-Byrd File.
14. Pamphlet and envelope, letter Brookhart to A. MacEachron, July 24, 1926, FBY Collection.
15. *The Union Advocate and Open Forum*, May 20, 1926; *Labor*, May 22, 1926; *Register*, April 23, 1926.
16. Pierce to Cummins, January 17, 1925, Cummins Papers, Box 29, January-March 1925 File. Responding to a letter from Wallace Sherlock, circulation manager for the *Homestead*, Edwin Meredith wrote: "Your visit with Dante Pierce is interesting. Am really glad to know he is getting off Brookhart." (Meredith to Sherlock, September, 1923, Meredith Papers, Box 17, Item 11656.); Rawson to Butler, April 24, 1925, Dante Pierce Papers, University of Iowa

Library, Iowa City, Folder 1, 1-1-1. Rawson to Skelly, March 14, 1925, Pierce Papers, Folder 1, 1-1-3.

17. Baldwin to Cummins, October 21, 1925, Cummins Papers, Box 30, October–December 1925 File. In the records of the Senate Committee on Privileges and Elections is an unsigned and undated holograph note alleging that the writer could get check stubs and books showing that Stone "paid out tens of thousands of dollars out of the B.L.E. Treasury to help the man Brookhart carry Iowa. That is where Brookhart got his money for his campaigns. Get a chance to search the accts (sic) of the B.L.E. & you will [find] that the Iowa man was practically on their payroll. They sent him to Russia." (Record Group 46, "Records of the United States Senate," Committee on Privileges and Elections, Drawer 72.); Circular letter, May 3, 1926, Mercer Johnston Papers, Box 52; Wheeler Circular Letter, April 23, 1926, Mercer Johnston Papers, Box 52. Writing to Brookhart to explain the Wheeler Fund refund plan, Johnston told Brookhart "I trust that everything is going well and that the Progressive Goose is hanging high, and that the scalp of Brother Cummins will hang much higher by the time the primaries come around, in fact as high as Haman." (Johnston to Brookhart, May 6, 1926, Mercer Johnston Papers, Box 52.); Brookhart to Johnston, June 29, 1926, Mercer Johnston Papers, Box 52.

18. *Register*, June 5, 1962; Ralph Mills Sayre, "Albert Baird Cummins," p. 551.

19. Allen to Judson Welliver, May 13, 1926, A. F. Allen Papers, University of Iowa Libraries, Iowa City, Box 2.

20. *Iowa Official Register, 1927–1928* (Des Moines: Iowa State Printer, 1927), pp. 348–349.

21. *Register*, June 8, 1926; "Why Iowa Smashed the Windows," *The Literary Digest* LXXXIX, No. 12 (June 19, 1926): 5; *Register*, June 9, 1926.

22. Rawson to Cummins, June 10, 1926, Cummins Papers, Box 33, June 1926 File; Burnquist to Cummins, June 22, 1926, Cummins Papers, Box 33, June 1926 File; *Register*, July 14, 1926.

23. MacNider to Robbins, May 24, 1926, MacNider Papers, Robbins, Col. C. B.; Cummins to Kelly, June 8, 1926, Cummins Papers, Box 33, June 1926 File; Cummins to Rawson, June 20, 1926, Cummins Papers, Box 33, June 1926 File.

24. *Journal*, June 9, 1926.

25. *Register*, June 13, 1926; June 21, 1926.

26. *Register*, June 13, 1926.

27. *Register*, June 20, 1926; July 18, 1926; July 20, 1926; July 21, 1926.

28. *Register*, July 22, 1926; *Iowa Official Register, 1927–1928* (Des Moines: Iowa State Printer, 1927) pp. 258ff.

29. *Register*, July 22, 1926.

30. Ibid.

31. *Register*, July 22, 1926; *The Union Advocate*, August 5, 1926.

32. Ibid.

33. *Homestead*, July 29, 1926.

34. *Register*, July 31, 1926.

35. *Register*, August 3, 1926; August 2, 1926.

36. *Register*, August 3, 1926; *Des Moines Capital*, August 3, 1926; August 4, 1926.

37. *Des Moines Capital*, August 6, 1926; August 7, 1926.

38. *Register*, August 7, 1926. Stewart's first reaction to the nomination was to exclaim: "What will my wife think about this? She didn't dream of my being mentioned as a candidate." (*Register*, August 7, 1926.); *Register*, August 12, 1926; Stewart served his seven months in the Senate and returned to Sioux City where he practiced law and was active in a number of the usual community service groups, the YMCA, Boy Scouts, Community Chest and the like. He also served on the board of a bank and for a time was president of the Board of Trustees of

Morningside College. His service in the Senate, however, was his last and only political office.

39. MacNider to Robbins, August 16, 1926, MacNider Papers, Robbins, Col. C. B. 1926 August-1928; Allen to George Roberts, August 31, 1926, Allen Papers, Box 2; Stewart to John Carey, September 7, 1926, John Carey Papers, University of Iowa Libraries, Iowa City.

40. Porter had served in the Iowa House of Representatives from 1896 to 1900 and in the Iowa Senate from 1900 to 1904. He ran for Secretary of State in 1898; governor of Iowa in 1906, 1910, and 1918; and the Senate in 1908, 1909, 1911, 1920, and 1926. He was unsuccessful in all of these races; *Register*, July 29, 1926; Allen to George Roberts, August 31, 1926, Allen Papers, Box 2.

41. *Register*, August 30, 1926; September 3, 1926; Meredith to Steck, September 10, 1926, Meredith Papers, Box 32, Item 19457.

42. *Register*, October 2, 1926; October 4, 1926; *Journal*, October 14, 1926.

43. *Register*, September 2, 1926.

44. Harlan to Brookhart, June 9, 1921, Edgar Harlan Papers, State Historical Society of Iowa, Des Moines, File 10E, Part 11, Group 2.

45. *Register*, September 11, 1926; September 12, 1926.

46. *Register*, October 3, 1926; October 10, 1926; October 21, 1926.

47. *Iowa Official Register, 1927-1928*, (Des Moines: Iowa State Printer), pp. 458-459.

48. *Register*, November 3, 1926; November 4, 1926.

49. Brookhart to Smith W. Brookhart, Jr., November 9, 1926, Smith W. Brookhart, Jr. Collection.

50. Arthur F. Allen wrote a friend in August, 1926, that it was "practically certain" that Brookhart would win the election. The fact that he did not get the nomination for the short term was "not to be regarded as an indication of changed sentiment" about Brookhart, Allen said, adding, "Brookhart, in his way, is a shrewd politician." Like Cummins in 1901, Brookhart made his appeal directly to the people. Cummins, however, was careful to see that his supporters were elected as delegates to the county conventions. Brookhart, Allen continued, had "neglected county conventions." (Allen to George Roberts, August 31, 1926, Allen Papers, Box 2)

51. *Press*, March 20, 1913; September 25, 1913. No doubt many Republicans in the 1920s thought Brookhart was the "blighting wrath."

52. Writing in *The Searchlight On Congress*, March 31, 1924, Walt Durand said: "'Regularity' to Brookhart means trusting in the true source of political power, which he finds to be in the mass of the people rather in the possessors of wealth and special privileges. His 'regularity' consists of looking out for the welfare of the plain men and women of the country, which he conceives to be the true mission of a political party." (Walt Durand, "What About Brookhart?" *The Searchlight On Congress IX*, No. 9 [March 31, 1924]: 18.)

53. See Peter L. Petersen, "A Publisher in Politics: Edwin T. Meredith, Progressive Reform, and the Democratic Party, 1912-1928" (Ph.D. diss., University of Iowa, 1971), pp. 336ff.

54. In 1922 Governor Kendall received a number of letters recommending MacNider for appointment to the Senate, but Kendall replied to all his correspondents that friends of MacNider's had told him MacNider would not accept the appointment. (Governor Kendall Papers, General Correspondence, File 212.); MacNider to Miles, June 8, 1926, MacNider Papers, Miles, Frank 1926 May-December. MacNider's son, Jack, has written that C. H. McNider had wanted Hanford to return to Mason City to devote more time to the family business. "Partly in deference to my grandfather's wishes, and partly because of [Hanford's] conviction that he could be more effective in politics as a private citizen rather than an elected official, he chose to return to Mason City and pursue a career as a banker and industrialist." (Jack MacNider to author, July 26, 1982)

12. REGULAR REPUBLICAN AND THE FIGHT FOR FARM RELIEF

1. *New York Times*, November 29, 1926.
2. *Congressional Record*, 68 Cong., 1 Sess., pp. 1081-1086.
3. Ibid.
4. Ibid., p. 1085.
5. Ibid., p. 1086.
6. Belle Case La Follette to Brookhart, May 17, 1927, La Follette Family Papers, Box D-27; Basil Manly to Robert M. La Follette, Jr., May 19, 1927, Ibid., Box C-6. The article appeared as "Nation Needs Economic Cooperation," *La Follette's Magazine 19* (June, 1927): 85-86.
7. The standard work on McNary-Haugen is Gilbert C. Fite, *George N. Peek and the Fight for Farm Parity* (Norman: University of Oklahoma Press, 1954).
8. Joan Hoff Wilson, "Herbert Hoover's Agricultural Policies, 1921-1928," in Ellis W. Hawley, ed. *Herbert Hoover as Secretary of Commerce: Studies in New Era Thought and Practice* (Iowa City: University of Iowa Press, 1981), p. 124.
9. U. S. Congress, House, Committee on Agriculture, *Hearing on H. R. 5563*, 68th Cong., 1st Sess., February 20, 1924, p. 299.
10. Fite, *Peek*, p. 93.
11. Smith W. Brookhart, "The Plight of the Farmer," *The Nation 122*, No. 3170 (April 7, 1926): 367-369; Sioux City *Union Advocate and Open Forum*, July 1, 1926.
12. Alex Moir to Frank O. Lowden, June 9, 1926, Frank Lowden Papers, University of Chicago Library, Chicago, Series III, Box 79, Folder 7; Charles H. Thomas to Lowden, June 22, 1926, Lowden Papers, Series III, Box 79, Folder 10; George Breitenbach to Henry C. Wallace, March 26, 1924, Record Group 16, "Records of the Office of the Secretary of Agriculture," General Correspondence, 1924, S. 2012 Iowa; George M. Titus to Andrew Mellon, June 11, 1926, Record Group 56, "General Records of the Department of the Treasury," Box 124.
13. LeRoy Rader to Lowden, August 13, 1926, Lowden Papers, Series III, Box 79, Folder 9; Harvey Ingham to Lowden, November 30, 1926, Lowden Papers, Series I, Box 24, Folder 1.
14. Frank Lund to Lowden, February 28, 1927, Lowden Papers, Series III, Box 79, Folder 5; Lowden to Lund, March 5, 1927, Ibid.
15. Lund to Lowden, April 15, 1927, Lowden Papers, Series III, Box 79, Folder 5.
16. H. O. Weaver to Lowden, March 4, 1927, Lowden Papers, Series III, Box 80, Folder 1; M. J. Tobin to Weaver, May 9, 1927, Lowden Papers, Series III, Box 79, Folder 10.
17. *Register*, April 11, 1927.
18. John D. Denison to Brookhart, April 13, 1927, Lowden Papers, Series III, Box 79, Folder 5.
19. Ingham to Lowden, June 15, 1927, Lowden Papers, Series III, Box 66, Folder 13; Edward P. Heizer to Clarence F. Buck, July 25, 1927, Lowden Papers, Series III, Box 79, Folder 3; See E. A. Burgess to H. O. Weaver, July 9, 1927, Lowden Papers, Series III, Box 78, Folder 6.
20. *Register*, August 3, 1927.
21. *New York Times*, December 3, 1926.
22. *New York Times*, December 3, 1927.
23. *New York Times*, February 4, 1927.
24. Iowa General Assembly, Senate, *Journal of the Senate*, 42nd General Assembly, March 31, 1927, p. 1110.

25. "Speech of Senator-Elect Smith W. Brookhart, Before the Open Forum at Baltimore, January 30, 1927," FBY Collection.
26. Iowa, *Journal of the Senate*, March 31, 1927, p. 1107; *Des Moines Tribune-Capital*, May 25, 1927.
27. Interview, Violet Brookhart Gunn, August 24, 1981.
28. Stewart H. M. Lund to author, June 29, 1981; Martha Mumma Keyes to author, May 16, 1990; Interview, Violet Brookhart Gunn, August 24, 1981.
29. Interview, Smith W. Brookhart, Jr., July 5, 1981; Martha Mumma Keyes to author, May 16, 1990; Interview, Violet Brookhart Gunn, August 24, 1981.
30. Interview, Smith W. Brookhart, Jr., July 5, 1981.
31. Jennie Brookhart to Smith W. Brookhart, Jr., April 24, 1925, Charles E. Brookhart Collection; Herbert Plummer, "A Washington Daybook," June 13, 1931.
32. Interview, Violet Brookhart Gunn, August 24, 1981; Jennie to Smith W. Brookhart, Jr., October 16, 1924; October 26, 1924; November 14, 1924, Charles E. Brookhart Collection.
33. *Journal*, August 9, 1927; August 3, 1927.
34. *New York Times*, August 15, 1927; August 18, 1927.
35. *Journal*, August 3, 1927.
36. *Register*, October 2, 1927; October 5, 1927; October 9, 1927.
37. Interview, Edith Brookhart Millard, January 23, 1981; April 17, 1981; Interview, Florence Brookhart Yount, July 7, 1981.
38. *Journal*, May 25, 1928; June 14, 1928.
39. Interview, Edith Brookhart Millard, April 17, 1981.
40. *New York Times*, September 15, 1927.
41. *New York Times*, October 27, 1927.
42. *New York Times*, November 21, 1927. Brookhart issued the statement in the name of Borah, Norris, Nye, Frazier, McMaster, and himself.
43. *Register*, November 28, 1927.
44. *New York Times*, November 12, 1927.
45. Ibid.
46. *Register*, November 28, 1927.
47. LeRoy Ashby, *The Spearless Leader, Senator Borah and the Progressive Movement in the 1920's* (Urbana: University of Illinois Press, 1972), p. 223; Richard Lowitt, *George W. Norris, The Persistence of a Progressive 1913-1933* (Urbana: University of Illinois Press, 1971), pp. 398-415.
48. George Norris to John F. Cordeal, January 9, 1929, George Norris Papers, Library of Congress, Box 4.
49. *New York Times*, November 3, 1927.
50. *Homestead*, December 8, 1927.
51. *New York Times*, December 4, 1927; December 7, 1927.
52. *New York Times*, December 7, 1927.
53. *Congressional Record*, 70 Cong., 1 Sess., p. 1246.
54. Fite, *Peek*, pp. 190ff.
55. *Congressional Record*, 70 Cong., 1 Sess., pp. 5821-5826.
56. Ibid., p. 6274.
57. Ibid., p. 6278.
58. Ibid.
59. Ibid., p. 6283; Fite, *Peek*, p. 192.
60. *New York Times*, April 16, 1928; *Congressional Record*, 70 Cong., 1 Sess., pp. 6170; Peek to Hearst, April 16, 1928, Lowden Papers, Series III, Box 67, Folder 4.
61. Hanford MacNider to C. H. McNider, April 13, 1928, MacNider Papers, Box 63;

McNider to MacNider, April 16, 1928, Ibid.

62. *Register*, September 12, 1928.

63. Fite, *Peek*, p. 193.

64. Alfred Lief, *Democracy's Norris, the Biography of a Lonely Crusade* (New York: Stackpole Sons, 1939), pp. 309ff; *Register*, September 21, 1928.

65. Lief, *Norris*, p. 310. The evidence for these events comes from Brookhart's speech before the Farmers' Union as reported in the *Register* on September 21. Lief gives more details about the events but it is difficult to tell exactly what his source is. His book uses general footnotes for an entire chapter. The footnotes for Chapter XIII, in which he tells about this episode, include a letter from Brookhart to Lief. It is not unreasonable to assume that Brookhart told Lief the details of the meeting in that letter.

66. Herman Steen to Donald Murphy, March 28, 1928, Lowden Papers, Series III, Box 79, Folder 7; M. J. Tobin to Andrew Mellon, May 18, 1928, Record Group 82, "Records of the Federal Reserve System, " Box 262. Tobin wrote a similar letter to Charles D. Hillis at the Republican National Committee, May 18, 1928, Lowden Papers, Series III, Box 79, Folder 10; Akerson to Pierce, March 10, 1928, Herbert C. Hoover Papers, Campaign and Transition, Box 12, Pierce; Robert P. Howard, *James R. Howard and the Farm Bureau* (Ames: Iowa State University Press, 1983), p. 213.

67. Roy V. Peel and Thomas C. Donnelly, *The 1928 Campaign, An Analysis* (New York: New York University Book Store, 1931), p. 13.

68. *Register*, March 8, 1928.

69. Peel and Donnelly, *1928 Campaign*, p. 18. Hoover received 837 out of a total of 1089 votes. (Burner, *Herbert Hoover*, p. 200.); Edgar Rickard Diary, June 10, 1928, Herbert Hoover Presidential Library.

70. *Register*, May 27, 1928.

71. MacNider to McNider, August 10, 1926, MacNider Papers, McNider, C.H.; *Register*, May 27, 1928.

72. Fite, *Peek*, p. 193. According to the Register the veto message was written by Ogden Mills. (*Register*, September 30, 1928.)

73. *Register*, May 24, 1928; *Congressional Record*, 70 Cong., 1 Sess., pp. 9875–9876.

74. Weaver to Buck, May 26, 1928, Lowden Papers, Series III, Box 80, Folder 1.

75. *Iowa Official Register, 1929–1930* (Des Moines: Iowa State Printer, 1929), pp. 254–264. The agricultural plank is found on pp. 259–260.

76. Ingham to Lowden, July 2, 1928, Lowden Papers, Series I, Box 23, Folder 10; E. N. Hopkins to Hoover, July 17, 1928, Herbert C. Hoover Papers, Campaign and Transition, 1928–1929, General Correspondence Hop-Ht, Box 36.

77. *Register*, July 17, 1928. See also Fite, *Peek*, p. 207.

78. *Des Moines Tribune and Capital*, June 29, 1928; Frank Moorhead to Akerson, July 29, 1928, George Akerson Papers, Herbert Hoover Presidential Library, Campaign and Transition, Moorhead, Frank G.

79. *Iowa Official Register, 1929–1930* (Des Moines: Iowa State Printer, 1929), pp. 269–277. The agricultural plank is found on pp. 271–272; See also Fite, *Peek*, p. 207; *Des Moines Tribune and Capital*, June 29, 1928; *Register*, June 29, 1928.

80. *Homestead*, July 12, 1928.

81. *Iowa Union Farmer*, July 4, 1928; *Register*, July 17, 1928.

82. *Register*, July 18, 1928; *Chicago Tribune*, July 15, 1928.

83. *Register*, July 19, 1928; *Iowa Official Register, 1929–1930* (Des Moines: Iowa State Printer, 1929), p. 267.

84. *Register*, July 19, 1928. Emphasis added.

85. *Homestead*, July 26, 1928; *Wallaces' Farmer*, July 20, 1928; *Iowa Union Farmer*, July

20, 1928.
86. *New York Times*, August 2, 1928; *Journal*, August 6, 1928.
87. *Mapleton Press*, August 9, 1928; *Journal*, August 7, 1928.
88. *Mapleton Press*, August 23, 1928.
89. *Mapleton Press*, September 20, 1928.
90. *Register*, September 25, 1928; September 13, 1928; *Journal*, September 21, 1928.
91. *Register*, September 21, 1928; *Wallaces' Farmer*, September 28, 1928.
92. *Register*, September 28, 1928.
93. *Wallaces' Farmer*, September 28, 1928; *Journal*, September 21, 1928; *Register*, September 21, 1928; *Wallaces' Farmer*, September 28, 1928. By November Reno's lament had turned to invective. Speaking in Ottumwa he called Brookhart a "liar, traitor, doublecrosser and without decent regard for the proprieties of life." (*Register*, November 5, 1928.)
94. *New York Times*, September 22, 1928.
95. *Register*, September 19, 1929; the *Iowa Union Farmer*, September 26, 1929.
96. Borah to Brookhart, July 18, 1928, William E. Borah Papers, Library of Congress, Box 260; Brookhart to Borah, July 31, 1928, Ibid; *Register*, July 31, 1928.
97. *Register*, August 13, 1928.
98. Ibid.
99. *Register*, August 22, 1928; *Cedar Rapids Gazette*, August 21, 1928.
100. *The New Day, Campaign Speeches of Herbert Hoover 1928*, (Stanford: Stanford University Press, 1928), p. 52.
101. Ibid., p. 53.
102. *Cedar Rapids Gazette*, August 22, 1928; August 23, 1928.
103. *Cedar Rapids Gazette*, August 24, 1928.
104. *New York Times*, August 27, 1928. "Hoover and the Farm Problem, Speech by Senator Smith W. Brookhart Delivered at Crown Point, Indiana, on August 26, 1928," (Chicago, Illinois: Republican National Committee, 1928).
105. "Hoover and the Farm Problem, p. 6.
106. *Register*, September 12, 1928.
107. *Journal*, August 28, 1928; August 31, 1928; *New York Times*, September 4, 1928.
108. *New York Times*, September 6, 1928.
109. *Register*, September 23, 1928; September 26, 1928; *Manning Monitor*, September 27, 1928; *Fort Dodge Messenger and Chronicle*, September 27, 1928.
110. Newspaper clipping, n.p., n.d., in Calvin Coolidge Papers, Reel 107; Newspaper clipping, n.p., n.d. in Black Scrapbook, FBY Papers, p. 161.
111. *Register*, October 18, 1928; September 22, 1928; *Manning Monitor*, September 27, 1928.
112. *Register*, September 22, 1928.
113. *Register*, September 29, 1928; *Fort Dodge Messenger and Chronicle*, September 26, 1928; *Register*, September 29, 1928; September 21, 1928.
114. *New York Times*, September 29, 1928; July 1, 1928; September 29, 1928. Hull was quoted as saying: "Secretary Hoover, I am sure, was in favor of giving the McNary-Haugen bill a chance and I gained the impression that he indicated to the President it should be given a trial, because he (Hoover) was anxious to help agriculture and this seemed to be the only opportunity. Senator Brookhart is substantially correct in his statement." There is nothing to indicate that Hoover's position in July was any different than it had been in May when he talked to Brookhart. But he may well have been as vague with Hull as he had been with Brookhart.
115. *Register*, September 30, 1928; Edwin H. Hopkins to Hoover, August 3, 1928, Herbert C. Hoover Papers, Campaign and Transition, General Correspondence; Ibid., September 30, 1928.

116. Peek to Hugh Johnson, October 4, 1928, Peek Papers, Joint Collection University of Missouri Western Historical Manuscript Collection-Columbia & State Historical Society of Missouri Manuscripts, File 244. A similar sentiment was expressed by Henry A. Wallace in a letter to Chester Davis at Republican Headquarters. (Wallace to Davis, October 2, 1927, Peek Papers, File 244.) On September 21 Herman Steen wrote L. W. Ainsworth, the Iowa Secretary of the Equality League to ask for a report of his activities to date and to submit a projected list of estimated expenses. (Steen to Ainsworth, September 21, 1928, Peek Papers, File 242.) Similar organizations also existed in Indiana, Minnesota, Missouri, Illinois, and Nebraska. Moreover, in Ohio, Wisconsin, North Dakota, South Dakota, and Montana organizational work was beginning. (Steen to Peek, September 21, 1928, Peek Papers, File 242.) Steen, however, was not very hopeful about Smith's chances in Iowa. Although Hoover had less support than Coolidge did four years before, to carry the state Smith would have to "overcome very deep-rooted religious and temperance views." Steen thought that this would be "impossible" and that the state would be "surely Republican." (Memorandum, "Iowa," c. September 20, 1928, Peek Papers, File 242.); *Register*, October 3, 1928.

117. *Des Moines Tribune-Capital*, October 11, 1928.

118. Myerly to Hoover, October 16, 1928, Herbert C. Hoover Papers, Campaign and Transition, General Correspondence, Box 50; Akerson to Pierce, October 17, 1928, Ibid.; Pierce to Akerson, October 18, 1928, Ibid.

119. *Iowa Union Farmer*, October 24, 1928.

120. *Register*, September 30, 1928.

121. *Register*, October 25, 1928; Lowitt, *George W. Norris*, pp. 410–414; *New York Times*, October 30, 1928. Brookhart said Norris had made only two mistakes in his career. One was his support of Al Smith. The other had been to vote for establishing the Federal Reserve Board, the "outstanding enemy of the farmer." Brookhart added, however, that he wished his record were as good. (*Register*, November 1, 1928.)

122. *New York Times*, October 27, 1928; *Register*, October 30, 1928; November 2, 1928; *Journal*, November 5, 1928; *Waterloo Evening Courier*, November 5, 1928.

123. *Iowa Official Register, 1929–1930* (Des Moines: Iowa State Printer, 1929) pp. 422f; *Register*, November 7, 1928; November 1, 1928. However, Brookhart did not convert every Iowan. Another writer in the same issue said that Brookhart was "too damn dumb to understand" that Peek had the best interest of farmers in mind; William S. Gilman to Hoover, June 12, 1930, Herbert C. Hoover Papers, President's Personal File, Gilman.

124. *Register*, November 11, 1928.

125. *New York Times*, December 28, 1928; David Burner, *Herbert Hoover, A Public Life*, (New York: Alfred A. Knopf, 1979), p. 208.

126. *Register*, January 23, 1929; January 9, 1929; Edgar Rickard Diary, January 6, 1929, Herbert Hoover Presidential Library.

127. *New York Times*, February 15, 1929; February 14, 1929; February 24, 1929.

128. *The Memoirs of Herbert Hoover, The Cabinet and the Presidency 1920–1933*, (New York: The Macmillan Company, 1052), 220. Hoover said of Hyde that he had "known no Secretary of Agriculture before or since who was his equal."; *Register*, March 3, 1929.

129. *Register*, February 5, 1929.

130. *Register*, March 17, 1929; April 7, 1929; March 24, 1929.

131. *New York Times*, March 12, 1929.

132. *New York Times*, March 15, 1929.

133. U. S. Congress, Senate, Committee on Agriculture and Forestry, *Hearings on S. 1*, 71st Cong., 1 Sess., March 25–26, 1929, p. 5.

134. Ibid., pp. 17–18.

135. Ibid., pp. 18–19.

136. Ibid.
137. *Register*, April 5, 1929.
138. *Register*, April 17, 1929.
139. *New York Times*, April 17, 1929; *Congressional Record*, 71 Cong., 1 Sess., p. 425-440.
140. *Congressional Record*, 71 Cong., 1 Sess., p. 428-436.
141. Ibid., pp. 435, 438.
142. *Register*, April 25, 1929; April 17, 1929; April 26, 1929.
143. *Congressional Record*, 71 Cong., 1 Sess., p. 3600.
144. Ellis W. Hawley, "Herbert Hoover, the Commerce Secretariat, and the Vision of an 'Associative State,' 1921-1928," *Journal of American History LXI* (1974): 116-140; Joan Hoff Wilson, *Herbert Hoover, Forgotten Progressive* (Boston: Little, Brown and Company, 1975), p. 105.
145. George H. Nash, *The Life of Herbert Hoover, The Humanitarian 1914-1917*, (New York: W. W. Norton and Company, 1988), p. 117.

13. THE POPULIST BECOMES A DEMOCRAT

1. Brookhart to Harlan, January 10, 1930, Edgar R. Harlan Correspondence, State Historical Society of Iowa, Des Moines, File 41C, Part 7, Group 13. Harlan to Brookhart, January 23, 1930, Harlan Correspondence, File 36D, Part 7, Group 10.

2. *Register*, November 29, 1927; U.S., Congress, Senate, Committee on Agriculture and Forestry, *Hearings on S. 1*, 71st Cong., 1st Sess., March 25, 1929, p. 9.

3. See Rowland Berthoff, "Independence and Enterprise: Small Business in the American Dream," in *Small Business In American Life*, ed. Stuart W. Bruchey (New York: Columbia University Press, 1980), pp. 28-48; Ruth L. Hoadley, "The Chain Store With Special Reference to Iowa," *Iowa Studies in Business No. IX* (Iowa City, Iowa: College of Commerce, University of Iowa, August, 1930), p. 16.

4. Iowa City *Press Citizen*, March 27, 1922; Smith W. Brookhart, "The Retail Merchant and Community Development," *National Grocers Bulletin*, (Special Convention Edition, 1928): 53-54; Smith W. Brookhart, "The Chain Store Monopoly," Speech, Institute of Public Affairs, University of Virginia, July 10, 1931. Manuscripts Department University of Virginia Library, Charlottesville; Smith W. Brookhart, "On Chain Stores," *The N.A.R.D. Journal, XLIX*, no. 1 (October 3, 1929): 36.

5. *Congressional Record*, 71 Cong., 3 Sess., pp. 3924-3926. The Des Moines example is on page 3926. Brookhart spoke on the chain store issue before the following groups: National Convention of Retail Grocers, National Association of Retail Druggists, Retail Meat Dealers Association.

6. *Congressional Record*, 70 Cong., 1 Sess., pp. 7857, 8522. The report that Brookhart asked for was issued in seven parts between December 1931 and June 1932. The were issued by the United States Senate, 72 Cong., 1 Sess., as: S. Doc. 12, "Chain Stores: Cooperative Grocery Chains"; S. Doc. 29, "Chain Stores: Wholesale Business of Retail Chains"; S. Doc. 30, "Sources of Chain-store Merchandise"; S. Doc. 31, "Chain Stores: Scope of Chain-store Inquiry"; S. Doc. 51, "Chain Stores: Chain-store Leaders and Loss Leaders"; S. Doc. 82, "Chain Stores: Cooperative Drug and Hardware Chains"; S. Doc. 100, "Chain Stores: Growth and Development of Chain Stores."

Brookhart had asked the FTC to discover whether the chain store system violated anti-trust laws and whether legislation was needed to correct any possible abuses by the chain store system. He had also asked the FTC to report (a) the extent to which the chain store system was a monopoly, (b) evidences of unfair practices by the chains, (c) the advantages and disadvantages of the chain store system, and (d) how much the increase in the number of chains was based on actual savings. He had also wanted legislative recommendations based on this information.

The FTC used a nationwide survey to compile data on chain stores but the survey only addressed sections (c) and (d) and ignored the other information that Brookhart's resolution requested. Thus not only did the reports come too late to help Brookhart they did not answer his fundamental question: what effect did the chains have on the survival of small independent businesses.

7. *The Congressional Digest*, 9, nos 8-9, (August-September, 1930): 202; *Congressional Record*, 71 Cong., 3 Sess., p. 3925; "Senator Brookhart of Iowa for Price Fixing," *The Home Owned Store* (May, 1932): 3, 6.

8. *Congressional Record*, 70 Cong., 1 Sess., pp. 554-545. This first bill was S. 1667. For subsequent bills see: S. 1003, *Congressional Record*, 71 Cong., 1 Sess., pp. 927-928; S. 3770, *Congressional Record*, 72 Cong., 1 Sess., pp. 4493-4502; U.S., Congress, Senate, Committee on Interstate Commerce, *Hearings On S. 1667*, 70th Cong., 1st Sess., February 27, 1928, pp. 4-5.

9. *Congressional Record*, 71 Cong., 1 Sess., pp. 927-928; Smith W. Brookhart, speech, "Why I Am Interested in the Movies," Eleventh Annual Convention of The Motion Picture Theatre Owners of Michigan, October 8, 1930, in Smith Wildman Brookhart Papers, Iowa State Department of History and Archives, Des Moines; See also *The Allied Exhibitor*, 2 no. 4 (October 1930): pp. 3-5; *Greater Amusements*, 32, no. 19 (October 11, 1930): p. 8.

10. *Congressional Record*, 71 Cong., 1 Sess., p. 927.

11. *Register*, November 12, 1928; Frank J. Rembusch to Brookhart, March 19, 1928, Thomas Walsh Papers, Library of Congress, Box 189; P. S. Harrison to Brookhart, June 8, 1929. Published in *Harrison's Reports*, Vol. XI, No. 28, July 13, 1929. In Walsh Papers, ibid.

12. *Congressional Record*, 72 Cong., 1 Sess., p. 4500; Ibid., p. 4493; Brookhart seemed to stop just short of calling for prior censorship. He would rather have the community make the decision as to whether a movie would be shown. At about the same time he discussed the same question as it related to printed matter. Speaking about the importation of books alleged to be obscene he said that the legislature ought to define what was obscene and then have the courts try cases based on the legal definition. He was opposed to having the courts, or clerks in the same office, make the decision about obscenity. (See *Congressional Record*, 71 Cong., 1 Sess., pp. 4455-4456; 71 Cong., 2 Sess., p. 5248.); *Congressional Record*, 72 Cong., 1 Sess., p. 4494.

13. *Congressional Record*, 72 Cong., 1 Sess., pp. 4500-4501; pp. 4493-4502; 14838; 72 Cong., 2 Sess., pp. 174-175.

14. Interview, Edith Brookhart Millard, January 23, 1981.

15. Beverly J. Cox and Denna Jones Anderson, *Miguel Covarrubias Caricatures*, (Washington: Smithsonian Institution Press, 1985), pp. 84-85; Interview, Smith W. Brookhart, Jr., July 3, 1981.

16. Weaver, *Call*, p. 70; 73; 132.

17. *Press*, January 18, 1912; April 11, 1912; February 22, 1912.

18. *Congressional Record*, 71 Cong., 2 Sess., p. 3505.

19. *Congressional Record*, 71 Cong., 2 Sess., p. 3647; 6227; He opposed the World Court for the same reasons. In a speech delivered in 1929 he asked, ". . . who shall make the laws for this World Court? There is no legislative branch of this super-government for the making of laws. It will of its own volition make its own laws. This is a contradiction of the fundamental principles of Americanism." (Speech, "The World Court," Brookhart Papers, Des Moines.)

20. Smith W. Brookhart, "Has the Federal Reserve Act Failed?" *Plain Talk*, V, no. 1 (July, 1929): 1; *Congressional Record*, 71 Cong., 2 Sess., pp. 595-598.

21. *Congressional Record*, 70 Cong., 1 Sess., p. 2502; Andrew Mellon to Peter Norbeck,

March 15, 1928, Record Group 56, "Records of the Department of the Treasury," Office of the General Counsel, Non-Tax Legislative History File; *Congressional Record*, 71 Cong., 2 Sess., p. 1093; Andrew Mellon to Peter Norbeck, January 22, 1930, Record Group 56, "Records of the Department of the Treasury," Office of the General Counsel, Non-Tax Legislative History File; *New York Times*, February 10, 1930; Brookhart submitted the bill again and for a third time the Treasury Department opposed the bill and it died. (*Congressional Record*, 72 Cong., 1 Sess., p. 190. Secretary of the Treasury to Peter Norbeck, January 26, 1932, Record Group 56, "Records of the Department of the Treasury," Office of the General Counsel, Non-Tax Legislative History File.)

22. *New York Times*, December 11, 1931; *Congressional Record*, 72 Cong., 1 Sess., p. 10846.

23. *Congressional Record*, 72 Cong., 1 Sess., p. 10846; Smith W. Brookhart, "Let's Abandon the Gold Standard," *The Forum*, 88 (July, 1932): 10-12. See also *Congressional Record*, 72 Cong., 1 Sess., pp. 2629-2630.

24. *Des Moines Tribune*, June 16, 1930; Chautauqua Collection, University of Iowa Libraries, Iowa City, Box 34; *New Hampton Gazette*, June 27, 1930.

25. *Rock Valley Bee*, June 13, 1930. Similar articles appeared in the *Emmetsburg Democrat*, June 26, 1930, and the *Sheldon Sun*, June 11, 1930.

26. *Register*, July 15, 1930. In the event of a vote Brookhart had arranged a "pair." By this practice a senator who intended to vote the opposite of Brookhart would agree not to vote, thus the senator's absence would not affect the outcome of a vote.

27. *Register*, July 12, 1930; July 16, 1930.

28. George H. Haynes, *The Senate of the United States, Its History and Practice*, (Boston: Houghton Mifflin Company, 1938), pp. 346-363. In 1914 Iowa's Senator William S. Kenyon had said that "any Senators 'who are engaged in campaigns' ought to be excused [from attendance.]" (Ibid., p. 350.)

29. *Des Moines Tribune*, June 16, 1930; Smith W. Brookhart, Jr. to Ray S. Johnston, July 1, 1960; July 11, 1960, Ray S. Johnston Papers; *Congressional Record*, 70 Cong., 2 Sess., pp. 2058-2059.

30. *Congressional Record*, 70 Cong., 2 Sess., p. 2058; See also ibid., 71 Cong., 1 Sess., pp. 5166-5168; and ibid., 71 Cong., 2 Sess., pp. 6617-6622; *New York Times*, January 1, 1930.

31. *New York Times*, November 6, 1929; See for example, *Time*, XIV, no. 15 (October 7, 1929): 16-17; *Time*, XIV, no. 21 (November 18, 1929): 13-14; *The Nation*, 129, no. 3360 (November 27, 1929): 626; "For a Nobler Washington," *The Commonweal*, no. 23 (October 9, 1929): 573.

32. *Congressional Record*, 71 Cong., 2 Sess., pp. 2681-2682.

33. *New York Times*, January 18, 1930; *Cleveland Plain Dealer*, February 7, 1930; February 8, 1930.

34. *New York Times*, March 20, 1930; *New York Herald Tribune*, March 20, 1930; *New York Times*, March 30, 1930.

35. Edith Brookhart to Ned Brookhart, March 17, 1931, Charles E. Brookhart Collection.

36. Jennie to Ned Brookhart, April 6, 1931, ibid.; Jennie to Ned Brookhart, March 27, 1931, ibid.; *New York Times*, March 27, 28, 30, 31, 1931, April 16, 1931; *Register*, March 28, 1931; Roy T. Davis to Secretary of State, April 2, 1931, April 8, 1931, Record Group 59, "Records of the Department of State," State Decimal File 1930-1939, Box 5306½, Box 5308½.

37. *New York Times*, April 17, 1931; Donald Day, *Will Rogers, A Biography*, (New York: McKay Company, Inc., 1962), pp. 268-269.

38. *Register*, March 13, 1932.

39. *Congressional Record*, 71 Cong., 2 Sess., p. 2683.

40. Allen to Forrest Allen, November 4, 1929, A. F. Allen Papers, University of Iowa Libraries, Box 2.

41. I. A. Nichols, *Forty Years of Rural Journalism in Iowa* (Fort Dodge, Iowa: Messenger Press, 1938), p. 123; Interview, Henry F. Ashurst, Ray S. Johnston Papers.

42. Louis H. Cook, "Brookhart, Insurgent," *North American Review*, 231 (February, 1931): 179-180, 183-184.

43. W. M. Price to Turner, June 13, 1930, Dan Turner Papers, State Historical Society of Iowa, Des Moines, Box 4, File 14; Cole to Hoover, July 17, 1930, Herbert Hoover Presidential Library, President's Personal File, Cole.

44. Gilman to Walter Newton, February 13, 1931, Herbert Hoover Presidential Library, Presidential Papers, State File, Iowa, Post Office; John Horswell to Wallace, March 29, 1931, Henry A. Wallace Papers, University of Iowa Libraries, Reel 6, Frames 471-472.

45. Harvey Ingham to Frank Lowden, August 29, 1931, Lowden Papers, Series 1, Box 23, Folder 9; *Register*, April 26, 1931.

46. Florence Brookhart to Ned Brookhart, [Spring] 1931, Charles E. Brookhart Collection; Jennie to Ned Brookhart, June 14, 1931, Charles E. Brookhart Collection; Interview, Smith W. Brookhart, Jr., July 3, 1981.

47. *Register*, June 10, 1931.

48. *Register*, September 3, 1931.

49. *Register*, August 16, 1931.

50. The straw poll was not a poll in the modern sense. The paper distributed ballots and asked its readers to return them; *Register*, February 14, 1932; February 21, 1932; also see *Register*, January 31, 1932; February 7, 1932.

51. *Register*, March 6, 1932; Jennie to Ned, February 19, 1932; March 18, 1932, Charles E. Brookhart Collection.

52. *Register*, June 7, 1931; July 14, 1931; January 30, 1932.

53. *Register*, January 10, 1932; L. E. Jondro to Wallace, February 4, 1932, Henry A. Wallace Papers, Reel 12, Frame 378; Wallace to Charles Roos, February 4, 1932, ibid., Frame 379.

54. *Register*, May 8, 1932; June 9, 1932; The source of Eickelberg's vote total is the *Register*, June 9. But the paper only reported the total based on 2,420 out of 2,435 precincts. Eickelberg's vote total is not included in the official election returns published in the *Iowa Official Register*.

55. *Register*, May 8, 1932; April 19, 1932; *Iowa Official Register, 1933-1934*, (Des Moines: The State of Iowa, 1933), pp. 146-147.

56. *Register*, April 3, 1932; May 8, 1932; *Iowa Official Register, 1933-1934*, Ibid.

57. *Register*, June 9, 1932. Cook's vote is based on the same partial totals as Eickelberg's. Like him, Cook does not appear in the *Iowa Official Register*; *Atlantic News-Telegraph*, October 27, 1931; *Register*, October 28, 1931.

58. George Frederic Nieberg, "All in the Congressional Family," *The Atlantic Monthly*, 148 (October, 1931): 514-523. Portions of the article were reprinted in the *Register*, September 27, 1931; See for example, *Davenport Democrat*, October 28, 1931.

59. *Register*, March 6, 1932; April 10, 1932; April 13, 1932; Bob Birkby and Janice Nahra Friedel, "Henry, Himself," *The Palimpsest*, 64, no. 5 (September/October, 1983): 150-169.

60. A. N. Ahlgren to Hanford MacNider, June 23, 1932, MacNider Papers, Herbert Hoover Presidential Library, Canada, Minister to file; *Register*, March 20, 1932; March 22, 1932.

61. *Register*, April 13, 1932; George Norris to Henry Field, April 11, 1932, George Norris Papers, Library of Congress, Box 23; Norris to Field, April 16, 1932, ibid.

62. Field to Norris, April 13, 1932, ibid.

63. *Register*, April 18, 1932.

64. *Register*, March 22, 1932; As of April 10 there were six Republican challengers to Brookhart: Cook, Cosson, Field, Haynes, Eickelberg, and Vern Haig. There were six Democrats vying for the nomination of their party for the senate: Louis Murphy of Dubuque; Fred Hagemann, Waverly; former Senator Dan Steck; Nelson G. Kraschel, Harlan; C. F. Lytle, Sioux City; and John W. Ficken, State Center. (*Register*, April 10, 1932.)
65. *Journal*, May 3, 1932.
66. Ibid.
67. Ibid. See also *Congressional Record*, 72 Cong., 1 Sess., pp. 6786–6787; *Register*, July 11, 1931; September 20, 1931; *Journal*, May 3, 1932.
68. *Journal*, May 3, 1932; *Congressional Record*, 72 Cong., 1 Sess., pp. 13244–13227.
69. *Journal*, May 3, 1932; *Congressional Record*, 72 Cong., 1 Sess., pp. 6786–6787.
70. *Register*, May 4, 1932.
71. Louis H. Cook, "The Man Who Beat Brookhart," *The Saturday Evening Post*, 205, no. 4 (July 23, 1932): 72.
72. "Nepotism," *Time*, XIX, no. 22 (May 30, 1932): 9–10.
73. *Register*, May 4, 1932; May 10, 1932; Washington editor Dave Elder once asked Brookhart why he had hired his family. Brookhart told him that "they worked a lot harder and for a lot less money than any other help he could hire around the place." Elder continued: "Seeing how modestly he lived as a Senator, and knowing his ideas of thrift, I didn't doubt it for a moment." (Dave Elder to author, November 6, 1977.)
74. *Register*, May 15, 1932.
75. *Register*, May 7, 1932.
76. "Playing Brookhart Out With a Steam Calliope," *The Literary Digest*, 113, no. 12 (June 18, 1932): 5; *Register*, May 12, 1932; May 15, 1932.
77. *Register*, May 15, 1932.
78. *Register*, May 15, 1932; May 22, 1932.
79. *Register*, May 13, 1932; May 7, 1932.
80. *Register*, May 25, 1932; May 27, 1932; June 1, 1932.
81. *Register*, May 29, 1932; *Waterloo Courier*, May 29, 1932; *Register*, May 29, 1932; June 2, 1932; Bryon Allen to Norris, May 29, 1932; Norris to Allen, May 30, 1932, Norris Papers, Library of Congress, Box 23.
82. Clifton wrote an analysis for each Congressional District. They were published in the *Register* over a period of ten days. 1st District, May 28, 1932; 2nd District, May 27, 1932; 3rd District, May 26, 1932; 4th District, May 25, 1932; 5th District, May 30, 1932; 6th District, May 31, 1932; 7th District, May 29, 1932; 8th District, June 2, 1932; 9th District, June 3, 1932; *Register*, June 5, 1932.
83. *New York Times*, June 6, 1932; *Register*, June 5, 1932.
84. Jennie to Ned Brookhart, June 7, 1932, Charles E. Brookhart Collection; *Iowa Official Register, 1933–1934*, (Des Moines: The State of Iowa, 1933), pp. 146–147. The percentages are based on the figures in the IOR and thus do not include the votes for Cook and Eickelberg. Their totals were not large enough, however, to alter the figures significantly; *Register*, June 9, 1932.
85. *Journal*, June 8, 1932; *Register*, June 9, 1932.
86. James H. MacLafferty Diary, June 7, 1932, James H. MacLafferty Papers, Herbert Hoover Presidential Library; Lowden to Harvey Ingham, June 10, 1932, Lowden Papers, Series I, Box 23, Folder 9; E. N. Hopkins to Hoover, June 8, 1932, Herbert Hoover Presidential Library, Presidential Subject File, Republican National Committee, Iowa; R. L. Whelan to Brookhart, June 24, 1932, FBY Collection.
87. See for example: "Playing Brookhart Out With a Steam Calliope," *Literary Digest*; Louis H. Cook, "The Man Who Beat Brookhart," *Saturday Evening Post*, 205 July 23, 1934:

72; Clifton W. Gilbert, "And so do his Cousins and his Aunts," *Collier's*, 90, no. 3 (July 16, 1932): 19; Clifton W. Gilbert, "The Laugh Cure," *Collier's*, 90, no. 6 (August 6, 1932): 21.

88. Roland A. White, *Milo Reno, Farmers Union Pioneer, The Story of A Man and A Movement*, (Iowa City: The Iowa Farmers Union, 1941), p. 85; Congressman H. R. Gross to author, July 25, 1981.

89. Gilbert, *The Laugh Cure*, ibid.; "Chicken Stew," *Time*, XIX, no. 25 (June 20, 1932): 12.

90. *Congressional Record*, 72 Cong., 1 Sess., pp. 12535-12536.

91. *New York Times*, May 13, 1931; May 14, 1931.

92. In March Hoover believed that he would have Brookhart's support. James MacLafferty recorded a conversation with Hoover on March 11. Hoover told him that within a week he would have a "public statement from Brookhart to the effect that he [would] support" Hoover. MacLafferty asked Hoover if he had talked with Brookhart and Hoover replied that he had. MacLafferty wrote in his diary that he did not ask for any further information about Hoover's claim. He knew that Hoover had no love for Brookhart but that Hoover, "simply reaffirmed . . . the necessity for using every possible form of assistance in winning an election." (James H. MacLafferty Diary, March 11, 1932.) This is a curious episode because it does not seem likely that Brookhart would have given any indication of support to Hoover. Furthermore, there is no evidence that the two met. If true, however, it does indicate a political pragmatism usually thought to be absent in both men; Kirk H. Porter and Donald Bruce Johnson, *National Party Platforms, 1840-1956* (Urbana, The University of Illinois Press, 1956), pp. 342-343; *Congressional Record*, 72 Cong., 1 Sess., p. 13694.

93. Porter and Johnson, *National Party Platforms*, p. 343; Smith W. Brookhart, "Cooperative Economics or Illiterate Facts vs. Intellectual Fiction," Unpublished Manuscript, c. 1939, p. 54. The author has a copy of the manuscript.

94. Ibid.

95. For Hull's account of the drafting of the platform see *The Memoirs of Cordell Hull*, 2 vols. (New York: The MacMillan Company, 1948), pp. 150-154. Hull, however, does not mention the Brookhart episode. Hull agreed with Brookhart that production control was a bad policy. Such a program, Hull believed, would cut the United States off from the world economy. (*Memoirs*, p. 248.); See also Harold B. Hinton, *Cordell Hull, A Biography* (Garden City, New York: Doubleday, Doran & Company, Inc. 1942), pp. 287-288; U. S., Congress, Senate, Committee on Agriculture and Forestry, *Hearing on Substitute Legislation for the Invalidated Agricultural Adjustment Act*, 74th Cong., 2nd Sess., January 14, 1936, pp. 63-64; Brookhart, "Cooperative Economics," pp. 54-57.

96. Porter and Johnson, *National Party Platforms*, pp. 331, 333.

97. *New York Times*, August 22, 1929.

98. *New York Times*, March 15, 1931. In the Democratic National Committee Papers there is a note written on April 12, 1932, that Brookhart had said he "might mention Mr. Roosevelt's name in speech in the Senate in a few days. Doesn't wish to make statement regarding candidacy." (Democratic National Committee Papers, April 12, 1932, Franklin Delano Roosevelt Presidential Library, Hyde Park, New York, Correspondence 1928-1933, Box 208.); *New York Times*, August 21, 1932; *Register*, September 15, 1932.

99. Jennie to Ned Brookhart, July 25, 1932, Charles E. Brookhart Collection.

100. *New York Times*, June 8, 1932; *Register*, June 8, 1932; Jennie to Ned Brookhart, July 25, 1932; August 12, 1932, Charles E. Brookhart Collection.

101. *Register*, September 14, 1832.

102. The standard work on the Farmers' Holiday Association is John L. Shover, *Cornbelt Rebellion, The Farmers' Holiday Association* (Urbana: The University of Illinois Press, 1965); *Sioux City Journal*, September 20, 1932; September 22, 1932.

103. *Sioux City Journal*, September 20, 1932; September 22, 1932.
104. Letter, n.d., FBY Collection.
105. *Register*, September 27, 1932; *Journal*, September 26, 1932; September 27, 1932.
106. *Journal*, September 26, 1932; September 27, 1932.
107. Ibid.
108. *Journal*, September 27, 1932.
109. Series of letters to Turner, October, 1932, Dan Turner Papers, Box 6, File 22; *Register*, October 16, 1932.
110. Jennie to Ned Brookhart, September 30, 1932, Charles E. Brookhart Collection.
111. *Journal*, September 27, 1932; *Waterloo Courier*, October 13, 1932.
112. *Journal*, October 22, 1932. The figures were: Field, 243; Brookhart, 118; Murphy, 116; *Journal*, November 5, 1932.
113. *Iowa Official Register, 1933-1934*, (Des Moines: The State of Iowa, 1933), pp. 250-251; Brookhart to Roosevelt, November 9, 1932, Democrat National Committee Papers, Franklin Delano Roosevelt Presidential Library, Correspondence, 1928-1933, Box 216.
114. Jennie to Ned, November 9, 1932, Charles E. Brookhart Collection.
115. *Journal*, November 14, 1932; Jennie to Ned Brookhart, November 28, 1932; December 28, 1932; Charles E. Brookhart Collection; *Register*, December 20, 1932.
116. *Register*, January 27, 1933. Smith W. Brookhart, Jr., joined Senator Murphy's staff for about a month to help him become established in the Senate. (Interview, Smith W. Brookhart, Jr., July 5, 1981.); *Congressional Record*, 72 Cong., 2 Sess., p. 5504.

14. THE REPUBLICAN NEW DEALER

1. *Register*, March 5, 1933.
2. Brookhart to Roosevelt, November 7, 1933, Franklin Delano Roosevelt Papers, Franklin Delano Roosevelt Presidential Library, Hyde Park, Official File 2A, Box 4; Brookhart to Roosevelt, August 28, 1934, Ibid., Official File 4191, Box 7.
3. Interview, Otha Wearin, June 17, 1981; Interview, Smith W. Brookhart, Jr., July 3, 1981; Congressman Claude Pepper to author, July 29, 1983.
4. John Brookhart to Ned Brookhart, [Christmas], 1932, Charles E. Brookhart Collection; *Journal*, September 27, 1932.
5. Panama Canal Zone *American*, January 15, 1933; *Register*, March 5, 1933; F. E. Lamb to Roosevelt, March 25, 1933, Roosevelt Papers, Official File 10A, Box 9.
6. Brookhart to Milo Reno, March 17, 1933, Milo Reno Papers, University of Iowa Libraries, Iowa City, Box 4, Item 694.
7. *Register*, April 26, 1933.
8. *New York Times*, May 28, 1933.
9. *Register*, May 30, 1933.
10. *Register*, May 28, 1933; Peek to Brookhart, May 29, 1933, Record Group 145, "Agricultural Stabilization and Conservation Service," Agricultural Adjustment Administration, National Archives, Washington, D.C., Smith Wildman Brookhart File; *Register*, April 3, 1934.
11. *Register*, May 30, 1933; April 3, 1934; Murphy to A. J. Gary, August 18, 1933, August 29, 1933, Roosevelt Papers, Official File 2971.
12. *Register*, June 4, 1933; July 30, 1933.
13. *Register*, June 11, 1933; Arthur W. Watwood to Roosevelt, June 9, 1933, Roosevelt Papers, Official File 2971.
14. Reno to Brookhart, May 29, 1933, Milo Reno Papers, University of Iowa Libraries, Box 5, Item 1366.

15. Peek to Brookhart, May 29, 1933, Record Group 145; Jennie to Ned Brookhart, July 30, 1933; August 22, 1933, Charles E. Brookhart Collection; John Brookhart to Ned Brookhart, December 17, 1933, Charles E. Brookhart Collection.
16. Jennie to Ned Brookhart, May 29, 1933; July 30, 1933, Charles E. Brookhart Collection; Owen L. Scott, article, October 19, 1933, n.n.
17. W. Irving Shuman to Walter J. Cummings, August 12, 1933, Roosevelt Papers, Official File 220A, Box 2; *New York Times*, November 18, 1933; November 19, 1933.
18. John Henry Hopkins to Brookhart, August 11, 1933, Franklin Delano Roosevelt Papers, Official File 220A, Box 2; Hopkins to Brookhart, August 23, 1933, ibid.
19. Brookhart to Hopkins, August 18, 1933; September 16, 1933, ibid.
20. Brookhart to Hopkins, August 18, 1933; August 30, 1933; September 22, 1933; ibid.; Hopkins to Brookhart, September 20, 1933, ibid.
21. For the full account of the Catholic position, see George Q. Flynn, *American Catholics & The Roosevelt Presidency, 1932-1936*, (Lexington, University of Kentucky Press, 1968), pp. 122-149.
22. Jennie to Ned Brookhart, October 26, 1933, Charles E. Brookhart Collection; Walsh sent Roosevelt two articles that he said reflected what he would have "written publicly" had he chosen to do so. (Walsh to Roosevelt, November 7, 1933, Roosevelt Papers, Official File 220. The articles are "Russia and Religion," *The Commonweal*, XIX, Number 2 [November 10, 1933]: 29-30. Wilfrid Parsons, SJ, "An Open Letter to M. Litvinov," *America*, L, No. 5 [November 4, 1933]: 107-108.); Edmund A. Walsh to Roosevelt, November 7, 1933, Roosevelt Papers, Official File 220.
23. Smith W. Brookhart, "On Russian Recognition," *Register*, November 8, 1933.
24. *Register*, November 18, 1933.
25. Jennie to Ned Brookhart, November 21, 1933, Charles E. Brookhart Collection; Norris to Roosevelt, n.d., Roosevelt Papers, Official File 2971. Murphy to Roosevelt, November 11, 1933, ibid.
26. Jennie to Ned Brookhart, November 21, 1933, Charles E. Brookhart Collection; Interview, Edith Brookhart Millard, April 17, 1981.
27. Brookhart to Joseph T. Robinson, March 7, 1934, Roosevelt Papers, Official File 220, Box 1.
28. Gilbert C. Fite, *George N. Peek and the Fight for Farm Parity*, (Norman: University of Oklahoma Press, 1954): 243-266.
29. Ibid., pp. 268-269.
30. Jennie to Ned Brookhart, February 5, 1934, Charles E. Brookhart Collection; *New York Times*, March 17, 1934.
31. *Des Moines Tribune*, April 5, 1934.
32. Ibid.
33. *Register*, April 3, 1934.
34. Ibid.
35. Ibid.
36. *Register*, April 22, 1934; Jennie to Ned Brookhart, June 23, 1934, Charles E. Brookhart Collection; Peek's logs show Brookhart talked with Peek either in person or by telephone nine times between April and December, 1934. George N. Peek Papers, Joint Collection University of Missouri Western Historical Manuscript Collection-Columbia & State Historical Society of Missouri Manuscripts, Files 391, 1914, 1918, 1920, 1975, 1979, 1982-1985, 1987, 1989.
37. Telephone conversation, Chester Davis and George Peek, September 11, 1934, Peek Papers, File 1918.
38. *Register*, September 15, 1934; October 1, 1934; Guy Hottel to J. Edgar Hoover, February 10, 1941, Smith W. Brookhart File, Federal Bureau of Investigation.

39. Cliff Millen, "On Warpath Again," *Des Moines Tribune*, n.d.; *Prescott (Arizona) Courier*, November 29, 1938.

40. *Journal*, January 9, 1935; Jennie to Ned Brookhart, January 22, 1935, Charles E. Brookhart Collection.

41. Florence Brookhart to Ned Brookhart, March 29, 1935, Charles E. Brookhart Collection.

42. Jennie to Ned Brookhart, January 9, 1934; May 21, 1933; November 26, 1934, Charles E. Brookhart Collection.

43. *Register*, February 10, 1935.

44. *Register*, January 19, 1935; *Prescott Courier*, November 29, 1938; Jennie to Ned Brookhart, January 22, 1935; John Brookhart to Ned Brookhart, February 5, 1935, Charles E. Brookhart Collection.

45. Jennie to Ned Brookhart, May 24, 1934; November 26, 1934, Charles E. Brookhart Collection.

46. Harry M. Daugherty and Thomas Dixon, *The Inside Story of the Harding Tragedy*, (New York: The Churchill Company, 1932), p. 214.

47. D. M. Ladd, "Memorandum for the Director," January 5, 1932, Brookhart File, Federal Bureau of Investigation.

48. *Journal*, April 23, 1936; *Daily Iowan*, April 22, 1936, April 23, 1936; *Iowa City Press-Citizen*, April 23, 1936; *Journal*, April 23, 1936.

49. Memo to J. Edgar Hoover, February 10, 1941; J. Edgar Hoover to L. M. C. Smith, Chief, Special Defense Unit, September 30, 1941; Hoover to Special Agent in Charge, December 8, 1941; Attorney General Francis Biddle to Hoover, July 16, 1943; Hoover to Special Agent in Charge, Baltimore, July 19, 1945; Smith W. Brookhart File, Federal Bureau of Investigation.

50. Roosevelt to Marvin H. McIntyre, March 23, 1936; Charles West to McIntyre, March 24, 1936; March 28, 1936, Roosevelt Papers, Official File 300, Box 18.

51. William H. Cumberland, *Wallace M. Short Iowa Rebel* (Ames: The Iowa State University Press, 1983), pp. 112-127; *Iowa Official Register, 1935-1936*, (The State of Iowa, 1935), pp. 324-329.

52. Circular letter from Howard Y. Williams, May 20, 1935, Howard Y. Williams Papers, Archives/Manuscripts Division of the Minnesota Historical Society, Box 25; Archie Carter to Howard Y. Williams, n.d., ibid.

53. *Journal*, April 6, 1936; April 11, 1936; *New York Times*, April 7, 1936.

54. *Journal*, April 10, 1936.

55. *Journal*, April 24, 1936.

56. Roland M. Jones, *New York Times*, April 12, 1936; *Register*, April 9, 1936; April 19, 1936; April 16, 1936; *Time*, April 29, 1936, p. 19.

57. *Register*, April 14, 1936; *Journal*, April 16, 1936.

58. *Register*, May 14, 15, 16, 18, 19, 20, 21, 22, 23, 1936; May 24, 1936.

59. *Register*, May 31, 1936; *Journal*, May 28, 1936.

60. *Register*, May 28, 1936; *Journal*, May 28, 1936.

61. *Iowa Official Register, 1937-1938*, (Des Moines: The State of Iowa, 1937), pp. 196-197.

62. *Journal*, June 22, 1936; *Register*, August 2, 1936.

63. *Davenport Democrat and Leader*, July 27, 1936; *Dubuque Leader*, June 19, 1936.

64. *Register*, July 17, 1936.

65. *Journal*, July 25, 1936; *Register*, July 26, 1936; July 28, 1936; Jennie to Ned Brookhart, July 29, 1936, Charles E. Brookhart Collection.

66. Brookhart to Marvin H. McIntyre, n.d., Roosevelt Papers, Official File 1038, Box 1.

67. *Register*, August 9, 1936; August 7, 1936.
68. *Register*, August 17, 1936; George F. Buresh to Howard Y. Williams, August 17, 1936, Williams Papers, ibid.
69. *Register*, September 12, 1936; September 29, 1936; August 23, 1936; September 13, 1936; October 11, 1936; Jennie to Ned Brookhart, October 13, 1936, Charles E. Brookhart Collection; *New York Times*, October 23, 1936; *Register*, November 1, 1936.
70. George L. Berry to Roosevelt, September 17, 1936, Roosevelt Papers, Official File 2971.
71. Josephus C. Trimble to Roosevelt, January 7, 1936, Roosevelt Papers, Official File 5A, Box 3; Jennie to Ned Brookhart, January 12, 1937, Charles E. Brookhart Collection; Otha D. Wearin, Edward C. Eicher, William S. Jacobsen, Vincent F. Harrington to Roosevelt, March 12, 1937, Roosevelt Papers, Official File 5A, Box 3; U. S. Congress, Senate, Committee on the Judiciary, *Hearings on S. 1392*, 75th Cong., 1st Sess., March 10-16, 1937, p. 1613.
72. George L. Berry to Roosevelt, July 31, 1937, Roosevelt Papers, Official File 59B, Box 3.
73. Berry to Roosevelt, September 17, 1937, Roosevelt Papers, Official File 2971; Roosevelt to Marvin H. McIntyre, September 21, 1937, Roosevelt Papers, Official File 2971; Wallace to McIntyre, September 23, 1937, Roosevelt Papers, Official File 2971; McIntyre to Brookhart, October 9, 1937, ibid.
74. Brookhart to McIntyre, November 17, 1937, Roosevelt Papers, Official File 34, Box 2. Roosevelt to McIntyre, November 23, 1937, Roosevelt Papers, Official File 1060A, Box 18; Eicher to Roosevelt, August 27, 1938, Roosevelt Papers, Official File 18Z, Box 34.
75. Jennie to Ned Brookhart, August 17, 1939, Charles E. Brookhart Collection; William G. Kerr, "A Rough Draft of My Recollections of Smith W. Brookhart and Associated Events Attending It," April 19, 1957, Henry A. Wallace Papers, University of Iowa Libraries, IA 51-888-904.
76. "Who Speaks for Small Business?" *Business Week*, September 24, 1938, pp. 28-29.
77. *New York Times*, December 16, 1936; February 23, 1937; John P. Devaney, "The Quarterly," *National Lawyers Guild Quarterly*, Vol. 1, No. 1, December, 1937, p. 1;*Time*, March 1, 1937, p. 43; Resolutions Adopted at the Fourth Annual Convention, May 29 to June 2, 1940, *National Lawyers Guild Quarterly*, Vol. 3, No. 2, July, 1940, pp. 122.
78. Smith W. Brookhart, "Brief," December 13, 1935, Roosevelt Papers, Official File 41A, Box 49.
79. *Prescott Courier*, November 29, 1938; Smith W. Brookhart, Jr. to Ned Brookhart, December 10, 1939, Charles E. Brookhart Collection; Roosevelt to McIntyre, December 10, 1938, Roosevelt Papers, Official File 2971; Wallace to Roosevelt, March 22, 1940, Roosevelt Papers, Official File 2971.
80. A copy of the manuscript is in the possession of the author.
81. Interview, Otha Wearin, June 17, 1981.
82. Jennie to Ned Brookhart, January 3, 1941, Charles E. Brookhart Collection; See also Jennie to Ned, February 15, 1940; June 20, 1940; September 8, 1940; Della Brookhart to Florence Brookhart Yount, June 17, 1942, FBY Collection.
83. Jennie to Ned Brookhart, October 9, 1942, Charles E. Brookhart Collection.
84. Jennie to Lillian Brookhart Dolman, November 1, 1942, FBY Collection; Interview, Edith Brookhart Millard, April 17, 1981; Jennie to Ned Brookhart, November 16, 1942, Charles E. Brookhart Collection.
85. Jennie to Lillian Brookhart Dolman, January 20, 1943, FBY Collection; Jennie to Ned Brookhart, February 3, 1943, Charles E. Brookhart Collection.
86. *New York Times*, April 16, 1943; Jennie to Ned Brookhart, May 6, 1943, Charles E. Brookhart Collection.

87. Jennie to Ned Brookhart, July 8, 1943, Charles E. Brookhart Collection; John Brookhart to Ned Brookhart, August 16, 1943, ibid.
88. John Brookhart to Ned Brookhart, October 13, 1943, Charles E. Brookhart Collection.
89. Jennie to Ned Brookhart, November 27, 1943, Charles E. Brookhart Collection.
90. *Journal*, January 8, 1944.
91. Interview, Smith W. Brookhart, Jr., July 5, 1981.
92. *Journal*, November 23, 1944; November 17, 1944; November 16, 1944.
93. Della Brookhart to Florence Brookhart Yount, June 17, 1942, FBY Collection.

BIBLIOGRAPHY

MANUSCRIPT COLLECTIONS

Adjutant General of Iowa, State Historical Society of Iowa, Des Moines
George Akerson, Herbert Hoover Presidential Library, West Branch
Arthur F. Allen, University of Iowa Libraries, Iowa City
William Boyd Allison, State Historical Society of Iowa, Des Moines
William E. Borah, Library of Congress, Washington, D.C.
Gutzon Borglum, Library of Congress, Washington, D.C.
Thomas Bray, University of Iowa Libraries, Iowa City
Charles E. Brookhart, Private
Smith Wildman Brookhart, State Historical Society of Iowa, Des Moines
Smith Wildman Brookhart, Jr., Private
Ed Hoyt Campbell, University of Iowa Libraries, Iowa City
John W. Carey, University of Iowa Libraries, Iowa City
Chautauqua Collection, University of Iowa Libraries, Iowa City
Edward T. Clark, Library of Congress, Washington, D.C.
James S. Clarkson, Library of Congress, Washington, D.C.
Cyrenus Cole, State Historical Society of Iowa, Iowa City
Cooperative League of the USA, New York Public Library, New York City
Calvin Coolidge, Library of Congress, Washington, D.C.
James Couzens, Library of Congress, Washington, D.C.
John Walter Coverdale, University of Iowa Libraries, Iowa City
Albert B. Cummins, State Historical Society of Iowa, Des Moines
Bronson Cutting, Library of Congress, Washington, D.C.
Chester Davis, Joint Collection University of Missouri Western Historical Manuscript Collection, Columbia and State Historical Society of Missouri Manuscripts, Columbia
Democratic National Committee, Franklin D. Roosevelt Presidential Library, Hyde Park
Charles Almon Dewey, University of Iowa Libraries, Iowa City
Lester J. Dickenson, University of Iowa Libraries, Iowa City
Jonathan P. Dolliver, State Historical Society of Iowa, Iowa City
Edward Eicher, University of Iowa Libraries, Iowa City
Federal Bureau of Investigation, Washington, D.C.
Henry Field, State Historical Society of Iowa, Iowa City
Carl Franke, State Historical Society of Iowa, Iowa City
Carter Glass, University of Virginia, Charlottesville
Lynn Haines, Minnesota Historical Society, St. Paul
John Hammill, State Historical Society of Iowa, Des Moines

Warren G. Harding, Ohio Historical Society, Columbus
Edgar Harlan, State Historical Society of Iowa, Des Moines
Gilbert N. Haugen, State Historical Society of Iowa, Iowa City
Charles Hearst, University of Northern Iowa, Cedar Falls
Myron T. Herrick, Western Reserve Historical Society, Cleveland
Clyde Herring, University of Iowa Libraries, Iowa City
Herbert C. Hoover, Herbert Hoover Presidential Library, West Branch
Harvey Ingham, State Historical Society of Iowa, Des Moines
Institute of Public Affairs, University of Virginia, Charlottesville
Iowa State Banking Department, State Historical Society of Iowa, Des Moines
Walter Jessup, University of Iowa Libraries, Iowa City
Mercer Johnston, Library of Congress, Washington, D.C.
Ray S. Johnston, Private
Nate E. Kendall, State Historical Society of Iowa, Des Moines
Nelson Kraschel, University of Iowa Libraries, Iowa City
La Follette Family Papers, Library of Congress, Washington, D.C.
Fiorello LaGuardia, New York Public Library, New York City
Fred Dickinson Letts, University of Iowa Libraries, Iowa City
Frank Lowden, University of Chicago Library, Chicago
Frank Lund, Webster City Public Library, Webster City
James H. MacLafferty, Herbert Hoover Presidential Library, West Branch
Charles McNary, Library of Congress, Washington, D.C.
Hanford MacNider, Herbert Hoover Presidential Library, West Branch
Basil Manly, Library of Congress, Washington, D.C.
Verne Marshall, Herbert Hoover Presidential Library, West Branch
Edwin T. Meredith, University of Iowa Libraries, Iowa City
Ogden L. Mills, Library of Congress, Washington, D.C.
George Norris, Library of Congress, Washington, D.C.
Gerald P. Nye, Herbert Hoover Presidential Library, West Branch
George Peek, Joint Collection University of Missouri Western Historical Manuscript Collection, Columbia and State Historical Society of Missouri Manuscripts, Columbia
Charles E. Perkins, The Newberry Library, Chicago
George D. Perkins, State Historical Society of Iowa, Des Moines
Charles Pickett, University of Iowa Libraries, Iowa City
Christian W. Ramseyer, University of Iowa Libraries, Iowa City
Charles Rawson, State Historical Society of Iowa, Des Moines
Milo Reno, University of Iowa Libraries, Iowa City
Republican Conference, United States Senate, Washington, D.C.
Republican National Committee, Washington, D.C.
Edgar Rickard, Herbert Hoover Presidential Library, West Branch
George Roberts, State Historical Society of Iowa, Iowa City
Franklin Delano Roosevelt, Franklin D. Roosevelt Presidential Library, Hyde Park
Theodore Roosevelt, Library of Congress, Washington, D.C.
Theodore Roosevelt, Jr., Library of Congress, Washington, D.C.
Leslie Shaw, State Historical Society of Iowa, Des Moines
Brainard Hayes Shearer, University of Iowa Libraries, Iowa City
Upton Sinclair, Indiana University, Bloomington
William Howard Taft, Library of Congress, Washington, D.C.
Clifford Thorne, University of Iowa Libraries, Iowa City
Dan Turner, State Historical Society of Iowa, Des Moines

BIBLIOGRAPHY

Henry A. Wallace, University of Iowa Libraries, Iowa City
Thomas Walsh, Library of Congress, Washington, D.C.
Howard Y. Williams, Minnesota Historical Society, St. Paul
Burton Wheeler, Montana Historical Society, Helena
Lafayette Young, State Historical Society of Iowa, Des Moines
Florence Brookhart Yount, Private

MANUSCRIPTS: THE NATIONAL ARCHIVES

Record Group 16, "Records of the Department of Office of the Secretary of Agriculture."
Record Group 40, "General Records of the Department of Commerce."
Record Group 46, "Records of the United States Senate."
Record Group 56, "General Records of the Department of the Treasury."
Record Group 59, "General Records of the Department of State."
Record Group 60, "General Records of the Department of Justice."
Record Group 82, "Records of the Federal Reserve System."
Record Group 94, "Records of the Adjutant General's Office, 1780's–1917."
Record Group 145, "Records of the Agricultural Stabilization and Conservation Service."
Record Group 165, "Records of the War Department General and Special Staffs."

INTERVIEWS

Al Baldridge, July 21, 1981
Frank Brookhart, March 20, 1982
Smith W. Brookhart, Jr., July 3, 1981; July 4, 1981; July 5, 1981
Ophelia Miller Gallop, October 26, 1981
Violet Brookhart Gunn, August 24, 1981
Bertha Guther, July 21, 1981
James Hearst, October 26, 1982
A. Joseph Kelly, July 24, 1981
Dave Livingston, June 27, 1981
Stewart H. M. Lund, August 25, 1981
Richard McCleery, July 18, 1981
Merritt E. McDaniel, May 29, 1982
Edith Brookhart Millard, January 23, 1981; April 17, 1981
Frank Nye, July 20, 1981
Mabel Wildman Rice, August 7, 1981
Norman Sage, November 24, 1982
Fred Stover, August 25, 1981
Dwight Taylor, March 5, 1981; March 24, 1981
Arthur Thompson, March 26, 1982
Otha Wearin, June 17, 1981
William O. Weaver, July 14, 1981
George Wharam, August 26, 1981
Florence Brookhart Yount, October 16, 1980; July 7, 1981

BIBLIOGRAPHY

CORRESPONDENCE

Elsie Bayley
Walter G. Berger
Luther F. Bowers
Smith W. Brookhart, Jr.
Douglas Bukowski
Carl Cone
William Cumberland
Robert Day
John C. Drier
Lowell Dyson
Dave Elder
Ronald L. Feinman
Robert C. Fisk
John R. Fleming
Thomas E. Frantz
Robert K. Goodwin
Orville F. Grahame
H. R. Gross
John Harlee
Lement Harris
James Hearst
John Henry
Alger Hiss
David A. Horowitz
Chuck Hotle
Grant Humble
Ray S. Johnston
Philip D. Jordan

George Kennan
Martha Mumma Keyes
Leon H. Keyserling
Katie Louchheim
Richard Lowitt
Stewart H. M. Lund
Jack MacNider
Dorris B. Martin
Edith Brookhart Millard
George Mills
Edmund D. Morrison
George E. Mumma
Frank T. Nye
Claude Pepper
Jesse W. Radda
W. B. Ragsdale
Jennings Randolph
James Roosevelt
Leland L. Sage
John D. Sheaffer
Telford Taylor
Elizabeth Thorne
James W. Wallace
Otha Wearin
Trevor West
Roland A. White
Elsworth Woods
Florence Brookhart Yount

NEWSPAPERS AND PERIODICALS

The American Rifleman, 1923–1930
Arms and the Man, 1910–1923
Des Moines Register, 1920–1933
Iowa Homestead, 1920–1929
Iowa Legionnaire, 1922–1923
Iowa Magazine, 1920–1922
Iowa Union Farmer, 1920–1933
Locomotive Engineers Journal, 1919–1926
New York Times, 1920–1936
Washington County Press, 1892–1918
Washington Evening Journal, 1894–1936
Washington Gazette, 1892–1905

Many other individual issues of newspapers are cited in the endnotes. Many of these came from clipping scrapbooks covering the senate years and kept by Florence Brookhart Yount.

BIBLIOGRAPHY

GOVERNMENT PUBLICATIONS: FEDERAL

Congressional Record, 67 Cong., 4 Sess.—72 Cong., 2 Sess.

64 Cong., 1 Sess., 1916, Hearings Before the Joint Subcommittee on Interstate and Foreign Commerce Pursuant to Public J. Res. 25.

65 Cong., 2 Sess., 1917, Hearings Before the Joint Committee on Interstate and Foreign Commerce Pursuant to Public J. Res. 25.

65 Cong., 3 Sess., 1919, Hearings Before the Senate Committee on Military Affairs on Acquiring Land for Establishment of Mobilization and Training Fields for Artillery and Small Arms.

66 Cong., 1 Sess., 1919, Hearings Before Subcommittee No. 2 (Camps) of the House Select Committee on Expenditures in the War Department

66 Cong., 3 Sess., 1921, Hearing Before a Subcommittee of the Senate Committee on Interstate Commerce Amending Section 10 of the Clayton Act, s. 4576.

67 Cong., 1 Sess., 1921, Hearings Before the Joint Commission of Agricultural Inquiry Pursuant to Senate Concurrent Res. 4.

67 Cong., 4 Sess., 1923, Senate, Minutes of the Federal Reserve Board Conference, May 18, 1920, Document No. 310.

68 Cong., 1 Sess., 1924, Hearings Before the Senate Committee on Banking and Currency on Nominations of Members of the Federal Farm Loan Board.

68 Cong., 1 Sess., 1924, Hearings Before the House Committee on Agriculture, H. R. 5563.

68 Cong., 1 Sess., 1924, Hearings Before the Senate Select Committee on Investigation of the Attorney General Pursuant to S. Res. 157.

69 Cong., 1 Sess., 1926, Hearings Before a Subcommittee of the Senate Committee on Privileges and Elections on the Senator From Iowa, Pursuant to S. Res. 21.

69 Cong., 1 Sess., 1926, The Senate Committee on Privileges and Elections, Senate Committee Print No. 1 on the Senator From Iowa.

69 Cong., 1 Sess., 1926, Report of the Senate Committee on Privileges and Elections Pursuant to S. Res. 21, Report No. 498.

69 Cong., 1 Sess., 1926, Hearings Before the Senate Committee on Agriculture and Forestry To Promote Cooperative Marketing, S. 1910 and H. R. 7893.

69 Cong., 1 Sess., 1926, Hearings Before the Senate Commitee on Interstate Commerce on Consolidation of Railway Properties, S. 1870.

69 Cong., 1 Sess., 1926, Hearings Before a Senate Special Committee Investigating Expenditures in Senatorial Primary and General Elections on Senatorial Campaign Expenditures, S. Res. 195.

69 Cong., 2 Sess., 1927, Hearings Before the Senate Committee on Interstate Commerce on the Nomination of Cyrus Woods to be a Member of the Interstate Commerce Commission.

70 Cong., 1 Sess., 1928, Hearings Before the Senate Commitee on Civil Service Covering Certain Persons Into the Classified Civil Service Without Examination, S. 1995.

70 Cong., 1 Sess., 1928, Hearings Before the Senate Committee on Interstate Commerce on the Motion Picture Bill, S. 1667.

71 Cong., 1 Sess., 1929, Hearings Before the Senate Committee on Agriculture and Forestry on Farm Relief Legislation, S. 1.

72 Cong., 1 Sess., 1932, Hearing Before the House Committee on Agriculture on Farm Marketing Program.

73 Cong., 1 Sess., 1933, Hearings Before the Senate Committee on Agriculture and Forestry on Agricultural Emergency Act to Increase Farm Purchasing Power, H. R. 3835.

73 Cong., 2 Sess., 1934, Hearing Before the House Committee on Interstate and Foreign Commerce on the Regulation of Interstate Motor Busses and Trucks on Public Highways, H.

R. 6836.

74 Cong., 2 Sess., 1936, Hearing Before the Senate Committee on Agriculture and Forestry on Substitute Legislation For the Invalidated Agricultural Adjustment Act.

75 Cong., 1 Sess., 1937, Hearings Before the Senate Committee on the Judiciary on the Reorganization of the Federal Judiciary, S. 1392.

75 Cong., 1 Sess., 1937, Hearings Before a Subcommittee of the Senate Committee on Agriculture and Forestry on the Agricultural Equality Act of 1937, S. 2732.

75 Cong., 3 Sess., 1938, Hearings Before a Subcommittee of the Senate Committee on the Judiciary on the Federal Licensing of Corporations, S. 10 and S. 3072.

76 Cong., 1 Sess., 1939, Hearings Before the Senate Committee on Agriculture and Forestry To Regulate Commerce in Agricultural Products, S. 570.

76 Cong., 1 Sess., 1939, Hearings Before a Subcommittee of the Senate Committee on Agriculture and Forestry to Authorize Commodity Exchange Commission to Regulate Margin Requirements, S. 831.

76 Cong., 1 Sess., 1939, Hearings Before a Subcommittee of the Senate Committee on Banking and Currency To Provide for the Insurance of Loans to Business, S. 1482 and S. 2343.

76 Cong., 3 Sess., 1940, Hearings Before the Senate Subcommittee of the Committee on Appropriations on the Military Establishment Appropriation Bill for 1941, H. R. 9209.

76 Cong., 3 Sess., 1940, Hearing Before the Senate Committee on Military Affairs on the Johnson Semiautomatic Rifle, S. 3983.

77 Cong., 1 Sess., 1941, Hearings Before a Subcommittee of the Senate Committee on Agriculture and Forestry on a Formula for Determining Parity Prices, S. Res. 117.

77 Cong., 1 Sess., 1941, Hearings Before the House Committee on Banking and Currency on a Price-Control Bill, H. R. 5479.

77 Cong., 1 Sess., 1941, Hearings Before the Senate Committee on Banking and Currency on an Emergency Price Control Act, H. R. 5990.

77 Cong., 1 Sess., 1941, Hearings Before the Special Senate Committee to Study and Survey Problems of Small Business Enterprises on Small Business and the War Program Pursuant to S. Res. 298 (76 Cong.).

92 Cong., 1 Sess., 1972, Senate Document No. 92-7, "Senate Election, Expulsion and Censure Cases From 1793 to 1972."

92 Cong., 1 Sess., 1971, Senate Document No. 92-8, "Biographical Directory of the American Congress 1774–1971."

96 Cong., 2 Sess., 1981, Senate Document No. 96-63, "Herbert Hoover Reassessed, Essays Commemorating the Fiftieth Anniversary of the Inauguration of our Thirty-First President."

GOVERNMENT PUBLICATIONS: STATE OF IOWA

Iowa Official Register, 1890—1937-1938

Iowa, *Journal of the House of the Thirty-Eighth General Assembly*, Speech of Albert B. Cummins, March 27, 1919.

Iowa, *Journal of the Senate of the Fortieth General Assembly*, Remarks of Senator Smith W. Brookhart, January 11, 1923.

Iowa, *Iowa Yearbook of Agriculture 1922*, "Report of Iowa Farm Bureau Federation," Remarks by Senator Brookhart, January 11–12, 1923.

Iowa, *Journal of the House of the Fortieth General Assembly, Extra Session*, Remarks of the Honorable Smith W. Brookhart, January 3, 1924.

Iowa, *Journal of the Senate of the Forty-Second General Assembly*, Speech by Senator Smith W. Brookhart, March 31, 1927.

BIBLIOGRAPHY

THESES

Briley, Ronald F. "Challenge to Normalcy: Four Midwestern Political Mavericks, 1922-1924." Master's thesis, West Texas State University, 1972.

Bull, Cornelius Holland III. "Smith Wildman Brookhart: Neither God Nor Little Fish." A. B. Thesis, Princeton University, 1950.

Cornell, Corwin D. "Smith W. Brookhart and Agrarian Discontent in Iowa." Master's thesis, University of Iowa, 1949.

Culp, Dorothy, "The American Legion: A Study in Pressure Politics." Ph.D. dissertation, University of Chicago, 1939.

Derr, Nancy Ruth. "Iowans During World War I: A Study of Change Under Stress." Ph.D. dissertation, George Washington University, 1979.

Dollar, Charles Mason. "The Senate Progressive Movement, 1921-1933: A Roll Call Analysis." Ph.D. dissertation, University of Kentucky, 1966.

Doyle, Daniel Joseph. "Rochdale and the Origin of the Rochdale Society of Equitable Pioneers." Ph.D. dissertation, St. John's University, 1972.

Frederick, Richard George. "Old Visions and New Dreams: The Old Progressives in the 1920's." Ph.D. dissertation, The Pennsylvania State University, 1979.

Johnston, Ray S. "Smith Wildman Brookhart: Iowa's Last Populist." Master's thesis, State College of Iowa, 1964.

Kirschner, Don S. "Conflict in the Corn Belt: Rural Responses to Urbanization 1919-1929." Ph.D. dissertation, University of Iowa, 1964.

McDaniel, George William. "Over Here: The Mobilization of The Republican Service League to Defeat Smith Wildman Brookhart." Master's essay, University of Iowa, 1977.

McDaniel, George William. "Smith Wildman Brookhart: Agrarian Radical in New Era America." Ph.D. dissertation, University of Iowa, 1985.

Miller, David B. "Origins and Functions of the Federal Farm Board." Ph.D. dissertation, University of Kansas, 1973.

Olssen, Erik. "Dissent From Normalcy: Progressives in Congress, 1918-1925." Ph.D. dissertation, Duke University, 1969.

Petersen, Peter L. "A Publisher in Politics: Edwin T. Meredith, Progressive Reform, and the Democratic Party, 1912-1928." Ph.D. dissertation, University of Iowa, 1971.

Russell, Barry Alexander. "The Changing Concept of Iowa Progressivism: Smith W. Brookhart vs. Albert B. Cummins 1920-1926." Master's thesis, University of North Carolina, 1973.

Savage, Hugh James. "Political Independents of the Hoover Era: The Progressive Insurgents of the Senate." Ph.D. dissertation, University of Illinois, 1961.

Sayre, Ralph Mills. "Albert Baird Cummins and the Progressive Movement in Iowa." Ph.D. dissertation, Columbia University, 1958.

Visser, John E. "William Lloyd Harding and the Republican Party in Iowa, 1906-1920." Ph.D. dissertation, University of Iowa, 1957.

Webb, David Dea. "Farmers, Professors and Money: Agriculture and the Battle for Managed Money, 1920-1941." Ph.D. dissertation, University of Oklahoma, 1978.

BOOKS

Allen, Howard W. *Poindexter of Washington: A Study in Progressive Politics*. Carbondale and Edwardsville: Southern Illinois University Press, 1981.

[Allen, Robert S. and Pearson, Drew]. *Washington Merry-Go-Round*. New York: Horace Liveright, Inc., 1931.

BIBLIOGRAPHY

Ashby, LeRoy. *The Spearless Leader, Senator Borah and the Progressive Movement in the 1920's*. Urbana: University of Illinois Press, 1972.

Atherton, Lewis, *Main Street on the Middle Border*. Bloomington: Indiana University Press, 1954.

Atkins, Annette. *Harvest of Grief: Grasshopper Plagues and Public Assistance in Minnesota, 1873-78*. St. Paul: Minnesota Historical Society Press, 1984.

Ayer, N. W. *N. W. Ayer and Son's American Newspaper Annual, 1890*. Philadelphia: N. W. Ayer and Son, 1890.

Barnard, Harry. *Independent Man: The Life of Senator James Couzens*. New York: Charles Scribner's Sons, 1958.

Bray, Thomas James. *The Rebirth of Freedom*. Indianola, Iowa: Record and Tribune Press, 1957.

Brigham, Johnson. *James Harlan*. Iowa City: The State Historical Society of Iowa, 1913.

Brinkley, Alan. *Voices of Protest: Huey Long, Father Coughlin, and the Great Depression*. New York: Alfred A. Knopf, 1982.

Brookhart, Smith W. *Cooperative Economics or Illiterate Facts vs. Intellectual Fiction*. Unpublished Manuscript, 1939.

_____. *Government Ownership of Railroads*. Washington, Iowa: Washington County Press, 1913.

_____. *Hoover and the Farm Problem*. Chicago Republican National Committee, 1928.

_____. *The Invisible Government*. The National Council of Farmers' Co-Operative Associations, 1915.

_____. *Personal record of Col. Brookhart during rifle matches and part of [the] World War*. Unpublished Diary.

_____. *Rifle Training in War*. Washington, D.C.: The National Rifle Association, 1918.

Bruchey, Stuart W., ed. *Small Business in American Life*. New York: Columbia University Press, 1980.

Buck, Solon Justus. *The Granger Movement: A Study of Agricultural Organization and Its Political, Economic and Social Manifestations 1870-1880*. Cambridge: Harvard University Press, 1913.

Burke, Robert E., ed. *The Diary Letters of Hiram Johnson 1817-1945*. New York: Garland Publishing, Inc., 1983.

Burner, David. *Herbert Hoover: A Public Life*. New York: Alfred A. Knopf, 1979.

Burns, James MacGregor. *Roosevelt, The Lion and the Fox*. New York: Harcourt, Brace and Company, 1956.

Burrell, Howard A. *History of Washington County Iowa From the First White Settlements to 1908*, 2 Vols. Chicago: The S. J. Clarke Publishing Company, 1909.

Carr, Edward Hallett. *A History of Soviet Russia, The Interregnum, 1923-1924*. New York: The Macmillan Company, 1954.

_____. *A History of Soviet Russia, Socialism in One Country, 1924-1926*. New York: The Macmillan Company, 1958.

Clark, Dan Elbert. *History of Senatorial Elections in Iowa*. Iowa City: The State Historical Society of Iowa, 1912.

Cole, Cyrenus. *A History of the People of Iowa*. Cedar Rapids, The Torch Press, 1921.

_____. *Iowa Through the Years*. Iowa City, The State Historical Society of Iowa, 1940.

_____. *I Remember I Remember: A Book of Recollections*. Iowa City: The State Historical Society of Iowa, 1936.

Cosmas, Graham A. *An Army for Empire: The United States Army in the Spanish-American War*. Columbia: University of Missouri Press, 1971.

Cox, Beverly J. and Anderson, Denna Jones. *Miguel Covarrubias Caricatures*. Washington,

D.C.: Smithsonian Institution Press, 1985.

Cumberland, William H. *Wallace M. Short, Iowa Rebel*. Ames, Iowa: Iowa State University Press, 1983.

Dallek, Robert. *Franklin D. Roosevelt and American Foreign Policy, 1932-1945*. New York: Oxford University Press, 1979.

Daugherty, Harry M. and Dixon, Thomas. *The Inside Story of The Harding Tragedy*. New York: The Churchill Company, 1932.

Davidson, Osha Gray. *Under Fire, The NRA and the Battle for Gun Control*. New York: Henry Holt and Company, 1993.

Davis, Kenneth S. *FDR, The New Deal Years, 1933-1937: A History*. New York: Random House, 1986.

Day, Donald. *Will Rogers, A Biography*. New York: David McKay Company, Inc., 1962.

Dennis, Alfred Pearce. *Gods and Little Fishes*. Indianapolis: The Bobbs-Merrill Company, 1931.

Dilling, Elizabeth. *The Red Network: A "Who's Who" and Handbook of Radicalism for Patriots*. Chicago: Elizabeth Dilling, 1934.

Dreier, Thomas. *Heroes of Insurgency*. Boston: Human Life Publishing Company, 1910.

Duffield, Marcus. *King Legion*. New York: Jonathan Cape and Harrison Smith, 1931.

Dyson, Lowell K. *Red Harvest, The Communist Party and American Farmers*. Lincoln: University of Nebraska Press, 1982.

Fausold, Martin L., ed., and Mazuzan, George T., assoc. ed. *The Hoover Presidency, A Reappraisal*. Albany: State University of New York Press, 1974.

Feinman, Ronald L. *Twilight of Progressivism: The Western Republican Senators and the New Deal*. Baltimore: The Johns Hopkins University Press, 1981.

Fellows, S. N. *History of Prohibition in Iowa*. Des Moines: Iowa Anti-Saloon League, 1905.

Fine, Nathan. *Labor and Farmer Parties in the United States, 1828-1928*. New York: Rand School of Social Science, 1928.

Fisher, Kathy. *In the Beginning There Was Land: A History of Washington County, Iowa*. Washington, Iowa: The Washington County Historical Society, 1978.

Fite, Gilbert C. *American Farmers, The New Minority*. Bloomington: Indiana University Press, 1981.

_____. *George N. Peek and the Fight for Farm Parity*. Norman: University of Oklahoma Press, 1954.

Flynn, George Q. *American Catholics and the Roosevelt Presidency, 1932-1936*. Lexington: University of Kentucky Press, 1968.

Fuess, Claude M. *Calvin Coolidge: The Man From Vermont*. Boston: Little, Brown and Company, 1940.

Gelfand, Lawrence E., ed. *Herbert Hoover: The Great War and Its Aftermath, 1914-1923*. Iowa City: University of Iowa Press, 1979.

Giglio, James N. *H. M. Daugherty and the Politics of Expediency*. Kent: The Kent State University Press, 1978.

Goodwyn, Lawrence. *Democratic Promise: The Populist Movement in America*. New York: Oxford University Press, 1976.

_____. *The Populist Movement: A Short History of the Agrarian Revolt in America*. Oxford: Oxford University Press, 1978.

Grant, H. Roger. *Self-Help in the 1890s Depression*. Ames: The Iowa State University Press, 1983.

Greater Iowa Association. *Concerning the Greater Iowa Association*. c. 1918.

Hanley, Peter J. *Hanley's Political Primer*. Washington, Iowa: Peter J. Hanley, 1908.

Haynes, Fred Emory. *James Baird Weaver*. Iowa City: The State Historical Society of Iowa, 1919.

BIBLIOGRAPHY

_____. *Third Party Movements Since the Civil War With Special Reference to Iowa, A Study in Social Politics.* Iowa City: The State Historical Society of Iowa, 1916.

Haynes, George H. *The Senate of the United States, Its History and Practice*, 2 Vols. Boston: Houghton Mifflin Company, 1938.

Hawley, Ellis W. *The Great War and the Search for a Modern Order: A History of the American People and Their Institutions, 1917-1933.* New York: St. Martin's Press, 1979.

_____. *Herbert Hoover as Secretary of Commerce: Studies in New Era Thought and Practice.* Iowa City: University of Iowa Press, 1981.

Herrick, Myron T. *Rural Credits: Land and Cooperatives.* New York and London: D. Appleton and Company, 1914.

Hicks, John D. *The Populist Revolt: A History of the Farmers' Alliance and the People's Party.* Minneapolis: The University of Minnesota Press, 1931.

_____. *Republican Ascendancy, 1921-1933.* New York: Harper and Row, 1960.

Hines, Walker D. *War History of American Railroads.* New Haven: Yale University Press, 1928.

Hinton, Harold B. *Cordell Hull, A Biography.* Garden City, New York: Doubleday, Doran and Company, Inc., 1942.

Hoadley, Ruth L. *The Chain Store With Special Reference to Iowa.* Iowa City, State University of Iowa, 1930.

Hoover, Herbert. *The Memoirs of Herbert Hoover: Years Of Adventure, 1874-1920.* New York: The Macmillan Company, 1951.

_____. *The Memoirs of Herbert Hoover: The Cabinet and the Presidency, 1920-1933.* New York: The Macmillan Company, 1952.

_____. *The Memoirs of Herbert Hoover: The Great Depression, 1929-1941.* New York: The Macmillan Company, 1952.

_____. *The New Day: Campaign Speeches of Herbert Hoover, 1928.* Stanford, California: Stanford University Press, 1928.

Howard, Robert P. *James R. Howard and the Farm Bureau.* Ames: The Iowa State University Press, 1983.

Hull, Cordell. *The Memoirs of Cordell Hull, in Two Volumes.* New York: The Macmillian Company, 1948.

Hutchinson, William T. *Lowden of Illinois: The Life of Frank O. Lowden*, 2 Vols. Chicago: The University of Chicago Press, 1957.

Jensen, Richard. *The Winning of the Midwest: Social and Political Conflict, 1888-1896.* Chicago: The University of Chicago Press, 1971.

"If Elected . . ." Unsuccessful Candidates for the Presidency 1796-1968. Washington, D.C.: Smithsonian Institution Press, 1972.

Interstate Commerce Law Convention. *Amendments, Proceedings.* Washington, D.C.: Interstate Commerce Law Convention, 1904, 1905.

Isms: A Review of Alien Isms, Revolutionary Communism and Their Active Sympathizers in the United States. Indianapolis: National Americanism Commission of The American Legion, 1937.

Koenig, Louis W. *Bryan: A Political Biography of William Jennings Bryan.* New York: G. P. Putnam's Sons, 1971.

Kramer, Dale. *The Wild Jackasses: The American Farmer in Revolt.* New York: Hastings House, Publishers, 1956.

Krog, Carl E. and Tanner, William R., eds. *Herbert Hoover and the Republican Era.* Lanham, New York: University Press of America, 1984.

La Follette, Belle Case and La Follete, Fola. *Robert M. La Follette, June 14, 1855-June 18, 1925, in Two Volumes.* New York: The Macmillian Company, 1953.

BIBLIOGRAPHY

Larrabee, William. *The Railroad Question: A Historical and Practical Treatise on Railroads, and Remedies for Their Abuses.* 5th Edition, Chicago: The Schulte Publishing Company, 1893.
Leuchtenburg, William E. *Franklin D. Roosevelt and the New Deal, 1932-1940.* New York: Harper & Row, 1963.
_____. *The Perils of Prosperity, 1914-1932.* Chicago: The University of Chicago Press, 1958.
Lief, Alfred. *Democracy's Norris: The Biography of a Lonely Crusade.* New York: Stackpole Sons, Publishers, 1939.
Louchheim, Katie, ed. *The Making of the New Deal: The Insiders Speak.* Cambridge, Massachusetts: Harvard University Press, 1983.
Lowitt, Richard. *George W. Norris: The Persistence of a Progressive, 1913-1933.* Urbana: University of Illinois Press, 1971.
_____. *George W. Norris: The Triumph of a Progressive, 1933-1944.* Urbana: University of Illinois Press, 1978.
Luthin, Reinhard H. *American Demagogues Twentieth Century.* Boston: The Beacon Press, 1954.
MacKay, Kenneth Campbell. *The Progressive Movement of 1924.* New York: Columbia University Press, 1947.
Marsh, Benjamin C. *Lobbyist for the People: A Record of Fifty Years.* Washington, D.C.: Public Affairs Press, 1953.
Martin, Albro. *Enterprise Denied: Origins of the Decline of American Railroads, 1897-1917.* New York: Columbia University Press, 1971.
Martin, Edward Winslow. *History of the Grange Movement; or, The Farmer's War Against Monopolies.* Chicago: National Publishing Company, 1874.
Mayer, George H. *The Republican Party, 1854-1966,* Second Edition. New York: Oxford University Press, 1967.
McCleery, Hugh H. *Newspapers and Other Publications of Washington, Iowa: A Brief History.* Washington, Iowa: Washington Evening Journal, n.d.
McKenna, George, ed. *American Populism.* New York: G. P. Putnam's Sons, 1974.
Moley, Ryamond, Jr. *The American Legion Story.* New York: Duell, Sloan and Pearce, 1966.
Moos, Malcolm. *The Republicans: A History of Their Party.* New York: Random House, 1956.
Mowry, George E. *The Era of Theodore Roosevelt and the Birth of Modern America, 1900-1912.* New York: Harper and Brothers, 1958.
Murray, Robert K. *The Harding Era: Warren G. Harding and His Administration.* Minneapolis: University of Minnesota Press, 1969.
Nash, George H. *The Life of Herbert Hoover, The Humanitarian 1914-1917.* New York: W. W. Norton and Company, 1988.
Neprash, Jerry Alvin. *The Brookhart Campaigns in Iowa, 1920-1926: A Study in the Motivation of Political Attitudes.* New York: Columbia University Press, 1932.
Nichols, I. A. *Forty Years of Rural Journalism in Iowa.* Fort Dodge, Iowa: Messenger Press, 1938.
Nordin, D. Sven. *Rich Harvest: A History of the Grange, 1867-1900.* Jackson University Press of Mississippi, 1974.
Nye, Russel B. *Midwestern Progressive Politics: A Historical Study of Its Origins and Development, 1870-1958.* East Lansing: The Michigan State University Press, 1959.
Official Report of the Proceedings of the Eighteenth Republican National Convention, 1924. New York: The Tenny Press, 1924.
Official Report of the Proceedings of the Nineteenth Republican National Convention, 1928. New York: The Tenny Press, 1928.
Overton, Richard G. *Burlington Route: A History of the Burlington Lines.* Lincoln: University

of Nebraska Press, 1965.

Peel, Roy V. and Donnelly, Thomas C. *The 1928 Campaign: An Analysis*. New York: New York University Book Store, 1931.

Peterson, Trudy Huskamp, ed. *Farmers, Bureaucrats, and Middlemen: Historical Perspectives on American Agriculture*. Washington, D.C.: Howard University Press, 1980.

Plumb, Glenn and Roylance, William G. *Industrial Democracy, A Plan for Its Achievement*. New York: B. W. Huebsch, Inc., 1923.

Pollack, Norman, ed. *The Populist Mind*. Indianapolis: The Bobbs-Merrill Company, Inc., 1967.

Porter, Kirk H. and Johnson, Donald Bruce. *National Party Platforms, 1840–1956*. Urbana: The University of Illinois Press, 1956.

Portrait and Biographical Album of Jefferson and Van Buren Counties, Iowa. Chicago: Lake City Publishing Company, 1890.

Portrait and Biographical Album of Washington County, Iowa. Chicago: Lake City Publishing Company, 1887.

Raiguel, George Earle and Huff, William Kistler. *This is Russia*. Philadelphia: The Penn Publishing Company, 1932.

Richardson, Reed C. *The Locomotive Engineer, 1863–1963: A Century of Railway Labor Relations and Work Rules*. Ann Arbor: University of Michigan Press, 1963.

Ross, Earle D. *Iowa Agriculture: An Historical Survey*. Iowa City: The State Historical Society of Iowa, 1951.

Ross, Thomas Richard. *Jonathan Prentiss Dolliver: A Study in Political Integrity and Independence*. Iowa City: The State Historical Society of Iowa, 1958.

Russell, Francis. *The Shadow of Blooming Grove: Warren G. Harding in His Times*. New York: McGraw-Hill Book Company, 1968.

Sage, Leland L. *A History of Iowa*. Ames: The Iowa State University Press, 1974.

_____. *William Boyd Allison: A Study in Practical Politics*. Iowa City: The State Historical Society of Iowa, 1956.

Saloutos, Theodore and Hicks, John D. *Twentieth-Century Populism, Agricultural Discontent in the Middle West, 1900–1939*. Madison: University of Wisconsin, 1951.

Schapsmeier, Edward L. and Frederick H. *Henry A. Wallace of Iowa: The Agrarian Years, 1910–1940*. Ames: The Iowa State University Press, 1968.

Schlesinger, Arthur M., Jr. *The Coming of the New Deal*. Boston: Houghton Mifflin Company, 1959.

Shambaugh, Benjamin F., ed. *The Messages and Proclamations of the Governors of Iowa, Volume III*. Iowa City: The State Historical Society of Iowa, 1905.

Sheenan, Marion Turner, ed. *The World at Home, Selections From the Writing of Anne O'Hare McCormick*. New York: Alfred Knopf, 1956.

Shideler, James H. *Farm Crisis, 1919–1923*. Berkeley: University of California Press, 1957.

Shover, John L. *Cornbelt Rebellion: The Farmers' Holiday Association*. Urbana: The University of Illinois Press, 1965.

Soule, George. *Prosperity Decade From War to Depression: 1917–1929*. New York: Holt, Rinehart and Winston, 1947.

Sparke, George R. *A Many-Colored Toga: The Diary of Henry Fountain Ashurst*. Tuscon, Arizona: The University of Arizona Press, 1962.

Sternsher, Bernard. *Rexford Tugwell and the New Deal*. New Brunswick, New Jersey: Rutgers University Press, 1964.

Stiles, Edward H. *Recollections and Sketches of Notable Lawyers and Public Men of Early Iowa*. Des Moines: The Homestead Publishing Co., 1916.

Swisher, Jacob A. *The American Legion in Iowa, 1919–1926*. Iowa City: The State Historical Society of Iowa, 1929.

BIBLIOGRAPHY

Thelen, David P. *Robert M. La Follette and the Insurgent Spirit*. Boston: Little, Brown and Company, 1976.

Thomas, John L. *Alternative America: Henry George, Edward Bellamy, Henry Demarest Lloyd and the Adversary Tradition*. Cambridge, Massachusetts: The Belknap Press of Harvard University Press, 1983.

Trefethen, James B., Compiler, Serven, James E., ed. *Americans and Their Guns: The National Rifle Association Story Through Nearly a Century of Service to the Nation*. Harrisburg, Pennsylvania: Stackpole Books, 1967.

Tucker, Ray and Barkley, Frederick R. *Sons of the Wild Jackass*. Seattle: University of Washington Press, (1932) 1970.

United States Senate, Republican Conference. *Minutes of Republican Caucus and Republican Conference and Index, April 4, 1911–June 2, 1936*.

Wall, Joseph Frazier. *Iowa: A History*. New York: W. W. Norton and Company, Inc., 1978.

Weaver, James B. *A Call to Action*. Des Moines: Iowa Printing Company, 1892.

Weissman, Benjamin M. *Herbert Hoover and Famine Relief to Soviet Russia: 1921–1923*. Stanford, California: Hoover Institution Press, Stanford University, 1974.

Wheeler, Burton K. with Healy, Paul F. *Yankee From the West*. Garden City, New York: Doubleday and Company, Inc., 1962.

White, Roland A. *Milo Reno Farmers Union Pioneer: The Story of a Man and a Movement*. Iowa City: The Iowa Farmers Union, 1941.

White, William Allen. *Politics: The Citizen's Business*. New York: The Macmillian Company, 1924.

_____. *A Puritan in Babylon, The Story of Calvin Coolidge*. New York: The Macmillian Company, 1938.

Wicker, Elmus. *Federal Reserve Monetary Policy, 1917–1933*. New York: Random House, 1966.

Wiebe, Robert H. *Businessmen and Reform: A Study of the Progressive Movement*. Cambridge: Harvard University Press, 1962.

_____. *The Search for Order, 1877–1920*. New York: Hill and Wang, 1967.

Wilson, Joan Hoff. *Herbert Hoover, Forgotten Progressive*. Boston: Little, Brown and Company, 1975.

ARTICLES

"A. B. A. Rival." *Time*, January 18, 1937, pp. 50–51.

"A. B. A. Rival (Cont'd)." *Time*, March 1, 1937, pp. 42–43.

"Again, Brookhart." *Time*, April 20, 1936, p. 19.

"An Amazing Revelation of Secret Financial Meeting." *Manufacturers Record*, February 22, 1923, pp. 53–62.

Ashby, Darrel LeRoy. "Progressivism Against Itself: The Senate Western Bloc in the 1920's." *Mid-America* 50 (October, 1968):291–304.

Baldwin, W. W. "Apples and Freight Rates." *Railway Review* 72:770.

"Bandwagon." *Time*, July 16, 1928, p. 8.

Bellamy, Edward. "The Programme of the Nationalists." *The Forum* 17 (March, 1894):81–91.

Black, John D. "The McNary-Haugen Movement." *The American Economic Review* 18 (September, 1928):405–427.

_____. "The Progress of Farm Relief." *The American Economic Review* 18 (June, 1928):252–271.

"Blazing the Trail for a Co-operative Bank Law." *Co-operation* IX (April, 1923):64–65.

Blythe, Samuel G. "The Parade of the Wooden Soldiers." *The Saturday Evening Post*, October 13, 1923, p. 12.

Bowers, William L. "The Fruits of Iowa Progressivism, 1900-1915." *Iowa Journal of History* 57:34-60.

Boyd, William R. "Liquor and Common Sense in Iowa." *Harper's Weekly* 53 (June 19, 1909):13.

Bradley, Phillips. "The Farm Bloc." *The Journal Of Social Forces* 3: 714-718.

Brant, David. "Source Material Of Iowa History, David Brant's Iowa Political Sketches." *Iowa Journal Of History* 53: 341-366.

Bray, Thomas James. "The Cummins Leadership." *Annals of Iowa* 32: 241-296.

Briggs, John E. "The Iowa Primary Interpreted." *National Municipal Review* 11:282-286.

Briley, Ronald F. "Smith W. Brookhart and Russia." *Annals of Iowa* 42: 541-556.

Briley, Ron. "Insurgency and Political Realignment: Regionalism and the Senatorial Elections of 1922 in Iowa, Nebraska, North Dakota, and Minnesota." *Mid-America* 72 (January, 1990):49-69.

Brookhart, Smith W. "Brookhart Reports to Iowa Farmers." *The Iowa Homestead*, July 26, 1923, p. 6.

_____. "Causes of the Agricultural Depression." *The Reference Shelf* 4:45-60.

_____. "Col. Brookhart Replies to Senator Cummins." *The Locomotive Engineers Journal* 54:525-527.

_____. "Co-operative Banking Legislation—Why We Need It." *Co-Operation* 11:24-25.

_____. "Co-operative Economics." *Co-operation* 12:89-90.

_____. "Cooperative Economics." *The Iowa Liberal* 1:3-4.

_____. "Criticism of Federal Reserve System by Senator Brookhart." *The Commercial and Financial Chronicle* 125:337-339.

_____. "The Dry Viewpoint." *New York Times*, March 23, 1930, p. X-4.

_____. "Eyes and Sights." *Arms and the Man* LXV (November 30, 1918):187,190.

_____. "The Farm Situation, Address of United States Senator Smith W. Brookhart, of Iowa." *Proceedings of a Conference of Progressives*, March 11-12, 1931, pp. 58-62.

_____. "Governmental Aid For Cooperative Marketing." *Proceedings of the Academy of Political Science in the City of New York* 10:569-580.

_____. "Greed at the River Crossings." *American Motorist* 29 (April, 1929):10ff.

_____. "Has the Federal Reserve Act Failed?" *Plain Talk* 5: 1-11.

_____. "Hoover and the Farm Problem." Republican National Committee.

_____. "Issues of the Senatorial Primary." *Des Moines Register*, May 23, 1922, p. 6.

_____. "Let's Abandon the Gold Standard." *The Forum* 88: 10-12.

_____. "Nation Needs Economic Co-Operation." *La Follette's Magazine* 19:85-86.

_____. "Norwegian Co-ops As Model for Farmers." *Des Moines Register*, July 2, 1923, p. 1.

_____. "[On Chain Stores] Senator Brookhart's Address." *The N. A. R. D. Journal* 49:36-40.

_____. "[On Cooperation.]" *The Fifty-Fifth Annual Co-operative Congress 1923*, Plunkett Foundation:437.

_____. "[On Renomination.]" *New York American*, June 9, 1924.

_____. "A Plan to Assure Equality to Agriculture." *The Missouri Farmer*, December 1, 1936, pp. 3-4.

_____. "The Plight of the Farmer." *The Nation* 122:367-369.

_____. "[The Progressive Program.]" *New York World*, November 10, 1930.

_____. "Public Ownership of Railroads." *Public Ownership of Public Utilities* 16:68-70.

_____. "Railroads are Wasting Millions." *La Follette's Magazine* 15:88.

_____. "The Retail Merchant and Community Development." *National Grocers Bulletin*, Special Convention Issue, June 11-14, 1928, pp. 53-55.

_____. "Rifle and Pistol Practice." *Arms and the Man* 55 (November 13, 1913):125-126.
_____. "Rifle Training in War." *Arms and the Man* 64 Part 1, April 6, 1918, 23ff; Part 2, April 13, 1918, 45ff; Part 3, April 29, 1918, 65ff; Part 4, April 27, 1918, 85ff; Part 5, May 4, 1918, 107ff; Part 6, May 11, 1918, 127ff.
_____. "Russia As I Saw It." *The Locomotive Engineers Journal,* October, 1923, pp. 791-792.
_____. "Shall the Farmers Organize?" *The Iowa Homestead*, December 11, 1919, pp. 13, 21.
_____. "Toll Bridges Menace Road Program." *La Follette's Magazine* 21:5-6.
_____. "What Co-Operation Means to The Iowa Producers." *The Iowa Union Farmer*, May 19, 1920, p. 4.
_____. "What I Really Saw and Learned in Europe in 1923." *The Saturday Evening Post*, March 15, 1930, p. 23.
_____. "Why the Farmers Should Oppose the Cummins Bill." *Des Moines Register*, January 5, 1920, p. 6.
_____. "Why I Am a Candidate Against Senator Cummins." *The Iowa Homestead*, May 27, 1920, pp. 12-13.
_____. "Why I am Interested in the Movies." *The Allied Exhibitor* 2:3-5.
_____. "Why I am Interested in the Movies." *Greater Amusements* 32:8.
Brookhart, Smith W. and Pettijohn, Charles C. "Will the Brookhart Bill Help the Exhibitors?" *The Congressional Digest* 7:305-307.
"Brookhart and the Resentful West." *The Outlook* 143:235-236.
"Brookhart at League Dinner." *Co-operation* 16:7-8.
"Brookhart Hauls Railway President Over Coals." *The Railway Maintenance of Way Employees Journal* 32:5-6.
"Brookhart-LaFollette Bloc Begins Radical Government Ownership Fight." *Railway Review* 72:171-175.
"Brookhart Loses." *The Independent* 116:372.
"Brookhart's Interest in Russia." *Annals of Iowa* 32:230-232.
"The Brookhart-Meredith Duel." *The Literary Digest*, September 8, 1923, pp. 13-14.
"Brookhart on Cloture." *The Searchlight on Congress* 10:7-8.
"Brookhart v. The Century." *Time*, February 10, 1930, pp. 13-14.
"The Brookhart Victory." *The Nation* 122:657.
"Brookhart's Victory in Iowa." *The American Review of Reviews* 66:17.
Buenker, John D. "The Progressive Era: A Search For A Synthesis." *Mid-America* 51:175-193.
"Campaign Notes." *Time*, October 13, 1924, pp. 3-4.
Campbell, Ballard C. "Did Democracy Work? Prohibition in Late Nineteenth-Century Iowa: A Test Cast." *Journal of Interdisciplinary History* 8:87-116.
"Chicken Stew." *Time*, June 20, 1932, p. 12.
Clark, Dan Elbert. "The Beginnings of Liquor Legislation in Iowa." *The Iowa Journal of History and Politics* 6:193-212.
_____. "The History of Liquor Legislation in Iowa, 1846-1861." *The Iowa Journal of History and Politics* 6:55-87.
_____. "The History of Liquor Legislation in Iowa, 1861-1878." *The Iowa Journal of History and Politics* 6:339-374.
_____. "The History of Liquor Legislation in Iowa, 1878-1908." *The Iowa Journal of History and Politics* 6:503-608.
"Congratulations, Senator Brookhart." *Locomotive Engineers Journal* 60: 325.
"Congress Has a Shouting Progressive in Brookhart, of Iowa." *Current Opinion* 74:538-540.
Cook, Louis H. "Brookhart, Insurgent." *North American Review* 231: 178-184.
_____. "The Man Who Beat Brookhart." *The Saturday Evening Post*, July 23, 1932, p. 12.
_____. "A New Sort Of U. S. Senator." *The Iowa Magazine*, December 7, 1922, p. 287.

BIBLIOGRAPHY

Cornwell, John J. "Brookhart's Government Ownership Plan." *Railway Age* 83:983.

Cowles, John. "Urges Legion to Help Nail Lies on Russia Here." *Iowa Legionnaire*, November 23, 1923, p. 8.

Creel, George. "What Do These Senators Want?" *Collier's*, March 10, 1923, pp. 9–10.

"Cummins Versus Plumb." *The Nation* 109:361.

Cushing, Charles Phelps. "A Glass of Political Fashions." *Collier's*, October 7, 1922, p. 11.

Davis, James C. "New Capital Needed in Fight Against Nationalization." *Railway Review* 72:558–561.

"Debating the Senatorship." *Iowa Forum*, May 3, 1922, p. 1.

"A Democratic Senator From Iowa!" *The Literary Digest*, April 24, 1926, p. 11.

Dennis, Alfred Pearce. "The European Education of Senator Brookhart." *The Saturday Evening Post*, December 14, 1929, p. 10.

Devaney, John P. "The Quarterly." *National Lawyers Guild Quarterly* 1 (December, 1937):1–2.

Dickinson, Lester J. "What Republicans Will Do Next." *Liberty* 11 (August 18, 1934):20–22.

Dileva, Frank D. "Iowa Farm Price Revolt." *Annals of Iowa* 32:171–202.

Durand, Walt. "What About Brookhart?" *The Searchlight on Congress* 9: 17–19.

English, Emory H. "Evolution in Iowa Voting Practices." *Annals of Iowa* 29:249–289.

Evans, Arthur. "Railroad Before Brookhart's Demand." *Railway Review* 72: 509–510.

"Ex-Senator Brookhart." *Railway Age* 80:1127.

"The Farmer Will Decide the Future of the Railroads." *Railway Review* 72:509–510.

"Farms and Russia: Brookhart's Appointment Renews Question of Soviet Recognition." *Newsweek* 1 (June 3, 1933):6.

Fausold, Martin L. "President Herbert Hoover's Farm Policies 1929–1933." *Agricultural History* 51:362–377.

Feinman, Ronald L. "The Progressive Republican Senate Block and the Presidential Election of 1932." *Mid-America* 59:73–92.

Filene, Peter G. "An Obituary for 'The Progressive Movement.'" *American Quarterly* 22:20–34.

"Financial Conference At Washington." *Federal Reserve Bulletin*, June, 1920, pp. 556–557, 579–582.

Fite, Gilbert C. "The Agricultural Issue in the Presidential Campaign of 1928." *The Mississippi Valley Historical Review* 37:63–672.

"For a Nobler Washington." *The Commonweal*, October 9, 1929, p. 573.

"Former Senator Brookhart." *American Economist* 72:121–122.

Fraker, Fleming. "The Beginnings of the Progressive Movement in Iowa." *Annals of Iowa* 35:578–593.

Friday, David. "The Course of Agricultural Income During the Last Twenty-Five Years." *The American Economic Review* 13:147–158.

Garlock, Fred L. "Bank Failures in Iowa." *The Journal of Land and Public Utility Economics* 2:49–66.

"A Gigantic Program of Confiscation." *Railway Age* 74:315–316.

Gilbert, Clinton W. "And So Do His Cousins and His Aunts." *Collier's*, July 16, 1932, p. 19.

Gilbert, Clinton W. "The Laugh Cure." *Collier's*, August 6, 1932, p. 21.

"G. O. P. Rebels Shown the Door." *The Literary Digest*, December 13, 1924, p. 10.

"Guild Organization, Constitution, By-Laws, and Resolutions." *National Lawyers Guild Quarterly* 2 (April, 1939):81–93.

Haines, Austin. "Smith W. Brookhart, Dissenter." *The Nation* 115:465–467.

Hard, William. "Our Leading 'Menace.'" *Hearst's International*, October, 1923, p. 79.

Harrington, Elbert W. "A Survey of the Political Ideas of Albert Baird Cummins." *Iowa Journal of History and Politics* 39:339-386.

Hawley, Ellis W. "Herbert Hoover, the Commerce Secretariat, and the Vision of an 'Associate State,' 1921-1928." *Journal of American History* 61:116-140.

Haynes, Frederick Emory. "La Follette and La Follettism." *Atlantic Monthly* 134:536-544.

_____. "The New Sectionalism." *The Quarterly Journal Of Economics* 10 (April, 1896):269-295.

_____. "Third-Party Backgrounds." *The Independent* 113:71-74.

Hearst, James. "The Demand of the Iowa Farmers." *McNaught's Monthly* 5 (March, 1926):70-71.

_____. "Reminiscences." *The North American Review* 259 (Fall, 1974):3943.

Herbst, Josephine. "The Farmer Looks Ahead." *The American Mercury* 34 (February, 1935):212-219.

_____. "Feet in the Grass Roots." *Scribners* 93 (January, 1933):46-51.

Hicks, John D. "The Persistence of Populism." *Minnesota History* 12:3-20.

_____. "Some Parallels with Populism in the Twentieth Century." *Social Education* 8:297-301.

Hines, Charles Delano. "A Reply to Senator Brookhart." *Proceedings of the Academy of Political Science in the City of New York* 10:581-584.

Hines, Walker D. "The Director-General's Position." *The Nation* 109: 202-203.

Hoover, Herbert. "Why Cooperative Marketing Should Receive Universal Support." *Country Gentleman*, October 21, 1922, p. 11.

Horwill, Herbert W. "The Progressive Conference, An Englishman's Impressions." *The Nation* 115:663.

"How Brookhart Would Change The Steel Trust into a Co-operative." *Co-operation* 10 (July, 1924):128.

"How Demagogues Misrepresent Railways." *Railway Age* 81:620.

Huntington, Samuel P. "The Election Tactics of the Nonpartisan League." *Mississippi Valley Historical Review* 36 (March, 1950):613-632.

"Impossible interviews—no. 10, Senator Brookhart vs. Marlene Dietrich." *Vanity Fair* 39 (September, 1932):36.

"Insurgents Resurgent." *Time*, January 26, 1931, pp. 12-14.

"Investigation." *The Outlook* 136 (March 12, 1924):413.

"The Iowa Fly in the G. O. P. Ointment." *The Literary Digest*, June 21, 1924, p. 13.

"The Iowa Primary." *American Economist* 77 (June 11, 1926):188-189.

"The Iowa Primary Election." *Locomotive Engineers Journal* 60:410.

Kern, Jean B. "The Political Career of Horace Boies." *Iowa Journal of History* 47:215-246.

Kerr, William G. "An Epoch in Iowa Politics." *Annals Of Iowa* 33:153-171.

Koerselman, Gary H. "Secretary Hoover and National Farm Policy: Problems of Leadership." *Agricultural History* 51:378-395.

"Labor and Farmers Start on United Political Drive." *The New Majority*, March 4, 1936, pp. 1ff.

La Follette, Robert M., Jr. "The Case of the People of Iowa and Smith W. Brookhart Against the Republican-Democratic Coalition in the United States Senate." *La Follette's Magazine*, May, 1926, pp. 76-78.

_____. "Iowa Repudiates Old Guard." *La Follette's Magazine*, May, 1926, p. 83.

"The Legal Left." *Time*, March 7, 1938, p. 16.

"Limitation of Business Profits." *Railway Age* 85:648-649.

Link, Arthur S. "What Happened to the Progressive Movement in the 1920's?" *American Historical Review* 64:833-851.

Lissner, Edward. "Iowa's Political War and its Bearing Upon the Destiny of the Republican Party." *Harper's Weekly*, April 21, 1906, p. 549.

Luthin, Reinhard H. "Smith Wildman Brookhart of Iowa: Insurgent Agrarian Politician." *Agricultural History* 25:187-197.
Lyman, Charles A. "Why Co-Operators Are Afraid of Uncle Sam." *The Spotlight* 8 (September, 1923):13-17.
McDaniel, George William. "'Martial Sons of Martial Sires.'" *The Palimpsest* 70 (Spring, 1989):32-48.
_____. "New Era Agrarian Radicalism: Smith W. Brookhart and the Populist Critique." *Annals of Iowa* 49 (Winter/Spring, 1988):208-220.
_____. "Prohibition Debate in Washington County, 1890-1894: Smith Wildman Brookhart's Introduction to Politics." *Annals of Iowa* 45 (Winter, 1981):519-536.
_____. "The Republican Party in Iowa and the Defeat of Smith Wildman Brookhart." *Annals of Iowa* 48 (Winter/Spring, 1987): 413-434.
_____. "The Search for Smith Wildman Brookhart: A Pilgrim's Progress." *Books at Iowa* 52 (April, 1990):53-69.
_____. "Smith Wildman Brookhart." *The Palimpsest* 63 (November/December, 1982):174-183.
_____. "Smith Wildman Brookhart: 'The Man Who Taught the Army How to Shoot.'" *The Palimpsest* 75, No. 1 (Spring, 1994): 30—45.
"The Meaning of Brookhart." *The Outlook* 131:363
Merz, Charles, "The Line-Up in Iowa." *The New Republic* 22:267-228.
Miles, Frank F. "Senator Brookhart Almost Alone In Ideas On Russia." *Iowa Legionnaire*, September 21, 1923, p. 5.
"Misquoted." *Time*, June 21, 1926. p. 10.
Mitchell, J. G. "Cooperative Marketing—An Iowa View." *Iowa Law Bulletin* 9:6-25.
Morrow, James B. "A Hunter of Wall Street Devils." *The Nation's Business*, March, 1923, pp. 21-22.
The Nation 115:717; 122;435; 129:626; 134:692.
Nelson, Lawrence J. "The Art of the Possible: Another Look at the 'Purge' of the AAA Liberals in 1935." *Agricultural History* 57 (October, 1983):416-435.
"Nepotism." *Time*, May 30, 1932, pp. 9-10.
"The New 'Bloc' System." *Railway Review* 72:259-260.
"A New 'Iowa Idea.'" *The Literary Digest*, June 24, 1922, pp. 8-9.
Nieberg, George Frederic. "All in the Congressional Family." *Atlantic Monthly* 148:514-525.
Nixon, Herman C. "Agrarian Influence in the Political Revolt of the Middle West." *The Iowa Agriculturist* 23 (January, 1923):189.
O'Brien, Patrick G. "A Reexamination of the Senate Farm Bloc 1921-1933." *Agricultural History* 47:248-263.
Olssen, Eric. "The Progressive Group in Congress, 1922-1929." *The Historian* 42:244-263.
"One Instance of Valuation Progress." *Railway Age* 82:635.
"Organized Labor Must Help in Colonel Brookhart's Campaign in Iowa." *Locomotive Engineers Journal* 54:523-524.
"Our Friend, Mr. Brookhart." *Railway Age* 81:1.
"Our National Soviet." *Railway Review* 72:186.
"Our Supposed Policy of Regulation and Our Real One." *Railway Age* 85: 441-442.
"Out of the Economic Dark Ages." *Nation's Business* 11:41.
Palermo, Patrick F. "The Midwestern Republican Tradition." *Capitol Studies, A Journal of the Capitol and Congress* 5:43-56.
Parsons, Stanley B.; Parsons, Karen Toombs; Killilae, Walter; Borgers, Beverly. "The Role of Cooperatives in the Development of the Movement Culture of Populism." *The Journal of American History* 69: 866-885.
Parsons, Wilfrid. "An Open Letter to M. Litvinov." *America* 50 (November 4, 1933): 107-108.

BIBLIOGRAPHY

Petersen, Peter. "The Reluctant Candidate: Edwin T. Meredith and the 1924 Democratic National Convention." *The Palimpsest* 57:146-156.
Pew, Marlen. "Shop Talk at Thirty." *Editor and Publisher the Fourth Estate* 64 (January 16, 1932):44.
"Playing Brookhart Out With a Steam Calliope." *The Literary Digest*, June 18, 1932, p. 5.
Plumb, Glenn E. "How to Value the Railroads." *The Nation* 109:78-79.
_____. "Labor's Solution of the Railroad Problem." *The Nation* 109:200-201.
_____. "What the Plumb Plan Means." *The Forum* 42:358-369.
"The Plumb Plan and the Railways." *The American Review of Reviews* 60 (September, 1919):278-281.
"The Plumb Plan to the Front." *The Nation* 109:196.
"The Political Explosion in Iowa." *The Literary Digest*, October 18, 1924, pp. 10-11.
Potts, E. Daniel. "The Progressive Profile in Iowa." *Mid-America* 47:257-268.
"Preparedness the Policy for Carriers on Political Issues." *Railway Review* 72:289-290.
"President Felton Replies to Statement Made by Senator Brookhart." *Railway Review* 76:664-666.
"President Felton of Great Western Writes Senator Brookhart." *The Iowa Magazine*, March 1, 1923, p. 406.
"The Primaries." *Time*, June 14, 1926, p. 6.
"Problems That Are Fundamental." *Railway Age* 92:1005-1007.
"Progressives of the Senate." *The American Mercury* 16 (April, 1929): 385-393.
"Prohibition." *Time*, October 7, 1929, pp. 16-17.
"'Railroad' Cummins Sidetracked." *The Searchlight on Congress* 9:17-19.
"Railway Employees and Senator Brookhart." *Railway Age* 92:854-855.
"The Railway Problem—Discussion." *The American Economic Review* 10 (March, 1920):186-212.
"Resignations from the Lawyers' Guild." *The Commonweal* 29 (March 10, 1939):547-548.
Rich, Edgar J. "The Transportation Act of 1920." *The American Economic Review* 10:507-527.
"Rival to A. B. A.: Lawyers Form New Progressive Guild and Favor Innovations." *The Literary Digest* 123 (March 27, 1937):8.
Roberts, George E. "The Origin and History of the Iowa Idea." *Iowa Journal of History and Politics* 2:69-82.
Roberts, Kenneth L. "Filibusters." *The Saturday Evening Post*, May 12, 1923, p. 6.
Rowell, Chester H. "Brookhart, Howell, and 'Brother Charley' Bryan, The Radical Revolt in Iowa and Nebraska." *World's Work* 46:478-485.
Ruggles, Clyde O. "The Economic Basis of the Greenback Movement in Iowa and Wisconsin." *Proceedings of the Mississippi Valley Historical Association* 6:142-165.
"Russia and Religion." *The Commonweal* 19 (November 10, 1933):29-30.
Sage, Norman. "Iowa's Son of the Wild Jackass." Unpublished, Author's Possession.
Sapiro, Aaron. "Cooperative Marketing." *Iowa Law Bulletin* 8:193-210.
"Senator Brookhart as an Aid to Wall Street." *Railway Age* 74:548-549.
"Senator Brookhart Censured." *American Economist* 24:1-2.
"Senator Brookhart . . . To Address Forum Meeting . . ." *City Club Life* (Boston), November 25, 1929, p. 1.
"Senator Brookhart of Iowa for Price Fixing." *The Home Owned Store*, May, 1932, p. 3.
"Senator Brookhart on the Air." *Law and Labor* 13:4-5.
"Senator Brookhart's Radical Railroad Bill." *Railway Age* 74:503-504.
"Senator Brookhart Returns From European Survey." *Co-operation* 9: 155-158.
"Senators Study Co-Operation Abroad." *Co-operation* 9:84.
"72nd Made." *Time*, November 17, 1930, pp. 16-18.

"Smith W. Brookhart." *Vanity Fair*, January, 1932, p. 48.
"Silver Flasks." *Time*, November 18, 1929, pp. 13-14.
"Sons of the Wild Jackass." *The Literary Digest*, November 23, 1929, pp. 10-11.
"Speed the Parting." *Railway Review* 78:609.
"Steck Wins Against Brookhart." *Review of Review*, May, 1926, pp. 461-462.
Sullivan, Mark. "The 'Progressive Group' in the Senate." *World's Work* 45:384-393.
"Teaching Co-Operation to the U. S. Senate." *Co-Operation* 9:48-49.
Thelen, David P. "Social Tensions and the Origins of Progressivism." *The Journal of American History* 66:323-341.
"Three Radicals' Schemes of Railroad Valuation." *Railway Age* 76:969.
Throne, Mildred. "Iowans in Congress, 1847-1953." *Iowa Journal of History* 51:329-368.
_____. "The Anti-Monopoly Party in Iowa, 1873-1874." *Iowa Journal of History* 52:289-325.
Titus, George M. "The Battle for Biennial Elections." *Annals of Iowa* 29:163-175.
Tucker, Ray. "The Customer is Always Right." *Collier's* 92 (October 21, 1933):26f.
Turner, James. "Understanding the Populists." *The Journal of American History* 67:354-373.
"USA-USSR: 40 Years of Diplomatic Relations." *Soviet Life* 11 (November, 1973):36-38.
"United States Senate Unseats Senator Smith W. Brookhart of Iowa—D. F. Steck, Who Contested Seat, Sworn In." *The Commercial and Financial Chronicle* 122:2145.
Upham, Cyril B. "Historical Survey of the Militia in Iowa 1865-1898." *The Iowa Journal of History and Politics* 18 (January, 1920):3-93.
"A Vest-Pocket Geography, Iowa." *The Saturday Evening Post*, October 6, 1928, p. 178.
Vietor, Richard H. K. "Businessmen and the Political Economy: The Railroad Rate Controversy of 1905." *The Journal of American History* 64:47-66.
"War on the Supreme Court." *The Literary Digest*, March 1, 1930, pp. 7-9.
"What Railway Officials Think of the Radical Legislative Program." *Railway Review* 72:226-228.
"What Senator Brookhart Saw in Europe." *The Spotlight* 8:11-12.
"What the Brookhart Bill Provides." *The Congressional Digest* 7:304.
"What the World is Doing." *The Independent*, June 19, 1926, pp. 723-724.
Wheeler, Senator Burton K. "Shall We Recognize Russia?" *Zion's Herald*, July 11, 1923, pp. 882-883.
Whiting, Edward W. "Why You Should Come To Hear Senator Brookhart." *City Club Life* (Boston), November 25, 1929, p. 4.
"Who Speaks for Small Business?" *Business Week*, September 24, 1938, pp. 28-29.
"Who's Who—And Why, Senator Brookhart." *The Saturday Evening Post*, May 5, 1923, p. 36.
"Why Iowa Smashed the Windows." *The Literary Digest*, June 19, 1926, pp. 5-7.
"Why the Voter Voted Discontent." *The Literary Digest*, November 25, 1922, pp. 8-9.
Wiebe, Robert H. "The Progressive Years, 1900-1917." Cartwright, William H. and Watson, Richard L. *The Reinterpretation of American History and Culture*, 1973, pp. 425-442.
Williams, William Appleman. "The Legend of Isolationism in the 1920's." *Science and Society* 18:1-20.
"Without a Peer." *Barron's* 10 (December 22, 1930):14.
"Yes, Travel Broadens One So." *Collier's*, September 8, 1923, p. 17.

INDEX

AAA. *See* Agricultural Adjustment Administration
Adams, John T., 130, 154
Agricultural Adjustment Administration (AAA)
   B. is advisor for Russian trade, 274-76, 279-80
   B. leaves in frustration, 281-83
Agricultural depression, 93-95. *See also* Farm relief
   B.'s analysis of causes, 94-95, 98-99, 120, 199-200
   Hoover's analysis of causes, 233
   in 1922 senatorial campaign, 133-34, 196
   in 1926 senatorial campaign, F185-86, 187, 189, 190, 192, 194, 197-98
Ahlgren, A. N., 257
Akerson, George, 214, 217, 226
Allen, Arthur F., 188, 193, 194, 252
Allen, Byron, 258, 266
Allison, William Boyd, 51, 52, 53, 56-57, 62-63, 83
American Farm Bureau Federation. *See also* Howard, James R.; Iowa Farm Bureau Federation
   absent from progressives' conference, 103
   in 1920 senatorial campaign, 76, 80
   in 1922 senatorial campaign, 102, 105-6, 108-10, 112, 120
   supports McNary-Haugen Bill, 201
   Wallace is close to, 276
American Legion. *See also* Republican Service League
   opposes Esch-Cummins Bill, 76
   in 1928 presidential campaign, 220
   in 1924 senatorial campaign, 150-52, 158-60, 193
   in unseating of B., 172, 173
American Society for Equity, 75, 103
Ames, Asa L., 74-75
Andrews, L. A., 94
Anti-Monopoly Party, 14, 96, 297
Army. *See also* Marksmanship
   B. favors citizens' army, 40-41, 285
Arrow ballots, 163, 167-68

B. of L. E.. *See* Railroad brotherhoods
Bacon, Edward, 58, 59, 60
Bailey, Josiah W., 281
Bailey, Marsh W., 53-54
Baker, Newton, 40, 42, 45
Baker, Norman, 210
Baldwin, W. W., 167
Bancroft, William A., 22
Banks. *See also* Federal Reserve Board
   cooperative, 79, 98-99, 144-45, 204-5, 248, 271
   fail during depression, 94, 157, 199
   tighten credit for farmers, 94-95
Bayard, Thomas F., 213
Bell, William B., 13, 14
Berry, Don, 110
Berry, George L., 292
Beveridge, Albert, 66-67
Blaine, John J., 137, 208, 211, 213
Blease, Coleman L., 171, 213
Blythe, James E., 52
Blythe, Joseph W.
   challenged by Cummins, 51-53, 58, 61-62
   dies suddenly, 63
   seeks B.'s support, 56-57, 62, 67
Boies, Horace, 51
Boies, William D., 101

367

INDEX

Bolters Convention, 131-32
Borah, William, 117, 208, 210, 213, 221-22, 262
Bradshaw, Charles S., 193
Bremmer, John E., 219, 220
Brewer, Luther, 161-62, 163-64
Brookhart, Abram Colar (father), 5-6, 7, 9, 17
Brookhart, Charles Edward (son)
  birth, 17
  correspondence from Florence, 283
  correspondence from John, 274
  correspondence from mother, 255, 262, 267, 268, 279, 282, 292, 295
Brookhart, Cynthia Wildman (mother), 5, 6, 9, 17
Brookhart, Edith (daughter)
  with aging parents, 279, 295
  childhood in Iowa, 30, 42
  moves to Washington, D.C., 208
Brookhart, Florence (daughter)
  with aging parents, 283, 284, 295-96
  childhood in Iowa, 30, 43
  marries, 289
  moves to Washington, D.C., 208
Brookhart, James L. (brother)
  and bank failure, 157
  in 1920 Congressional campaign, 73
  as county attorney, 21
  illness and death, 195-96
  as land speculator, 28-29
  as Smith's law partner, 16, 26, 39
Brookhart, Jennie Hearne (wife)
  and bank failure, 157
  becomes senator's wife, 143
  and 1920 Congressional campaign, 73
  early married life, 17-18, 30-31, 42-43, 47
  final years, 283, 292, 293, 295-96
  during husband's AAA tenure, 274, 276, 279, 280, 282
  moves to Washington, D.C., 206-8
  and 1936 presidential campaign, 290
  role in marriage, 206, 283-84, 296
  and 1924 senatorial campaign, 164, 165
  and 1932 senatorial campaign, 255, 262, 266, 267-68
  travels with husband, 205, 251
Brookhart, John (son)
  adulthood in Duluth, 207, 265, 274, 295-96
  youth in Iowa, 30, 43, 157, 206
Brookhart, Joseph (son), 30, 42, 295
Brookhart, Ned. See Brookhart, Charles Edward
Brookhart, Odes (brother), 205

Brookhart, Samuel Colar (son), 30, 43
Brookhart, Smith Wildman
  absenteeism from Senate, 249-50, 263
  in army, 44-48, 73
  attention to detail, 25, 49
  bank failure liability, 157, 187, 205, 249, 276, 295
  business investments, 16, 27, 28-29
  childhood, 5-6
  as county attorney, 13-16, 21, 26, 53-54
  education, 6-7
  European trip, 143-49
  as export consultant, 284, 288
  as farmer, 31, 43, 206
  final illness and death, 295-97
  lack of political skills, 272
  law practice after Senate, 142, 294-95
  law practice before Senate career, 7-8, 10, 15, 16, 25, 26, 29, 57
  as marksman, 32-35, 37-42, 44-49
  moral values, 42-43
  moves to Washington, D.C., 206-8
  in National Guard, 19-24, 32, 33-37
  as New Dealer, 273
  passionate style, 271-72
  patriotism, 25, 104
  populism, 95-98, 120, 242-43
  portraits by painters, 242
  progressivism, 4, 68, 95, 259, 270, 273
  prohibitionism, 11, 13-14, 26, 34, 250-52, 269
  as regular Republican, 191, 216, 218-19, 228, 229, 270, 272
  religious attitudes, 42, 277-78
  reluctance to support third parties, 287
  remote personality, 16, 42, 272
  as schoolteacher, 7
  simplicity, 44-45, 142-43, 298
  in Washington, D.C., social life, 136, 142-43, 208
  in Washington, Iowa, civic life, 27-28, 30
Brookhart, Smith Wildman, Jr. (son)
  and aging parents, 293
  assesses father's politics, 273
  correspondence from mother, 206
  son's accidental death, 289
  works for father, 157, 254
  youth in Iowa, 30, 43, 157
Brookhart, Thompson (brother), 16, 289
Brookhart Railroad Bill, 141-42
Brotherhood of Locomotive Engineers. See Railroad brotherhoods
Brown, Benjamin F., 13-14
Bryan, William Jennings, 53, 69
Bureaucracy
  and farm relief, 201, 216

vs. Populism, xviii
Buresh, George F., 289
Burgess, E. A., 154
Burnquist, B. B., 130, 132, 133, 159, 162, 189
Burrell, Howard A., 4, 11, 12, 13, 15-16, 54, 55
Business. *See* Corporate power; Small business
Butler, William M.
  in 1926 senatorial campaign, 185, 187, 195
  works with MacNider for Steck, 160, 163, 168-69, 170, 171, 172, 173
Byers, Howard W., 65, 100
Byers, Melvin H., 32, 34, 36
Byers, Web, 114, 115

C. B. & Q.. *See* Chicago, Burlington and Quincy Railroad
Call, George C., 84
Campbell, Frank T., 59
Campbell, Thomas D., 229
Camp Cuba Libre, 21-23, 24
Camp Dodge, 45, 47
Camp McKinley, 20-21, 24
Camp Perry, 45-48, 129
Canfield, Fred, 76
Cannon, Joseph, 73
Capper, Arthur, 94, 111-12, 130, 132
Capper-Kelly Bill, 244
Caraway, Thaddeus H., 167, 170, 230
Carey, John W., 193
Carroll, Beryl F., 63, 131, 150
Carter, Archie, 287
Cedar Rapids Gang, 123, 223
Chain stores, 243-44, 293
Chamber of Commerce, 82, 225
Chautauqua speeches, 249-50
Chicago, Burlington and Quincy Railroad, 3, 28, 51, 58, 154, 167
Clark, Howard J., 75-76, 100, 254
Clarkson, James S., 50, 53
Clarkson, Richard, 53
Clifton, C. C., 164, 165, 190, 262, 288, 291, 297
Cole, Cyrenus, 81, 165, 253
Commercial Club, 27
Committee of 17, 95
Committee of 48, 81, 83
Communism
  anti-communism in 1920s Iowa, 82
  as charge against B., 141, 260, 284-86
  vs. cooperation, 98
  praised by B., 281, 282
  in rhetoric of 1920 campaign, 83

in rhetoric of 1924 campaign, 156
Company D. *See* Iowa National Guard
Conference for Progressive Political Action, 102-4, 116, 126, 142
Conference of Farm and Labor Organizations, 99
Congressional campaign (1910), 3-4, 63-65
Congressional reform, 64
Cook, Louis H., 134, 252-53, 256, 257, 260
Coolidge, Calvin
  alleged meeting with B., 214, 215, 225-26
  declares won't run in 1928, 203
  farm policy, 190, 209-10, 211
  and national rifle matches, 49
  1924 presidential campaign, 155, 156, 160, 161
  punishes B. for supporting La Follette, 166
  and 1924 senatorial campaign, 162, 165, 173-74
  and 1926 senatorial campaign, 187, 190
  vetoes McNary-Haugen, 201, 204, 216
Cooper, Harry L., 48
Cooperative associations. *See also* Populism
  B. studies European examples, 143, 145, 146, 147, 148, 149
  B. writes book on, 294
  banking cooperatives, 79, 98-99, 144-45, 204-5, 248, 271
  in B.'s 1920 farm relief analysis, 74, 75, 84
  in B.'s 1922 farm relief analysis, 95, 98-99, 106, 139
  in B.'s 1926 farm relief analysis, 185
  in B.'s program as senator, 200, 201, 209, 248
  in Democrats' 1932 farm plank, 265
  in Hoover's farm policies, 201, 216, 218, 223, 231-32, 233
  in McNary-Haugen Bill, 201, 212
  of nineteenth-century farmers, 96
  Rochdale principles, 77-78, 97-98, 145, 271
  for small businesses, 243
Cooperative League of America, 145
Copeland, William W., 64, 67, 80-81, 107
Corey, Frank, 80
Corliss-Nelson bill, 58
Corn Belt Committee, 217, 218
Corn Belt Meat Producers Association, 69
Corporate power. *See also* Railroads
  and agriculture, 243, 271
  in B.'s 1920 campaign rhetoric, 77-78
  in B.'s 1922 campaign rhetoric, 126

369

Corporate power (*continued*)
  in B.'s 1932 campaign rhetoric, 259
  Cummins' opposition to, 57-58
  and depression, 242-43
  monopolies, 120, 243-46, 293
  populist analysis, 95-96
  progressives' position, 59-60, 67
  trusts, 69, 74-75
Cosson, George, 256, 261
Coughlin, Father Charles E., 289, 290
Couzens, James, 138
Coverdale, J. W., 108, 110
Cozad, W. T., 167, 169, 173
Crawford, Marion, 57
Cummins, Albert Baird. *See also* Esch-Cummins Act
  alliance with B., 54-58, 61-63, 66, 67, 72
  appoints B. as Inspector of Small Arms Practice, 37, 58, 62
  breaks with B., 72, 74-80, 196-97
  challenges Blythe, 51-53, 58
  dies, 192
  escorts B. into Senate, 135, 136
  railroad reform position, 71-72
  in Senate's internal politics, 154-55, 166
  and 1922 senatorial appointment, 101
  and 1924 senatorial campaign, 153, 154-55, 156
  in 1920 senatorial campaign, 80-86
  in 1926 senatorial campaign, 185-89
  and 1922 senatorial election, 121, 122, 123, 124, 125, 126, 129
  and 1922 senatorial primary, 107-8, 109, 112, 114, 115, 117
  in unseating of B., 169, 171, 172
Cummins railroad bill, 72, 74, 75
Cunningham, Edward H., 94, 101, 105-6, 122, 157-58
Curtis, Charles, 140, 192

Dale, Porter H., 171
Darling, Ding, 255
Darrow, Clarence, 251
Daugherty, Harry M., 155, 170, 187, 188, 285
Davis, Chester C., 280, 282-83
Davis, James C., 141
Dawes, Charles G., 156, 162, 172, 204, 213
Dawson, Albert F., 94-95
Dawson, Anna, 135
Deemer, Horace, 65
Democracy, and cooperative associations, 77-78
Democratic Party
  adopts reformist legacy, 273
  in 1928 presidential campaign, 216-17
  in 1920 senatorial campaign, 84
  in 1922 senatorial campaign, 111, 117, 125-26, 131-32
  in 1924 senatorial campaign, 158, 164-65, 169-70, 171-72
  in 1926 senatorial campaign, 194, 197
  in 1932 senatorial campaign, 261-62, 265, 268
Deneen, Charles S., 192
Denison, John D., 203
Dennis, Alfred Pearce, 144, 145, 146, 148-49
Depression. *See* Agricultural depression; Great Depression
Dewey, Almon, 54, 55
Dickinson, Lester J., 101, 153, 254, 280-81, 286, 287, 289, 291
Dolliver, Jonathan Prentiss, 4, 52, 63, 64
Douglas, William O., 295
Dows, William G., 123, 124
Duval, Minnie, 291

Eicher, Edward, 268, 284, 293
Eickelberg, Louis E., 254, 255-56
Elkins railroad bill, 58
Ellington, John, 146
Engle, Perry, 127, 131
Equality, in B.'s populism, 243
Equalization fee
  in McNary-Haugen Bill, 200, 212, 214, 216, 226
  in progressives' farm program, 209
  in 1928 Republican platform, 218
Ernst, Richard P., 166, 167, 170, 171, 195
Esch-Cummins Act
  B. works for repeal, 141-42
  labor opposition, 74, 76, 78, 79-80
  section 15-A, 72, 94, 105, 123, 141
  in 1920 senatorial campaign, 76, 78, 79-80
  in 1922 senatorial campaign, 106, 113, 122, 123, 126, 129
  in 1926 senatorial campaign, 188

Farm Bloc, 99, 100, 111, 134, 136
Farm Bureau. *see* American Farm Bureau Federation
Farmer-Labor Party, 286-87, 289, 290, 291
Farmers Alliances, 96
Farmers' and Merchants' Bank
  and B.'s financial problems, 205, 249, 276, 295
  failure, 157, 187
  founding, 27-28
Farmer's Cooperative Association, 143
Farmers' Holiday Association, 266

Farmers' Institute, 27
Farmers' National Council, 75, 103
Farmers' Protective Association, 97
Farmers' Union. *See also* Reno, Milo
  absent from progressives' conference, 103
  B. speaks to, 98-99
  Farmers' Holiday Association, 266
  in 1928 presidential campaign, 218, 219, 220-21, 225
  in 1920 senatorial campaign, 76, 80-81, 84
  in 1922 senatorial campaign, 105, 117, 119, 132
  in 1932 senatorial campaign, 253-54, 263
Farm relief. *See also* Agricultural depression; McNary-Haugen Farm Relief Bill
  B.'s program, 200, 271
  B.'s 1928 Senate bill, 212, 213
  B.'s 1929 Senate bill, 230
  Coolidge's program, 211
  Hoover administration bill, 230-33
  in 1928 presidential campaign, 202-3, 214-18, 222, 223
  in 1932 presidential campaign, 264-65
  progressives' program, 208-10
  in 1932 senatorial campaign, 254, 259
Fay, Louis, 161
FBI investigates Brookhart, 284-86
Federal Land Banks, 99
Federal Reserve Board
  B. blames for agricultural depression, 94, 95, 99, 194, 199
  B. blames for 1929 crash, 248
  B. calls for farm and labor representation, 139
  B.'s monetary policy, 249
  farmer member added, 100
  issue in 1922 senatorial campaign, 106, 123, 124
Felton, Rebecca Latimer, 135
Fess, Simeon D., 171
Feuling, E. J., 132, 133, 171, 172
Field, Henry, 257-58, 260-64, 267, 268
Filibuster, 140
Fisher, Elizabeth, 135
Fites, Ray, 194
Folger, A. S., 13, 14
Fraker, Fleming, 52
Francis, Leslie, 105, 108, 115, 116
Frazier, Lynn, 134, 137, 166, 208, 211
Frazier-Lemke Act, 290
Funk, Abraham B., 52, 65

Gage, H. M., 131
Galer, Roger S., 81
Galloway, William, 257
Garst, Warren, 63
Gear, John H., 8, 51, 52-53
George, Walter F., 167
Gilman, William S., 253
Glasgow, J. D., 101, 112
Gompers, Samuel, 137, 150
Good, James W., 222
Government ownership, 83
  of land, 82, 280
  of railroads, 69-72, 75, 79, 82, 96, 128, 141, 142
  of utilities, 96, 128
Government regulation. *See also* Farm relief; Railroad rates
  vs. corporate values, xvii-xviii
  to curb monopolies, 4, 244-46
  vs. government ownership, 69-72
Grange, 96, 97, 103, 105, 297
Gray, N. C., 219-20
Great Depression. *See also* Agricultural depression
  B.'s analysis of causes, 242-43, 248, 259
Greater Iowa Association, 82, 85, 127
Greenback Party, 8, 96
Griffith, Gladys W., 224
Grimes, James W., 52
Gross, H. R., 263

Haig, Vernon, 257
Haines, Austin P., 78, 133
Halligan, Bert L., 159, 173
Hammill, John, 130, 156, 193, 254
Harding, George, 130
Harding, Warren G.
  appoints Kenyon to judgeship, 99-100
  cool relationship with B., 73, 135-36, 166
  criticized by B., 259
  criticized by progressives, 137-38
  and 1920 senatorial campaign, 85-86
  and 1922 senatorial campaign, 117, 118, 122, 130, 133
  shipping subsidy bill, 136, 138-39, 140
Harding, William, 115
Harlan, Edgar R., 134, 136, 194-95, 242
Harlan, James, 52-53
Harrison, Benjamin, 8
Harrison, P. S., 245
Harrison, Pat, 170
Haugen, Gilbert N., 197, 227. *See also* McNary-Haugen Farm Relief Bill
Haynes, Glenn C., 256, 261
Hays, Will H., 73, 245

INDEX

Hearst, Charles E., 193, 213, 214, 216
Hebner, E. T., 20
Hedge, Thomas, 51
Henderson, David, 53
Herrick, Myron T., 144-45, 149
Herring, Clyde L.
   and 1924 election dispute, 164
   in 1922 senatorial campaign, 126, 127, 129, 130, 131, 132
   in 1936 senatorial campaign, 289, 291
Hillquit, Morris, 104, 131
Hoover, Herbert
   allegedly supports McNary-Haugen Bill, 214-16, 226-27
   B. feels betrayed by, 231-34
   B. supports for president, 217-28
   chooses Hyde for Agriculture Secretary, 228-29
   as Commerce Secretary, 143, 144
   farm relief bill, 230-33
   is pleased when B. loses, 263
   opposes McNary-Haugen Bill, 201, 202, 226, 227
Hopkins, Edwin N., 226
Hopkins, Rev. John Henry, 277-78
Houser, Walter, 65
Howard, James R.
   and Esch-Cummins Act, 74, 105, 106
   and 1922 senatorial appointment, 100, 101
   and 1922 senatorial campaign, 102, 103, 108-13
   supports Hoover, 214-15
Howell, Robert, 134, 208, 213
Hubbell, Frederick, 186
Huffman, George, 164
Hughes, Charles Evans, 72, 149-50, 247
Hughes, William E., 59-60
Hull, Cordell, 117, 265
Hull, William, 226
Hunt, C. W., 102, 106, 108
Hyde, Arthur M., 229, 230, 231
Hylen, Mrs. Ingar, 136

Industrial Association, 27
Infantry School of Arms, 47-48
Ingham, Harvey, 202, 203, 216-17
Interstate Commerce Commission
   B. litigates rate cases, 69
   in Brookhart Railroad Bill, 141
   under Plumb Plan, 79
   T. Roosevelt's policy, 59, 60
Interstate Commerce Committee, of Senate, 142, 154-55
Interstate Commerce Law Convention, 58-59

Iowa Agricultural Equality League, 226
Iowa Board of Railroad Commissioners, 58
Iowa Farm Bureau Federation, 74, 78, 94, 95, 108, 136-37. *See also* American Farm Bureau Federation
Iowa Federation of Labor, 99
Iowa Grain Dealers Association, 71
Iowa National Guard
   B. becomes Second Lieutenant, 16-17
   Company D returns home, 24-25
   Company D sits out the war, 19-23
   marksmanship, 33, 38, 42
   Mexican border service, 40-41
   new Company D organized, 32, 34-37
Iowa Threshers Union, 75

Jackson, Andrew, 95
Jackson, John, 38, 39
Jardine, William, 190, 229
Jay, Peter, 148
Jefferson, Thomas, 95, 243
Johnson, Andrew, 220
Johnson, Hiram, 170, 172
Johnson, Hugh S., 226
Johnston, Mercer, 188
Johnston, William H., 102
Jones, Andrieus A., 170
Jones, Mrs. T. H., 267
Jones, Wiley A., 8-9
Judiciary
   B. loses bid for, 55
   B.'s views on, 247-48, 293-94

Kellogg, Frank, 130
Kelly, Ed, 169, 172, 186, 192
Kendall, Nathan, 100-102, 124, 130, 132, 134, 150, 156, 193
Kennedy, Charles A., 3, 63-64, 73, 80, 135
Kenyon, William S.
   leaves Senate for judgeship, 99-100
   mentioned to replace Cummins, 193
   as senator, 65, 71, 85, 86, 118, 133, 135
Kern, John W., 61
Kimball, Clem F., 156
King, William H., 170
Klein, Carl W., 184-85, 267, 296
Kopp, William F., 73, 100, 135
Kraschel, Nelson, 261
Ku Klux Klan, 159, 171, 172
Kurtz, Louis, 115

Labor. *See also* Railroad brotherhoods
   common interests with farmers, 74-75, 76, 78-79, 80-81, 98, 99
   at Conference for Progressive Political Action, 102-3

372

INDEX

fear of unions in 1920s Iowa, 82, 85
opposes Cummins, 80
opposes Esch-Cummins Act, 74, 78, 79-80
in Populist vision, 96
supports B. in 1922, 105
supports B. in 1924, 154, 155
supports B. in 1926, 187
supports Brookhart Railroad Bill, 141-42
Ladd, Scott, 100, 193
La Follette, Robert M., Jr., 200, 208, 210, 211, 262, 264
La Follette, Robert M., Sr.
and Daugherty investigation, 155
and 1904 Iowa Republicans, 57
opposes Cummins railroad bill, 75
in People's Legislative Service, 137
as 1911 presidential candidate, 65-66
as 1924 presidential candidate, 161, 162, 166
and 1920 senatorial campaign, 78
and 1922 senatorial campaign, 105-6, 108-9, 115, 117, 118, 132
and 1924 senatorial campaign, 153, 162, 164, 165-66
supported by B. of L. E., 79
La Guardia, Fiorello, 251, 262
Landis, Kenesaw Mountain, 150-51
Landon, Alf, 290, 291-92
Larrabee, William, 58-59, 60, 126, 133
Lee, Harry F., 163
Lemke, William, 290, 291-92
Lenihan, James J., 158, 162
Letts, F. Dickinson, 165
Lewis, J. C., 143, 154, 187
Liberty Bonds, 77, 107
Lincoln, Abraham, 64, 65, 115
Lincoln, James Rush, 20
Little Business Men's League, 293
Livingston, Schuyler, 78
Loan and Building Association, 27
Logan, D. H., 11, 12, 14, 16, 26, 57
Long, Huey, 290
Lowden, Frank O., 202, 203, 209, 210, 215, 216, 263
Lund, Frank, 186, 190, 192, 202-3, 215, 218, 266
Lytle, Charles F., 261

Machinist Union, 102
MacNider, Hanford
and B.'s vote for McNary-Haugen, 213-14
and contested 1924 election, 167-69, 171-74
mentioned for 1922 Senate vacancy, 100

opposes B.'s Russia policy, 151
and 1928 presidential campaign, 223
and 1924 senatorial campaign, 158-61, 163
and 1926 senatorial campaign, 185-87, 189, 193, 197-98
Manly, Basil, 137, 200
Marksmanship. *See also* National Rifle Association
army policy on, 41-42, 43
army vs. National Guard, 40-41
B. is army rifle instructor, 44-48
B. writes army rifle manual, 46
national matches, 37-38, 39-40, 43, 47, 48-49, 162
Palma Trophy, 38-39
after World War I, 48-49
Marsh, Benjamin, 75
Marshall, Verne, 169, 171, 288
McAdoo, William Gibbs, 284
McBirnie, Robert, 80
McClean, William, 57
McCleery, Hugh, 119
McClure, Martha, 193
McCord, J. H., 116
McCormick, Medill, 117, 130
McInerney, Thomas, 281
McIntyre, Marvin, 292-93
McKinley, William, 53
McMaster, William, 212
McNary, Charles, 200, 213, 214
McNary-Haugen Farm Relief Bill, 200-202
B. votes for, 213-14
Coolidge vetoes, 201, 204, 216
Dante Pierce opposes, 187
Farm Bureau supports, 201
Hoover allegedly supports, 214-16, 226-27
Hoover opposes, 201, 202, 226, 227
new version, 212-15, 216
Peek originates ideas, 275
vs. progressives' 1927 plan, 209, 210
rejected by 1928 convention, 218, 219
in 1926 senatorial campaign, 190
McNider, C. H., 167, 185-86, 194, 213-14
Mellon, Andrew, 202, 214, 248, 250
Meredith, Edwin T., 164, 169-70, 194, 197
Metz, Charles, 82
Miles, Frank, 161, 198
Miller, Alex, 111, 118
Miller, Mrs. Alex, 268
Mills, J. H., 134
Monopolies. *See also* Trusts
block booking of movies, 244-46
chain stores, 243-44, 293
in Populist vision, 120

373

INDEX

Moore, Ernest R., 110
Moorhead, Frank, 217
Moses, George H., 171
Movie industry, block booking in, 244-46
Mulct law, 12-14
Mullan, Charles W., 54
Mumma, Morton C., 38, 44, 45, 46, 47, 48, 205
Murphy, Donald, 214
Murphy, Frank, 225
Murphy, Louis, 267, 268, 269, 275, 279, 290
Myerly, J. I., 226-27
Myers, Sherman, 191

National Association of Manufacturers, 59
National Board for the Promotion of Rifle Practice, 37, 39-40, 41-42, 46, 47, 48-49
National Conference of Progressives, 137-38
National Conference on Valuation of American Railroads, 142
National Council of Farmers' Cooperative Associations, 70
National Guard. *See also* Iowa National Guard
 conflict with army, 40
 in national rifle matches, 37, 39-40
 rifle matches at Camp Perry, 129
 trained by NRA, 32-33
Nationalization. *See* Government ownership
National Lawyers Guild, 293-94
National Rifle Association (NRA)
 B. is president of, 39, 48
 founded, 32-33
 publishes B.'s rifle manual, 46
 supports national matches, 37-38, 41, 43, 48-49
National School of Public Ownership, 69-70
Neal, Samuel Wakefield, 11, 12, 13, 14, 16, 57, 58
Neely, Matthew M., 170
Neiswanger, Jasper, 36
Nepotism, 256-57, 260-61, 263
Newberry, Truman H., 100, 106, 138
New Deal, supported by B., 272-73
Newspapers. *See* Press coverage
Nichols, I. A., 252
Nonpartisan League, 97, 134
Norbeck, Peter, 262
Norris, David W., 108
Norris, George
 as B.'s friend, 135, 207, 279, 292
 endorses Al Smith, 227

and Hoover's farm policy, 230
at National Conference of Progressives, 137
as possible presidential candidate, 203, 210, 264
as progressive senator, 208, 211
and 1922 senatorial campaign, 117
and 1924 senatorial campaign, 173
and 1932 senatorial campaign, 257-58, 262
Norris farm relief bill, 139, 224
Nourse, E. G., 94
NRA. *see* National Rifle Association
Nye, Gerald, 208, 211

O'Hare, Kate Richards, 127, 131

Palma Trophy, 38-39
Palmer, David J., 55, 57, 58, 78, 107
Parry, David M., 59
Parsons, James, 167
Paul, George H., 28-29
Payne, W. O., 125
Peek, George
 at AAA, 275, 276, 279-80, 281-83
 in Hoover presidential campaign, 223, 226
 and McNary-Haugen Bill, 200, 213, 214, 219, 220
 supports Al Smith, 217
People's Legislative Service, 103, 137, 142
People's Party, 95, 96
People's Reconstruction League, 142
Pepper, Claude, 273
Perkins, Charles E., 154
Pershing, John J., 43, 45
Philbrick, Allen, 242
Phipps, Lawrence C., 172
Pickett, Charles E., 100, 101, 102, 104, 108, 116, 122
Pierce, Dante
 B. supports for Agriculture Secretary, 229
 becomes regular Republican, 187-88, 191
 at Conference for Progressive Political Action, 103
 opposes McNary-Haugen Bill, 187
 personal association with B., 103, 134, 135, 140, 150
 and 1928 presidential campaign, 214, 227
 and 1922 senatorial campaign, 105-7, 110, 113, 114, 117, 127, 132, 138
 and 1924 senatorial campaign, 153, 154
Pierce, James M., 75-76, 78, 81, 83, 133

Pitt, Milton, 131
Plumb, Glenn, 79
Plumb Plan, 79, 80, 81, 83, 103
Plunkett, Sir Horace, 149
Populism, 95-98, 247. *See also* Cooperative associations
    of B. after Hoover disappointment, 242-43
    and banking system, 248-49
    of B.'s 1922 victory, 120
    in evolution of liberal politics, 270, 273
    and judicial power, 247-48
    in 1932 senatorial campaign, 259
    and small business, 243-46
Porter, Claude R., 65, 164, 194, 195, 197
Press coverage
    B. buys *Washington County Press,* 65-66
    B. writes for newspapers, 60, 65-66, 74
    of B.'s career, xv, 252-53, 296-97
    of B.'s regular Republicanism, 229
    of 1910 Congressional campaign, 4, 63-64
    of 1928 Republican National Convention, 219
    of 1920 senatorial campaign, 78-79, 82-83, 84
    of 1922 senatorial campaign, 113-18, 133-34
    of 1932 senatorial campaign, 260
Price controls, retail, 244, 293
Price supports, agricultural
    in 1928 Brookhart bill, 213-14
    Coolidge opposes, 211, 216
    in Eicher bill, 284
    Hoover advocates in wartime, 233
    Hoover opposes, 231, 232
    in McNary-Haugen Bill, 200, 212
    vs. production controls, 264-65
    in progressives' 1927 plan, 209
Primary reform, 122, 124, 137
Production controls
    AAA calls for, 282-83
    B. opposes, 264-65, 282-83, 297
    in McNary-Haugen Bill, 212
Progressive Party
    in 1912 presidential election, 66-67
    in 1924 presidential election, 161, 287
Progressive Party of Iowa (1932), 267
Progressives
    Conference for Progressive Political Action, 102-4
    farm program in Senate, 208-10
    in Iowa Republican Party, 52, 64-66
    National Conference of Progressives, 137
    support FDR, 291
    want alternative to Hoover, 264

Progressivism, of Brookhart
    in 1910 Congressional campaign, 4
    and New Deal, 273
    origins in railroad reform, 68, 270
    and populism, 95
    in 1932 senatorial campaign, 259
Prohibition
    B. opposes repeal, 250-52, 269
    Cummins opposes, 57
    Iowa after repeal, 284
    Iowa mulct law, 12-14
Public Ownership League of America, 103

Rader, LeRoy, 116, 202
Radicalism
    accusations by railroads, 141
    accusations in 1920 campaign, 78-79, 80, 82-83, 84
    accusations in 1922 campaign, 103-4, 105, 119, 128-29
    accusations in 1926 campaign, 194
    B.'s real radicalism, 271
Railroad brotherhoods
    cooperative bank, 79, 144
    and farm relief, 75, 99
    support B. for Senate, 78, 79-80, 102, 116, 117
    support Brookhart Railroad Bill, 142
Railroad rates
    and agricultural depression, 94, 99, 199
    B. litigates rate cases, 68-69
    in Brookhart Railroad Bill, 141
    and competition, 28
    in Esch-Cummins Act, 72
    at Interstate Commerce Law Convention, 58-61
    under Plumb Plan, 79
    in 1922 senatorial campaign, 105, 124-25
    in 1926 senatorial campaign, 185
Railroads. *See also* Esch-Cummins Act
    Brookhart bill (1923), 141-42
    Cummins bill (1919), 72, 74, 75
    government ownership, 69-72, 75, 79, 82, 96, 128, 141, 142
    political power in Iowa, 51, 56-57, 154, 167
    strike of 1922, 123
    wartime nationalization, 71-72
Ramseyer, C. William, 80
Rankin, Jeanette, 73
Rankin, Roy, 132, 135, 154, 161, 254
Rawson, Charles A.
    appointed to Senate, 100, 101-2
    introduces B. in Senate, 135
    and 1928 presidential election, 203

INDEX

Rawson, Charles A. (*continued*)
  and 1924 senatorial campaign, 154, 155, 157-58, 161, 162
  and 1926 senatorial campaign, 187-88, 189, 193
  and 1922 senatorial election, 121, 122, 123, 124, 132, 133
  and 1922 senatorial primary, 104, 109, 110, 116, 117
Record, George, 142
Redistribution of wealth, 242-43, 259-60
Reed, David A., 166, 171
Reeves, Ira L., 44
Regency, 51
Regular Republicans. *See also* Standpats
  B. starts out as, 270
  B. temporarily becomes, 191, 216, 218-19, 228, 229, 272
Remley, Milton, 54
Reno, Milo
  estranged from B., 218, 219, 220-21, 227
  and Hoover farm policy, 227, 232
  and Roosevelt farm policy, 274, 276
  and 1922 senatorial campaign, 117, 132
Republican National Convention (1912), 66
Republican National Convention (1916), 72
Republican National Convention (1924), 154
Republican National Convention (1928), 218-19
Republican Party. *See also* Senatorial campaign; Standpats
  attitude toward B., xv-xvi
  B.'s independence of, 125, 133, 272
  Iowa conflicts of 1920s, 196-98, 272
  Iowa establishment, 50-53
Republican Service League, 159-60, 162, 163, 167, 169, 173
Reservation, 51, 62, 69, 80, 85
Rickard, Edgar, 215
Rifle training. *See* Marksmanship
Rifle Training in War (Brookhart), 46, 49
Robbins, Charles B., 159, 167, 169, 171, 172, 173
Roberts, Jackson, 10, 12, 13, 14, 15
Robinson, Joseph T., 170, 279
Rochdale Conference, 145
Rochdale principles, 77-78, 97-98, 271
Roosevelt, Franklin D.
  asked to give B. a job, 279, 292-93
  B. supports, 265, 273, 290-91
  Iowa support, 268, 286, 290-92
  recognition of Soviet Union, 278-79
  removes Peek from AAA, 280
Roosevelt, Theodore
  B. admires, 3, 61, 259, 273

  B. supports, 66, 72
  and Iowa politics, 57, 62
  railroad policy, 59, 60, 61, 69-70
Roosevelt, Theodore, Jr., 159, 160
Russia. *See* Soviet Union

Sanders, Everett, 168
Schilling, LeRoy, 37
Schwartz, Alexander, 150
Section 15-A, 72, 94, 105, 123, 141
Senatorial campaign (1920)
  B. challenges Cummins, 75-81, 196
  Cummins wins, 84-86, 93
  radicalism issue, 82-83
  state convention waffles, 83-84
Senatorial campaign (1922)
  B. campaigns after primary, 116-20
  B. wins, 132-34
  candidates line up, 104-9, 114-15
  Democrats attack, 125-26
  radicalism issue, 126-29
  regulars work to defeat B., 107-16, 129-32, 196
  state convention goes to standpats, 121-25
Senatorial campaign (1924)
  B. apparently wins, 164-66
  B. emerges from primary and convention, 153-57
  B. is unseated, 167-74, 189
  regular Republicans promote Steck, 157-64, 196
Senatorial campaign (1926)
  B. runs on agricultural issues, 184-88
  B. wins election easily, 194-95, 197-98
  B. wins primary, 188-89
  convention supports B., 190-92
Senatorial campaign (1932)
  B. loses badly, 268
  B. loses primary, 262-64
  B. runs as independent, 266-68
  B. runs on populist issues, 258-62
  B. starts out vulnerable, 253-57
Senatorial campaign (1936), 286-89
Seventieth Congress, 204, 211, 228
Seventy-first Congress, 228, 245
Shaw, Leslie M., 19, 24, 52, 132
Shearer, Brainard, 140
Shipping subsidies, 136, 138, 139, 140, 200
Shipstead, Henrik, 134, 171, 208, 211
Shoemaker, Ray, 163
Short, Wallace M., 267, 286, 290
Sieh, John, 116
Simmons, Furnifold McLendel, 170
Sims bill, 79
Sixty-eighth Congress, 166

INDEX

Sixty-ninth Congress, 204
Sixty-seventh Congress, 138
Skelly, W. G., 188
Skromme, Lars J., 254
Slade, C. Arnold, 242
Sloan, Hugh B., 56
Small business
   vs. chain stores, 243-44, 293
   vs. movie companies, 243-46
Smith, Al, 216-17, 220, 225, 226, 227, 228
Smith, Ellison DuRant, 154, 170
Smith, Gerald L. K., 290
Smith, U. S., 134
Socialism. *See also* Cooperative associations
   accusations by railroads, 59, 71, 141
   accusations in 1920 campaign, 78-79, 82, 83, 84, 85
   accusations in 1922 campaign, 104, 119, 126-28, 130, 131
   accusations in 1924 campaign, 156, 196
   B. repudiates, 69, 131
   B. turns epithet on opponents, 125, 204
   at Conference for Progressive Political Action, 103-4
   socialists support B., 127-28
Social welfare
   as 1920 campaign issue, 77
   as 1922 campaign issue, 105
Sound Money Club, 53
Soviet Union
   B. is trade advisor, 274-83
   B. passed over for ambassador, 279
   B. visits, 143-44, 145-48
   B.'s conclusions are criticized, 149-52
   diplomatic recognition of, 146, 147, 149-51, 274, 276, 277-79
   food relief to, 145-46
Spanish-American War, 19, 23
Spanish American War Veterans, 76
Speaks, John C., 49
Spence, R. H., 76
Standard Oil, 69
Standpats
   B. is accused of becoming one, 221
   B. starts out as one, 55-56, 62
   in 1910 Congressional campaign, 3, 63-64
   in 1920 senatorial campaign, 81, 84, 85
   in 1922 senatorial campaign, 107, 123, 124
   in 1924 senatorial campaign, 154, 162
   in 1926 senatorial campaign, 191
   at turn of century, 52
   in 1911 vote on Dolliver's replacement, 64-65

   in 1912 Washington County convention, 66
Stanley, Claude M., 1114
State Federation of Labor, 75, 76
Steck, Albert, 158
Steck, Daniel F., 197
   attacks B. on farm relief, 209, 225-26
   contests 1924 election, 167-74
   refuses to escort B. into Senate, 211
   in 1924 senatorial campaign, 158-61, 163-65
   in 1932 senatorial campaign, 254, 261
Stedman, James, 80
Steen, Herman, 214
Stephens, Hubert D., 170-71, 173
Sterling, Thomas, 130
Stern, Willis, 195, 223
Stewart, David W., 193, 203, 254
Stone, John Y., 50
Stone, Warren S., 78, 79-80, 144, 188
Subsidies
   for agriculture, 201, 211, 212, 218, 223, 224, 230
   for private enterprise, 139, 199-200, 201-2
   for railroads, 199
Sullivan, Mark, 114, 128, 140-41, 215
Surpluses, agricultural. *See also* Production controls
   B. addresses problem, 149, 207, 212, 259
   in Eicher bill, 284
   foreign markets for, 147, 274, 276-77
   in Hoover administration bill, 231
   in McNary-Haugen Bill, 200-201, 216
   in Norris Bill, 139
   in progressives' 1927 plan, 209
Sutherland, William, 119
Swanson, Claude A., 170
Sweet, Burton, 101, 104-5, 153, 155, 193

Taft, Charles, 29
Taft, William Howard, 4, 39, 63, 64, 66, 69
Taft Republican Clubs, 63
Tariff reform, 55, 64, 72, 200, 222
Taxpayers League, 99
Taylor, Dean, 80
Thorne, Clifford, 61, 68-69, 75, 108-15, 117-19
Titus, George, 54, 202
Titus Amendment, 54
Tobin, Michael J., 100, 203, 214
Towner, Horace M., 100
Townsend, Francis, 286, 289, 290
Transportation Act. *See* Esch-Cummins Act
Trewin, James W., 100, 124
Trotsky, Leon, 146

Trusts, 69, 74-75. *See also* Monopolies
Turner, Dan, 51, 190-91, 253, 267, 281, 284

Unemployment relief, 77, 259, 264
Union Party, 290
United Society of Agriculture, 103
United Taxpayers League, 75

Van Vechten, Ralph, 167
Veterans' benefits
  Fordney Bill, 159
  in 1920 senatorial campaign, 76-77
  in 1922 senatorial campaign, 105, 106, 124
  in 1932 senatorial campaign, 259

Waite, J. L., 80
Wallace, Henry A.
  B. is disappointed by, 283, 292
  and Coolidge veto of McNary-Haugen, 216
  Hoover rules out for cabinet, 229
  as Secretary of Agriculture, 274, 276, 279-80, 287, 294
  and 1932 senatorial campaign, 253, 255
  supports Lowden for president, 202
Wallace, Henry C.
  and 1922 senatorial appointment, 99, 100
  and 1922 senatorial campaign, 109, 110, 112, 118, 121, 124
  and 1924 senatorial campaign, 162
  and 1926 senatorial campaign, 193
  supports McNary-Haugen Bill, 201, 202, 224
  welcomes B. to Senate, 136
Wall Street
  B. wants appointment to SEC, 292-93
  in B.'s analysis of depression, 199, 242-43
  in 1920 campaign rhetoric, 75
  in 1922 campaign rhetoric, 123, 126, 129

  in 1924 campaign rhetoric, 161, 162
Walsh, Rev. Edmund A., 278, 279
Walsh, Thomas J., 170
War Department. *See* Army
War profits, 99, 103, 105, 106
Washington, Iowa
  in 1890s, 10-11
  after turn of the century, 27-28
Washington County Press
  B. buys, 65-66
  B. writes for, 23, 97
  published by Burrell, 11
Washington Gazette
  B. writes for, 60
  published by Logan and Neal, 11
Watson, James E., 86, 167, 171, 223
Wearin, Otha, 273, 294
Weaver, H. O., 203, 216
Weaver, James B., 8-9, 95-96, 120, 247
Weaver, James B., Jr., 193
Weeks, John W., 122
Welliver, Judson, 188
Wheeler, Burton, 137, 161, 162, 188, 285, 292
Wheeler Defense Fund, 188
Wilde, Daniel, 97
Williams, George, 36
Williams, Howard Y., 286-87
Willis, Frank B., 171
Wills, H. E., 102
Wilson, Charles J., 13, 14, 78, 81, 165, 185
Wilson, Clarence S., 227
Wilson, James F., 51, 53
Wilson, L. J., 84
World War I
  marksmanship for, 43-44
  nationalization of railroads, 71-72

Young, John Alex, 13, 14, 39, 57, 58
Young, Lafayette, 64-65, 99, 107, 114, 134
Yount, Clarence E., 289

378